Caribbean
Ports of Call

WESTERN REGION

KAY SHOWKER WITH MARY BRENNAN

NINTH EDITION

gpp
travel
Guilford, Connecticut

To buy books in quantity for corporate use
or incentives, call **(800) 962–0973**
or e-mail **premiums@GlobePequot.com.**

Text design by Nancy Freeborn
Photo research by Sue Preneta
Cartography by Multi-Mapping, Ltd. © Morris Book Publishing, LLC.

ISSN 1536-6235
ISBN 978-0-7627-4539-5

Printed in the United States of America
10 9 8 7 6 5 4 3 2 1

Please bear in mind that prices, exchange rates, schedules, etc., change constantly. Readers should always check with a cruise line regarding its ships and itineraries before making final plans.

Caribbean Ports of Call

WESTERN REGION

a photo essay

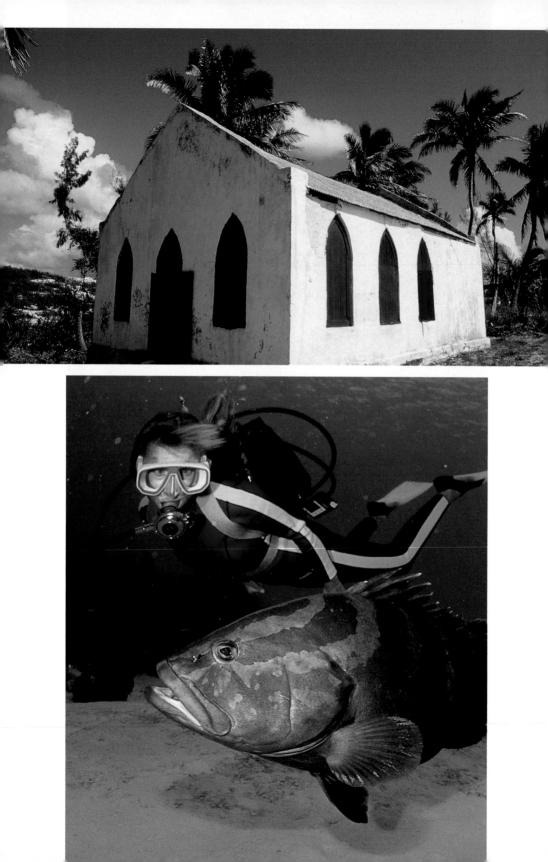

Bahamas  **Bahamas**

Costa Rica  **Costa Rica**

Belize   **Guatemala**

Guatemala   **Guatemala**

Jamaica   **Jamaica**

Jamaica  **Honduras**

Honduras **Honduras**

Bahamas

Bahamas

Riviera Maya

Riviera Maya

Riviera Maya

Cayman Islands

Cayman Islands

Cayman Islands

Key West

Cozumel

Contents

List of Maps

The Caribbean

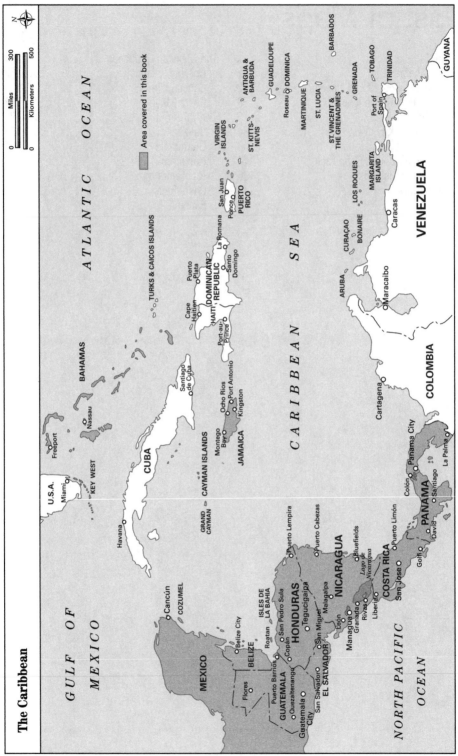

GULF OF MEXICO

ATLANTIC OCEAN

Miles 0 · 300
Kilometers 0 · 500

N

Area covered in this book

U.S.A.
Miami
KEY WEST
Freeport
Havana

BAHAMAS
Nassau

TURKS & CAICOS ISLANDS

CUBA

Santiago de Cuba

CAYMAN ISLANDS
GRAND CAYMAN

Cape Haitien
Puerto Plata
La Romana
Santo Domingo
HAITI
DOMINICAN REPUBLIC
Port-au-Prince

San Juan
Ponce
PUERTO RICO

VIRGIN ISLANDS

ST. KITTS-NEVIS
ANTIGUA & BARBUDA
GUADELOUPE
Roseau DOMINICA
MARTINIQUE
ST. LUCIA
ST. VINCENT & THE GRENADINES
BARBADOS
GRENADA
TOBAGO
Port of Spain
TRINIDAD

Montego Bay
Ocho Rios
Port Antonio
Kingston
JAMAICA

CARIBBEAN SEA

MEXICO
Cancún
COZUMEL

Belize City
Roatan
ISLES DE LA BAHIA
BELIZE

Flores
Puerto Barrios
GUATEMALA
Guatemala City
Quezaltenango
San Salvador
San Miguel
EL SALVADOR
Copán
San Pedro Sula
HONDURAS
Tegucigalpa
Puerto Lempira
Puerto Cabezas
Bluefields
NICARAGUA
Managua
Granada
León
Rivas
Liberia
Lago de Nicaragua
San José
COSTA RICA
Puerto Limón
Golfito
David
PANAMA
Santiago
Colón
Panama City
La Palma

NORTH PACIFIC OCEAN

Cartagena
COLOMBIA

ARUBA
CURAÇAO
BONAIRE
LOS ROQUES
MARGARITA ISLAND
Maracaibo
Caracas

VENEZUELA

GUYANA

The Caribbean and the Bahamas Ports of Call

Ports of Call

Basseterre, St. Kitts
* Belize City, Belize
Bequia, the Grenadines
* Bimini, the Bahamas
* Bluefields, Nicaragua
Bridgetown, Barbados
* Calica, Mexico
* Cancún, Mexico
Cap Haitien, Haiti
Castries, St. Lucia
* Caye Caulker, Belize
Charlestown, Nevis
Charlotte Amalie, St. Thomas, US Virgin
  Islands
Christiansted, St. Croix, US Virgin Islands
* Colón, Panama
* Costa Maya, Mexico
Cruz Bay, St. John, US Virgin Islands
Fort Bay, Saba
Fort-de-France, Martinique
Frederiksted, St. Croix, US Virgin Islands
* Freeport, Grand Bahama, the Bahamas
* Guanaja, Bay Islands, Honduras
* Grand Cayman, Cayman Islands
* Great Guana Cay, Abaco, the Bahamas
Gustavia, St. Barthélemy (St. Barts)
Iles des Saintes, French West Indies
Jost Van Dyke, British Virgin Islands
* Key West, USA
* Kingston, Jamaica
Kingstown, St. Vincent
Kralendijk, Bonaire
* La Ceiba, Honduras
* Livingston, Guatemala
Marigot, St. Martin
Mayreau, the Grenadines
* Montego Bay, Jamaica
* Nassau, New Providence, the Bahamas
Philipsburg, St. Maarten

* Playa del Carmen, Mexico
* Placencia, Belize
Plymouth, Montserrat
Pointe-à-Pitre, Guadeloupe
Ponce, Puerto Rico
* Port Antonio, Jamaica
Port-au-Prince, Haiti
Port-au-Spain, Trinidad
* Port Cristobál, Panama
* Porto Progreso (Mérida), Mexico
* Puerto Barrio, Guatemala
* Puerto Cortes, Honduras
* Puerto Limón, Costa Rica
Puerto Plata, Dominican Republic
* Punta Gorda, Belize
* Ocho Rios, Jamaica
Oranjestad, St. Eustatius
Oranjested, Aruba
* Roatan, Bay Islands, Honduras
Roseau, Dominica
St. George's, Grenada
St. Johns, Antigua
Sandy Ground, Anguilla
* San Blas Islands, Panama
San Juan, Puerto Rico
* San Miguel, Cozumel, Mexico
* San Pedro, Ambergris Caye, Belize
Santo Domingo, Dominican Republic
* Santo Tomás de Castella, Guatemala
Scarborough, Tobago
Tortola, British Virgin Islands
Virgin Gorda, British Virgin Islands
Willemstad, Curaçao

* Ports covered in this volume. The balance
  appear in the companion volumes, *Caribbean
  Ports of Call: Northern and Northeastern
  Regions* and *Caribbean Ports of Call: Eastern
  and Southern Regions.*

PART ONE

Cruising and the Caribbean

The Winning Combination

Every year more than thirteen million people take cruises, and almost half of them cruise in the waters of the Bahamas and the Caribbean. Superb year-round weather, proximity, prices, and the region's great variety—of cultures, activity, scenery, sports, and attractions—all are reasons that make the combination of cruising and the Caribbean a vacation choice that's hard to beat.

Caribbean Ports of Call: Western Region is one of three books in the Caribbean Ports of Call series. From its first publication in 1987, the series has been intended to fill the gap between two kinds of books: books about cruising and books about the Caribbean.

- Typically, books about cruising describe the ships in great detail and are useful in selecting a cruise; however, these books give little or no attention to ports of call. Generally, once you are on board your ship heading to the Bahamas or the Caribbean, their value is marginal.

- Guidebooks on the Bahamas and the Caribbean invariably assume that their readers will arrive at a destination by plane and remain several days or longer and have plenty of time to explore the attractions. They are not written for cruise passengers who spend only a few hours in port and need a special kind of guidance.

Indeed, neither the standard cruise guide nor the typical Caribbean guidebook has the kind of information that cruise passengers need to help them plan and set priorities for their time in port. And that has been the aim of my series from the outset.

Caribbean Ports of Call: A Guide for Today's Cruise Passenger was the first of its kind when it was first published, and although other cruise guides and Caribbean books have appeared with "Ports of Call" added to their titles, a comparison of their content would show that the books in our series are still the only ones designed specifically with the goal of helping readers plan their time in each port of call as well as serving as a guide to be taken along in port.

Caribbean Ports of Call: A Guide for Today's Cruise Passenger has been divided into three volumes for the most practical reasons. We want each of the three books to be portable and their inclusion of ports to reflect the pattern of Caribbean cruises.

Caribbean Ports of Call: Western Region is the result of the growing popularity of the Western Caribbean as an area for new cruise itineraries, with the number of ships offering cruises in this region more than tripling in the past decade. It also reflects a certain maturing of Caribbean cruising. As the number of cruise lines and cruise ships grows and the reservoir of past passengers expands, cruise lines need to develop new itineraries to keep up with or stay ahead of their competition to attract new passengers and stimulate repeat passengers to return.

Caribbean Ports of Call: Western Region covers the ports on the itineraries that depart regularly from Florida to the Bahamas and Western Caribbean for lengths of two to seven days, as well as those that sail from Florida and other ports, such as Houston and New Orleans, for the Western Caribbean and Central America or en route to the Panama Canal.

The majority of the cruises to the Bahamas are three- and four-day trips from Miami, Fort Lauderdale, and Port Canaveral in Florida. Those to the Western Caribbean are generally five- to seven-day cruises from Miami and Tampa. Many ships alternate their Bahamas cruises with Western Caribbean ones, thus enabling passengers to combine two itineraries.

The companion volumes are *Caribbean Ports of Call: Northern and Northeastern Regions* and *Caribbean Ports of Call: Eastern and Southern Regions*. The first covers the ports of call for ships departing from Florida on one-week cruises and longer for the Northern and Eastern Caribbean, and the second book covers the ships departing from Florida or based in San Juan, Barbados, and elsewhere that cruise in the Eastern and Southern Caribbean on seven-day cruises or longer, as well as those sailing through the Eastern and Southern Caribbean en route to the Panama Canal.

How to Use This Guide

In deciding what information to include, we recognized that cruise passengers are a diverse group of travelers, and their interests and needs change, sometimes from port to port. Therefore, we knew the books had to address a variety of readers' needs. For example, you may be sports-oriented—or more interested in history, art, and culture. Someone else might want only to stroll around and shop. Some people will only venture beyond their cruise ship if they can take a tour; others would not take an organized tour if it were offered to them for free. At the same time, many people who normally do not take tours will take one on their first visit to a new place to gain a quick, overall impression. Yet for others the very newness of a place inspires them to be independent and explore on their own. Some ports lend themselves to organized touring, and others are best seen by walking on your own.

To ensure that the book has the broadest possible application and can be used by many different kinds of cruise passengers, it is organized in an easy-to-use format that enables readers to find the information they need quickly.

Part 1 introduces you to the delights of the Caribbean in general, to the Western Caribbean specifically, and to the delights of a cruise.

Part 2 has a profile of each cruise line with cruises to the Bahamas and the Caribbean. It is designed to help you find the line and ship most likely to match your tastes and pocketbook. A convenient chart listing the ships, their ports of call, and range of prices appears at the end of the book.

Part 3 covers the ports visited on Bahamas and Western Caribbean cruises. For easy reference, an alphabetical list of ports follows the table of contents.

Ports of Call

The ports of a cruise itinerary provide a kaleidoscope of a region's history and cultures, scenery and sights, language and music. In the Caribbean, and particularly the Western Caribbean, the destinations are very distinctive, which is one of the reasons they are the basis for such interesting itineraries. The differences are topographic and cultural, ranging from English-speaking Jamaica, Cayman Islands, and Belize to Spanish-speaking Mexico and Central America. Some places are tropical and lush like Jamaica; others are sandy and arid like Cozumel. There are places that have towering mountains, rain forests, vast jungles, deserts, and low-lying islets—sometimes all within one country.

Port chapters start with an introduction to the country and a general map, Fast Facts, Budget Planning, and the Author's Favorite Attractions in addition to a port profile with information on embarkation, facilities, and local transportation. For those who prefer to tour with a group, there are descriptions of the most frequently available shore excursions sold aboard ships. If you prefer to be on your own, each chapter has a walking tour with a map, where appropriate, and descriptions of attractions to see if you were to rent a car or hire a taxi. In any case, the objective is to help you organize and maximize your time in port to ensure you get the most out of the visit. Other sections cover shopping, sports, dining, and entertainment.

All ports, except those covered very briefly, open with At a Glance, a generic list of attractions with ★ to ★★★★★ stars. The purpose is to give you an instant picture of the destination so you can judge how best to use your time. The stars are not used in the same sense as a restaurant critique; they are simply intended as an objective guide to what the destination has to offer. My personal list of favorite attractions can also be a guide.

A cruise is the best and sometimes the only way to visit several Caribbean destinations in one vacation. That's one of the main attractions of cruising. But if you don't plan, you may come back thinking that the islands are all alike. Using this book will enable you to have a balanced and varied itinerary by planning your activity in each port. In other words, if you were to spend all your time on a walking tour in Nassau or Key West, you might want to play golf or go horseback riding in Jamaica and try snorkeling or diving in the Cayman Islands.

Each port has a Budget Planning section. Prices are not uniform in the region. Generally, they tend to be highest in the most popular places. You might sometimes have the feeling there's a *soak-the-tourist* attitude, but do remember that a place like Nassau must import almost all its food and supplies. Caribbean destinations cater mainly to Americans, and American tastes often cost a great deal to satisfy. That means costs are high.

The islands depend on tourism. Local people want you to have a good impression of their country so you will come back and bring your friends. They are on your side. On the other hand, don't blame them for your own gullibility or lack of planning. There are as many bad apples in New York or Miami as in Nassau or Montego Bay. This book gives you guidelines to help you avoid the bad ones. We hope you will use these guidelines and have a pleasant and memorable cruise.

As with our other books, we invite you to send us your comments and suggestions and tell us about your experiences—good or bad. Please let us hear from you.

The Delights of the Caribbean

Take a cruise to the Caribbean, and you will discover a world that is foreign but familiar, close yet far. It is an exotic world of vivid color and gentle trade winds. Paradise, the Caribbean is often called, and you will see why as your ship glides gently through aquamarine and sapphire waters to reach places thick with tropical greenery down to their white-sand shorelines.

The seas of the Bahamas and the Caribbean stretch across more than a million square miles from the coast of Florida to the shores of Central and South America. On the east, the islands form an arc that cradles the Caribbean Sea and separates it from the Atlantic Ocean, and on the west, Mexico and Central America form the landmass that separates the Caribbean Sea from the Pacific Ocean. The Caribbean region, often called the Eighth Continent of the World, contains large and small countries, islands, and tiny islets, some no more than the peaks of long-submerged mountains. Others are larger than fifteen states of the United States and have the geographic variety of a continent. The Caribbean region has as many independent nations and island-states as there are countries in Europe, and they draw their heritage from around the globe.

Locating the Islands

On a map with the arm of the compass pointing north, the islands closest to the United States are known as the Greater Antilles, which include Cuba, Haiti, the Dominican Republic, and Puerto Rico. All but Cuba have daily air service from New York, Miami, and other major US cities. Puerto Rico is a major hub for cruise ships as well as airlines.

The Bahamas and the Turks and Caicos lie southeast of Florida and north of the Greater Antilles. They are entirely in the Atlantic Ocean, but because their tropical environment is so similar to that of the Caribbean, they are thought of as part of the region. Both have daily air service from the United States, but only the Bahamas is a major cruise destination.

Farther along, with the compass pointing east, the area known as the Eastern Caribbean includes the Lesser Antilles, starting with the Virgin Islands on the north and curving south to Grenada. The northern group of these many small islands is called the Leewards and comprises the US and British Virgin Islands, Anguilla, St. Maarten, St. Barts, Saba, St. Eustatius, St. Kitts, Nevis, Antigua, Barbuda, Montserrat, and Guadeloupe. The south group, called the Windwards, includes Dominica, Martinique, St. Lucia, Barbados, St. Vincent and the Grenadines, and Grenada. Most, but not all, have direct air service from the United States. The others can be reached by local airlines, and most are stops for cruise ships.

On the south side of the Caribbean are Aruba, Bonaire, Curaçao, and Trinidad and Tobago, which lie off the coast of Venezuela.

To the west are Jamaica and the Cayman Islands; Mexico's Yucatán Peninsula, with the islands of Cancún and Cozumel; Belize and Honduras, with long coastlines fronting the longest barrier reef in the Western Hemisphere; plus the Central American countries of Guatemala, Nicaragua, Costa Rica, and Panama, bracketing the Caribbean's western shores.

Along the 2,000 miles of the Caribbean, whether to the east or the west, nature has been extravagant with its color, variety, and beauty. Verdant mountains rise from sun-bleached shores. Between the towering peaks and the sea, rivers and streams cascade over rocks and hillsides and disappear into mangrove swamps and deserts. Fields of flowers, trees with brilliant scarlet and magenta blossoms, and a multitude of birds and butterflies fill the landscape. The air, refreshed by quick tropical showers, is scented with spices and fruit.

And this is only nature's act above the ground. Below the sea is a wonderland of exotic species in a setting often called the most beautiful in the world. Rainbows of brilliantly colored fish of every size and shape dart endlessly through the crystal waters to hide in caves and grottos, mingle between the swaying purple sea fans, and burrow into boulders of coral and sponge.

Yet what makes the Caribbean region unique is not simply its beauty or geography but rather the combination of this lovely and exotic scenery and the kaleidoscope of rich and diverse cultures. Like the vibrant landscape they reflect, the people and their cultures have evolved from a wide range of traditions, music, dance, art, architecture, and religions from around the world into the greatest of the world's melting pots.

Enter Columbus

Before 1492, when Columbus sighted the New World, the lands of the Caribbean region were populated by Indian tribes, some of whom may have migrated to the region from Asia 20,000 years ago. In more recent history we know that the Ciboneys, who probably came from South America, arrived in the Caribbean region about 3,000 years ago. They were followed by the peaceful Tainos (known as the Arawaks, their more frequently used linguistic name) and the fierce Caribs, who had been in the region for about 600 years when Columbus arrived. It is from the latter group that the Caribbean Sea takes its name.

But in less than a century after Columbus's voyages, the Native population in the islands had almost vanished because of war, disease, and enslavement. Their only survivors are a small group of the descendants of the Carib Indians on the island of Dominica and the Afro-Amerindians, known as Black Caribs in St. Vincent and as Garifunas, after their distinct language, in Belize and Honduras.

Columbus's discoveries brought waves of explorers, conquerors, settlers, merchant sailors, pirates, privateers, traders, and slavers from Europe, the Middle East, Africa, and Asia. For two centuries the West Indies, as the region came to be known, were a pawn in the battle for the New World that raged among the European nations. While they fought, they plundered the region's riches and searched for a route to the East. These were savage times that disgraced even the noblest of aims.

By the dawn of the eighteenth century, Spain, England, France, Denmark, and Holland had sliced up the region, had planted their flags on various islands, and had begun to colonize their new territories. Gradually the decimated Indian population was replaced with African slaves to work the land that yielded fortunes in sugar, rum, cotton, and tobacco. After slavery was abolished in the British colonies in the nineteenth century (three decades before its abolition in the United States), the Africans were replaced by indentured laborers from Asia. They were in turn followed by waves of immigrants from the Mediterranean to the Americas in search of a better life.

Once entrenched in the Caribbean, the European governments began to make burdensome demands on their colonies. There were many rebellions. Haiti's revolt was the only one to succeed in a complete break and led to the establishment of the first black republic in the Western Hemisphere two decades after the American Revolution.

Following abolition and the invention of the steam engine and cotton gin, the West Indies lost the base of their economy and soon became neglected outposts of European empires. With the end of the Spanish-American War, Spain gave up its holdings in the New World, and after World War II, Britain, France, and the Netherlands were forced to change their relationships with most of their colonies, granting them independence in most cases.

But the road to independence was a rough one. The troubled 1960s in the United States, with their shock waves of black power demands and rising expectations, washed ashore in the Caribbean simultaneously. Adding to their burdens, the 1970s, with the oil crisis, inflation, and the worldwide recession, were particularly hard on the islands, which have few resources other than their people and natural beauty. But from the experience a new Caribbean has taken shape.

Caribbean Culture

Down through the centuries, those who came to the Caribbean—conquerors and settlers, sailors and slaves, merchants and workers, and visitors and vacationers—brought with them parts of their cultures: their church steeples, temples, brogues, high tea, High Mass, masks, drums, colors, songs, dances, high-rises, and hamburgers. Out of this mélange has grown a new Caribbean as colorful, rich, and diverse as the landscape in which it flowers.

Although it might be difficult to single out a Caymanian or a Cruzan by sight, there is no mistaking the lilt of a Jamaican's voice when she speaks or a Trinidadian when he sings. Haitian art is instantly recognizable. The beguine began in Martinique, the merengue in the Dominican Republic. Calypso and steel bands were born in Trinidad, reggae in Jamaica, and salsa in Puerto Rico.

Today the region pulsates with creative energy in the arts. The best time to see the evidence is during Carnival, when tradition vies with innovation as part of the show. Trinidad's Carnival is the best known and is held at the traditional pre-Lenten time, but Carnival in the Caribbean often developed from local events and is held at different times of the year. For example, Crop-Over in Barbados in July stems from the celebration of the harvest, and Antigua's Carnival in August started as a welcome to the British monarch during her visit in the 1960s.

Caribbean architecture, like its art, is a composite of world cultures. English churches and Spanish cathedrals stand alongside warm-weather adaptations of Dutch farmhouses and French manors. Victorian gingerbread mansions are pauses in the tango of brightly painted houses in the towns and villages of Haiti. Minarets and steeples pierce the sky of Trinidad; the oldest synagogue in the Western Hemisphere is a Curaçao landmark.

New Cuisine

Caribbean cuisine, too, is a cornucopia of tastes from the four corners of the world—a unique blend that evolved over the centuries and combines nature's bounty with the richness of the region's culinary heritage. The Spaniards discovered not only the New World but also a continent of exotic foods, fruits, and vegetables Europeans had never seen—avocado, cassava, maize, peppers, papaya, chocolate, and potatoes, to name a few. From the Natives the Spaniards learned how to use the new ingredients and eventually adapted them for their own cooking; many became basic elements in classic Spanish and French cuisine. The Danes, Dutch, Portuguese, English, Africans, Chinese, Indians, Greeks, Turks, Indonesians, and Arabs all made their contributions.

Out of this potpourri evolved a Creole or West Indian cuisine that includes such standards as Cuban and Puerto Rican black bean soup, Jamaican pepperpot, St. Kitts goat water or mutton stew, Grenadian callaloo, and Guadeloupan accra.

Following independence, a new generation of hotel and restaurant chefs began developing a new and sophisticated Caribbean cuisine. Their creativity has been encouraged by their restaurant and hotel associations, which stage annual competitions judged by international food critics. The new cuisine has resulted in such wonderful creations as cold papaya bisque, crab and callaloo soup, breadfruit vichyssoise, callaloo quiche, chicken Creole with mango, and avocado ice cream, to name a few.

The starting point in the making of Caribbean cuisine is the market—a cultural potpourri where Africa meets the Caribbean and mixes with Asia. Mountains of mango, melon, and banana and pyramids of papaya, pineapple, and pomegranate are stacked next to the plantain, okra, dasheen, coconut, cassava, cloves, coffee, and cinnamon—alongside piles of clothes and shoes to be haggled over by the townfolk and villagers. Visitors, too, frequently join the mélange because there is no better place than a market to take in the Caribbean kaleidoscope.

A Wealth of Activity

Against the Caribbean's rich and varied geographic and cultural landscape, visitors enjoy a cornucopia of sports and recreational facilities, entertainment, sightseeing, and shopping possibilities.

For sports the Caribbean has few rivals. Across its million square miles, sailing is suited for any type of boat, from Sailfish to ocean yachts. Yachters often call the stretch south from St. Vincent through the Grenadines the finest sailing water in the world. Snorkeling and scuba diving are excellent throughout the warm and exceptionally clear waters of the region. And while divers wander through the magnificent reefs and look for sunken treasures, nonswimmers need not miss the excitement. They can see it from the comfort of a glass-bottomed boat, recreational submarine, or underwater observatory.

Golf on championship layouts created by the most famous names in golf course design is available at many ports of call. The Bahamas and Puerto Rico each offers more than a dozen championship courses; Jamaica has six of them. And they have the added attraction of the Caribbean's beautiful and colorful landscape decorating the greens. Most cruise lines have golf programs or can arrange for their passengers to play golf at most ports of call.

You can also play tennis, squash, or polo and fish in the ocean or in mountain streams. There is horseback riding, jogging, hiking, biking, surfing, windsurfing, rafting, kayaking, tubing, waterskiing, parasailing, and more.

If you are less athletically inclined or simply want to enjoy nature and the outdoors, there are mile-long, powdery sand beaches where you can stretch out for the day with no more company than a couple of birds. You can spend the morning gathering shells, have a picnic by a secluded cove, stroll along bougainvillea-decorated lanes, or wander mountainsides overlooking deep green valleys and sapphire seas. Throughout the region are national parks, bird sanctuaries, mountain trails, and panoramas of magnificent scenery. Visitors can have a close-up look at a rain forest, drive into the crater of a volcano, bike over rolling meadows, hike through deep ravines, and explore some caves along the way.

Diversity of Destinations

No two Caribbean destinations are alike: Each has a personality, distinctive geographic features, and special charm with which it beguiles its admirers. Some places are tiny idyllic hideaways far from the beaten path with names familiar only to mapmakers and yachters. Others are big in size or seem big because of their strong character and regional influence, while still others are big on action, with gambling, shopping, and sophisticated dining and nightlife. Some locales have enough sports and entertainment to keep you busy every hour of the day; others test your ability to enjoy simple pleasures.

Few Caribbean destinations fit neatly into only one category: Most have features that contrast and overlap. One of the great advantages of a cruise is the chance to visit several places during one vacation and sample some of this variety. This is particularly true on a Western Caribbean cruise, where the kaleidoscope might change from lush, mountainous Jamaica to the low-lying Caymans, and from America's Caribbean at Key West to Mexico's Caribbean at Cozumel and Cancún, or from Mayan temples in Belize to river jungles in Guatemala.

A visit to any Caribbean destination is a visit to a foreign country—including those such as Puerto Rico and the US Virgin Islands, which are under the American flag. You can have a Dutch treat in St. Maarten, order lunch in French in Martinique, and pick up some golf tips in Spanish in Costa Rica. You will be able to count euros in Guadeloupe, pesos in the Dominican Republic, lempira in Honduras, and gilders in Curaçao, and add to your kids' stamp collections from such offbeat places as Antigua, Dominica, Saba, and Grenada.

The Caribbean is a learning experience, too. The region is rich in historic monuments, old forts, plantation homes, sugar mills, churches, and synagogues that have been beautifully restored and put to contemporary use as art galleries, boutiques, cafes, restaurants, inns, and museums. They help bring the region's history to life.

The New Caribbean

Learning about its history is also a way to help understand the region today. It is bound to Europe

---

by history, language, and culture; to Africa or Latin America by sentiment and emotion; and to the United States by economic and strategic necessity. So far, the region has shown it has the ability to survive on its own, but its problems have not disappeared.

The brightest prospect is tourism. Already tourist dollars pay for schools, roads, hospitals, and many other necessities. But tourism has limits. Too much can destroy the very elements that make the Caribbean so attractive.

Finally, a word about the people and pace of Paradise. Life in the Caribbean is leisurely. It is easy for Americans to become impatient with the slow pace of things, but remember, if you can, it's precisely the unhurried atmosphere you have come to enjoy. Americans often misinterpret a shyness and conservative nature toward strangers as unfriendliness. But after traveling from one end of the Caribbean to the other for almost three decades, we know from experience that the people of the Caribbean are as friendly as their music and as warm as their sunshine. They have wit, talent, dignity, and grace. They are generous and kind and will go out of their way to be helpful if you meet them with respect and greet them with a genuine smile.

We love the Caribbean. It's like magic. We recognize the elements that create the magic, although we don't quite know what makes it happen. Yet the experience is so delightful that we're happy to let the mystery remain.

The Delights of Cruising

People take cruises for various reasons. Some people are looking for fun, companionship, excitement, and romance—whether it's the romance of the sea or romance at sea. A cruise offers a change of pace and relaxation, new faces, new places, and a foreign environment. It is a different kind of holiday. Indeed, a cruise is so completely unlike other holiday experiences, it is difficult for those who have never taken one to imagine its pleasures or realize its true built-in value.

But to understand cruising today, let's step back a moment to consider the changes in the nature of steamship travel that have helped create today's cruising. Prior to the 1960s, most ships sailed between New York and Europe; Caribbean cruising was limited to the winter season, mainly because ships were not air-conditioned then. With the advent of the jet, which all but sank transatlantic steamship passenger travel, many ships shifted to the Caribbean in search of new markets.

Once the ships had taken up their new home ports, the pressure was on the cruise lines to get passengers from big centers in the northern United States to southern warm-weather ports with a minimum of difficulty. And this led to the birth of air/sea packages—value-packed holidays hard to beat.

In other words, the steamship companies whose very existence was threatened by the jet in the early 1960s had realized by the 1970s that the airlines were their best friends. Savings in fuel and the elimination of travel to and from northern ports in inclement weather were boons. At the same time, the cruise companies broadened their appeal by changing the old image of cruising from that of a pleasure only for the rich and idle to a new one that would attract people from all walks of life.

Changing Lifestyles

In the past, people saved all their lives to make a single trip. The ultimate dream was a trip around the world by ship. Today the stresses of modern life and the pressures of work and urban living have made it desirable—even necessary—to get away often, if only for a few days. Shorter, less expensive cruises have enabled more people to take them and to take them more often.

Speedier modes of transportation combined with greater affluence have made the short break the norm, especially for city dwellers. And nothing could be more ideal for a short, recuperative break than a cruise. No matter what your job or profession, a cruise offers a more complete break from the workaday world than almost anything else you can do. The expanse of sea and open sky brings a freedom and an awareness of space that can be totally therapeutic.

Convenience and Hassle-Free Travel

A cruise ship is no farther away than the nearest airport. When cruise lines began combining air transportation with the cruise and selling them as one product—an air/sea package—they made the trip not only more economical but also easier and more convenient for vacationers, even those from Salt Lake City or Detroit who had never before dreamed of taking a cruise. By assembling all the parts of a vacation in advance, cruise lines can provide a hassle-free holiday from the moment the passenger's travel begins. The air/sea combination becomes an extension of what the ship offers: namely, accommodations, meals, recreation, entertainment, sports, and transportation from port to port.

Once you have checked in at the airport in your hometown, you won't have to bother with your luggage again. It will be waiting in your cabin. You will be brought from the airport by motorcoach to the ship that awaits you at your port of embarkation without having to tote bags or give out tips.

The ease and comfort with which you can visit places that are hard to reach on your own are part of cruising's great attractions. Almost anyplace in the Caribbean can be reached by plane, but if you tried visiting Key West, Jamaica, and Cozumel or Nassau, St. Thomas, and Martinique in a week, you would spend most of your vacation in airports! Indeed, the more complex the travel—the more changes of hotels, trains, buses, and planes that a similar itinerary by land requires—the more attractive travel by ship can be. Your ship is not only your transportation, it is also your hotel. And that's where you gain the ultimate convenience—you pack and unpack only once. In our book, that's a real vacation!

Cruising is the ultimate escape. For a few days you can turn off your worries and live out your fantasies. There are no phones ringing and no computers blinking. Without even working at it, you relax. The pure air, the gentle movement of the ship gliding through the water, and the unhurried rhythm of shipboard life are instant antidotes to the noise, pollution, and pressures of daily life.

Because people travel to escape does not mean they seek isolation. On the contrary, meeting people is part of the fun of travel, and there is no better or easier place to do this than on ship. You feel the friendly atmosphere as soon as you start up the gangplank, where the smiling staff welcome you aboard, eager to serve you and see you enjoy yourself. You meet people from all over the country and from other parts of the world in an atmosphere of camaraderie. Yet if you really don't like to socialize, you can stand aside. Or if you are shy about meeting people, the ship's staff have dozens of clever ways to make it easier.

Onboard Activities

A cruise is what a vacation should be—fun! In fact, there are more ways to have fun on a cruise than there are hours in the day to enjoy them all. People often have the false notion they will become bored on a cruise, but there's little chance of boredom if you take advantage of all that is available.

For active people there are swimming, fitness classes, yoga, deck tennis, table tennis, workout gyms, and exercise and dance classes. Even rock climbing is sometimes offered! On some ships, onboard sports and fitness programs are combined with organized in-port snorkeling, diving, sailing, windsurfing, tennis, golf, and fishing. Or you can simply head for a beach and participate in these activities on your own.

With lavish meals so much a part of the cruise experience, it might seem incongruous that cruise lines spend millions on elaborate facilities and fitness programs to turn their floating resorts into floating health spas. But once again, this has come in response to changing lifestyles. Most have added new light dishes to their menus and designated their dining rooms and most lounges as non-smoking venues.

Those who like to learn are kept busy, too. Ships frequently have instructors and tournaments for bridge, language, arts and crafts, wine tasting, cooking, and computers, to name a few subjects. These enrichment programs, as the cruise lines call them, vary from ship to ship and cruise to cruise. Some ships build a cruise around a special theme such as mystery or photography; others offer annual cruises featuring classical music or jazz festivals at sea. Bingo is alive and well on ships, and so are other competitive games, along with casinos and slot machines.

Movies—new releases and old favorites—are shown daily in the ship's theater or on closed-circuit television in your cabin. The theater is also used for such special events as concerts by visiting artists, fashion shows, or Broadway-style shows.

Every evening before you go to bed, a schedule of the next day's activities is slipped under your door. You can take in all of them, pick and choose, or ignore the lot of it.

A Movable Feast

Cruising has given new meaning to the term *movable feast*. The feasting starts with morning coffee and tea for the early birds and breakfast in the dining room or on one of the parlor decks. Midmorning bouillon, afternoon tea, and the midnight buffet are cruise traditions. These snacks are provided in addition, of course, to lunch by the pool and the regular lunch and dinner served in the dining room. There, every day at every meal, the menu has three, four, or more selections for each course and half a dozen courses for each meal. All the new, large ships have several alternative restaurants; those of Norwegian Caribbean Line have up to eleven dining venues. The ships also cater to special dietary requirements and can provide salt-free, diabetic, vegetarian, or kosher meals.

Needless to say, every line believes it offers the best cuisine on the high seas, and all work hard to distinguish themselves. But dining on a cruise is a more important part of the cruise experience than simply eating a meal. In addition to sampling specialties and new dishes, you have the chance to get to know your traveling companions in a relaxed and congenial atmosphere and to enjoy the best part of shipboard service by dining room staffs who take pride in their work. The food, wine, music, dances, language, and people all give a ship its personality and ambience and make a cruise a special kind of holiday.

Nightlife is another attraction on a cruise. Cruise lines go out of their way to provide a variety of entertainment for different age groups and interests. All but the smallest ships have nightclubs and discos, and most have casinos. Most large ships offer full-scale Broadway- and Las Vegas–style shows. Best of all, they're there to enjoy only one or two decks from your cabin.

Cruising with Children

A cruise is one of the best possible vacations for families with children. There is no end to a child's fascination with a ship. It is a totally new experience, with an environment different from anything he or she has known at home. It's also an education. The crew members—many of whom are away from their own children—are wonderful with young passengers. There are always babysitters around, and you are never far from the children when you want to spend time on your own.

Once strictly adult territory, some cruise ships are so well equipped for children, they could be called floating camps. Trained youth counselors, often teachers and counselors on holiday or leave from their regular jobs, plan and supervise shipboard activities geared to specific age groups. Some ships have year-round counselors; others provide them during summer and other traditional vacation periods.

On the first day at sea, the counselors meet with parents and their children to review the week's activities and answer questions about facilities. Each morning a printed schedule especially for children is slipped under their door with the program for the day. Preteens are kept busy with pool parties, arts and crafts projects, movies, masquerades, scavenger hunts, and special entertainment such as magic shows, sports tournaments on deck, "Coketails," ice-cream parties, and talent shows.

Teenagers are likely to shun structured activities, and many prefer to be on their own. But the ship helps them get acquainted with a party. There are also pizza, hamburger, and disco parties to help ensure that the shy ones don't miss out on the fun. Some ships give the teenagers exclusive use of the disco while the adults are at cocktails or dinner. Dance contests, sports tournaments, fitness classes, language lessons, and theatrical productions are some of the other activities.

Shows with magicians, puppets, dancers, and singers are big hits with kids and parents alike.

And, too, there is children's favorite pastime—eating. Four servings of ice cream, if they want them. A cruise might be the one time in your life you will hear your children say, "I can't eat any more."

Children often get their own tours of the ship and even get to meet the captain. They often learn more about the ship and how it operates than many adults do. They learn about travel etiquette and different foods, experience new kinds of service, and learn how to socialize in new environments.

In port, the family can take the ship's organized tours or explore on its own. One of the great advantages of a cruise is its room for flexibility. If one member of the family does not want to go on a tour, it should not cause a family crisis. The ship is in full operation even when it is in port, so you never need worry about being left alone.

Family Reunions

Cruises are great for not only families with children but those with grandchildren, too. And they are ideal for family reunions, especially for families scattered around the country who find it hard to gather in one place—and do all that cooking! A cruise gives all members of the family equal time to spend with their favorite aunts, uncles, and cousins. Thanks to a ship's wide range of activities, there's always plenty to do, regardless of age. By sailing together, family members across the country can take advantage of group rates. Your travel agent can piece the parts together for you. All you need to do is agree on the cruise and the date.

Ideal Honeymoon

A cruise is what a honeymoon should be—romantic, relaxing, glamorous, different, and fun. It is a fairy tale come true. And it has the ingredients for a perfect honeymoon: privacy when you want it, attention when you need it; sports, music, dancing, and entertainment to share; sightseeing to enjoy. The atmosphere is a happy one. Honeymooners need not have a worry in the world. Everything is at their fingertips, including breakfast in bed. There are no big decisions to make, no travel hassles to face.

A cruise offers them total flexibility in making plans. No matter what the wedding date, they will be able to find a cruise. And thanks to the all-inclusive nature of a cruise, a couple can know the cost of the honeymoon in advance and plan accordingly.

A travel agent can also arrange for the honeymooners' extras that most ships offer. These might include champagne on the first night, flowers in the cabin, a wedding cake, an album for honeymoon photos, and a reception by the captain. Almost all ships have tables for two and cabins with double beds, which a travel agent can request when the reservations are made.

Ship captains cannot perform marriages aboard ship unless they are state-licensed. Some ships offers a ceremony during the cruise for reaffirmation of vows, and couples are given certificates as a remembrance. Some ships also double as a wedding chapel in their home port. The cruise line will provide a notary to conduct the wedding ceremony, or you can bring your own clergy member aboard to officiate. The ceremony can be simple or lavish and can be followed by a reception. Some couples have been known to take their wedding parties with them on their cruises!

Princess Cruises' *Grand Princess,* the largest cruise ship ever built when it was launched in 1998, has a real wedding chapel where you can be married by the captain in full ceremony in a lovely setting. Now other new Princess ships have a wedding chapel, too. You need to contact Princess Cruises in advance of your cruise to make the arrangements. The even larger Royal Caribbean's Voyager class and Freedom class of ships and the Carnival Cruises' newest ships also have wedding chapels.

Selecting a Cruise

Hints, Tips, and Advice

With so many cruises going to so many different places, selecting one can be difficult. Our suggestion is to start your planning at a travel agency. About 85 percent of all cruises are purchased through travel agents. It will not cost more than buying a cruise directly from a cruise line, and it will save you time.

Using a Travel Agent

A good travel agency stocks the brochures of the leading cruise lines; these show prices and details of each ship's itineraries and facilities. An experienced agent will help you understand the language of a cruise brochure, read a deck plan, and make reservations. The knowledgeable agent can help you make comparisons and guide you in the selection of a ship and an itinerary to match your interests. Your agent can book your dining room table and handle a particular request, such as for an anniversary party or a special diet. Agents also know about packages and discounts that can help you save money.

In recent years, with the boom in cruising, there has been rapid growth in travel agencies that sell only cruises. Such specialized agencies are more likely than general agencies—which sell all the products of travel—to have staffs with first-hand knowledge of many ships and should be able to give you a profile of the ship, its crew, and its personality. If not, you should go to another agency.

The Built-In Value of a Cruise Vacation

Of all the attractions of cruising, none is more important than value. For one price you get transportation, accommodations, meals, entertainment, use of all facilities, and a host of recreational activities. The only items not included are tips, drinks, personal services (such as hairdressers), and shore excursions. There are no hidden costs.

Dollar for dollar, it's hard to beat a cruise for value. To make an accurate assessment of how the cost of a cruise compares with that of other types of holidays, be sure to compare similar elements. A holiday at sea should be compared with a holiday at a luxury resort, because the quality of service, food, and entertainment on most cruises is available only at posh resorts or top-level all-inclusive resorts.

The average brochure price of a one-week Caribbean cruise can range from $100 to $300 per

person per day including all the ingredients previously described—but with discounts and advance purchase plans, these prices can often be cut in half. Shorter three- and four-day Bahamas cruises range from $100 to $250 per day, and there are plenty of low promotional fares available for them, too. No luxury resorts give you a hotel room, four full meals plus two or three snacks each day, nightly entertainment, and myriad activities—all for the one price of $100 to $300.

Stretching Your Budget

Air/sea combinations are available in two forms: an all-in-one package combining a cruise and air transportation in one price; or a second type in which the cruise is priced separately and an air supplement is added on to the cruise price, or a credit for air transportation from your hometown to the ship's nearest departure port is offered. The amount of the supplement or credit varies from one cruise line to another. But usually the supplement grows slightly higher the farther away from the departure port you live. Still, the total cost is less to you than if the cruise and air transportation were purchased separately. The details are spelled out in the cruise line's brochure. Ask your travel agent to explain how the package works; it can be confusing.

Is "Free" Air Free?

If you are skeptical—*you don't get something for nothing*—every cruise company publishes pamphlets that show the rates for every cabin on its ships, regardless of how passengers elect to get to the ship. If the cruise offers "free" air transportation and quotes one price for the package without a breakdown for each component, you can still discover the value by reading the section intended for those prospective passengers who live in or near the departure port of the ship.

Although air/sea packages save you money, it goes without saying that some definitely represent larger savings than others, depending on the cruise line, the cruise, and the time of year. Every line's policy is different, and policies vary not only from line to line but even from cruise to cruise on any specific ship. The introduction of new cruise lines and the addition of new cruise ships, particularly in the Caribbean, have created a buyer's market with real bargains. It pays to shop around.

Cruise-Only Fares

More and more, cruise line brochures quote "cruise-only" fares, rather than air/sea packages. The reasons: Crowded airplanes and crowded skies have often made it difficult for cruise lines to negotiate the low airfares of the past. Even when they can, the airlines—not cruise lines—control the routings, which often have deviations that lead to passenger complaints. Also, many cruise passengers have acquired frequent-flier miles they want to use for vacation travel.

Selecting a Ship

The ship's and the cruise line's reputation are other considerations in making your selection. Not only do ships differ; so do their passengers. You are more likely to enjoy a cruise with people who are seeking a similar type of holiday and with whom you share a community of interests and activities. A good travel agent who specializes in selling cruises is aware of the differences and should be able to steer you to a ship that's right for you. But before you visit an agent or begin to cull the colorful and enticing brochures, here are some tips on the items affecting cost that can help you in making a selection.

Selecting a Cabin

The largest single item in the cost of a cruise is the cabin, also known as a stateroom. The cost of a cabin varies greatly and is determined by its size and location. Generally, the cabins on the top deck are the largest and most expensive; the prices drop and the cabins narrow on each deck down from the top. (Elevators and stairs provide access between decks.) But the most expensive cabins are not necessarily the best. There are other factors to consider.

Almost all cruise ship cabins have private bathrooms, but the size and fittings vary and affect cost. For example, cabins with full bathtubs are more expensive than those with showers only. Greater standardization of cabins is a feature of most new cruise ships.

Outside cabins are more costly than inside ones. There is a common misconception that inside cabins are to be avoided. It dates from the days before air-conditioning, when an outside cabin above the waterline was desirable because the porthole could be opened for ventilation. Today's ships are climate-controlled; an inside cabin is as comfortable as an outside one. What's more, on a Caribbean cruise particularly, you will spend very little time in your cabin. It is mainly a place to sleep and change clothes. An inside cabin often provides genuine savings and is definitely worth investigating for those on a limited budget.

For the most stable ride, the deck at water level or below has less roll (side-to-side motion), and the cabins in the center of the ship have the least pitch (back-and-forth motion). But these cabins also cost more than those in the front (fore) or the back (aft) of the ship. Fore (or the bow) has less motion and is therefore preferable to aft (or the stern), where sometimes there is vibration from the ship's engines.

A ship's deck plan shows the exact location of each cabin and is usually accompanied by diagrams of the fittings in the cruise line's brochures. It does not give the dimensions of the cabin, but you can easily make a reasonable estimate by remembering that beds are standard single size—about 3 by 6 feet. Some ships have double beds, but most have twin beds that can be converted to doubles on request.

A few ships have single cabins; otherwise, a passenger booking a cabin alone pays a rate that is one and a half times the price per person for two sharing a cabin. A few ships offer special single rates on certain cruises or reserve a few cabins for single occupancy at the same rate as the per-person rate on a shared basis plus a small supplement. Your travel agent should be able to give you specific information about single rates.

Other Cost Factors

As might be expected, rates for the winter season in the Caribbean are higher than those in spring, summer, or fall. Cruises over Christmas, New Year's, and other major holidays are usually the year's most expensive, but often real bargains are to be found on cruises immediately before or after a holiday season, when demand drops and lines are eager to stimulate business.

The length of the cruise bears directly on its cost. Longer cruises provide more elegance and fancier dining and service. The cost also varies depending on the ship's itinerary. For example, it is more economical for a cruise line to operate a set schedule of the same ports throughout the year, such as the ships departing weekly from Florida to the Caribbean, than it is to change itineraries every few weeks.

Family Rates

If you are planning a family cruise, look for cruise lines that actively promote family travel and offer special rates for children or for third and fourth persons in a cabin. It means a bit of crowding but can yield big savings. Family rates vary from one cruise line to another. As a rule of thumb, children sharing a cabin with two paying adults get discounts of 50 percent or more from the minimum fare. Qualifying ages vary, too, with a child usually defined as two to twelve, and sometimes up to seventeen years. Some lines have teen fares, while at certain times of the year others have free or special rates for the third or fourth person sharing a cabin with two full-fare adults, regardless of age. Most lines permit infants under two years to travel free of charge.

Cruise Discounts

In today's highly competitive market, discounts have become a way of life. Cruise lines use them to publicize a new ship or itinerary and to attract families, younger passengers, singles, and a diversity of people. Some low fares are available year-round but may be limited to a certain number of cabins on each sailing, while others are seasonal or may apply to specific cruises.

You can take advantage of fare discounts in two ways. If you book early, you can usually benefit from early-bird discounts, often 50 percent or more, and of course you can be sure you take the cruise you want. On the other hand, if you are in a position to be flexible, you can wait to catch the last-minute "fire sales." To take advantage of this situation, you need to have maximum flexibility.

And remember, when you are buying a cruise, you will have already paid for all your accommodations, all meals (three meals a day is only the beginning; most ships have seven or more food services daily), all entertainment, and all recreational facilities aboard ship—and in many cases round-trip airfare to the ship's departure port (in air/sea packages), baggage handling, and transfers. It is this all-inclusive aspect of a cruise that makes it a good value—a particularly significant advantage for families with children and those who need to know in advance the cost of a vacation.

Shore Excursions

Sightseeing tours, called shore excursions by the cruise lines, are available for an additional cost at every port of call in the Caribbean. A pamphlet on the shore excursions your cruise line offers is usually included in the literature you receive prior to sailing. If not, ask for one. Also, many cruise lines now describe their shore excursions on their Web sites, and more and more are enabling you to book your excursions in advance online.

A few lines encourage travel agents to sell their shore excursions in advance; most don't. If you have not booked your excursion online in advance, you can buy them onboard ship from the purser, cruise director, or tour office. First-time cruisers are likely to prefer buying them onboard since, frequently, their interests and plans change once the cruise is under way.

A word of caution: When we first wrote this book, in 1987, we found that there was very little difference between the cruise ships' prices for tours and those of local tour companies if you were staying in a hotel. Since that time, however, the situation has changed so dramatically that we must alert you. In their need to keep their cruise prices down in the face of intense competition and rampant discounting, many cruise lines have come to regard shore excursions (as well as ancillary services such as shipboard shopping, bars, and spa facilities) as profit centers, and some are selling their tours at exorbitant prices.

In a preliminary survey, we found prices jacked up 30 to 50 percent; some are even double the prices you would pay on shore. To take an example, on Western Caribbean cruises, the most popular excursion, Tulum/Xel-Ha, varies from an overpriced US$75 for a three-hour trip from Playa del Carmen, and reasonable $55 to $68 for five- to six-hour trips from Cozumel, to a modest $39 for a seven-hour trip from Cancún—all for what is essentially the same trip.

To help you in your selection and to gauge fair prices, each port of call in this book includes descriptions of sample shore excursions offered by the majority of cruise lines, as well as some that you must arrange on your own. The approximate price of each excursion when you buy it directly from a tour company on shore is noted, where possible, along with the current price at which it is sold aboard ship. The prices were accurate at press time, but of course they are not guaranteed.

Since tours vary from vendor to vendor and cruise ship to cruise ship, it is difficult to generalize. When you check prices, then, it is important that you compare like items—and when necessary factor in such additional costs as transportation from the pier to the vendor's office or starting point. The information and prices provided here are intended as guidelines. Even if they change, the increase is not likely to be more than a dollar or two. If you come across shore excursion prices that appear to be out of line in comparison with those found in this book, please write to us in care of the publisher and enclose a copy of the tours with their descriptions and prices sold on your cruise.

The good news is that cruise lines have finally gotten the message that passengers want to do more than shop, so they have been making a great effort to expand the type and variety of their shore excursions, especially creating programs that appeal to active passengers. Now, in almost every Caribbean port of call, passengers can go hiking, biking, kayaking, tubing, horseback riding, diving, snorkeling, and more. Another piece of good news is that on the television in your cabin, you can watch a video of the tours being offered by your ship.

Port Talks

All ships offer what is known as a port talk—a brief description of the country or island and port where the ship will dock, as well as shopping tips.

The quality of these talks varies enormously, not only with the cruise line but also with the ship, and can depend on such wide-ranging considerations as the knowledge and skill of the cruise staff member giving the talk and the policy of the cruise line as to the true purpose of the information.

You should be aware that most cruise lines in the Caribbean have turned these port talks into sales pitches for certain products and stores with which they have exclusive promotional agreements and in which the cruise lines take commissions or are paid directly by the stores. You will receive a map of the port with "recommended" shops. What that really means is that the shop has paid the cruise line for being promoted in port talks and advertising in the ship's magazine that might appear in your cabin. Also, sometimes cruise directors or shore excursion companies receive commissions from local stores, even though they deny it. Hence, their vested interest could color their presentation and recommendations.

There are three ways to avoid being misled. If a cruise line, a cruise director, a guide, or anyone else recommends one store to the exclusion of all others, that should alert you to shop around before buying. The recommended store may actually be the best place to buy—but it may not. Second, if you are planning to make sizable purchases of jewelry, cameras, or china, check prices at home before you leave and bring that list of prices with you. Be sure, however, you are comparing like products. Finally, check the prices in shipboard shops, which are usually very competitive with those at ports of call.

Happily, because you have this book, you do not need to rely on port talks for information, but if you do attend your ship's port talks and find that they are more sales pitch than enlightenment, please write and tell us about your experience.

What You Should Know Before You Go

Luggage and Wardrobe: There are no limits on the amount of luggage you can bring aboard ship, but most staterooms do not have much closet and storage space. More important, since you are likely to be flying to your departure port, you need to be guided by airline regulations regarding excess baggage. Many are charging for excess over fifty or fifty-five pounds. Life on a cruise, especially a Caribbean one, is casual. It is needless to be burdened with a lot of baggage, as you will spend your days in sports clothes—slacks, shorts, T-shirts, bathing suits. Men usually are asked to wear a jacket at dinner.

The first and last nights of your cruise and the nights your ship is in port almost always call for casual dress. At least one night will be the captain's gala party, where tuxedos or dark suit for men and long or cocktail dress or evening pantsuit for women are requested but not mandatory. Indeed, the need is less and less with each passing year. Another night might be a masquerade party; it's entirely up to you whether or not to participate.

A gentleman who does not have a tuxedo should bring a basic dark suit and white shirt. Add a selection of slacks and sport shirts, one or two sport jackets, and two pairs of bathing trunks. Women will find nylon and similar synthetics are good to use on a cruise because they are easy to handle, but these fabrics can be hot under the tropical sun. It largely depends on your tolerance for synthetic fabrics in hot weather. Personally, we find cottons and cotton blends to be the most comfortable. You will need two cocktail dresses for evening wear. A long dress for the captain's party is appropriate but not required. Add a sweater or wrap for cool evening breezes and the ship's air-conditioning in the dining room and lounges. Take cosmetics and sun lotion, but don't worry if you forget something. It will most likely be available in shipboard or portside shops.

You will need rubber-soled shoes for walking on deck and a comfortable pair of walking shoes for sightseeing. Sunglasses and a hat or sun visor for protection against the strong Caribbean sun are essential. A tote bag comes in handy for carrying odds and ends; include several plastic bags for wet towels and bathing suits upon returning from a visit to a beach. You might also want to keep camera equipment in plastic bags as protection against the salt air and water and sand. And don't forget to pack whatever sporting equipment and clothes you will need. If you plan to snorkel, scuba dive, or play tennis, often you can save on rental fees by bringing your own gear.

Documentation: Requirements for vaccinations, visas, and so on depend on the destinations of the ship and are detailed in the information you receive from the cruise lines. Among the Caribbean's many advantages is that normally, no destination (except Cuba, which is not covered in this book) requires visas of US and Canadian citizens arriving as cruise passengers. However, US government regulations that took effect in January 2007 require all US citizens returning from the Caribbean to have a passport in order to reenter the United States. Actually, every traveler should have a passport—it's the best identification you can carry.

Mealtimes: All but the most luxurious Caribbean cruise ships have two sittings for the main meals. Early-sitting breakfast is from 7:00 to 8:00 A.M.; lunch is from noon to 1:00 P.M.; and dinner is from 6:15 to 7:30 P.M. On the late sitting, breakfast is from 8:00 to 9:00 A.M.; lunch is from 1:30 to 2:30 P.M.; and dinner is from 8:15 to 9:30 P.M. If you are an early riser, you will probably be happy with the early sitting. If you are likely to close the disco every night, you might prefer the late one. Of course, you will not be confined to these meals as there is usually a buffet breakfast, lunch on deck, a midnight buffet, and afternoon tea.

Also, more and more ships, particularly the new ones, have alternative dining venues, plus turning the Lido restaurant into a casual evening dining venue. Some ships also have added specialty restaurants. In another effort to provide flexibility, many ships have open seating for breakfast and lunch and assigned seats for dinner only.

Norwegian Cruise Lines (NCL) has introduced FreeStyle Cruising, which provides the most flexibility of all—passengers dine when, where, and with whom they want. NCL's newest ships have as many as eleven restaurants. Princess Cruises and Carnival Cruises have followed suit with similar programs.

Requesting a Table: Your travel agent can request your table in advance, if you want a table for two or for your family, as well as your preference for early or late seating. Some cruise lines will confirm your reservation in advance; others require you to sign up for your dining table with the maître d'hôtel soon after boarding your ship. In this day of computers, it's hard to understand why any cruise line would want to put a passenger through this unnecessary inconvenience, but some do.

Electrical Appliances: Cabins on almost all new ships have outlets for electric razors and have hair dryers or are wired for them, but older ships do not. Instead, rooms with special outlets are provided. Few ships allow you to use electric irons in your cabin because of the potential fire hazard. Electric current is normally 115 to 120 volts—but not always—and plugs are the two-pronged American type. Check with your cruise line for specific information.

Laundry and Dry Cleaning: All ships have either laundry service for your personal clothing (for which there is an extra charge) or coin-operated laundry rooms. Only a very few have dry-cleaning facilities. In the Caribbean this is not an important consideration, as the clothes required are cotton or cotton blends and should be easy to wash.

Beauty Salons and Spas: All but the smallest Caribbean cruise ships have beauty salons and spas for both men and women. New, big ships have large, elaborate spas with a wide range of treatments. Prices are comparable to those at deluxe resorts.

Religious Services: All ships hold interdenominational services; many also have a daily Catholic Mass. Services will be conducted by the captain or a clergy member. At ports of call you will be welcome to attend local services.

Medical Needs: All cruise ships are required by law to have at least one doctor, nurse, and infirmary or mini hospital. Doctor visits and medicine cost extra.

Seasickness: First-time cruise passengers probably worry more about becoming seasick than about any other aspect of cruising. Certainly they worry more than they should, particularly on a Caribbean cruise, where the sea is calm almost

year-round. Ships today have stabilizers, which steady them in all but the roughest seas. But if you are still worried, there are several types of nonprescription medicines such as Dramamine and Bonine that help to guard against motion sickness. Buy some to bring along—you may not need it, but having it with you might be comforting. Also, the ship's doctor can provide you with Dramamine and other medication that will be immediately effective should you need it.

Sea Bands are a useful product for seasickness prevention. They are a pair of elasticized wristbands, each with a small plastic disk that, based on the principle of acupuncture, applies pressure on the inside of the wrist. We use Sea Bands and have given them to friends to use and can attest to their effectiveness. They are particularly useful for people who have difficulty taking medication. Sea Bands are found in drug, toiletry, and health care stores and can be ordered from Travel Accessories, P.O. Box 391162, Solon, OH 44139; call (216) 248-8432. Sequined covers are even available in a dozen colors to wear over the bands for evening.

There are two important things to remember about seasickness: First, don't dwell on your fear; and second, remember that even the best sailors and frequent cruisers need a day to get their sea legs. If you should happen to get a queasy feeling, take some medicine immediately. The worst mistake you can make is to play the hero, thinking it will go away. When you deal with the symptoms immediately, relief is fast, and you are seldom likely to be sick. If you wait, the queasy feeling will linger, and you run a much greater risk of being sick.

Caution against the Caribbean sun: You should be extra careful about the sun in the tropics. It is much stronger than the sun to which most people are accustomed. Do not stay in the direct sun for long stretches at a time, and use a sunscreen at all times. Nothing can spoil a vacation faster than a sunburn.

Shipboard Shops: There's always a shop for essentials you might have forgotten or that can't wait until the next port of call. Many ships—particularly the new ones—have elaborate shops competitive with stores at ports of call. It's another reason to pack lightly, since you are almost sure to buy gifts and souvenirs during the cruise.

Tipping: Tipping is a matter of a great deal of discussion but much less agreement. How much do you tip in a restaurant or a hotel? Normally, the tip should be about $3.50 per person per day for each of your cabin stewards and dining room waiters. On some ships, particularly those with Greek crew and on small adventure-type ships, the custom is to contribute to the ship's common kitty in the belief that those behind the scenes such as kitchen staffs should share in the bounty. On some ships, dining room staffs also pool their tips. More recently, some cruise lines have begun adding a specific amount for gratuities to passengers' shipboard accounts at the end of a cruise, and passengers are at liberty to increase or decrease the levy. Any such charges will be explained. Tipping guidelines are sometimes printed in literature your cruise line sends in advance, enabling you to factor the expense into your budget even before booking a cruise. The cruise director, as part of the advice-giving session at the end of the cruise, also explains the ship's policy and offers guidelines.

Communications: New ships have telephones in cabins with international direct-dialing capability and fax facilities in their offices. Be warned, however: The service is very expensive—$6 to $15 per minute. If someone at home or in your office needs to reach you in an emergency, she or he can telephone your ship directly. Those calling from the continental United States would dial 011 plus 874 (the ocean area code for the Caribbean), followed by the seven-digit telephone number of your ship.

Someone calling from Puerto Rico should dial 128 and ask for the long-distance operator.

Instructions on making such calls, how to reach the ship, or whom to notify in case of an emergency are usually included in the information sent to you by your cruise line along with your tickets and luggage tags. If not, your travel agent can obtain them. You should have this information before you leave home.

Most ships sailing the Caribbean have e-mail and Internet facilities; some have Internet access in their cabins. The trend toward equipping ships with wireless capabilities has recently picked up steam, enabling passengers to use their wireless-enabled computers at sea. The fees that cruise lines charge for the use of Internet access usually range from 40 to 75 cents per minute. Some ships have packages of a hundred or more minutes, which can bring down the cost. In the case of wireless, the charge is usually $10 per day. Keep in mind that almost all ports in the Caribbean have conveniently located Internet cafes where the cost is generally much cheaper than on cruise ships.

The ability to use a cell phone equipped for international calling is becoming more and more widely available. Norwegian Cruise Lines' *Norwegian Jewel* and *Norwegian Sun* were the first ships equipped with the technology to enable cell phone connection virtually anywhere they sail. Now all NCL ships have this capacity, and it's rapidly becoming a standard feature on new ships. Be aware, however, that you will be billed by your phone company at long-distance or international rates—likely about $5 per minute. Information on cell phone use aboard your ship should be provided in advance by your cruise line. If not, ask for it.

PART TWO

Caribbean Cruise Lines and Their Ships

A Guide

Every effort has been made to ensure the accuracy of the information on the cruise lines and their ships, their ports of call, and prices, but do keep in mind that cruise lines change their ships' itineraries often, and for a variety of reasons. Always check with the cruise line or with a travel agent before making plans. For specific information on the itineraries of ships cruising to the Caribbean, see the chart at the end of this book.

American Canadian Caribbean

461 Water Street, Warren, RI 02885; (401) 247-0955; (800) 556-7450; fax (401) 245-8303; www.accl-smallships.com

Ships (passengers): *Grande Caribe* (100); *Grande Mariner* (100)

Departure ports: Various ports

Types of cruises: 11 days of Bahamas; Virgin Islands; Turks and Caicos

Lifestyle tips: Family-style dining; mature and experienced passengers; light adventure; no frills; emphasis on natural attractions and local culture

If you are looking for tranquility, informality, and conversation with fellow passengers instead of floor shows and casinos, American Canadian Caribbean Line offers low-key cruises around the Bahamas archipelago and the Caribbean during the winter season.

In 1964 the late Luther Blount designed his first small ship for cruising Canada's inland waterways. By 1988 the line had expanded to the extent that it could add Caribbean to its name. In the intervening years, ACCL remained faithful to the concept that small, intimate ships with limited planned entertainment can be successful. The ships' innovative bow ramps and shallow drafts give passengers direct access to beaches, coves, and places that are inaccessible to larger ships.

ACCL's ships are popular with mature, well-traveled passengers who like hearty American menus and the informal atmosphere of family-style dining. It is an atmosphere for instant friendships and complete relaxation. The line's large number of

repeaters would seem to indicate that passengers agree with its concept and appreciate the "in-close" facility the ships bring to the cruise experience.

Carnival Cruise Lines

3655 Northwest Eighty-seventh Avenue, Miami, FL 33178-2428; (305) 599-2600; (800) 438-6744; fax (305) 599-8630; www.carnival.com

Ships (passengers): *Carnival Conquest* (2,974); *Carnival Destiny* (2,642); *Carnival Dream* (3,652); *Carnival Freedom* (2,974); *Carnival Glory* (2,974); *Carnival Legend* (2,124); *Carnival Liberty* (2,974); *Carnival Magic* (3,652); *Carnival Miracle* (2,124); *Carnival Pride* (2,124); *Carnival Spirit* (2,124); *Carnival Splendor* (3,006); *Carnival Triumph* (2,758); *Carnival Valor* (2,974); *Carnival Victory* (2,758); *Celebration* (1,486); *Ecstasy* (2,052); *Elation* (2,052); *Fantasy* (2,056); *Fascination* (2,052); *Holiday* (1,452); *Imagination* (2,052); *Inspiration* (2,052); *Paradise* (2,052); *Sensation* (2,052)

Departure ports: Miami, Port Canaveral, Tampa, New Orleans, San Juan, Galveston, Jacksonville, Mobile, Fort Lauderdale, year-round; New York, Charleston, Norfolk, summer/fall

Types of cruises: 3, 4, and 5 days to Bahamas and Key West; 4 to 10 days to Western, Northern, Eastern, and Southern Caribbean, and the Panama Canal

Lifestyle tips: The "Fun Ships"; youthful, casual, action-filled; high value for money

Carnival Cruise Lines is the stuff of legends. In 1972 the late Florida-based cruise executive Ted Arison and an innovative Boston-based travel agency bought the *Empress of Canada*, which they renamed the *Mardi Gras* to start a cruise line that would stand the stodgy old steamship business on its ear. But alas, the *Mardi Gras* ran aground on her maiden cruise. After staring at losses three years in a row, Arison took full ownership of the company, assuming its $5 million debt, buying its assets—the ship—for $1, and launched the "Fun Ships" concept that is Carnival's hallmark.

The idea was to get away from the class-conscious elitism that had long been associated with luxury liners and to fill the ship with so much action-packed fun that the ship itself would be the cruise experience. The line also aimed at lowering the average age of passengers by removing the formality associated with cruising and providing a wide selection of activity and entertainment to attract active young adults, young couples, honeymooners, and families with children at reasonable prices. In only a few months, Carnival turned a profit, and in the following two years it added two more ships.

The line's next move was as surprising as it was bold. In 1978, when shipbuilding costs and fuel prices were skyrocketing—threatening the very future of vacations at sea—Carnival ordered a new ship, larger and more technologically advanced than any cruise ship in service. It changed the profile of ships and enhanced the "fun" aspects of cruises. But it was Carnival's *next* move that really set the trend of the 1980s and beyond.

In 1982, less than ten years after its rocky start, Carnival ordered three "superliners," *Holiday*, *Jubilee*, and *Celebration*, each carrying 1,800 passengers, with design and decor as far removed from the grand old luxury liner as could be imagined. The decor was so different, it was zany. The owners called it "a Disney World for adults." On the *Holiday*, the main promenade deck, called "Broadway," complete with boardwalk and a Times Square, had as much glitz and glitter as the neon on Broadway. In the 1990s Carnival outdid itself with the *Fantasy* group, eight megaliners even more dazzling than the earlier superliners. A ship for the twenty-first century, the *Fantasy*, with its flashy decor and high-energy ambience, has at its heart an atrium, awash in lights, towering seven decks high. Here and in the entertainment areas, 15 miles of computerized lights are programmed to change color—constantly, but imperceptibly—from white and cool blue to hot red, altering the ambience with each change. The ships have full-fledged gyms and spas and so many entertainment and recreation outlets that you need more than one cruise to find them all. The eight megaliners were followed by *Carnival Destiny*, the world's largest cruise ship when it was put in service in 1996. Since then Carnival has added two new classes of ships—four 110,000-ton megaliners and four 88,500-ton superliners—and is building

another, even larger class, 130,000-ton ships carrying 3,652 passengers. Carnival's largest ships are called "post-Panamax," meaning that they are too large to transit the Panama Canal. All Carnival ships have Internet cafes and are fitted for wireless connections.

Now headed by Arison's son, Micky, Carnival is directed by an energetic and aggressive team that seems determined to entice everybody—single, married, families, children, retirees, disabled, first-time cruisers, repeat cruisers, people from the North, South, East, and West, and all walks of life—to take a cruise. Toward that end, the cruises are priced aggressively and offer among the best values in cruising.

Carnival has a 24-hour toll-free hotline to help passengers who encounter a travel emergency, such as severe weather or an airline delay or strike, en route or returning from their cruise. The US number is (800) 885-4856; outside the United States, call collect (305) 406-4779. The service is staffed by Carnival employees.

Do all these ideas work? You bet they do! Carnival has twenty-two cruise ships in service, carrying more than three million passengers a year; three more very large ships are under construction. That's up from 80,000 passengers in its first year. Carnival Cruise Lines is a public company and owns the long-established Holland America Line, Costa Cruises, Cunard, Princess Cruises, and Seabourn Cruise Line. Altogether, Carnival Corporation operates eighty-three cruise ships, accounting for more than 49 percent of the US cruise market. These lines operate under their own banners, but the combination makes Carnival one of the world's largest cruise lines and gives it enormous marketing clout across the widest possible spectrum.

Celebrity Cruises

1050 Caribbean Way, Miami, FL 33132; (305) 539-6000; (800) 646-1456; fax (800) 437-5111; www.celebrity.com

Ships (passengers): *Azamara Journey* (710); *Azamara Quest* (710); *Celebrity Century* (1,750); *Celebrity Constellation* (1,950); *Celebrity Eclipse* (2,850); *Celebrity Equinox* (2,850); *Celebrity Galaxy* (1,750); *Celebrity Infinity* (1,950); *Celebrity Mercury*

(1,750); *Celebrity Millennium* (1,950); *Celebrity Solstice* (2,850); *Celebrity Summit* (1,950); *Celebrity Xpedition* (94)

Departure ports: Fort Lauderdale, San Juan, Jacksonville, Miami, Cape Liberty

Types of cruises: 2 to 5 nights to the Bahamas; 7 to 14 nights to Northern, Southern, Western, and Eastern Caribbean; Bermuda

Lifestyle tips: Modestly deluxe cruises at moderate prices

When John Chandris, the nephew of the founder of Chandris Cruises, announced the creation of a new deluxe midpriced cruise line in 1989, he said the goal was "to bring more luxurious cruises to experienced travelers at affordable prices." He was met with a great deal of skepticism; *deluxe* and *midpriced* seemed a contradiction in terms. But three years later he had made believers out of all his doubters.

Not only did Celebrity Cruises accomplish what it set out to do, it did it better than anyone had imagined and in record-breaking time. A Celebrity cruise is not only deluxe, but also offers true value for the money.

Celebrity was a completely new product with a new generation of ships designed for the 1990s and beyond. It defined the ideal size of a cruise ship and the appropriate layout, cabins, decor, and ambience for its market and set new standards of service and cuisine in its price category.

Celebrity's ships are not as glitzy as some of the new megaliners, but they are spacious and have a similar array of entertainment and recreation. The once-standard one-lounge-for-all was replaced by small, separate lounges, each with its own decor, ambience, and entertainment, and a variety of bars to give passengers a range of options. They have stunning, stylish decor that brought back some of the glamour of cruising in bygone days, but with a fresh, contemporary look.

From its inception, Celebrity Cruises aimed at creating superior cuisine as one way to distinguish itself. It engaged as its food consultant an award-winning master French chef with two Michelin three-star restaurants in England and other food enterprises. The food is high quality, sophisticated but unpretentious. Celebrity was launched with stylish, elegant ships that were classic and very contemporary at the same time. They have mostly outside staterooms equipped with television service that carries daily programs of events, first-run movies, and world news; a piano bar; a nightclub; a duplex show lounge with state-of-the-art sound and lighting systems; a disco; a casino; and an observation lounge. There are shops, a sports and fitness center, two swimming pools, three Jacuzzis, and Internet cafes. In the suites, butler service is available. As a send-off on the last day of the cruise, all passengers may enjoy a classic high tea with white-glove service and classical music.

In 1992 Celebrity introduced three new megaliners even more spacious and luxurious than the first ships. In 2000 the line launched the millennium with another new class of four ships, even larger, more spacious, and more elegant than the previous ones. In 2004 the line acquired the deluxe 94-passenger *Celebrity Xpedition*, based year-round in the Galapagos. Three years later, Celebrity acquired two 710-passenger ships, creating a small ship brand, Azamara Cruises, and announced construction on *Celebrity Solstice,* the first of an even larger class of three 118,000-ton ships to carry 2,850 passengers apiece and to be introduced between 2008 and 2010. Celebrity Cruises was bought by Royal Caribbean in 1997, but operates as a separate company.

Costa Cruise Lines

Venture Corporate Center II, 200 South Park Road, Suite 200, Hollywood, FL 33021-8541; (954) 266-5600; (954) 266-2100; (800) GO-COSTA; www.costacruise.com

Ships (passengers): *Costa Allegra* (1,000), *Costa Atlantica* (2,114); *Costa Classica* (1,356); *Costa Concordia* (3,300); *Costa Europa* (1,494); *Costa Fortuna* (2,720); *Costa Magica* (2,720); *Costa Marina* (1,000); *Costa Mediterranea* (2,114); *Costa Romantica* (1,356); *Costa Serena* (3,300); *Costa Victoria* (1,928)

Departure ports: Miami, Fort Lauderdale, Guadeloupe

Types of cruises: 7 days to Western, Northern, and Eastern Caribbean

Lifestyle tips: More European atmosphere and service than similar mass-market ships

"Cruising Italian Style" has long been Costa Cruise Lines' stock in trade, with a fun and friendly atmosphere created by its Italian staff. The emphasis is on Italian food, which means pasta and pizza (there are other kinds of cuisine, too); European-style service, particularly in the dining room; and, not to forget the Italians' ancestry, a toga party, which is usually a hilarious affair, one night of the cruise.

Founded by the Genoa-based Costa family, which has been in the shipping business for more than a hundred years and in the passenger business for almost sixty, Costa began offering one-week Caribbean cruises from Miami in 1959. It was the first to offer an air/sea program, introduced in the late 1960s.

Costa launched the 1990s with new ships, introducing interesting new features in its design, combining classic qualities with modern features and boasting unusually large cabins for their price categories. Among the ships' nicest features are canvas-covered outdoor cafes and pizzerias serving pizza throughout the day without additional charge. The ships also have Internet cafes.

Catalina Island is Costa's "private" beach off the southeast coast of the Dominican Republic, featured on Eastern Caribbean cruises. The island is near the sprawling resort of Casa de Campo, which has, among its many facilities, three of the best golf courses in the Caribbean, a tennis village, horseback riding, and polo. With Casa de Campo's new marina and seaside village, Costa ships usually call at the island during the day and move to the marina for the nightlife. Costa's ships have fitness centers and spas (most services are extra), along with a health and fitness program to suit individual needs. Costa lets you combine two consecutive cruises into one fourteen-day trip, at a price considerably less than that of two separate cruises. Another popular feature: During a Caribbean cruise a couple can renew their wedding vows in a special shipboard ceremony.

Costa is owned by Carnival Cruise Lines but operates as a separate entity.

Crystal Cruises

2049 Century Park East, Suite 1400, Los Angeles, CA 90067; (310) 785-9300; fax (310) 785-3891; www.crystalcruises.com

Ships (passengers): *Crystal Serenity* (1,080); *Crystal Symphony* (960)

Departure ports: Miami and worldwide

Types of cruises: 10- to 17-day Eastern/Western with transcanal

Lifestyle tips: Ultraluxury for sophisticated travelers

The launching of Crystal Cruises in 1989 was one of the most anticipated in the cruising world. The owners spared no expense to ensure that the sleek *Crystal Harmony* (transferred in 2005 to a new sister company of its owners, Mitsubishi) would live up to its advance billing. Its goal was to create luxury cruises that would return elegance and personalized service to cruising and be designed for an upscale mass market at deluxe prices.

The *Crystal Harmony* exceeded expectations and quickly became the ship by which others in its class—or trying to be in its class—are measured.

Crystal Symphony is essentially a copy of the *Crystal Harmony*, with some refinements and new features. For example, there are no inside staterooms. The *Crystal Serenity* has taken luxury to another level with larger cabins, more cabins with balconies, a larger spa, and more dining options, including a specialty restaurant by famed master chef Nobu Matsuhisa. The ships are magnificent, with exquisite attention to detail. The food is excellent and the service superb, with the staff at every level smiling and gracious and always willing to go the extra mile.

These are spacious ships for experienced travelers with sophisticated lifestyles. The luxury is evident from the moment you step aboard. The atrium lobby, the ship's focus, is accented with greenery and hand-cut glass sculptures. The piano bar features—what else?—a crystal piano.

Staterooms have sitting areas, mini bars, spacious closets, and such amenities as hair dryers, plush robes, VCRs, and 24-hour hookup with CNN and ESPN; more than half have verandas. The ships' penthouses have Jacuzzis and butler service. Facilities include spa and fitness centers and full promenade decks for jogging. The indoor/outdoor swimming pools have swim-up bars and lap pools with adjacent whirlpools. The ships have casinos.

The ships' most innovative feature was the choice of dinner restaurants—Japanese, Asian, and Italian—at no extra cost, which set a new trend for cruising. These restaurants are in addition to standard meal service in the main dining room and 24-hour room service.

Crystal's ships offer Computer University@Sea, with hands-on lab sessions. Laptop computers can be rented. Crystal also offers passengers their own e-mail address to use on board.

Cunard

24303 Town Center Drive, Suite 200, Valencia, CA 91355-0908; (661) 753-1035; (800) 7-CUNARD; fax (661) 259-3103; www.cunard.com

Ships (passengers): *Queen Mary 2* (2,620); *Queen Victoria* (2,014)

Departure ports: New York, Fort Lauderdale

Types of cruises: 8 to 14 days for Caribbean on seasonal schedules

Lifestyle tips: Deluxe, and no mistaking the British touch; caters mostly to affluent travelers

The 150,000-ton *Queen Mary 2,* the largest cruise ship ever built, is heir to a family of transatlantic liners whose history reaches back more than a century and a half. Of these, it's the only ship still on regular transatlantic service, from April to December.

The *Queens* set the standard of elegance at sea in times of peace and served their country with distinction in times of war. Today the *QM2,* which made its maiden voyage in January 2004, set the tone for Cunard for the years to come. An ocean liner reminiscent of the great steamships, it is—in Cunard's words—meant to "relaunch the golden age of travel for those who missed the first one."

Costing more than $800 million, the *QM2* is one of the world's fastest ships, with speeds up to 30 knots. It carries 2,620 passengers in a "quasi-class system," with cabin category determining

assignments in each of three restaurants—one with a grand staircase similar to that moviegoers saw in *Titanic.* Seventy-five percent of the cabins have balconies.

The *QM2* boasts the largest spa afloat, designed by the famous Canyon Ranch, which also operates it.

In 1998 Cunard was purchased by Carnival Cruises but operates as a separate company.

Even though Cunard is one of the oldest lines afloat, it has been an innovator, responding to today's changing lifestyles with gusto and recognizing the impact of the electronic revolution on people's lives—including their vacations. Its ships were the first to have full-fledged spas, computer learning centers, and satellite-delivered world news at sea.

Upon the arrival of the *QM2,* the *QE2* was transferred to England and marketed primarily to the British market. In 2007 Cunard announced that the *QE2* had been sold and would make its last voyage for the line in spring 2008.

Disney Cruise Line

210 Celebration Place, Suite 400, Celebration, FL 34747-4600; (407) 566-3500; (800) 939-CRUISE; fax (407) 566-6910; www.disneycruise.com

Ships (passengers): *Disney Magic* (1,760); *Disney Wonder* (1,760)

Departure port: Port Canaveral

Types of cruises: 3-, 4-, 5, and 7-day Eastern and Western cruises combined with Disney World vacations

Lifestyle tips: Family-oriented but designed for all ages

Disney Cruise Line was launched in July 1998, with its first ship, the *Disney Magic,* followed by a sister ship the *Disney Wonder* in 1999. Both have classic exteriors reminiscent of the great transatlantic ocean liners of the past, but inside they are up-to-the-minute in Disney innovation and family entertainment.

The line combines a three- or four-day stay at a Walt Disney World resort with a three- or four-day cruise, sailing round-trip from Port Canaveral. The itinerary includes Nassau and a day at Castaway Cay, Disney's own private island. In 2000 the line introduced a seven-day itinerary combining the Bahamas with the Eastern Caribbean; the following year it added Western Caribbean cruises.

In addition to catering to families, *Disney Wonder* and *Disney Magic's* major innovations are three themed restaurants as well as an adults-only alternative restaurant, a swimming pool, and a nightclub on each ship.

Nightly entertainment features Disney-produced shows with Broadway-quality entertainers, cabaret, and a comedy club.

The children's programs are the most extensive in the industry, with the largest children-dedicated space, age-specific activities, and numerous counselors. The ships have a separate pool, lounge, teen club, and game arcade for older kids.

The ships sport spacious suites and cabins, with 73 percent outside; almost half boast small verandas.

Disney Cruises has announced its intention to build two new megaliners to be added to its fleet in 2011 and 2012.

Holland America Line

300 Elliott Avenue West, Seattle, WA 98119; (206) 281-3535; (800) 426-0327; fax (206) 301-5327; www.hollandamerica.com

Ships (passengers): *Amsterdam* (1,380); *Eurodam* (2041); *Maasdam* (1,266); *Noordam* (1,848); *Oosterdam* (1,848); *Prinsendam* (794); *Rotterdam* (1,316); *Ryndam* (1,266); *Statendam* (1,266); *Veendam* (1,266); *Volendam* (1,440); *Westerdam* (1,848); *Zaandam* (1,440); *Zuiderdam* (1,848)

Departure ports: Fort Lauderdale, Tampa, New York; Boston, Norfolk seasonally

Types of cruises: 5 to 11 days to Western and Eastern Caribbean; 10 days to Southern Caribbean; 10 to 23 days to Panama Canal

Lifestyle tips: Classic but contemporary

Begun in 1873 as a transatlantic shipping company between Rotterdam and the Americas, Holland America Line stems from one of the oldest

steamship companies in the world. Through the years and two world wars, its ships became an important part of maritime history, particularly significant in the westward passage of immigrants to America. The line also owned Westours, the Seattle-based tour company that pioneered tours and cruises to Alaska in the 1950s. The following year the group was purchased by Carnival Cruise Lines, but the lines operate as separate entities.

Holland America now has one of the newest fleets in cruising, having added ten magnificent, brand-new ships in less than ten years. The ships combine the Old World with the New in decor and ambience and boast million-dollar art and antiques collections reflecting Holland's association with trade and exploration in the Americas and Asia. Their Dutch officers and Indonesian and Filipino crews are another reminder of Holland's historical ties to Asia.

The ships have the space and elegance for the two-week-plus cruises for which they were designed. They feature a three-level atrium lobby with unusual sculpture, an elegant two-level dining room, small lounges and bars, a disco, a casino, a large state-of-the-art spa, a sliding-glass dome for the swimming pool, spacious cabins, and premium amenities. All suites and 120 deluxe cabins have private verandas, whirlpool baths, mini bars, and VCRs. There are bathtubs in all outside cabins.

In 1997 Holland America bought the uninhabited 2,400-acre Bahamian island of Little San Salvador, located between Eleuthera and Cat Island, renaming it Half Moon Cay and developing it as a private island that's now included on all its Caribbean itineraries. Ships anchor offshore and tender passengers ashore. There the line's multimillion-dollar facility, covering forty-five acres along a gorgeous white-sand beach, has three areas—an arrival marina and plaza built to resemble the ruins of an old Spanish fort, a shopping area in the style of a West Indian village, and a food pavilion—all connected by walkways and a tram.

The market area has shops as well as an ice-cream parlor, coffee shop, bar, and art gallery. There is a children's playground and wedding chapel; a post office sells Bahamian stamps and has its own postmark. The sports center offers snorkeling and diving on nearby reefs, Sunfish sailing and other water sports, volleyball, and basketball. Parts of the island were designated as a bird sanctuary by the Bahamian National Trust; nature trails lead to areas with the best bird-watching.

Signature of Excellence is a program that Holland America launched in 2004 to update its ships with new features—such as Internet cafes, extensive spa facilities, alternative dining venues, and expanded children's facilities—in order to make the ships more relevant to boomers and multigenerational families. Both markets are becoming more and more important to cruise lines.

Life aboard the ships of Holland America proceeds at a leisurely pace. Traditionally the line has attracted mature, experienced travelers and families. During winter the fleet sails on Caribbean and Panama Canal cruises, some departing from Tampa—a port that Holland America helped to develop for cruise ships—and New Orleans to the Western Caribbean and the Panama Canal; others leave from Fort Lauderdale for the Eastern Caribbean.

MSC aims for a mix of 85 percent American and 15 percent international passengers when its Florida-based ship sails the Caribbean. Onboard, MSC made changes to appeal to American tastes, such as prices being in dollars rather than euros, cabin television with CNN and American movies, and breakfast and lunch buffets with choices that American passengers prefer.

The *Lirica* (or *Lyric* in English) made its debut in 2003, with actress Sophia Loren doing the christening honors. The *Lirica* is powered by an advanced propulsion system that reduces engine noise and increases comfort. Among other amenities it features two swimming pools, a gym and jogging track, two hot tubs and a sauna, a virtual-reality center, and an Internet cafe. The ship also has a disco and a theater with shows nightly, a supervised Mini Club for children, and a shopping gallery. All cabins have satellite television, mini bar, safe, radio, and 24-hour room service. Of 795 cabins, 132 have verandas, and 4 are designed for disabled passengers. *Lirica* has two restaurants as well as a grill and pizzeria that serve authentic Italian cuisine.

MSC Cruises

6750 North Andrews Avenue, No. 605, Fort Lauderdale, FL 33309; (954) 772-6262; (800) 666-9333; fax (954) 776-5881; www.msccruises.com

Ships (passengers): *Lirica* (1,590); *Musica* (3,000); *Opera* (1,756); *Orchestra* (3,000)

Departure port: Fort Lauderdale

Types of cruises: 7, 10, and 11 days to Eastern and Western Caribbean and Panama Canal

Lifestyle tips: Classic but contemporary; Italian style

Part of a Swiss group operating a global fleet of container ships and fast ferries, Mediterranean Shipping Company (MSC) acquired three cruise ships in less than four years and had added another six ships by 2007. (All but one sail primarily in Europe.) Its almost overnight expansion launched the line's bid to be a major player in Europe and North America.

With an Italian staff and ambience, the ships offer classic cruises with good food and service.

Norwegian Cruise Line

7665 Corporate Center Drive, Miami, FL 33126; (305) 436-4000; (800) 327-7030; fax (305) 436-4120; www.ncl.com

Ships (passengers): *Norwegian Dawn* (2,240); *Norwegian Dream* (1,748); *Norwegian Gem* (2,376); *Norwegian Jewel* (2,376); *Norwegian Majesty* (1,462); *Norwegian Pearl* (2,376); *Norwegian Spirit* (1,966); *Norwegian Star* (2,240); *Norwegian Sun* (2,002)

Departure ports: Miami, New York, San Juan, Houston; Boston, Charleston, New Orleans seasonally

Types of cruises: 2, 3, 4, and 7 days to the Bahamas; Northern, Eastern, and Western Caribbean; Bermuda

Lifestyle tips: Mainstream of modern cruising

Norwegian Cruise Line (NCL) was started in 1966 by Knut Kloster, whose family has been in the steamship business in Scandinavia since 1906.

Kloster is credited with launching modern cruising when he introduced year-round three- and four-day cruises from Miami to the Bahamas, thus creating the first mass-market packaging of cruises.

By 1971 NCL had added three new ships and pioneered weekly cruises to Jamaica and other Caribbean destinations. The company introduced a day-at-the-beach feature in the Caymans and bought a Bahamian island to add a day-on-a-private-island to the line's Bahamas cruises. The idea has since been adopted by most cruise lines sailing the Bahamas and Caribbean.

Yet in a history loaded with firsts, nothing caused as much excitement as the entry of the *Norway* (now retired) in 1980. After buying the former *France* for $18 million, NCL spent $100 million to transform it from the great ocean liner it had been to the trendsetting Caribbean cruise ship it became.

The 2,000-passenger *Norway* was the largest passenger ship afloat. Its size enabled NCL to create a completely new onboard environment with restaurants, bars, and lounges of great diversity; shopping malls with "sidewalk" cafes; full Broadway shows and Las Vegas revues in its enormous theater; a full casino; and sports and entertainment facilities that could keep passengers in motion almost around the clock. These innovations set the pattern for all cruise ships that followed.

NCL is known for its entertainment, ranging from comedy clubs and cabaret stars to Broadway shows. The line has an extensive youth and children's program as well.

In 2000 NCL was bought by Star Cruises, the largest cruise line in Asia, which stepped up NCL's expansion with seven new megaliners in five years, keeping its promise to add a new ship every year for the remainder of the decade. The newest ships reflect NCL's FreeStyle Cruising, one of the line's most significant innovations. The program aims at providing passengers with the utmost flexibility, enabling them to dine where, when, and with whom they choose, with up to ten restaurants, along with choice of attire, among other features. NCL was one of the first cruise lines to provide wireless capability on its newest ships.

Oceania Cruises

8300 Northwest Thirty-third Street, Suite 308, Miami, FL 33122; (305) 514-2300; (800) 531-5658; fax (305) 514-2222; www.oceaniacruises.com

Ships (passengers): *Insignia* (684); *Nautica* (684); *Regatta* (684)

Departure port: Miami

Types of cruises: 10 to 16 days to Caribbean, Panama Canal, Central and South America in winter

Lifestyle tips: Casual country-club elegance without pretension

Formed in late 2002 by two well-known cruise industry veterans, Frank Del Rio and Joe Watters, Oceania Cruises has carved out a niche between the premium and luxury categories similar to that of now-defunct Renaissance Cruises, using three of the former line's ships and appealing to discerning, sophisticated travelers.

The cruise line has created an outstanding product with its cuisine, service, and destination-oriented itineraries and offers it at reasonable prices. The relaxed onboard atmosphere is meant to resemble the casual elegance of a country club, neither stuffy nor pretentious. Formal wear is never a requirement for dining; passengers dress comfortably to enjoy their evenings.

The 30,277-ton ships—small compared with today's more typical megaships—provide an intimate atmosphere while, at the same time, having the facilities of larger ships. For example, each ship has four restaurants with open seating, enabling passengers to dine when, where, and with whom they choose.

Each restaurant offers a different type of cuisine and a different ambience. Menus have been crafted by master chef Jacques Pepin, the line's executive culinary director and one of America's best-known chefs as food columnist, cookbook author, and host of numerous public television shows. He has also served as the personal chef to three French heads of state, including Gen. Charles de Gaulle.

Of the total 340 spacious cabins and suites, 92 percent are outside, and almost 70 percent have verandas. The Owner's and Vista Suites, each encompassing nearly 1,000 square feet, have floor-to-ceiling glass doors that lead to a veranda. The ships have spas where passengers can be pampered with aromatherapy massage and hot stone treatments, among other offerings. The fitness center has state-of-the-art equipment and an aerobic area; personal trainers are available.

Oceania@Sea, the 24-hour computer center, has Internet access, and there's a library, card room, medical center, self-service launderette, and four elevators. The ships have a high staff-to-guest ratio, with more than one crew member per cabin to provide a high degree of personal service.

The *Regatta*, inaugurated in July 2003, spends its winters in the Caribbean and its summers in Europe. Some itineraries have been tailored to include overnight port stays, allowing passengers to immerse themselves in the history, culture, and flavor of a region. The *Insignia* sails in Central and South America; the third ship, the *Nautica,* cruises in Asia and Europe. The cruise line is building two new ships to debut in 2010 and 2011. Passengers are registered in the line's repeaters club from their first cruise, making them eligible for travel rewards and other benefits.

Princess Cruises

24305 Town Center Drive, Santa Clarita, CA 91355; (800) 774-6237; fax (661) 284-4771; www.princess .com

Ships (passengers): *Caribbean Princess* (3,100); *Coral Princess* (2,000); *Crown Princess* (3,100); *Dawn Princess* (1,950); *Diamond Princess* (2,700); *Emerald Princess* (3,100); *Golden Princess* (2,600); *Grand Princess* (2,600); *Island Princess* (2,000); *Pacific Princess* (700); *Royal Princess* (700); *Ruby Princess* (3,100); *Sapphire Princess* (2,700); *Sea Princess* (1,950); *Star Princess* (2,600); *Sun Princess* (1,950)

Departure ports: Fort Lauderdale, San Juan, Acapulco, Los Angeles, New York (summer), Barbados (winter)

Types of cruises: 7 to 14 days, combining Western, Eastern, and Southern Caribbean, and Panama Canal

Lifestyle tips: Casually stylish and modestly affluent

Princess Cruises, a West Coast pioneer begun in 1965, is credited with helping to create the relaxed and casual atmosphere that typifies life aboard today's cruises. One of its ships, the former *Pacific Princess* (now retired), was the ship used in the popular television series *The Love Boat.* It's impossible to calculate, but that show probably did more to popularize modern cruising than all other cruise publicity combined. It was certainly a factor in dispelling cruising's elitist image and enabling people who might have never considered a cruise holiday to identify with it.

The former *Royal Princess* (now retired), which was christened by the princess of Wales, made its debut in 1983. The ship set new standards in passenger comfort with all outside cabins, refrigerators, televisions, and bathrooms fitted with tubs as well as showers in every cabin category. All suites, deluxe cabins, and some of those in lesser categories had private outside balconies—a first for cruising.

In 1995 and for the next decade, Princess launched two new classes of megaships. First came the *Sun Princess* in 1995, followed by its twin, the *Dawn Princess,* and the *Grand Princess,* the largest cruise ship ever built when it was launched in 1998. These were followed by nine even larger ships.

Designed by Njal Eide, the architect of the elegant *Royal Princess,* the *Sun Princess* is one of the most beautiful large ships afloat, with exquisite interiors of the finest Italian workmanship. It introduced many new features, including two atrium lobbies and two main show lounges, a true theater at sea, and a restaurant offering 24-hour dining. About 70 percent of the outside cabins have verandas. The *Grand Princess* and her sister ships have even more choices—three show lounges with different shows each night, three dining rooms, three alternative restaurants, and more. All have elaborate spas and Internet cafes.

With the new ships, the cruise line introduced a flexible dining program enabling passengers to dine when and with whom they wish as in a restaurant, along with traditional dining in the main dining room.

In recent years Princess has had one of the strongest presences in the Caribbean in the winter season. The line has a private beach, Princess Cays (on southern Eleuthera in the Bahamas), where the ships call. This facility has just about every water sport a passenger could want, as well as nature trails with guided walks, games, kiosks for local crafts, and a large dining pavilion where passengers are served lunch.

In 2003 Princess Cruises was purchased by Carnival Corporation, outbidding Royal Caribbean Lines for this prize. Princess continues to operate as a separate company.

Princess caters to a modestly affluent clientele from thirty-five years of age on up, with a median age of fifty to fifty-five. It is very aggressive with promotional fares and seasonal savings.

Regent Seven Seas Cruises

600 Corporate Drive, No. 410, Fort Lauderdale, FL 33334; (954) 776-6123; (800) 477-7500; fax (954) 772-3763; www.rssc.com

Ships (passengers): *Paul Gauguin* (320); *Seven Seas Mariner* (729); *Seven Seas Navigator* (490); *Seven Seas Voyager* (708)

Departure ports: Fort Lauderdale and worldwide ports seasonally

Types of cruises: 7 to 14 days; transcanal, Eastern Caribbean

Lifestyle tips: Luxury for affluent travelers

Diamond Cruises, a joint venture of Finnish, Japanese, and US interests, formed a partnership with Radisson Hotels International, and in 1995 Radisson Diamond joined with Seven Seas Cruises to form a new company, Radisson Seven Seas, renamed Regent Seven Seas in 2006.

In the years that followed, the cruise line built four new ultraluxurious ships that sail the world. They are among the most spacious ocean liners afloat. The Seven Seas Mariner and Seven Seas Voyager were cruising's first all-suite-with-balcony ships. Throughout the fleet, the decor is one of understated elegance. The ships have several lounges and bars, a spa, and a fitness center with a gym sauna and jogging track. The dining rooms and alternative restaurants serve cuisine as fine as

you'll enjoy at top restaurants in New York or Paris.

Only one of the newest ships sails in the Caribbean, and only for a limited time in winter. These cruises are usually combined with the Panama Canal or South America. The cruises are expensive and cater to affluent passengers who are accustomed to the best.

Royal Caribbean International

1050 Caribbean Way, Miami, FL 33132; (305) 539-6000; (800) 659-7225; (800) 722-5329; fax (305) 373-4394; www.royalcaribbean.com

Ships (passengers): *Adventure of the Seas* (3,114); *Brilliance of the Seas* (2,000); *Empress of the Seas* (1,602); *Enchantment of the Seas* (1,950); *Explorer of the Seas* (3,114); *Freedom of the Seas* (3,600); *Grandeur of the Seas* (1,950); *Independence of the Seas 2008* (3,634); *Jewel of the Seas* (2,100); *Legend of the Seas* (1,808); *Liberty of the Seas* (3,634); *Majesty of the Seas* (2,354); *Mariner of the Seas* (3,114); *Monarch of the Seas* (2,354); *Navigator of the Seas* (3,114); *Radiance of the Seas* (2,000); *Rhapsody of the Seas* (2,000); *Serenade of the Seas* (2,100); *Sovereign of the Seas* (2,276); *Splendor of the Seas* (1,800); *Vision of the Seas* (1,950); *Voyager of the Seas* (3,114); *Project Genesis* (5,400) 2009

Departure ports: Miami, San Juan, Fort Lauderdale, Port Canaveral, Bayonne, Philadelphia, Baltimore, Boston, Tampa, Galveston, New Orleans

Types of cruises: 3 to 10 days to Bahamas and Western, Eastern, and Southern Caribbean

Lifestyle tips: Active, wholesome ambience

Royal Caribbean Cruise Line, launched in the early 1970s, was the first line to build a fleet of ships designed specially for year-round Caribbean cruising. The ships were established so quickly that within five years, RCCL needed more capacity. It achieved this by "stretching" two of the vessels. They were literally cut in half, and prefabricated midsections were inserted. Although the method had been used on cargo and other vessels, RCCL's work was the first for cruise ships.

For the 1980s it added superliners with unique design features, and in 1988 it got a head start on the future with the *Sovereign of the Seas,* the first of the new generation of megaliners and the largest cruise ship afloat at the time. Few ships in history have received so much attention.

Over the next decade RCCL added a new group of six megaliners. The first ship, *Legend of the Seas,* introduced the first miniature golf course at sea and a spectacular "solarium"—an indoor/outdoor swimming, sunning, and fitness facility. The cruise line entered the new millennium with another new group of ships, dubbed the Eagle class. The *Voyager of the Seas,* the first of these three ships, was, at 142,000 tons, the largest ship ever built when it debuted in 1999. It came with such unusual features as a rock climbing wall, a skating rink, cabins overlooking the atrium, and more. These were followed by four smaller Radiance class ships, the most beautiful of the fleet, noted particularly for their walls of glass. Next came the 158,000-ton Freedom class, with the largest cruise ships ever built. The first one, *Freedom of the Seas,* arrived in May 2006, followed by two sister ships in 2007 and 2008. And now, an even larger ship of 220,000 tons for 5,400 passengers is under construction and is scheduled to enter service in 2009. Known as *Project Genesis,* it will be the largest cruise ship ever built. Her sister will follow in 2010.

It would be impossible for even the most active passenger to participate in all the daily activities offered on an RCCL ship. Fitness folks have a ½-mile outside deck encircling the vessel and one of the best-equipped health clubs at sea, complete with ballet barres, sophisticated computerized exercise equipment, and a high-energy staff to put them through their paces. The sports deck has twin pools and a basketball court.

For those with something less strenuous in mind, there are small, sophisticated lounges for drinks, dancing, and cabaret entertainment. Enrichment programs run the gamut from napkin folding to wine tasting. The library resembles a sedate English club with wood paneling and leather chairs. Two feature films run daily in twin cinemas; the shopping boulevard has a sidewalk cafe; the show lounge, a multitiered theater with unobstructed views, runs two different Las Vegas–style revues and variety shows.

Somewhere there's music to suit every mood, from big band, steel band, Latin, country, rock, or strolling violins to classical concerts. The Schooner is a lively piano bar; Music Man has entertainers from blues to country; and the disco projects holograms on the mirrored walls and music videos around the dance floor. Casino Royale offers blackjack, 216 slot machines, and American roulette. The chic Champagne Bar is a quiet corner where fifty people clink flutes and scoop caviar.

Designed as they are for Caribbean cruising, RCCL ships have acres of open sundecks and large pools. The line offers low-fat, low-calorie fare and has a ShipShape program on all ships in the fleet. It is often combined with sports in port. Golf Ahoy! enables passengers to play at courses throughout the Caribbean.

The cabins are compact—in fact, they are small—but functional and spotless. A top-deck lounge cantilevered from the funnel provides fabulous views from twelve or more stories above the sea. These lounges are RCCL's signature.

RCCL blankets the Caribbean year-round. It has cruises year-round on the West Coast and Mexico, and in Alaska and Europe in summer. Coco Cay, a small island in the Bahamas, is used for the ships' day at the beach. Labadee, RCCL's private resort on the north coast of Haiti, is very popular.

Founded in 1969 as a partnership of three prominent Norwegian shipping companies, RCCL went public in April 1993. In 1997 RCCL purchased Celebrity Cruises, which it operates as a separate company.

RCCL caters to a moderately upscale market. The atmosphere is friendly and casual, and the activities are so varied that there is something for everyone at almost every hour of the day. All RCCL ships have programs for children and teenagers: The line believes that a happy kid on a cruise now will still be a customer in 2025.

Seabourn Cruise Line

6100 Blue Lagoon Drive, Suite 400, Miami, FL 33126; (305) 463-3000; (800) 929-9391; fax (305) 463-3010; www.seabourn.com

Ships (passengers): *Seabourn Legend* (214); *Seabourn Pride* (214); *Seabourn Spirit* (214)

Departure ports: Fort Lauderdale, Barbados, Aruba, San Juan, Antigua, St. Thomas

Types of cruises: 3 to 21 days in Eastern and Southern Caribbean and Panama Canal in winter; worldwide schedules year-round

Lifestyle tips: The ultimate luxury cruise

When Seabourn was formed in 1987, it set out to create the world's most deluxe cruises on the most elegant, luxurious ships afloat. Despite very high per-diem rates, Seabourn quickly won enough fans to add more ships.

The ships and cruises were designed with a certain type of person in mind—one who normally stays in the best rooms at a luxury hotel and books a deluxe suite on a luxury liner. The staterooms are luxuriously appointed in soft, warm colors and have television with CNN, CD and DVD players, stocked bars, refrigerators, walk-in closets, and large marble bathrooms with tub and shower. Each has a roomy sitting area beside a large picture window with electrically manipulated shades and outside cleaning mechanisms. In 2000 French balconies replaced the picture windows in thirty-six suites of each of the Seabourn trio; an expanded spa, a computer learning center, and other improvements were added as well.

Passengers dine on gourmet cuisine served on Royal Doulton china and have open seating. They may also dine from the restaurant menu in their suites, and there is a 24-hour room service menu with a wide selection and a choice wine list.

Seabourn's ships have sleek profiles that resemble the most modern of yachts. A water sports platform at the stern has a "cage" that can be lowered into the water for passengers to swim in the open sea without fear. The ships carry sailboards, snorkeling and dive equipment, and two high-speed boats. Their itineraries take them to all parts of the world, but at least one spends some of the winter in the Caribbean.

In 2007 Seabourn announced its intention to build two new 32,000-ton ships for delivery in 2009 and 2010. Seabourn is owned by Carnival Cruise Lines but operates as a separate company.

SeaDream Yacht Club

2601 South Bayshore Drive, Penthouse 1B, Coconut Grove, FL 33133-5417; (305) 631-6100; (800) 707-4911; fax (305) 631-6110; www.seadreamyacht club.com

Ships (passengers): *SeaDream I/SeaDream II* (110)

Departure ports: San Juan, Barbados, St. Thomas, St. Maarten

Types of cruises: 7 day Caribbean, seasonally

Lifestyle tips: Luxurious but casual

SeaDream Yacht Club, a venture of two cruise industry veterans, began operating in late 2001 with the luxury twin ships *SeaDream I* and *II* (formerly *Sea Goddess I* and *II*). The handsome twins, which the line calls mega-yachts, are meant to provide a totally different experience from today's typical cruise, one that more closely resembles yachting. Like yachts, the ships offer an open, unstructured ambience for passengers to move at their own pace. *No clocks, no crowds, no lines, no stress* could be the company's motto.

According to SeaDream, what make its cruises different are flexible schedules and itineraries: SeaDream's yachts depart their first port and arrive at their last port as scheduled, but the port calls in between are not run by a strict timetable. Captains have the authority to adjust for local opportunities. For example, they might make an unscheduled visit to an island fish market so the chef can pick up the day's catch. Also, while most cruise ships arrive at ports of call at about 8:00 A.M. and sail at 5:00 or 6:00 P.M. the same day, SeaDream yachts overnight at popular ports where the action doesn't get started until late evening.

While the ship is in port, passengers may visit a small-town pastry shop with the chef, go snorkeling with the captain, or go hiking, biking, or golfing with the officers. What better guides to have?

The ships have alcoves for sunning on double sun beds, a private massage tent on deck, a large-screen golf simulator that can also be used to watch sports events or movies, and a water sports marina at the stern equipped for kayaking, water-skiing, windsurfing, snorkeling, and Sunfish sailing. Tai chi, yoga, and aerobics classes are also offered.

Indoors, passengers have an Asian-style spa and fitness center. The ships also have a Main Lounge, a piano bar, a casino, and a library with books, CDs, DVDs, and computer outlets. Laptops are available. Passengers are given their own onboard e-mail address.

Of the fifty-five cabins, thirty-eight are 195 square feet; sixteen are 390 square feet with his-and-hers bathroom facilities and a dining area accommodating four. The 450-square-foot Owner's Suite has a bedroom, a bathroom with a tub and separate shower with a view of the sea, a living room/dining area, and a guest bath. Bathrooms have multiple-jet massage showers and lighted magnifying mirrors. All cabins are Internet-ready and have an entertainment center with a flat-screen television, CD and DVD systems with movies and other selections, and a personal jukebox with more than one hundred digital music programs.

SeaDream has no dress code; rather it stresses the casual nature of yachting.

Silversea Cruises

110 East Broward Boulevard, Fort Lauderdale, FL 33301; (954) 522-4477; (800) 722-6655; fax (954) 522-4499; www.silversea.com

Ships (passengers): *Silver Cloud* (306); *Silver Shadow* (388); *Silver Whisper* (388); *Silver Wind* (306)

Departure ports: Fort Lauderdale, Barbados

Types of cruises: Caribbean, seasonally

Lifestyle tips: Ultraluxurious surroundings in a relaxing, friendly—not stuffy—atmosphere

Silversea Cruises was launched in late 1994 with the luxurious all-suite *Silver Cloud,* designed by Oslo-based Petter Yran and Bjorn Storbraaten, the architects of the Seabourn ships. Its twin, the *Silver Wind,* made its debut the following year.

The Silversea ships mirror Seabourn's in many ways but carry 306 passengers (100 more than Seabourn's); 107 of the Silversea's 155 suites have verandas.

Silversea's large suites, averaging 300 square feet, have a spacious sitting area, walk-in closet, fully stocked bar, hair dryer, TV with VCR, direct-dial telephone, and marble-floored bathroom with tub. Passengers are welcomed to their staterooms with fresh flowers, a bottle of champagne, a basket of fruit replenished daily, personalized stationery, and plush terry robes for use during their cruise.

There is open seating in the dining room and 24-hour room service. The ship has a tiered show lounge spanning two decks, with a nightclub at the upper level, plus a casino, a spa, and a library.

In 2000 and 2001 the line added two new, slightly larger and even more spacious ships, the *Silver Shadow* and *Silver Whisper,* but both are almost identical in style to the earlier models. Silversea Cruises' newest build is again, slightly larger at 36,000 tons; it will be launched in late 2009.

The ships sail on worldwide itineraries throughout the year, but at least one is in the Caribbean for transcanal, Central, and South American itineraries in winter. The co-owners of the line are passenger and shipping veterans Francesco Lefebvre of Rome and the Vlasov Group of Monaco. Silversea sails under the Italian flag, with Italian officers and a European staff.

Star Clippers, Inc.

7200 Northwest Nineteenth Street, Suite 206, Miami, FL 33126; (305) 442-0550; (800) 442-0551; fax (305) 442-1611; www.starclippers.com

Ships (passengers): *Royal Clipper* (224); *Star Clipper* (180); *Star Flyer* (180)

Departure ports: St. Maarten; Barbados

Types of cruises: 7 to 14 days on alternating itineraries in Eastern Caribbean

Lifestyle tips: For active travelers looking for the romance of sailing to out-of-the-way places

Star Clippers is the brainchild of Swedish shipping entrepreneur Mikael Krafft, whose passions for sailing and building yachts and his love of the clipper ship (which he says is one of America's greatest inventions) led him to create a cruise line with clipper ships. Launched in 1991, the cruises are priced to fit between budget-conscious cruises and pricey yachtlike vessels.

Star Clippers is truly distinctive. The *Star Clipper* and *Star Flyer*—each accommodating 180 passengers in 90 staterooms—are direct descendants of the fast, sleek clipper ships that ruled the seas in the mid-1800s. Built in Belgium, the vessels are 357 feet long with four masts and square-rigged sails in the forward mast—a Barguentine configuration—with a total of seventeen sails (36,000 square feet of sail area). They are human-operated, not computerized, and capable of attaining speeds of 19.4 knots. At 208 feet tall, they are among the tallest of the tall ships.

Today's clippers retain the romance of sailing under canvas coupled with the excitement of participating in the sailing of an authentic square-rigger. They are further enhanced by the out-of-the-way Caribbean destinations they visit. Passengers quickly get to know the youthful crew, who double as deckhands, as sports instructors, and in other capacities.

Responding to many vacationers' wish to de-emphasize ostentatious food and the crowds of big ships, the cruises focus on an active, casual, and even educational experiences—it's more like being on a private yacht. The food is good but not gourmet. Dress is very casual, with shorts and deck shoes the uniform of the day, and only slightly less casual in the evening. Fellow passengers will be kindred souls—you hope—and 50 percent or more might be Europeans, depending on the time of the year. The cruises are also a great environment for families with children ages seven to seventeen.

All cabins have air-conditioning, carpeting, and private bathrooms with showers. Most face the outside and are fitted with twin beds that can be converted to a bed slightly larger than the standard queen size. Eight inside cabins are furnished with upper and lower beds, and eight cabins can accommodate three passengers. The top staterooms on the main deck have marble bathrooms with bathtubs and hair dryers. Cabins are equipped with multi-channel radio and video players. Videotapes are available from the ship's library. There is storage for luggage, golf clubs, scuba gear, and other such items.

Facilities include a small piano bar, located midship on the main deck. It has brass-framed panoramic windows, carved paneling, and cush-ioned banquettes. The unusual lighting comes from the skylight overhead—it's actually the transparent bottom of the sundeck pool, one of the ship's two small pools. The piano bar is on the landing of a double staircase leading into the Clipper Dining Room on the deck below. All passengers dine at one seating, although when the ship is full the room can be very crowded. In addition to regular meal service, the dining room converts into a meeting room with screen projectors and video monitors.

Adjoining the aft end of the Piano Bar is the Tropical Bar, protected from the elements by a broad canvas awning, under which are found the bar, a dance floor, and the stage where the captain holds daily talks and much of the entertainment takes place during the cruise. Breakfast and lunch buffets are occasionally served here, too. Also on the main deck is a library that resembles an English club with large brass-framed windows, carved paneling, and a marble fireplace. It doubles as a reception desk and is used for small meetings.

The line's newest 5,000-ton ship, the *Royal Clipper,* is the largest sailing vessel in the world—more than twice the size of its sister ships—but with a capacity for only 224 passengers, compared with their 180. Built for more than $75 million, the ship is 439 feet in length with a 54-foot beam and has five masts with thirty-nine sails.

The *Royal Clipper* is also more upscale. It has three small swimming pools, one with a glass bottom that allows light into the three-deck atrium below; an observation lounge with wraparound windows on the deck below the bridge; and a dining room, accommodating all passengers at a single seating, which is built on two connecting levels. The ship also has a water sports platform and an inflatable floating raft for swimmers.

Cabins are larger than those on the sister ships, and some have a third fold-down bed. The suites have private verandas and bathrooms with whirlpool tubs.

The *Royal Clipper* sails the Caribbean in winter from Barbados. The *Star Clipper* is based in St. Maarten in winter, sailing on alternating seven-day cruises in the Eastern Caribbean. An unduplicated fourteen-day itinerary is possible with back-to-back cruises. The clippers can anchor in bays that large cruise ships cannot reach. Launches take passengers to isolated beaches and scuba and snorkeling spots or to enjoy other water sports. Snorkeling gear, water skis, sailboards, and volleyballs are carried on board.

Windstar Cruises

300 Elliot Avenue West, Seattle, WA 98119; (206) 281-3535; (800) 258-7245; fax (206) 281-0627; www.windstarcruises.com

Ships (passengers): *Wind Spirit* (148); *Wind Star* (148); *Wind Surf* (308)

Departure ports: Barbados, Puerto Caldera, St. Thomas

Types of cruises: 7 days to Eastern and Southern Caribbean, Costa Rica, Belize, and Panama Canal

Lifestyle tips: Combination of sailing yacht and deluxe cruise ship; for active people

Imagine a deck one and a half times the length of a football field and half its width. Now look up to the sky and imagine four masts in a row, each as high as a twenty-story building and each with two enormous triangular sails. If you can picture these dimensions, you will have a mental image of the windcruiser, which was, when it debuted, the most revolutionary vessel since the nineteenth-century steamship. The six great sails are controlled by computers instead of deck hands. The computer is designed to monitor the direction and velocity of the wind to keep the ship from heeling no more than six degrees. The sails can be furled in less than two minutes.

The windcruiser marries the romance and tradition of sailing with the comfort and amenities of a cruise ship. The ship has seventy-five identical, 182-square-foot outside staterooms (comparable in size to those on regular cruise ships). The well-designed cabins make optimum use of space and are fitted with twin- or queen-size beds, mini bar, color television, VCR, satellite phone communications, and individual safes.

Cabins, gym, and sauna are on the bottom two of four passenger decks. The third deck has a main lounge and dining salon; both are handsome rooms that have the ambience of a private yacht. The dining room, which has open seating, serves sophisti-

cated gourmet cuisine. The ship has a tiny casino, boutique, and beauty salon. The top deck has a swimming pool, bar, and veranda lounge used for lunch during the day, plus a disco at night. Through the overhead skylight of the lounge, passengers can have a dramatic view of the majestic sails overhead.

The vessel's shallow 13½-foot draft enables it to stop at less visited ports and secluded beaches and coves. It's fitted with a water sports platform that gives passengers direct access to the sea. Sailboats and windsurfing boards are carried on board, as are Zodiacs (inflatable boats) to take passengers snorkeling, scuba diving, waterskiing, and fishing. The gear for these activities is available for use without additional charge. Any passenger lucky enough to hook a fish can have it cooked to order by the ship's chefs.

In April 1997 Windstar Cruises bought the *Club Med I*, one of two identical ships in the Club Med fleet that are large versions of Windstar's ships. It was remodeled and renamed *Wind Surf*. Among many renovations, thirty-one deluxe suites were created, and a 10,000-square-foot spa was added—both moves intended to enhance the ship's appeal and offset its larger size and capacity (it can carry more than twice as many passengers as other Windstar ships). In addition to the standard amenities, the suites boast his-and-hers bathrooms with shower, complete with teak flooring, plush terry towels and robes, and vanity lighting. More recently the ship added a computer center, an outdoor barbecue station, and an improved gangway and access to the ship. There's a complimentary water sports program off its marina deck and a fully equipped conference center.

Windstar's cruises are planned to be part cruise, part yacht charter. They are geared toward working professionals who can afford to take a cruise and like the luxury of a cruise ship or resort but want a more active and unusual vacation than that associated with traditional cruises. Thus the company attracts experienced cruise passengers and boat owners as well as people who may have shunned cruise ships in the past.

In 2007 Windstar Cruises was purchased by Majestic America Cruises, a specialist in cruises on US rivers. Windstar, however, continues to operate its own unique cruises as a separate entity.

PART THREE

Ports of Call

The Bahamas

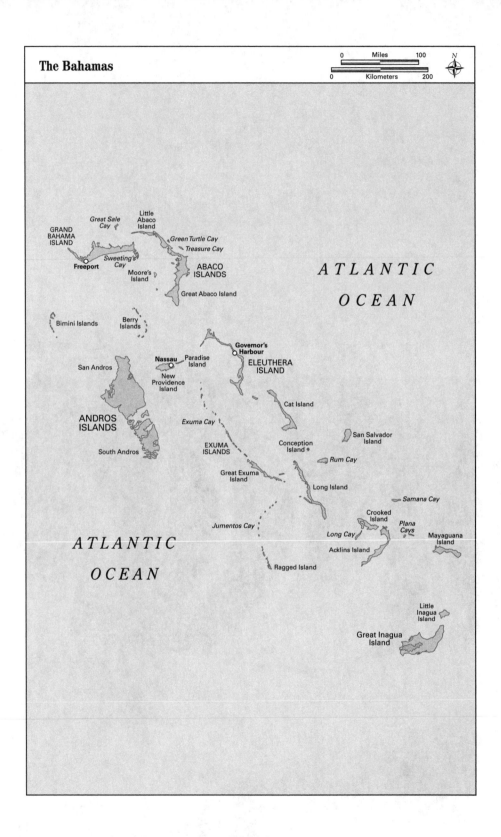

The Bahamas

| 0 | Miles | 100 |
| 0 | Kilometers | 200 |

N

GRAND BAHAMA ISLAND

Great Sale Cay

Little Abaco Island

Green Turtle Cay

Treasure Cay

Sweeting's Cay

Freeport

Moore's Island

ABACO ISLANDS

Great Abaco Island

ATLANTIC

OCEAN

Bimini Islands

Berry Islands

Governor's Harbour

San Andros

Nassau

Paradise Island

New Providence Island

ELEUTHERA ISLAND

ANDROS ISLANDS

Exuma Cay

Cat Island

San Salvador Island

South Andros

EXUMA ISLANDS

Conception Island

Rum Cay

Great Exuma Island

Long Island

Samana Cay

Crooked Island

Plana Cays

Jumentos Cay

Long Cay

Mayaguana Island

Acklins Island

ATLANTIC

OCEAN

Ragged Island

Little Inagua Island

Great Inagua Island

Distant Neighbors

Whether your destination is Nassau, Freeport, or one of the Family Islands, your first impression of the Bahamas and the image you are likely to carry away with you is of water. Intensely beautiful with shades of aqua, turquoise, cobalt, and peacock blue, these waters have long attracted boating and fishing enthusiasts, and now they are being discovered by snorkelers, scuba divers, and cruise passengers.

The Bahamas is an archipelago of more than 700 low-lying tropical islands and islets dotting 100,000 square miles of sea. They start only 50 miles from the eastern coast of Florida and stretch for 750 miles to the northern coasts of Haiti and Cuba. They are strategically situated between the Atlantic on the north, south, and east and the Gulf of Mexico on the west. About half of the archipelago lies north of the Tropic of Cancer.

The Bahamas derives its name from the Spanish *baja mar*, shallows—a term that early explorers used in mapping the group. Of the hundreds of islands, islets, and cays that make up the island-nation, only about three dozen are populated. Of these, three ports—Nassau, Paradise Island, and Freeport—get the lion's share of visitors and almost all of the cruise passengers.

The Bahamas is so close to the US mainland that many people hop over for the weekend in their own boats or private planes, and ships board thousands of passengers every week for one-, two-, three-, and four-day cruises between Florida and Bahamian ports.

Yet the Bahamas is foreign. A British colony for more than two centuries and independent since 1973, the Bahamas in many ways is still more British than the queen. This despite the fact that throughout the history of the islands—from the time Columbus made his first landfall on the Bahamian island of San Salvador and Ponce de León came in search of the Fountain of Youth—the Bahamas has been as closely linked to events in the United States as to any in Britain.

Today the British flavor combined with American familiarity, the magnificent waters and endless days of clear skies, the outstanding facilities, the variety of sports and entertainment all have made the Bahamas the most frequently visited destination in the tropics, with more than five million visitors a year—of whom 71 percent arrive by cruise ship.

On any given day in port, you can play tennis and golf or bike and jog in the countryside. The shallow, warm waters provide a carnival of life for snorkelers and scuba divers. Protected bays and shallow waters near shore are ideal for windsurfing, waterskiing, Jet Skiing, and parasailing. You'll find an abundance of fish in the deep waters only a short distance from port and excellent opportunities for deep-sea fishing year-round.

If the sporting life is not your first requirement, a walking tour of Nassau is a stroll through history and a chance to check out the bargains in the shops and straw markets along the way. You can do it on your own or in the company of a Bahamian host arranged for through the Tourist Office's People-to-People Program. Evening entertainment in

At a Glance

Antiquities	★
Architecture	★★★
Art and Artists	★★
Beaches	★★★★★
Colonial Buildings	★★★★
Crafts	★★
Cuisine	★★
Dining/Restaurants	★★★
Entertainment	★★★★
Forts	★★
Gambling Casinos	★★★★★
History	★★
Monuments	★★
Museums	★
Nightlife	★★★★
Scenery	★★★
Shopping	★★
Sightseeing	★★
Sports	★★★★★
Transportation	★★

port can range from the music of a scratch band in a rustic tavern by the sea to an extravaganza with Las Vegas sizzle at a cavernous casino.

Columbus and the Aftermath

The diversity of the Bahamas is the result of its variegated past. The islands' recorded history begins on the most significant date in the annals of the New World—October 12, 1492—with Christopher Columbus making his first landfall on an island the Native Lucayans called Guanahani and that Columbus christened San Salvador, the Savior.

When the Spaniards who followed Columbus found no gold, they abandoned all interest in the Bahamas, but not before enslaving the entire Lucayan Indian population of 20,000 and shipping them to work the mines in Cuba and Hispaniola. Ponce de León was apparently an exception. He came to the Bahamas in search of the Fountain of Youth before moving on to Florida to continue his quest. Today four places on the island of Bimini claim to have been stops in his epic journey.

In 1648—a century after the Spaniards departed from the islands, English settlers fleeing religious conflict in Bermuda arrived on Sigatoo Island, which they named Eleuthera after a Greek word meaning "freedom." Following a dispute within the group, which was known as the Company of Eleuthran Adventurers, many of the settlers left and founded another settlement at or near Spanish Wells.

In time, the Bahamas was granted to the lords of the Carolinas, absentee landlords whose lack of interest allowed the infestation of pirates, such as the infamous Edward Teach, known as Blackbeard, and Henry Morgan. The hundreds of harbors were ideal havens for smuggling and piracy; their reefs and shallows ensured—by accident or design—frequent wrecks.

Finally in 1718 the ironfisted British captain Woodes Rogers took command of the Bahamas and established order. Rogers gave the scavengers a clear choice: Give up piracy and be pardoned, or be hanged. Eight who tested Rogers's will were hanged in public, thus helping to bring a chapter of the Bahamas's history to a close. Ten years later, the islands were officially made a British colony, with Rogers the first royal governor.

In an effort to destroy British supply lines during the American Revolution, the American navy captured Nassau and held it for two weeks. Later the Spanish held it for a year and did not leave until they were forced out by Col. Andrew Deveaux, a Loyalist from the Carolinas and one of 8,000 who had fled to the Bahamas after the Revolution. Deveaux and the other Loyalists brought with them all their possessions, including slaves, and in the Bahamas they replicated the plantation society they had left behind. The old order lasted until slavery was abolished in 1834.

Twice again events in the United States led to direct Bahamian involvement and a boom: gunrunning during the Civil War and rumrunning during Prohibition. After that, the American–Bahamian connection became more respectable, but no less flamboyant. During World War II the royal governor of the Bahamas was none other than the duke of Windsor, who along with his glamorous American-born duchess set the style for what was to become the Bahamas's most important postwar enterprise, tourism.

The New Bahamas

After the war, a weak and weary Britain welcomed foreign investments that would enable its colonies to become self-supporting. At the same time, several wealthy Americans saw the opportunity to create playgrounds in the Bahamas, which could benefit from the islands' proximity to the US mainland. The most significant venture turned a spit of land facing Nassau Harbor into the most complete resort in the tropics.

In the 1950s A&P heir Huntington Hartford bought most of Hog Island, as it was known, from another millionaire and renamed it Paradise. His estate, set in landscaped gardens adorned with classic marble statues and enclosed with stones from a twelfth-century French monastery, became the centerpiece of the fashionable Ocean Club.

During the following decade Paradise Island was acquired by Resorts International, which added hotels, a casino, and extensive sporting facilities. It also made Paradise more accessible by building a multimillion-dollar bridge between the island and Nassau, and later by adding an airline. Then, in 1989, famed television star Merv Griffin bought

Fast Facts

Population: 350,000, of which two-thirds live in New Providence (Nassau). Except for Nassau and Freeport, there are no towns with more than 1,500 people.

Government: The Parliament, more than 250 years old, has two houses. The House of Assembly has members elected every five years; the Senate is an advisory group of sixteen appointed members. The Bahamas is a member of the Commonwealth, and the British queen is its monarch, too.

Climate: Strictly speaking, the Bahamas is not part of the Caribbean, but it enjoys a similar idyllic tropical climate. The Gulf Stream bathes the western coast with clear warm waters, and easterly trade winds caress the shores. As a result, temperatures in the northernmost islands seldom drop below 60°F or rise above 90°F.

Clothing: Casual but proper. Bahamians tend to be conservative and are offended by the overly revealing dress of some tourists on the streets. Informal spring/summer sportswear for day and evening will suit most occasions, although elegant attire is not out of place in the evening, depending on your choice of dining place and activities. Generally, men neatly dressed in slacks, sport shirt, and jacket will be comfortable at any nightspot in the islands. For women, a cocktail dress or stylish pantsuit is appropriate.

Currency: The Bahamian dollar (B$) is freely exchanged with the US dollar at par.

Departure Tax: When you leave the Bahamas by air, you pay $15 ($18 departing Grand Bahama) per adult and per child ages six and older. Children ages five and under are not charged.

Electricity: 120-volt, 60-cycle AC. Standard US shavers, hair dryers, and other appliances can be used.

Entry Formalities: All US citizens must have a passport.

Language: English—more British than American—with a lilt and influences from the early settlers, African slaves, and Caribbean islanders who came here to work.

Postal Service: A letter to the United States costs 65 cents per half ounce; a postcard, 50 cents. The post office nearest the pier in Nassau is at Parliament and East Hill Streets, 3 blocks south of Rawson Square. In Freeport, the post office nearest the pier is at Adventurer's Way. Hours: 9:00 A.M. to 5:00 P.M.

Public Holidays: January 1, New Year's Day; Good Friday, Easter Sunday and Monday; Whit Monday (six weeks after Easter); Labor Day (first Friday in June); July 10, Independence Day; Emancipation Day (first Monday in August); October 12, Discovery Day; December 25, Christmas; December 26, Boxing Day.

Telephone Area Code: 242. (Dial exactly as you do for a long-distance call within the United States.)

Time: Eastern Standard Time. Daylight saving time is adopted in the summer months as in the United States.

Vaccination Requirement: None.

Airlines: Direct flights from major US gateways by Air Jamaica, American Airlines, American Eagle, Bahamasair, Comair, Continental, Delta, Fly First Class, Gulfstream, Hooters Air, JetBlue, Northwest, Paradise Island Airways, Song, Spirit Airlines, United, USAirways, and USAir Express, and from Canada by Air Canada.

Information: www.bahamas.com.

In the United States:

Bahamas Tourist Offices: (800) 422-4262, (800) BAHAMAS.

Chicago: 8600 West Bryn Mawr Avenue, No. 820, IL 60631; (773) 693-1500; (800) 449-5385; fax (773) 693-1114.

Los Angeles: 11400 West Olympic, Suite 200, CA 90064; (213) 385-0033; (800) 439-6993; fax (213) 383-3966.

Miami: 1200 South Pine Island Road, Suite 700, Plantation, FL 33324; (954) 236-9292; (800) 224-3681; (800) 327-9019; fax (954) 236-0733. Grand Bahamas Tourist Bureau, (242) 352-8044; (800) 448-3386; fax (242) 352-7840. Bahamas Out Islands Promotion Board, (305) 931-6612; (800) 688-4752; fax (305) 931-6867.

New York: 60 East Forty-second Street, Suite 1850, New York, NY 10165; (212) 758-2777; (800) 823-3136; fax (212) 753-6531.

In Canada:

Toronto: 6725 Airport Road, Suite 202, Mississauga, ON, L4V 1V2; (905) 672-9017; (800) 667-3777 (Canada only); fax (416) 968-6711.

In Nassau:

The Ministry of Tourism has information booths at Prince George Dock, (242) 325-9155; Ministry of Tourism Headquarters, Bolam House, George and Marlborough Streets, (242) 322-7500; (800) BAHAMAS (224-2627).

In Freeport:

The Tourist Information Centre is located in the Sir Charles Hayward Library, (242) 352-8044, and there are booths at Freeport Harbor, (242) 352-9651, and in the International Bazaar. Hours: 8:30 A.M. to 5:00 P.M. Monday through Saturday.

Resorts International and put his stamp on the island. But the greatest transformation of all came after Sun International bought out Griffin and transformed Resort International's holdings into a new resort named Atlantis, creating an entirely new landscape of lakes, parks, and attractions. It renovated all the hotels and added new ones, a marina, and a second bridge between Paradise Island and Nassau, investing almost a billion dollars to make it the largest resort and theme park in the tropics.

About the same time that Hartford was creating Paradise, American financier Wallace Groves was transforming Grand Bahama Island, a little-known stretch of limestone and pine forest only 60 miles from Florida. Freeport, as it is better known, became the showplace of its day with hotels, casinos, a flashy international shopping bazaar, and six championship golf courses.

In the 1970s, with the recession, inflation, oil crisis, and competition from newer resorts in Florida and the Caribbean, Freeport lost a great deal of its luster. But by the mid-1980s a renaissance was under way, with millions of dollars being invested by the government and private developers. Now a second renaissance, particularly in the Lucayan area, where old hotels were demolished, has seen new, elaborate ones built to replace them.

Another transformation took place in the 1980s at Cable Beach, a 5-mile stretch west of downtown Nassau. The multimillion-dollar Cable Beach Hotel and Casino opened in 1983 (now a Sheraton hotel), followed by the thousand-room Wyndham Nassau Resort and Crystal Palace Casino, one of the largest hotels in the tropics.

The Royal Bahamian Hotel, the colonial grande dame of Cable Beach, which served as the fashionable resort of royalty and heads of state in its heyday as the Balmoral Beach Club when the duke of Windsor was governor, was also renovated. In 1994 it was purchased by Sandals, the Jamaican-based, all-inclusive group, and after extensive renovation and expansion reopened in 1996 as the chain's most luxurious resort. Down the road Breezes Bahamas, formerly the Ambassador Beach, was the first Bahamas member of Superclubs, also a Jamaican all-inclusive chain. On the west side of Nassau, the landmark British Colonial Hotel was gutted and rebuilt as the British Colonial Hilton International. But all this seems to be merely a prelude to the current developments at Cable Beach (see the description later in the Attractions West of Nassau section). As your ship steams into Nassau Harbor, look south and you can spot Cable Beach on the ship's starboard side. The stretch of green north of the harbor on the port side of the ship is Paradise Island. Long before it became a famous playground, the island served as a natural breakwater for Nassau Harbor, protecting the only safe entrance to New Providence. In the distance the arched bridges connecting Paradise Island to Nassau are the most visible evidence of the long-standing American–Bahamian connection.

An Introduction to Nassau
www.nassauparadiseisland.com

Old World charm and New World glamour come together in Nassau and its elaborate resorts of Cable Beach and Paradise Island. Nassau is one of the most sophisticated and popular destinations in the tropics.

For most people Nassau *is* the Bahamas. However, Nassau is not an island but a town—to be sure, the main town—on the island of New Providence, located at the center of the Bahamas archipelago. As the seat of government, the hub of commercial activity, and the crossroads of the nation's air and sea-lanes, Nassau has acquired the bustle and worldliness of an international capital. Yet it is the only place throughout the 700 islands of the Bahamas archipelago, including Freeport, that comes even close to having this character.

For cruise passengers Nassau's combination of the old and the new in an international city surrounded by lovely beaches is perfect. Stretched along the north coast of the island, the town is compact and easy to explore on foot in a leisurely morning or afternoon. It is situated on a low-lying island only 21 miles long and 7 miles wide that is easy to see by car, bus, or moped in a few hours. It is also possible to combine some sightseeing with a sport or a shopping expedition and have time at the beach.

Perhaps more than any other place in the Bahamas, Nassau reflects the country's British past visually in the colonial buildings of Old Nassau and in the trappings of tradition that have lasted through three centuries. Cruise passengers encounter the British legacy almost from the moment they step off their ship. Street traffic is directed by "bobbies" whose uniforms—white jacket, blue trousers with a red stripe, and pith helmet—are a tropical version of their London counterparts' garb. Driving is on the left, as in Britain.

The graceful colonial buildings of Parliament Square are the backdrop for a statue of Queen Victoria, and visitors on hand for the annual opening of Parliament will see the members of the legislature dressed in striped pants and morning coats. Were you to step into the Supreme Court while it is in session, you would find the judges and lawyers dressed in robes and wearing the traditional white wigs.

Nassau's Origins

Nassau, originally known as Sayle's Island, was settled for the first time around 1666 by a group of Bermudians and English, and within five years it had more than 900 settlers. By the time the Bahamas was granted to the Six Lords Proprietors of Carolina by the British Crown in 1670, the population had reached almost 1,000, including slaves. But the settlement developed into a pirate stronghold, which led to Spanish raids in 1684—raids so effective, apparently, that the town was abandoned. Some settlers returned two years later, but growth was slow until 1695, when one of the governors, Nicholas Trott, laid out a town plan for Charlestown, as it was called. To protect the western entrance to the harbor, he built Fort Nassau, which he named in honor of the prince of Orange-Nassau, who later became William III of England.

Except for Trott, however, the Carolina landlords were not interested in the Bahamas and allowed it to become a haven for pirates and privateers. Finally, from 1718 to 1721 and again from 1729 to 1732, under the first royal governor, Woodes Rogers, Nassau was cleaned up, Fort Nassau restored, an assembly established, and a town plan created, which has remained, more or less, the same to the present day. To protect the

eastern entrance to the harbor, Fort Montagu was added in 1741.

Nassau had a burst of prosperity later in the century when Loyalist refugees fleeing the American Revolutionary War came here to settle. Both administratively and architecturally, the new arrivals made a major impact on the island and transformed the scrappy little port into a pretty and prosperous town with new streets and wharfs and city ordinances for fire and health.

In 1787 the last royal governor of Virginia, John Murray, better known to history as Lord Dunmore, became the governor of the Bahamas. Arrogant, incompetent, and thoroughly disliked, Dunmore left an indelible mark on the Bahamas with his passion for building. He cost both the Crown and the Bahamians a great deal of money and grief. To fortify the island he built Fort Charlotte on the west, Fort Fincastle and Fort Winton on the east; he added gun emplacements on Hog (Paradise) Island. His home, Dunmore House, served as the governor's residence until Government House was completed. On the eastern end of New Providence, he built the Hermitage as his summer home. The present mansion, reconstructed in the early 1900s, is the residence of the Roman Catholic bishop of Nassau.

Port Profile: Nassau

Embarkation: In Nassau the piers are located on the north side of New Providence Island, less than a ten-minute walk from the heart of town. Ships pull dockside to the modern piers, known as Prince George Wharf, 1 block from Bay Street, the main shopping street of Nassau, accessible by an attractive pedestrian walk from the piers to the square. Taxis and motorcoaches are waiting for passengers at the dock when ships arrive.

Passengers are allowed to come and go freely between their ship and town. On returning to your ship, however, you will have to show your passport, your government-issued ID and cabin key, or some other form of identification distributed by your ship. After leaving the pier, en route to Rawson Square, you can pass through the large, brightly colored building marked FESTIVAL PLACE with the Welcome Center of the Bahamas Ministry of

Tourism, where you can pick up maps, brochures, and other information. Festival Place also has a post office and about two dozen shops for books, spices, souvenirs, and the like.

Local Transportation: Taxis are readily available and are zoned, but you can also request to be put on the meter. Rates are supposed to be fixed at $3 flag-fall and 40 cents each ⅕ mile for one or two passengers, $2 for each additional passenger. Some zone rates are: Cable Beach to downtown $17; Cable Beach to Paradise Island $17, each additional passenger $3, and $1 bridge toll. For a typical city and country tour, through Nassau, Cable Beach and Montague Foreshore, in the inner city areas and residential areas, a party of four pays approximately $60 for two hours. Unfortunately, some Nassau taxi drivers pretend their meters do not work in order to overcharge tourists.

If you plan to engage a taxi for sightseeing, negotiate the price in advance. Be aware that there are freelancers who are not legal taxis and who will charge whatever they think they can get. Look for a taxi with a BAHAMA HOST sticker on its windshield. The drivers are reliable and the best informed to be tour guides.

In Nassau, city buses or jitneys (US$1 to $2 fare) run frequently throughout the day and early evening from two downtown departure points only 3 blocks from the pier. At Bay and Frederick Streets is the station for buses to the northern and eastern parts of the island; those to Cable Beach and residential areas on the western side of the island leave from Bay Street and Navy Lion Road, next to the British Colonial Hilton. For Paradise Island, you'll need to take a taxi or ferry. The Paradise Island Bridge Toll is $1 per motorized vehicle. Taxis from Prince George Wharf to Paradise Island charge $8 plus toll for a one-way trip.

Surreys—horse-drawn carriages that can be hired at Rawson Square—are strictly for tourists and cost $10 per person. If there are more than two of you or if you want to keep the surrey for a longer period than the usual half hour, be sure to negotiate the price in advance.

Ferry Services: Ferries for Paradise Island depart from Woodes Rogers Wharf every thirty minutes from early morning until 6:00 P.M. and cost $3 per person. Bahamas Fast Ferries (323-2166; www.bahamasferries.com) offers regularly scheduled service to Harbour Island as well as to Spanish Wells, North Eleuthera, and Governor's Harbour. The Harbour Island tour costs $110 adults, $70 children round-trip.

Car Rentals: Car rentals from major US companies are available at major hotels and various locations throughout Nassau. Those with offices nearest the pier are Avis (377-7121) and Dollar Rent-a-Car (377-8300) at the British Colonial Hilton. Expect to pay $50 and up for a subcompact with unlimited mileage. If you rent a car with a credit card, you must be twenty-one years or older; without the card, twenty-five or older. Americans may use US driver's licenses for up to three months. Remember: Bahamians drive on the left. The speed limit is generally 30 mph, but not many drivers observe it, least of all the bus drivers.

Mopeds/Bicycles: Rental agencies for motor scooters and bicycles are located by the pier and on Marlboro Road near the British Colonial Hilton. A valid driver's license and a helmet supplied by the rental agency are compulsory for using a motorbike, and you must be eighteen or over. Inside Festival Place, there is a counter for renting motorbikes. The price is $30 per hour, $40 for two hours, and $50 for a full day, plus $5 gassing charge, or you can opt to get gas yourself. You must leave a $20 deposit, and insurance is $5. To repeat, driving is on the **LEFT.**

Emergency Numbers: Police: Nassau, call 919 or 322-4444. **Medical Services:** Nassau, Princess Margaret Hospital, call 322-2861. **Ambulance:** Nassau, call 322-2221.

Budget Planning

Nassau is not a cheap port. Taxis, car rentals, admission fees to privately operated sightseeing and other attractions, deluxe restaurants, and drinks are usually 20 percent higher than comparable facilities in the United States and other Caribbean ports of call. These costs, however, can be avoided or offset. Here are some ways, particularly for visitors on limited budgets.

- Walk. Nassau is a compact town that's easy and pleasurable to cover on foot.
- Use public transportation, which is good and low cost.
- Enjoy the abundant, beautiful, free, easy-to-reach beaches.
- Dine in restaurants serving local specialties. They are reasonably priced and clean.

Drugs, Crime, and Today's Realities

The Bahamas, like other places, is not immune to today's social ills. Although you might be approached to buy drugs, the possession, sale, or purchase of drugs is prohibited. Penalties for breaking the law apply to tourists as much as to Bahamians. They are severe, and the jails unpleasant.

Theft and crime, particularly in Nassau and Freeport, are on the rise. As a tourist, you are an easy target. Rented cars and motor scooters, for example, have special plates that make them easy to identify. However, you can reduce your vulnerability with prudence.

Do not park in secluded or isolated areas, particularly on the south coast of Nassau. Never leave valuables in your car or on the beach, including hotel beaches. Do not walk alone in remote or lightly trafficked areas, and most of all, do not engage someone as a guide who approaches you on the street or beach. All guides and taxi drivers in the Bahamas are licensed; if you have any doubt about a person's credentials, you need only step into the nearest tourist office or police station.

Nassau Shore Excursions

Because Nassau is easy to manage on your own and has a wide selection of activities to enjoy, shore excursions offered by cruise lines tend to be limited. The attractions and sports on these tours are described elsewhere in this chapter.

Combination Tour: Three to four hours; $25 to $36. A drive through Old Nassau and around the island is combined with a visit to the Ardastra Gardens. Some visit Paradise Island, including Versailles Gardens, or Crystal Cay. This is suggested for those on their first visit who cannot make the walking tour and whose interest in sports is marginal. A shorter two-hour city tour is hardly worthwhile since most of it can be covered in a walking tour on your own. Crystal Cay's tour with transportation by ferry to and from the port costs US$22.

Excursion Boat Trips: Glass-bottomed boats, catamarans, and other excursion boats depart from the pier area frequently throughout the day on guided tours to nearby reefs, beaches, and Blue Lagoon. Some boats stop for a swim and snorkeling. Some offer sunset and moonlight dinner cruises, too. Prices range upward from $40. The trips will probably be sold as shore excursions on your ship.

The *Seaworld Explorer:* $45 adult; $25 child. This semi-submarine drops about 5 feet below the surface of the water for you to view the gardens. The tour (356-2548) begins and returns from the port and goes on a fifteen-minute ride to the underwater marine park, known as the Sea Gardens, at Athol Island.

Half-Day Sail and Snorkel Excursion: Three hours; $60 adult; $30 child. Several large catamarans and "pirate" sailing ships offer full party cruises to nearby beaches for swimming, snorkeling, and rum punch.

Golf: Most cruise lines offer packages, or you can make your own arrangements. Majestic Tours (322-2606), one of the major local companies, has golf packages to the Cable Beach Golf course starting at $155. See the Sports in Nassau section later in this chapter.

- ★ Walking Tour of Old Nassau
- ★ Snorkeling/scuba
- ★ Golf
- ★ People-to-People program

Dolphin Encounters: At Blue Lagoon, an islet off Nassau, Close Encounters with dolphins are available for $85 per person, and swimming with dolphins for $165 per person. Call 363-1003; fax 363-4438; www.dolphinencounters.com.

Biking Excursions: See the Sports in Nassau section later in this chapter.

Nightclub Tour: $30; $50 with dinner. The tour includes admission to a nightclub with Bahamian and West Indian music and show, drink, tips, and transfers. It is suggested for those who are more interested in local entertainment than casinos but are reluctant to go out on their own.

Casino/Show: $35, cocktail show; $55, dinner show, including transportation to/from hotel at Crystal Palace or Atlantis. Las Vegas–style musical revue with long-legged showgirls and visit to the casino. Either can be done on your own, but you will not be saving money, as the round-trip fare by taxi costs $12 or more.

People-to-People

The Bahamas Ministry of Tourism gives you the opportunity to meet Bahamians as you would a friend through its People-to-People program, which brings tourists together with Bahamians who have volunteered to host visitors.

People-to-People volunteers—more than 1,200 on seven islands—come from a cross section of the community. They might belong to the same service club, such as Rotary or Kiwanis, as you do; or practice your profession or trade; or share your hobby. Many have traveled themselves and know what it is like to be on your own in a strange place. They know, too, how much more meaningful a visit can be when it is enriched with a personal experience.

These nice folks are *volunteers*. Although the program is operated by the Bahamas Ministry of Tourism, the volunteers are neither employed nor subsidized by the government. They offer their time and friendship without compensation and neither ask nor expect anything in return. They are involved because they enjoy meeting people from other countries and they want visitors to know their country in a natural, noncommercial atmosphere.

The form that the welcome takes depends on your Bahamian hosts. Because they, too, work for a living, they generally entertain in the evenings or on weekends. They might take you sightseeing or to their favorite beach for a picnic or to a Sunday service at their church. Or hosts might invite you to share an afternoon or evening of conversation with light refreshments, join a family gathering, or take a meal at their home. If so, you will most likely have a chance to sample food and drink you will not normally find on restaurant menus. You will be enjoying facets of Bahamian life that most visitors never see.

To participate in the People-to-People program, contact an office of the Bahamas Ministry of Tourism for a request form to be submitted about two to three weeks in advance of your visit. Write to the Ministry of Tourism, P.O. Box N-3701, Nassau, Bahamas; or P.O. Box F-251, Freeport, Bahamas. You can also visit www.bahamas.com or e-mail peopletopeople@bahamas.com. You will be contacted by a Ministry of Tourism People-to-People coordinator about the arrangements that have been made especially for you.

Cruise directors often have the forms. However, it's better to make your request in advance to give the People-to-People coordinator time to match you with your Bahamian host, especially if you have a particular interest in a social, fraternal, or religious organization, or a hobby, vocation, or profession that you would like to share.

Garden tea parties, sponsored jointly with the Bahamas Ministry of Tourism, are another part of the People-to-People program. In Nassau the parties are held January through November on the fourth Friday of the month at historic Government House and hosted by the wife of the governor-general. In Freeport the Garden of the Groves is the venue. In Exuma, high tea is held every other month from November through March/April; the venue revolves among Grand Isles Villas and Spas, Peace and Plenty Club, and the Palm Bay Beach Club. Call 366-2430.

Nassau on Your Own

Unless you have already been to Nassau several times, you will probably find a walking tour of Old Nassau or a boat excursion as interesting a way to enjoy your day in port as any alternative. Neither requires transportation from the pier, but visiting the attractions east and west of town and on Paradise Island does. Public buses are available, but they do not take you directly to the sites; from the main road, you will have a short walk. If you engage a taxi to a specific location, be sure to arrange your return transportation and set the price in advance.

A Walking Tour of Old Nassau

The entire walk, following the sequence as numbered, takes three to four hours depending on your pace. At several points along the way, you can stop for a refreshment or break off entirely and return to your ship or to Bay Street for shopping.

A walking tour of Old Nassau in the heart of town is a stroll through Bahamian history, particularly its British past. The town plan, laid out in grid fashion in 1788, is virtually intact and comprises four long, parallel east-west streets crossed by ten small north-south streets running from the harbor and Bay Street on the north to a hillside (East Hill and West Hill Streets) on the south. Although modern encroachments are everywhere, many streets have retained enough of their eighteenth- and nineteenth-century buildings, gardens, and broad steps to give visitors a real sense of Nassau in bygone days.

Prince George Wharf (1): From Prince George Wharf where the cruise ships dock, it is only a few steps to Rawson Square, the **Tourist Information Office (2)** inside Festival Place, and Parliament Square, the heart of downtown. En route you will pass a statue dedicated to the women of the Bahamas, by Randolph Johnston of Abaco.

The docks have been upgraded with a Welcome Plaza, a taxi dispatch station, and shelter for the horse-drawn surreys. Festival Place contains a Welcome Centre, as well as information, communication, and banking services; shops selling Bahamian products; and the **Junkanoo Expo (12)**

(Junkanoo is described later in the chapter). Either now or at the end of your walk, a detour to the museum is very worthwhile. Admission: $2 adult; 50 cents child.

Rawson Square (3): In 1985, as part of the beautification project for the visit of Queen Elizabeth II and the meeting of the Commonwealth nations, Old Nassau's stately buildings and monuments in the heart of downtown were spruced up, and a garden and mosaic walkways were laid to connect Rawson Square and Parliament Square on the south side of Bay Street. The square is named for Sir William Rawson, governor of the Bahamas from 1864 to 1869, and it has a small statue of Sir Milo Butler, the first governor-general of the Bahamas after independence in 1973. The Churchill Building on the east side of the square was formerly the prime minister's office. On the west side, you can engage a horse-drawn surrey for a tour or stop to have your hair braided for $2 per braid at the open-air pavilion.

Woodes Rogers Walk (4): The waterfront walkway west of Rawson Square, known as Woodes Rogers Walk, was named for the first British governor of the Bahamas. The tiny lanes are lined with shops. The town's famous **Straw Market (34),** a lively bazaar of Bahamian crafts, was destroyed by fire in 2001, but its merchants and stalls have been temporarily relocated 2 blocks west of the former location on Bay Street, the town's oldest street and main thoroughfare. It is lined with department stores and boutiques selling anything from $2 T-shirts to French perfumes and English china at about 20 percent less than stateside prices. The **Ministry of Tourism (35),** formerly housed in the same building as the Straw Market, was also destroyed and relocated in the Commerce Centre at the British Colonial Hilton Hotel, farther west at the end of Bay Street. Plans have been approved to rebuild the Straw Market in its original location, but construction has not begun.

If you were to continue west on Bay Street beyond the British Colonial Hilton, you would be on West Bay Street, the road leading to Ardastra Gardens and Cable Beach. East on Bay Street about 2 miles is the bridge to Paradise Island. Potters Cay has a native market where Bahamians buy fresh fish and provisions.

Parliament Square (5): The traditional center of Bahamian government activity, Parliament

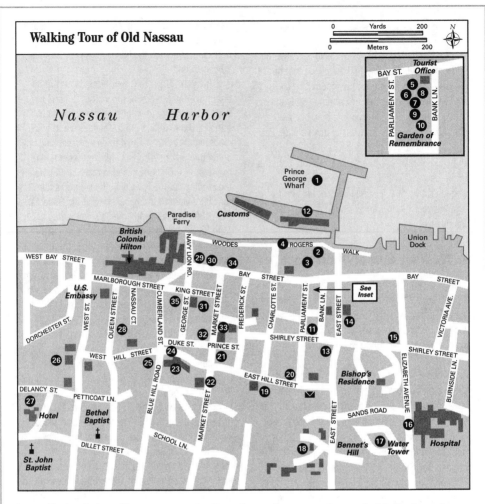

Walking Tour of Old Nassau

0 — Yards — 200
0 — Meters — 200
N

Nassau Harbor

Tourist Office
BAY ST.
PARLIAMENT ST.
BANK LN.
⑤
⑥ ⑧
⑦
⑨
⑩
Garden of Remembrance

Prince George Wharf ①

⑫

Paradise Ferry
Customs
British Colonial Hilton
WOODES ④ ROGERS
② WALK
③
Union Dock

WEST BAY STREET
MARLBOROUGH STREET
NAVY LION RD.
㉙ ㉚ ㉞
BAY STREET
BAY STREET
See Inset

U.S. Embassy
QUEEN STREET
WEST ST.
DORCHESTER ST.
NASSAU CT.
CUMBERLAND ST.
KING STREET
㉟ ㉛
GEORGE ST.
MARKET STREET
FREDERICK ST.
CHARLOTTE ST.
PARLIAMENT ST.
BANK LN.
EAST STREET
⑭
VICTORIA AVE.

㉘
㉜ ㉝
DUKE ST.
PRINCE ST.
SHIRLEY STREET
⑪
⑬
㉕
WEST HILL STREET
⑮
SHIRLEY STREET

㉖
BLUE HILL ROAD
㉔
㉓
㉑
EAST HILL STREET
⑳
ELIZABETH AVENUE
BURNSIDE LN.

DELANCY ST.
㉒
⑲
Bishop's Residence

㉗
PETTICOAT LN.
Hotel
Bethel Baptist
MARKET STREET
SANDS ROAD
⑯

DILLET STREET
SCHOOL LN.
⑱
Bennet's Hill
EAST STREET
⑰ Water Tower
Hospital

St. John Baptist

NOTE: Numbers in the walking tour correspond to the numbers on the accompanying map. An "x" after the number means the house or building is not open to the public; "s" means it can be visited by special arrangement.

1. Prince George Wharf
2. Tourist Information Office
3. Rawson Square
4. Woodes Rogers Walk
5. Parliament Square
6. House of Assembly
7. Senate Building
8. Colonial Secretary's Office and Treasury
9. Supreme Court
10. Central Police Station
11. Public Library
12. Junkanoo Expo
13. Curry House and Zion Church
14x. Cascadilla
15. Bahamas Historical Society and Museum
16. Queen's Staircase
17. Fort Fincastle and Water Tower
18. Police Headquarters
19. Ministry of Foreign Affairs

20x. Jacaranda House
21. St. Andrew's Presbyterian Church
22. Gregory's Arch
23s. Government House
24. Christopher Columbus Statue
25. Graycliff House
26. Cathedral of St. Francis Xavier/The Priory (Dunmore House)/National Art Gallery/ Junkanoo Museum
27. Buena Vista
28. The Deanery
29. Cable Beach/West End Bus Stand
30. Vendue House/Pompey Museum
31. Christ Church Cathedral and Pirates of Nassau Museum
32. Balcony House
33. Central Bank/Trinity Place
34. Straw Market; North and East End Bus Stand
35. Ministry of Tourism

Square is graced by a marble statue of a youthful Queen Victoria seated upon a throne and holding a sword and scepter. Framing the statue is the lovely Georgian architecture of the **House of Assembly (6)** on the west, the **Senate Building (7)** on the south, and the old **Colonial Secretary's Office and Treasury (8)** on the east. The buildings were constructed from 1805 to 1813 and are based on Tryon's Palace of New Bern, the old capital of North Carolina, praised as the most beautiful building of its time. South of these buildings facing the Garden of Remembrance, with a cenotaph commemorating the dead of the two world wars, is the **Supreme Court (9)**. The garden with stately royal palms and tropical flowers is one of the prettiest spots in the downtown area. On the east side of the square on Bank Lane is the **Central Police Station (10)**.

Public Library (11): The octagonal structure, built in about 1798 as a prison, was made into a library and museum in 1879. The structure, contemporary with buildings in Williamsburg, Virginia, is thought to have been modeled after the Old Powder Magazine there. The first and second floors had prison cells on each of their eight sides; a central open area provided fresh air. These alcoves now hold library stacks. A domed gallery on the third floor was originally unroofed; it once held a bell that was rung to summon members of the House of Assembly to meetings. The upper floor has a collection of books and artifacts on the Bahamas, including old maps dating from 1750 and prints from 1891. Hours: 10:00 A.M. to 8:00 P.M. Monday through Thursday, 10:00 A.M. to 5:00 P.M. Friday, 10:00 A.M. to 4:00 P.M. Saturday. Call 322-4907.

Magistrate's Court No. 3 on Parliament Street was originally built in 1894 as a chapel for the Salem Union Baptist congregation on a site known as the Livery Stable Grounds. It is still owned by the church. South of the library, the old Royal Victorian Gardens was the site of the once grand Victorian Hotel, the center of social activity when it opened in 1861 during the American Civil War. Among its first guests were those fleeing the war; others were blockade-runners, officers of the Confederacy, spies of the northern states, and "ladies of high quality" who were invited to the nightly parties.

In 1876 the hotel was leased to the brother of Grover Cleveland, US president from 1885 to 1889

and 1893 to 1897; and according to a plaque in the gardens, the hotel was purchased in 1898 by Henry M. Flagler. The American railroad czar connected Florida with the rest of the nation and drew up plans for a rail/ferry service to connect the Bahamas to the US mainland. In its heyday the hotel hosted a long list of distinguished guests that included Winston Churchill, Prince Albert, and an array of European royalty and celebrities. The hotel changed hands many times before it closed in 1971 and was later destroyed by fire.

Curry House (13), located on Shirley Street immediately west of Zion Church, is a three-story building that opened in 1890 as a private hotel. Later it became an annex of the Royal Victoria Hotel, and in 1972 it was acquired by the government and is used by the Ministry of Finance.

From here, you have a choice of walking east to Bennet's Hill and the Water Tower or west to Government House. If you plan to cover this entire walking tour on foot, you might do well to take the uphill climb to the Water Tower first. To reach the Water Tower, walk east on Shirley Street and turn south onto Elizabeth Avenue. It leads directly to the Queen's Staircase and hence the Water Tower.

Cascadilla (14x) is one of the Nassau houses thought to have been built by ships' carpenters—the island's only craftsmen for many decades. (Certain Bahamian architectural features later transplanted to Key West by Bahamians derive from this origin.) The oldest part of the house dates from 1840, when it marked the eastern boundary of town. The ruins of kitchens and other buildings indicate that it was once part of a plantation house. The property has had many owners over the years and now belongs to a real estate broker.

Bahamas Historical Society and Museum (15): Founded in 1959, the society is a nonprofit cultural and educational organization dedicated to stimulating interest in Bahamian history and collecting and preserving material related to it. Admission: $1 adult; 50 cents ages five through twelve. Hours: 10:00 A.M. to 4:00 P.M. Tuesday through Friday, 10:00 A.M. to 1:00 P.M. Monday, 10:00 A.M. to noon Saturday. For information: Bahamas Historical Society, Box SS-6833, Nassau. Call 322-4231.

Queen's Staircase (16): At the head of Elizabeth Avenue is a passageway of sixty-six steps carved out of limestone, draped with thick tropical foliage, and cooled by a waterfall. Local lore says the steps represent each year of Queen Victoria's reign. Actually, they were carved by slaves a century earlier and form a passageway to Fort Fincastle, thus enabling troops to reach the fort from town without being exposed to fire from enemy ships. Call 326-9772.

Fort Fincastle (17): Situated on Bennet's Hill overlooking the town, Paradise Island, and the eastern approaches to New Providence, Fort Fincastle was built in 1793 and takes its name from Lord Dunmore's title as the Viscount Fincastle. The fort was constructed in the shape of a ship's bow and has served as a lighthouse and signal station. Hours: 8:00 A.M. to 4:00 P.M. Monday through Friday, 9:00 A.M. to 6:00 P.M. Saturday and Sunday.

Water Tower (17): Next to the fort, the 126-foot Water Tower built in 1928 is the highest point on the island, 216 feet above sea level. An elevator (or a circular stairway of 202 steps) goes to an observation deck at the top for a lovely panoramic view of the city, harbor, and Fort Fincastle below. The tower was closed for repairs and had not reopened at press time. Open from 9:00 A.M. to 5:00 P.M. daily; the elevator ride costs 50 cents. (You may be hustled for tips by the elevator operator and self-appointed guides on the tower's observation deck; you should simply ignore them.) Call 326-9781.

From the tower you can continue your walking tour by returning to East Street via Sands Road or Prison Lane and walking north to East Hill Street. The **Police Headquarters (18)** was built in 1900. The green-and-white building on the north side of the complex is a typical example of Bahamian wooden architecture and is reminiscent of houses built in Key West by Bahamian transplants.

When the Loyalists came to Nassau after the American Revolution, they brought with them ideas about colonial architecture, particularly of the South. Although it evolved into a decidedly Bahamian version with different types of building materials, the influence is evident. Typical building materials included limestone with pink-washed walls and peaked roofs; wood was used in colonnades, fretwork balconies, and jalousies, or louvered shutters that shielded the verandas from the hot sun and allowed the air to circulate. In the late nineteenth and early twentieth centuries, economic hardship forced many Bahamians to leave the

islands. Some became the early settlers of Key West, bringing their building habits with them.

From East Street, turn west onto East Hill Street. You will pass the modern post office building and the former East Hill Club, which houses the **Ministry of Foreign Affairs (19).** The club was built around 1850 by the socially prominent Matthews family, who were lawyers and government officials. The Georgian Colonial house was first renovated when it was owned by Lord Beaverbrook.

Jacaranda House (20x), on the corner of East Hill and Parliament Streets, was built about 1840 by Chief Justice Sir George Anderson, of Georgia stone previously used as ship's ballast. During World War II the house was owned by Capt. Vyvian Drury, aide-de-camp to the duke of Windsor. It was bought in 1949 by the widow of Sir Harry Oakes and later passed to her daughter. The house is furnished with lovely antiques and has exterior features typical of classical Bahamian architecture, such as interlocking corners of large projecting stones used for strength (known as chamfered quoins).

St. Andrew's Presbyterian Church (21): The pretty white church at the corner of Prince and Market Streets was begun in 1810 and expanded many times over the next five decades. It was completely renovated early in the twentieth century.

Gregory's Arch (22): Spanning Market Street is a picturesque entrance to Grant's Town, one of the early settlements of former slaves, referred to locally as "Over the Hill" as it is literally over the ridge that divides north Nassau from the south side. The arch, named for Governor John Gregory, was built in 1852 by J. J. Burnside, the surveyor-general who laid out Grant's Town. The English iron railings were added two years later. Broad stone stairways at the foot of Charlotte and Frederick Streets lead from East Hill Street directly to Bay Street.

Government House (23s): The imposing Government House (at Blue Hill Road and East Hill Street) stands on Mount Fitzwilliam, a hillside overlooking Nassau. It is home of the governor-general, the queen's personal representative to the Commonwealth of the Bahamas. A previous structure is thought to have housed governors from Richard Fitzwilliam in 1733 to Lord Dunmore in 1787. Dunmore moved to the house he built on West Street (now a priory) and sold the former government house and its land to another Loyalist. The present house was built between 1803 and 1806 and expanded several times. The east wing dates from 1909.

The hurricane of 1929 caused a great deal of damage to the structure, and, subsequently, the interior and front facade were entirely redesigned, the main entrance changed, and the main hall added. In 1940 the house was extensively redecorated, and living quarters in the west wing, known as the Windsor Wing, were added for the personal staff of the duke of Windsor, who lived here for four years as the royal governor of the Bahamas.

More changes were made in 1964 and again in 1977 for the visit of Queen Elizabeth II. In addition to the queen, many members of the royal family, heads of state including President John F. Kennedy, and other celebrities have been guests here. Monthly, the Bahamas Ministry of Tourism and the People-to-People program hold a garden party for tourists, hosted by the governor-general's wife. Call 322-1875.

Christopher Columbus Statue (24): The entrance to Government House is marked by a 12-foot-tall statue of Christopher Columbus, made in London by an aide to American novelist and historian Washington Irving and placed here in 1830 by Governor Sir James Carmichael Smyth. It commemorates Columbus's arrival in the New World on the Bahamian island of San Salvador. The ceremonial Changing of the Guard with the famous Royal Bahamas Police Force Band takes place on alternate Saturdays at 10:00 A.M. sharp. Call 322-3622.

From the statue you can walk down George Street in front of the Columbus statue to the Straw Market on Bay Street, or continue your walking tour to see some of Nassau's oldest and loveliest houses.

Graycliff House (25): This Georgian mansion set in a lovely tropical garden dates from about 1726. Now a hotel and restaurant, it was originally built by a notorious pirate, Capt. John H. Graysmith, as his home. The building may have been used as a garrison for the British West Indies Regiment, judging from the thick walls and other structural elements in the cellars, which are now used by the hotel for its wine collection. The house is known to have been a hotel as early as 1844, but it

became a private residence again in 1937 when it belonged to a Canadian couple who added a swimming pool and made alterations. In 1966 the estate was bought by Lord Dudley, earl of Staffordshire, as his winter home. The present owners acquired it in 1974.

Farther west on West Hill Street are several beautifully restored private homes and the **Priory (26),** formerly known as Dunmore House. After serving as the governor's residence, the house became the officers' quarters and mess hall for the 22nd West Indies Regiment. It later became a military hospital and in 1893 was purchased by the Roman Catholic Church and made into the Priory; the Cathedral of St. Francis Xavier is adjacent.

National Art Gallery (26): Opened in 2003 and housed in a magnificently restored mansion built in the 1860s, the National Art Gallery of the Bahamas, at the corner of West and West Hill Streets, contains impressive examples of the Bahamas's art development from colonial times to the present. Although the collection is in its early stage of acquisition, it is the only place you can get a comprehensive view and gain an appreciation for the Bahamas's young art movement. Among the established artists in the collection are Amos Ferguson, Brent Malone, Maxwell Taylor, the brothers Jackson and Stanley Burnside, Alton Lowe, Edison G. Rolle, Edward Minnis, Dorman Stubbs, Ricardo Knowles, and others. The gallery renovation took three years to complete at the cost of $3.4 million. The museum shop sells the richly illustrated book *Bahamian Art, 1492–1992,* an excellent introduction to the Bahamas's art history, published to commemorate the Columbus Quincentennial. Admission: $5 adult; $3 senior, student; under 12 free. Hours: 10:00 A.M. to 4:00 P.M. Tuesday through Saturday. Call 328-5800; www.nagb.org.bs.

The annual national festival of the Bahamas, Junkanoo, held December 26 and January 1, is now an integral part of Bahamian culture, and the creation of its elaborate costumes has played an important role in the development of Bahamian art and artists. At the **Educulture/Junkanoo Museum (26)** (West and Delancy Streets), visitors see some of the costumes and get a comprehensive tour of Junkanoo by a guide who is an active and enthusiastic member of the festival. Admission: $20 adult; $10 child. Call 328-DRUM.

South of the museum on Delancy Street is **Buena Vista (27)**, a hotel with one of the town's leading restaurants, housed in a building dating from the mid-nineteenth century. Call 322-2811.

The Deanery (28): From West Hill Street continue north and turn into Queen Street to the Deanery, at No. 28. Built in 1710, it is thought to be the oldest house in the Bahamas. The building was acquired by the Anglican Church in 1800 and is the rectory of Christ Church Cathedral. The three-story house is built of stone with chamfered quoins; originally it had three tiers of verandas on three sides. A one-story building on the west side was the stone kitchen with an 8-foot fireplace and a domed oven; it has a small room thought to have been used as sleeping quarters for domestic slaves. Across the street is the US embassy.

In the next small lane is Nassau Court, built in 1830 as the West Chapel of the Wesleyan Methodist Church. In 1864 it was sold to the government and used as a school for almost a century, although the nature of the school changed several times. In 1960 it was turned over to the Ministry of Public Works and is now occupied by the Ministry of Economic Affairs.

On the north side of Marlborough Street is the British Colonial Hilton, the pink colonial building that dominates the waterfront. It is on the site of the town's first fortification, Fort Nassau, built in 1670. On its east side is the stand for buses to **Cable Beach (29).**

Vendue House/Pompey Museum (30): At the head of George Street facing Bay Street is the site of the former slave market, originally a colonnade structure without walls dating from about 1769. It was rebuilt in the early 1900s and occupied by the Bahamas Electricity Corporation. In 1992, as part of the Columbus Quincentennial, it was renovated to house a museum—Pompey Museum of Slavery and Emancipation—funded by a grant from Bacardi Corporation. The exhibit on the African experience in the Bahamas was named for Pompey, a slave on one of five estates in Exuma owned by Lord Rolle and a hero in Bahamian history. The Vendue House was damaged in the fire that destroyed the Straw Market in 2001 but reopened in 2007 and is currently hosting a special exhibition, Lest We Forget, which commemorates the 200th anniversary of the abolition of slavery. The collection of the paintings by Amos Ferguson, the internationally acclaimed Bahamian intuitive artist, which had been exhibited at the Pompey Museum, was saved from the fire and is now in safekeeping at the National Art Gallery. Admission: $3 adult; $2 senior; $1 child. Hours: 9:30 A.M. to 4:00 P.M., closed Thursday and Sunday. Call 356-0495.

Christ Church Cathedral (31): Turn east onto Marlborough Street and walk to the corner of King and George Streets to Christ Church Cathedral. In the original layout of the town, this area was a park known as George's Square, the site of the colony's first church.

Pirates of Nassau Museum (31) (King and George Streets). One of Nassau's newest attractions, two years in the making, is part museum, part Disneyesque entertainment. Housed in three adjoining structures, the 150-year-old Lofthouse, a 200-year-old slave kitchen, and the modern Marlborough Arms building, the museum offers an interactive, educational journey into the early eighteenth century when pirates such as Blackbeard ruled Bahamian waters. Designed and built in Canada, Switzerland, and Britain, as well as Nassau, the museum has as its centerpiece a 75-foot replica of the pirate ship *Revenge* and a re-created wharf. The scent of tar, the sound of water lapping against the wooden ships, scenes of life at sea, and a pirate marooned on a deserted island are some of the come-to-life details that depict the age of piracy at its zenith. A tour of the ship and other exhibits takes about forty-five minutes and is suitable for all ages. Hours: 9:00 A.M. to 5:00 P.M. Monday through Saturday, 9:00 A.M. to noon Sunday. Admission: $12 adult; $6 ages twelve or under. Call 356-3759; www.pirates-of-nassau.com.

Balcony House (32): Facing the Central Bank on Market Street is the two-story Balcony House, whose construction indicates it may have been built by ships' carpenters around 1790. The house was constructed of American soft cedar and has a second-floor balcony that hangs over the street. An unusual inside staircase is said to have come from a ship. The property, which includes three other houses and slave kitchens, was acquired by Lord Beaverbrook, who sold it in 1947. More recently it was acquired by the Central Bank and renovated as a museum by the Department of Archives to show life of a prosperous family in the nineteenth century. Hours: 10:00 A.M. to 5:00 P.M. weekdays except holidays. Call 302-2621.

The Central Bank (33) has a collection of the Bahamas's leading artists on display in its lobby. The bank is on Trinity Place, a small street between Market and Frederick Streets. One of the oldest streets in Nassau, Trinity Place is home to the Trinity Church. Both Market and Frederick Streets lead to Bay Street and the local bus stand for buses to the North and East End. You can return to your ship by walking east on Bay Street.

Nassau and Its Environs

New Providence has many good roads, making any section of the island accessible with a few minutes' drive. At least four highways cut the island north–south, making it easy to reach the south coast from Nassau by a direct route.

Attractions West of Nassau

In contrast with the Old World ambience of Old Nassau are the modern resorts of **Cable Beach** that stretch west from town along 5 miles of lovely, white-sand beaches on the north shore. Dubbed the Bahamian Riviera, they include the eye-popping Wyndham Nassau Resort & Crystal Palace Casino; Sheraton Cable Beach Resort; Breezes Bahamas, next to Nassau's oldest golf course; Nassau Beach; and Sandals Royal Bahamian. All are undergoing a transformation.

A joint venture between Baha Mar Resort and a subsidiary of Harrah's Entertainment, Inc., will create the largest destination resort in the Caribbean here, with a phase one investment of than $2.3 billion. Baha Mar will offer approximately 3,000 guest rooms and will feature the Caribbean's first-ever Caesar's Resort Hotel & Casino, the largest casino in the Caribbean at 10,000 square feet. Starwood has committed to operate hotels under its W, St. Regis, Westin, and Sheraton brands. An eighteen-hole golf course, twenty-acre pool and beachfront complex, retail village, restaurants, and entertainment venues are scheduled for completion in 2010. The $80 million Sheraton Cable Beach Resort—the former Radisson—opened in June 2007. Between Old Nassau and modern Cable Beach, in the shadow of Fort Charlotte, there are several attractions that usually can be visited in one tour.

If you visit any of the following places on your own by taxi, be sure to arrange for your return transportation. In most cases, public buses pass within walking distance.

Ardastra Gardens and Zoo: One mile west of town in the shadow of Fort Charlotte is a nature park with the world's only trained flamingo corps. The pink birds are put through their paces in a twenty-five-minute show thrice daily. The pretty birds, which are the national bird of the Bahamas, have a mating display of strutting that lends itself to being trained to parade. The five-acre gardens also offer the chance to see in one place a wide variety of tropical plants as well as endemic birds, four species of iguana (which look like miniature dinosaurs), and other wildlife remaining in the Bahamas.

Visitors are allowed to take photographs, including ones of themselves amid the flapping flamingos. The flamingos come from the southern island of Great Inagua, where 50,000 birds—the world's largest breeding colony—are protected in a nature preserve administered by the Bahamas National Trust. Ardastra also has several beautiful Bahama parrots in a captive breeding program with the trust. This endangered species, one of sixteen Amazon parrot species in the Caribbean, is found only in Inagua and the Abacos in a sanctuary within a large forest reserve. Hours: 9:00 A.M. to 5:00 P.M. daily. Admission: $12 adult; $6 child. Shows are Monday through Saturday, 10:30 A.M., 2:10 P.M., and 4:10 P.M. Call 323-5806; www.ardastra.com.

Nassau Botanical Gardens: Adjacent to Fort Charlotte is an eighteen-acre spread of tropical plants and flowers, a delightful oasis with a large variety of flora typical of the tropics. The gardens are popular for weddings. They also have a re-created Lucayan village. Admission: $1 adult; 50 cents child. Hours: 9:00 A.M. to 4:30 P.M. daily. Call 323-5975.

Fort Charlotte: One mile west of town. Named in honor of the wife of George III, the fort was begun by Lord Dunmore in 1787 and built in three stages. The eastern part is the oldest; the middle portion was named Fort Stanley; and the western section, Fort D'Arcy. Much of it was cut

New Providence Island

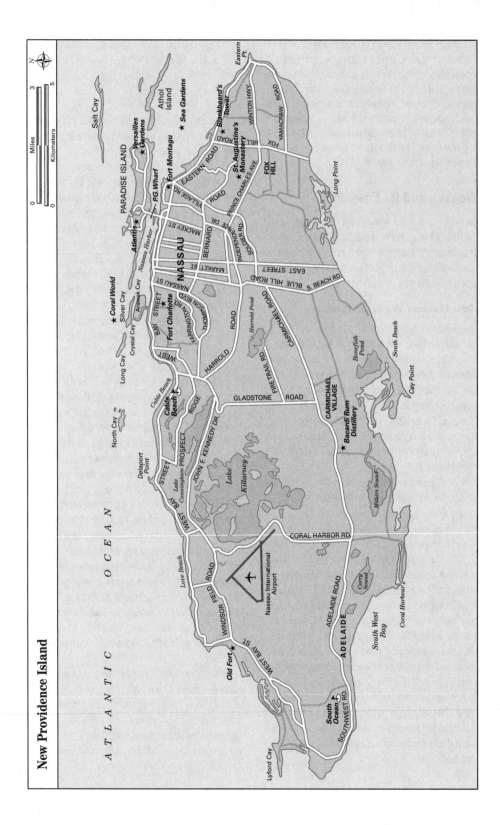

out of solid rock, and the walls were buttressed with cedar to "last to eternity," according to Dunmore. It still has its moat, open battlements, and dungeons, plus a good view of the harbor. The fort was restored extensively in 1992. Admission: $5 adult; $2 child under twelve. Hours: 9:00 A.M. to 4:00 P.M. daily. Tours throughout the day. Call 326-9772.

Arawak Cay: What started a few years ago as a few stalls of fishermen shucking conch—Bahamians' favorite food—for local conch lovers has blossomed into one of Nassau's main attractions. Here, at any of two dozen stalls, you can sample fresh conch prepared in one of several ways—cracked, fritters, jerk, and more. Those in the know agree that the best is conch salad, the Bahamian answer to seviche, the popular South American lime-and-onion-flavored fish appetizer. A fish fry with local bands making music is held here on Saturday and Sunday. For information: 323-2227.

From Cable Beach, a road hugging the coast continues west around the island to Love Beach, one of the island's loveliest beaches. Farther west is Lyford Cay, a private, 4,000-acre residential resort that you can visit only as a guest of a member. Lyford Cay, as much as any development, caused the Bahamas to be called the jet-set capital because of the many famous international personalities who own homes here.

The western end of the island has many elegant Bahamian mansions, frequently painted in the deep pink color associated with the Bahamas or other pastels with white trim, and surrounded by tropical gardens. Among the loveliest are the home of the former prime minister, on Skyline Drive; the residence of the US ambassador to the Bahamas, on Saffron Hill; and on Sandford Drive, the mansion of Canadian millionaire Sir Harry Oakes, one of the island's most famous residents and benefactors, whose murder in 1943 sent shock waves through the island and continues to be a mystery.

Large areas of the south side of the island are uninhabited and covered by miles of pine forests. From Adelaide and Carmichael Roads, you can circle back via Gladstone Road over Prospect Ridge to see one of the island's biggest surprises—Lake Killarney and Lake Cunningham—large bodies of water whose wooded shores are richly populated with birds.

Attractions East of Nassau

Fort Montagu: The first fortification at the northeastern end of the island was built in 1728 to protect the eastern approach to Nassau Harbor. In 1741 it was replaced by the present structure, designed by Peter Henry Bruce, an engineer previously employed by Peter the Great of Russia. The fort was seized by the Americans briefly during the Revolutionary War.

The Retreat, Bahamas National Trust: The trust's headquarters, east of Nassau near Queen's College, is on an eleven-acre site where Arthur and Margaret Langlois, beginning in 1925, created one of the world's largest private collections of palm trees—about 175 species from around the world. The property was donated to the trust and officially opened in 1985. The palm trees grow in a thick coppice forest with other native trees and shrubs. The gardens are maintained by volunteers from local garden clubs. Admission: $2. Hours: 9:00 A.M. to 5:00 P.M. Monday through Friday. Call 393-1317.

St. Augustine's Monastery: Near Fox Hill village. Father Jerome, the architect of several Anglican and Catholic churches in the Bahamas, designed the school and cloister of the monastery.

Wealthy colonialists originally settled in the area east of Nassau; there, dozens of fine mansions stand witness to the enormous wealth the early settlers amassed. Some sections also have small settlements of colorful West Indian–style houses built, after slavery was abolished, by former slaves granted plots of land. Four of the original settlements are Adelaide, Carmichael, Fox Hill, and Gambier.

Attractions on Paradise Island

Facing Nassau's north shore is Paradise Island, connected to Nassau by two ½-mile bridges and a ferry from Prince George Wharf. Initially, the island resort was put on the map by A&P heir Huntington Hartford, whose home became the centerpiece of the fashionable Ocean Club. In 1994 Sun International acquired Resorts International, changing the name to Atlantis and making major changes.

Atlantis Resort and Casino: The complex includes a dozen hotels, twenty restaurants, a cavernous casino, an enormous dinner theater, an eighteen-hole championship golf course, a twelve-court tennis complex, horseback riding, a marina, a full range of water sports, and an international airport with flights to several Florida cities. Atlantis's centerpiece is the new sixty-three-acre Aquaventure water experience with "master blaster" waterslides, water escalators, and wave surges all accentuated by smoke, fog, and video effects. There is a near-vertical 50-foot drop at the 120-foot tall Power Tower; you'll also find 7-foot ups-and-downs into white-water rapids on a mile-long river loop. The fourteen-acre Waterscape is said to have the largest outdoor, open-water aquarium in the world, six exhibit lagoons, more than forty waterfalls, five swimming pools, three underground grottos, and an underwater walkway with windows for viewing sharks and artificial coral reefs. Dig and Marine Aquarium Tour (given frequently throughout the day, 9:00 A.M. to 5:00 P.M. daily) admission: $29 adult; $14.50 ages four to twelve. Aquaventure: $105 adult; $75 child. Call 364-1317.

Versailles Gardens and French Cloister: Landscaped gardens, adjacent to the Ocean Club on the island's northeast side, are enclosed by the stones and arches of a twelfth-century Augustinian monastery, which Huntington Hartford had shipped from France stone by stone and reconstructed here. From the hotel's swimming pool, the gardens rise in seven terraces to the cloisters, which overlook a small garden and the sea. Each terrace is embellished with ancient as well as modern statues of historic figures, such as Empress Josephine of France, Franklin D. Roosevelt, and Dr. Stanley Livingstone.

Shopping

With the increase in the number of cruise passengers in recent years, shopping in Nassau has greatly improved in quality and selection and closely rivals St. Thomas, with goods from around the globe. The Tourist Information Center inside Festival Place in Rawson Square by the piers can provide information. There are shops and services here, too.

At Rawson Square you can turn east or west onto Bay Street, and you will find every type of shop—dress, sportswear, shoes, men's clothing, liquor, perfume, and more. The newest shops and small shopping plazas are east of the square, while the stores on the west are generally the more established ones. The free promotional booklet *Best Buys in the Bahamas* is useful for maps and store descriptions. It usually has coupons for free gifts and discounts, too.

Before the day has ended, you will certainly want to visit the Straw Market on Bay Street; it is open daily. One of the best of its kind in the tropics, it's crammed full of handcrafted baskets, hats, handbags, dolls, and other inexpensive gifts to take home to relatives and friends. You can watch the items emerge from the skilled fingers of a Bahamian craftswoman and even have them handmade to order with your own design and initials. Don't hesitate to bargain in the market; the women expect it and enjoy the exchange. And it's fun!

In addition to Bay Street, there are shopping arcades in hotels, particularly on Paradise Island at Atlantis, where the shopping arcade, Crystal Court, includes such high-fashion boutiques as Ferragamo, Versace, and Gucci, as well as more moderate ones such as Tommy Banana. The newest shopping mall, Marina Village, is also part of Atlantis but outside the hotel structures. In stores designed to resemble the houses in a Bahamian village are found art shops, clothing and jewelry boutiques, and a variety of restaurants. Some are included in the information below.

Nassau stores are open 9:00 A.M. to 5:00 or 6:00 P.M. Monday through Saturday. Many are also open on Sunday; some close on Thursday afternoon. All of the following stores are on Bay Street unless indicated otherwise.

Art and Antiques: Nassau Art Gallery (East Bay Shopping Center) and **Doongalik Art Gallery** (Marina Village; 363-1313) have limited selections of contemporary local artists. *The Plait Lady* (Marina Village; 363-1416), after an absence of several years, has reopened in the new shopping mall. The owner, Clare Sands, employs more than 1,000 craftspeople throughout the Bahamas who produce the most authentic, best-made straw products in Nassau. All are handmade from the silver top palm, mostly from Long Island, and the pond top from Eleuthera. The products are expensive. And indeed, it would appear that some of these craftspeople are supplying other vendors, such as the **Bahamas Craft Centre** (Paradise Island Shopping Centre), with similar, if not the same, finely woven baskets of improved style and design for modest prices.

For a humorous view, Jaff Cooper, a political cartoonist for local newspapers, has a kiosk at the new Marina Village, where he sells his Bahama Mama cartoon characters, children's coloring books, and other souvenirs.

Balmain Antiques (Bay Street at Charlotte Street, second floor; 323-7421; fax 323-7422) has a great collection of old prints and maps.

Bahamian Batiks: Native Bahamian designs on cotton and other fabrics are printed by Androsia on the Bahamian island of Andros and made into sportswear sold in high-quality stores. Selections are available at **Royal Palm Trading Co.** A similar, more expensive product, **Bahama Hand Prints** (Marina Village; 394-4111), is made in Nassau. Their silk-screened designs, usually on voile-type fabrics, have a more flowing look. New prints and colors are introduced each season.

Books: The **Island Book Shop** is something of a department store and sells everything from cameras to cashmeres, swimsuits, and sportswear. The book department on the second floor is the best in town.

Children's Gifts: If you want a fun, unusual, and interesting gift for a small child, bookstores, newsstands, and pharmacies stock a series of coloring books on Bahamian flowers, birds, fish, shells, ships, and Junkanoo. For expensive items, **The Linen Shop** (322-4266) has lovely hand-smocked and embroidered children's clothes.

China and Crystal: For the best selections of English bone china, Waterford, and other fine crystal, **Solomon Mines** (Bay Street; 356-6920) has a large selection, with savings of up to 35 percent on china and crystal, among some the best buys in duty-free goods in the Bahamas. You will be better prepared to recognize a bargain when you come with prices from home. Have the name of the pattern as well as the manufacturer for accurate comparisons. **Tiffany and Co.** (284 Bay Street) has a boutique inside John Bull, a major department store.

Dive Supplies: Bahamas Divers outfits divers and snorkelers; **Pyfrom's** carries T-shirts, Sea Island cotton shirts, and souvenirs, as well as masks and flippers for children and adults.

Jewelry: Coin of the Realm (14 Charlotte Street; 322-4682) has not only coins but also a large selection of precious and semiprecious stones, gold and silver jewelry, and stamps. **Bulgari** (Crystal Court, Atlantis) is the first boutique of the famous Italian designer in the Bahamas.

Leather: Leather Masters (Parliament Street; 322-7597) and the **Brass and Leather Shops** (14 Charlotte Street) carry fine Italian bags, briefcases, shoes, and other leather goods. Fendi and Gucci have their own shops in prime locations. Savings are about 20 percent, if that much, over US prices. Ferragamo, Versace, and other famous designers have shops at the Atlantis resort.

Perfumes: The Perfume Shop has several outlets on Bay Street and in the Paradise Island Shopping Centre. Their prices are as competitive as any we have found. Actually, French perfume prices are set by French perfume makers; any dealer who undercuts the price is cut off from the supply. For local products, **Bahamaspa** (Festival Place; 327-2772; bahamaspa@aol.com) has luxury soaps made in small batches by hand with natural ingredients and oils. At **Sundrop Creations** (Montrose Avenue and Sears Road; 325-4469; www.sundropcreations.com) offerings include bath salts made with sea salt from the local waters, hand-poured candles, body butter, and sea bubbles.

Sportswear: There are many low-priced and discount shoe stores and sports- and casualwear shops along East Bay Street. **Seventeen Shop** (Bay Street; 322-2456) has a large selection of mod fashions, in dresses as well as shorts, shirts, and slacks. **Venue** (Bay Street; 326-8079) has both casual and evening wear for women.

Watches: John Bull (Bay Street and Paradise Island; 322-4253; www.johnbull.com) is one of the oldest and largest stores in the Bahamas. It carries all the famous makes from novelty watches to Corum and Cartier, as well as a full line of cameras and photo equipment.

Women's Fashions: Calypso Carousel (Marina Village; 363-0380) sells the latest mod fashions with lots of glitter for $300 and up. **Cole's of Nassau** (Parliament Street, Lyford Cay, Crystal Court; 322-8393; www.colesofnassau.com) has the largest selection of sophisticated women's fashions, but many are familiar labels that sell for less in New York. For less expensive clothes, check the shops on Bay Street east of Rawson Square.

Dining and Restaurants

Restaurants and hotel dining rooms range from elegant and sophisticated—as befits a world capital—to simple and unpretentious, as suits an unhurried tropical resort. You can enjoy a barbecue on the beach, a fish fry by the harbor, or a gourmet treat in the romantic ambience of a colonial home.

The variety of international cuisine includes French, English, Italian, American, Chinese, Indian, and Greek, but you really should try some Bahamian specialties before the day is out. The best known are johnnycakes, a corn bread; conch chowder, spicy and delicious; conch fritters or deep-fried grouper; and pigeon peas with rice, to mention a few. Prices range from $4 for lunch at a typical local restaurant to $100 for dinner at the top gourmet havens.

Always check your bill before you leave a tip. Many restaurants in the Bahamas and the Caribbean have taken up the European custom of adding a 15 percent service charge to the bill. If so, you do not need to leave a tip, unless the service has been exceptional and you want to leave something more.

Bahamian Kitchen (Trinity Place; 325-0702), 1 block from the Straw Market. Has Bahamian specialties. Moderate.

Buena Vista (Delancy Street; 322-2811). Continental cuisine by candlelight in the elegant setting of a historic eighteenth-century house surrounded by beautiful gardens. Dinner only. Expensive.

Humidor Churrascaria (Graycliff, West Hill Street; 322-2796; www.graycliff.com) is a steak house like no other. Start at the salad and pasta bar, where selections can be a meal by themselves; then wait for the waiters to come to your table every few minutes with a skewer of hot roasted beef, lamb, pork, chicken, and more; and finish with a scrumptious dessert. Expensive. The *Humidor* part of the name comes from the cigar-rolling center adjacent to the restaurant.

Conch Fritters (Marlborough Street, across from British Colonial Hilton; 323-8778) offers rustic island decor and a thatched-roof bar. It specializes in seafood and Bahamian dishes. Inexpensive.

Dune (Ocean Club, Paradise Island; 363-2501; 800-321-3000). Set in the dunes at the water's edge, the restaurant of renowned chef Jean-Georges Vongerichten, and designed by famed French designer Christian Liaigre, is casual and elegant at the same time. Liaigre blended natural woods and fabrics with a sophisticated palette of color from the ash of weathered wood to the slate of the chairs and the charcoal of hardwood tabletops.

Dune offers signature dishes from Jean-Georges's top-rated New York restaurants—Jean Georges, Vong, and others—with Bahamian ingredients, often seasoned with herbs from the restaurant's small garden. Open daily for three meals. Diners may sit inside under a high-pitched, beamed ceiling and enjoy views of the turquoise sea; watch the activity in the display kitchen that runs across the back of the restaurant; or dine under white umbrellas on the outdoor patio by the beach. Reservations are necessary to get past the security gate at the hotel entrance. Jean-Georges's newest venture, **Café Martinique** (Marina Village), is an elegant French restaurant in the Atlantis complex.

The Taj Mahal (Parliament Street). A new restaurant from the operators of Gaylords, the international Indian restaurant chain. The menu includes tandoori, Punjabi, Nepalese, and Mughali dishes. It has carry-out service, too. Moderate.

Nobu (Atlantis, Royal Towers). Fans of the famous Japanese chef Nobu Matsuhisa will want to try out this Bahama-based version. Expensive.

Mama Lyddys (Market Street; 328-6849) serves seafood and authentic Bahamian cuisine in a lovely setting that was once an old Bahamian home. Inexpensive.

The Poop Deck (East Bay Street; 393-8175; www.thepoopdeckrestaurants.com) offers Bahamian and seafood specialties in a rustic atmosphere at lunch or dinner. The restaurant has great conch chowder, fritters, and Key lime pie in a fabulous setting by the water overlooking Paradise Island Bridge. Moderate. There's a more upscale version of The Poop Deck west of town at Cable Beach (327-3325).

Sun and . . . (Lakeview Drive; 393-1205; www .sun-and.com), one of the most popular restaurants in Nassau, serves continental cuisine on the patio of a Bahamian house created by a Belgian chef and his wife. Dinner only; closed Monday in August and September. Jacket required for men. Expensive.

Traveller's Rest (West Bay Street; 327-7633; www.travellersrestbahamas.com) is something of a drive from town, but it's worth it for the food and delightful country setting under huge shade trees overlooking the aqua sea. Here you can try fried grouper with peas and rice, and plantains, which are similar to fried bananas. Moderate.

There are also lots of places to satisfy your steak cravings—like Outback Steakhouse—or your pizza yearnings, including Domino's and Swank's. You'll also find a Hard Rock Cafe and a Señor Frog's.

Sports in Nassau

The Bahamas has some of the best sports facilities in the tropics, available in or near enough to Nassau or Freeport for cruise passengers to use them with relative ease. When facilities for sports such as tennis or golf are available at a hotel, contact the hotel or the sports operator in advance, particularly during the peak season, when demand is likely to be high. When you want specific information on any sport, phone the Bahamas Tourist Office, (800) 327-7678.

Beaches: So fine are the beaches that picking the best is difficult. For hotel beaches, the nearest to the port is the British Colonial Hilton, but if you go a little farther west, you have all of Cable Beach, dubbed the Bahamian Riviera. Most of Paradise Island is fringed by white sand.

Biking: The island is rather flat, and roads away from the main arteries with heavy traffic are easy for biking. Bikes can be rented for $15 per day and up. Inquire at the Bahama Tourist Office by the pier.

Bahamas Outdoors (362-1574; fax 362-2044; www.bahamasoutdoors.com) offers a variety of tours for bikers of average skill on easy trails through woodland and along the seashore, visiting historic Adelaide Village. Easier or more challenging tours are available. Tour includes off-road bicycle, water bottle, helmet, and backpack. Minimum age nine years; maximum weight 200 pounds. Half-day tours, $59, require advance booking; maximum six persons. Birding tours are available in winter and include an ecotour guide.

Boating: It may seem strange for a cruise passenger to get off one vessel only to climb aboard another, but many people find it a wonderful way to spend their day in port. How better to enjoy the magnificent waters than by chartering a boat? Almost any size or type, sail or power, with or without crew, is available. You can explore, swim, and picnic at your own pace. **Nassau Yacht Haven** (East Bay Street; 393-8173) can provide information on yachts and fishing boats.

Half- and full-day sailing/snorkeling ($30/$50) and sunset excursions ($30) are also offered by **Flying Cloud** (Paradise Island Ferry Dock; 363-4430; www.flyingcloud.info). **Seahorse Sailing Adventures** (Atlantis Marina; 363-5510; 800-821-4505; www.seahorsesailingadventures.com) has three catamarans departing at 9:00 A.M. and 1:00 P.M.; $60 adult; $30 under twelve. **Barefoot Sailing Cruises** (393-0820; www.barefootsailing cruises.com) also offers bareboats.

For more adventure, **Powerboat Adventures** (East Bay Street; 363-1466; www.powerboatadven tures.com) has fast boats to Exuma Cays (fifty-five minutes) for a day of drift snorkeling, shark and stingray feedings, nature walks, and more, departing at 9:00 A.M. and returning about 5:30 P.M.; $190 adult; $120 ages two through twelve, including transfers, lunch, open bar. A similar excursion to the Exumas is available from **Island World Adventures** (363-3333; www.islandworldadventures.com) for $190 adult; $140 ages three through twelve.

Canoeing Lake Nancy: (J. F. Kennedy Drive; 323-3382). Lake Nancy's clear, shallow waters are home to fish and bird life such as ospreys, coots, egrets, cranes, and endangered white-crowned pigeons. Canoes are available for rent by the hour or day. Refreshments and light snacks are available.

Deep-Sea Fishing: The Bahamas is a magnet for sportfishers. World records for marlin and other big game are made and broken year after year. Deep-sea fishing can be enjoyed almost anywhere in the Bahamas in ideal weather conditions throughout the year, and the variety of fish is endless. January to late April is the best season for white marlin and amberjack; June through August for blue marlin and kingfish. Ocean bonito, blackfin tuna, and Allison tuna are caught from May to September. Grouper can be found in reefy areas year-round, and you'll find bluefin tuna, sailfish, wahoo, and more. Andros calls itself the bonefishing capital of the world.

Boats depart from Nassau Yacht Harbor on regular half-day fishing trips at 8:30 A.M. and 12:30 P.M. for $60 per person, with six persons per boat. The price includes bait and tackle. Contact **Chubasco Charters,** Capt. Mike Russell (324-3474; www.chubascocharters.com). Charter rates, which include tackle, bait, ice, and fuel, are about $300 to $400 for a half day; $400 to $800 for a full day for boats accommodating up to six people. Other charter companies include **Born Free Charters** (393-4144; www.bornfreefishing.com), which offers fishing charters trolling around Nassau for trophy fish in the ocean less than a mile offshore or light-tackle or bottom fishing in more shallow water.

The Bahamas Tourist Office (800-327-7678) has copies of the *Bahamas Fishing Guide,* with pictures and descriptions of the main sportfishing targets and their seasons, plus a wealth of other information. The center can provide you with an up-to-date schedule of the fishing tournaments held during the year.

Golf: A baker's dozen of Bahamian courses, designed by famous architects, are as beautiful to see as they are challenging to play. The Bahamas's tropical island landscape provides lovely emerald fairways bordered by flowering trees and palms.

Most courses are part of resort complexes and have resident pros, pro shops, and clubhouses.

Nassau/Paradise Island has four courses. The closest to the port is the **Cable Beach Golf Course** (327-6000; 7,040 yards, par 72). This championship course was the Bahamas's first when it was built in 1926. Renovated in 1990 and again in 1996, it has a clubhouse, pro shop, and restaurant. Greens fees are $105 per person for nine holes, $125 for eighteen holes, including cart.

Ocean Club Golf Course (363-6680; 6,776 yards, par 72). The championship course, completely redesigned by well-known golfer Tom Weiskopf, reopened in late 2000. It is open to members and Atlantis and Ocean Club hotel guests only.

In development as part of the Baha Mar megaresort at Cable Beach is an eighteen-hole Jack Nicklaus Signature course that will be accessible via a specially designed waterway and will feature play for all skill levels. (For Freeport golf clubs, see the section on Grand Bahama Island.)

Horseback Riding Windsor Equestrian Centre Happy Trails Stables: (Coral Harbour; 362-1820; www.windsorequestrian centre.com), open daily except Sunday. A riding tour costs about $110, including round-trip transportation to the stables from town.

Snorkeling and Scuba Diving: www.bahamasdiving.com. The spectacular underwater world of the Bahamas has something for everyone, no matter what your level of expertise. Snorkelers and novice divers can simply swim off a beach to discover fantastic coral gardens only 10 or 20 feet below the surface of the water.

More experienced divers can explore drop-offs that start at 40 feet and plunge thousands. They can swim into underwater caverns and tunnels teeming with fish and roam through waters with visibility as great as 200 feet. Masks and flippers are readily available, as are diving equipment and instruction.

Most ships that sail on three- and four-day cruises from Florida visit their "own" island, usually one of the Out Islands. The highlight of the day is snorkeling or diving directly from shore in water so incredibly clear, you don't need a mask to see the colorful fish and fantastic coral. (It is, of course, more practical to wear a mask.)

Bahamas Divers Ltd. (East Bay Street; 393-6054; 800-398-DIVE; www.bahamasdivers.com) has daily snorkeling excursions for $39. It also offers dive trips (all gear provided) with one-tank dives for $55 and two-tank dives for $89. **Stuart Cove's Aqua Adventures** (South West Bay Road; 362-4171; www.stuartcove.com) offers the full range of dive excursions as well as shark diving. Prices start at $48 snorkeling; $89 diving. It also offers "Sub Bahamas," a personal underwater scooter. **Dive Dive Dive Ltd.** (362-1143; 800-368-3483) takes experienced divers to see bull, reef, and silky sharks several days a week.

Tennis/Squash/Racquetball: In the Bahamas, where the weather is ideal to play year-round, tennis is as popular as any water sport. There are no fewer than one hundred courts and excellent facilities with pros and pro shops, instruction, and daily clinics available at hotels and resorts in Nassau, Cable Beach, and Paradise Island. Many courts are lighted for evening play. Since most hotels do not charge guests for the use of courts, you will need to make special arrangements in advance by writing or calling the hotel to request court time.

Hotels nearest the port with the best facilities and night lights are on Cable Beach. Nicks Tennis Academy at the **Wyndham Nassau Resort** (327-7711; 800-223-5672) has three Plexipave courts. The resort also offers windsurfing, sailing, snorkeling, and other water sports.

Underwater Adventures: The **Seaworld Explorer** (Moses Plaza, Bay Street; 356-2548; www.seaworldtours.com). A semi-submarine, originally developed in Australia for use on the Great Barrier Reef, glides over Nassau Sea Gardens while you sit in air-conditioned comfort 5 feet below the surface of the water. Price: $49 per person, adults and children.

Hartley's Undersea Walk (Nassau Yacht Haven, East Bay Street; 393-8234; www.underseawalk.com). Explore the reefs like early marine biologists did before scuba was invented. Your head stays dry. It's safe for all ages, nonswimmers, and

those who wear contact lenses. Two trips daily. Price: $125 per person, adults and children.

Dolphin Encounters (Blue Lagoon Island; 363-1003; fax 363-4438; www.dolphinencounters.com) offers two options at Blue Lagoon, an islet off Nassau used by many cruise ships for beach and snorkeling excursions. The Close Encounters program with dolphins costs $85 per person; swimming with dolphins, $165 per person.

Waterskiing: It is easy to do in the calm Bahamian waters and available at hotels at about $40 for thirty minutes.

Windsurfing: The protection the shallows and reefs give to most parts of the Bahamian coast also makes its many bays excellent places to learn to windsurf. Try it once, and you'll be hooked! Instruction is available to get you started. The cost is about $20. The annual Windsurfing Regatta is held in January.

Entertainment

Bahamians—and visitors—make something of a ritual of watching the pretty sunsets. So when the air begins to cool and the sun starts its fall, you can grab a Bahama Mama (that's the local rum punch) and head for the beach. You'll probably be joined by kindred spirits, a scratch band, or other local musicians for some impromptu jamming.

After the sun disappears and the stars are out, you can stay on the beach with the calypso beat or change into something a bit dressier for a round of the Bahamas's razzle-dazzle nightlife. The 1,000-seat theater of the **Atlantis Show Room** (Paradise Island) hosts Las Vegas–style shows nightly.At the adjacent **Crystal Palace Casino** you can choose blackjack, roulette, craps, baccarat, or slot machines to play, and if your luck runs out, you can laugh it off at Atlantis's **Joker's Wild Comedy Club.** The same resort also offers discos, several bars, and restaurants.

Hard Rock Cafe (Charlotte Street; 325-7625; www.hardrock.com) is nearest the port, offering live music along with the chain's usual menu. Some other noted nightspots are **Bambu** (Prince George Dock; 326-6627), a music bar and lounge for dancing with a rooftop SkyLounge open from 9:00 P.M. when cruise ships are in port; **22 Above** (Wyndham Nassau Resort & Crystal Palace Casino, Cable Beach)—home to exotic cocktails like the award-winning "Cable Beach Sunset"—where DJs spin dance music and live bands often play; and **Club Waterloo** (East Bay Street; 393-7324), popular with the young crowd.

To sample the current sounds of the hot new generation of Bahamian musicians who blend Junkanoo whistles, cowbells, and goatskin drums with hip-hop and funk, check out **Charlies** (formerly Club 601) (East Bay Street), the hot nightspot where Baha Men (of "Who Let the Dogs Out" fame), Visage, Spank Band, and other local bands hang out.

For those who want something on the cultural side, the **Dundas Centre for the Performing Arts** (Mackey Street; 393-3728) offers plays, musicals, ballets, and folkloric shows.

Festivals and Celebrations

Bahamians love to celebrate. From January to December the calendar is full of sporting events, music festivals, historic commemorations, religious feasts, and national holidays. All are windows on island life not open to visitors at other times of the year. You can watch the fun from the sidelines or join in. And if you bring your camera, you'll run out of film before you run out of subjects to photograph.

Junkanoo, a National Festival

Of all the festivals, none compares to Junkanoo, an exuberant Bahamian celebration full of color and creativity, humor, rhythm and music, dance, fun, and festivity. The national extravaganza traces its origins to the West African dance and mask traditions kept alive throughout the West Indies by slaves brought to the New World in the seventeenth and eighteenth centuries. After emancipation in the early nineteenth century, Junkanoo was suppressed by religious zealots, both black and white. It had nearly died out when it was revived in the 1970s as part of the effort to preserve the Bahamas's multifaceted heritage.

Now, once again, Junkanoo is part of the Bahamian tradition reflected in the art, dance, and music. It has been taken into the schools, where the construction of costumes is part of the curriculum, and sent abroad by the musicians and entertainers, where it is receiving international recognition.

Junkanoo is the Bahamian version of Carnival, with parades, costumes, and music, but unlike traditional Carnival, it is held at the end of the year and the start of the new one. The first Junkanoo parade starts at daybreak on December 26, Boxing Day, a public holiday stemming from British tradition. Bahamians and visitors who feel the spirit don brilliant costumes and parade through downtown Nassau to the clatter of cowbells, horns, whistles, and the driving beat of African drums. Prizes are awarded to those with the most unusual and elaborate costumes—all made from cardboard and strips of paper laid down in tight layers. Every display must be able to be carried by one person; nothing on wheels is allowed.

Participants and viewers need to be on the street before daylight—it's all over by 8:00 A.M. (Photographers need fast film, as the light is still low at parade time.) Bleachers are set up in the judging area on Bay Street west of Rawson Square, and the judging takes place from 6:00 to 7:00 A.M. Costumes that do not win are often dumped in the street and make fine souvenirs.

The celebration is repeated on New Year's Eve after the private parties at homes and hotels wind down and the streets begin to fill with late-night revelers. It lasts through New Year's Day. But you don't have to wait to the year's end to see Junkanoo. You can sample it at some nightclub and folkloric shows and other celebrations throughout the year and visit the Junkanoo Expo by the port, where many of the winning costumes are displayed.

Goombay, a Summer Festival

Goombay Summer Festival is a series of special events for visitors featuring the music of Junkanoo and Goombay. Different events give visitors an opportunity to experience the Bahamians' Bahamas with their music and dance, culture, crafts, and cuisine.

Goombay has several derivations and has come to have several meanings. Historically, it referred to the drumbeats and rhythms of Africa brought to the Bahamas by slaves and free blacks.

The term was used during ring-play and jump-in dances; the drummer would shout "Gimbey!" at the beginning of each dance.

Today *Goombay* is used to refer to all Bahamian secular music, especially that using the traditional goat-skin drum, a barrel-shaped drum made from wooden kegs with goat or sheep skin covering one end, positioned between the legs and played with bare hands. The word *Goombay* is still used in West Africa, especially by Ibo tribes, who have a similar drum they call the Gamby.

Other Festivals and Events

Independence Week in early July is another holiday filled with festivities, parades, and fireworks to celebrate the independence of the Commonwealth of the Bahamas. It culminates on Independence Day, July 10, with fireworks at Clifford Park.

Emancipation Day, the first Monday in August, is a public holiday that commemorates the abolition of slavery in 1834. It is followed on Tuesday by Fox Hill Day. In the old days Fox Hill was isolated from Nassau; hence, the residents did not learn about the Emancipation until later. And so, symbolically, they celebrate on the second day.

October 12, Discovery Day, is a public holiday with special meaning in the Bahamas. It was on a Bahamian island, which the native Lucayan Indians called Guanahani, that Christopher Columbus landed in 1492. Columbus renamed the island San Salvador.

Another October highlight is the formal opening of the Supreme Court, when the chief justice, dressed in the traditional robe and wig, is escorted by the commissioner of police to inspect the Police Honor Guard while the famous Police Band strikes up. An equally colorful event with pomp and pageantry is the formal opening of Parliament, usually in February.

The Christmas festivities begin in mid-December with an annual candlelight procession staged by the Renaissance Singers. The group performs at the Government House ballroom and the Dundas Centre for the Performing Arts with a repertoire ranging from Renaissance classics to modern spirituals. For information on tickets, contact the Ministry of Education, Division of Cultural Affairs (322-8119). Although the performances are usually sold out early, the ministry makes an effort to accommodate visitors.

Grand Bahama Island
www.grand-bahama.com

When American financier Wallace Groves began to turn his dream into reality in the 1950s, Grand Bahama Island, 60 miles from Florida, was little more than limestone, pine trees, and brush. From the money he earned lumbering the pine, he began developing the island. Today Freeport, as it came to be known, developed into the second largest town and largest industrial area in the Bahamas and a major international resort. In recent years the name *Freeport* has been consigned to the port/airport area only; the Bahamians prefer their island be called by its proper name, Grand Bahama Island.

Freeport spent the 1960s in the limelight, particularly after Cuba went by the board as an American playground, but by the 1970s it had lost much of its luster. The recession, worldwide economic problems, and competition from new resorts in Florida and elsewhere resulted in a setback for the island.

A renaissance began in 1984 with the multi-million-dollar renovation of hotels and casinos. This was followed the next year by the development of Port Lucaya, a shopping and entertainment complex, along with the Dolphin Experience attraction.

Grand Bahama got another boost when it became a popular cruise stop, especially for short cruises from Florida. These cruises bring more visitors to the island in a month than many islands see in a year. And on a smaller scale, there is as much for them to enjoy here as in Nassau. The island has an active People-to-People program similar to that in Nassau, as well as a large variety of restaurants, casinos, golf courses, and a famous international shopping bazaar.

More recently a second renaissance has been under way, with almost $1 billion having been invested in the renovation of hotels and golf courses, the addition of new resorts and marinas, and the completion of an $11 million cruise passenger terminal at the port, renamed the Lucayan Harbour Cruise Facility.

In Brief

Location: Grand Bahama Island is about 80 miles from end to end. The cruise ship port, situated on the south coast at the mouth of Hawksbill Creek, is about 5 miles from the town of Freeport, where two golf courses and the International Bazaar are located. Another 5 miles east along Sunrise Highway takes you to the Lucayan residential and resort area, where major hotels front expansive white-sand beaches on the south shore and offer an array of water sports.

Transportation: Metered taxis are available at the port, downtown Freeport, and at hotels. Rates are supposed to be fixed at $3 for the first ¼ mile and 40 cents for each additional mile, $3 for each additional passenger over age two.

If you plan to engage a taxi for sightseeing, you should negotiate the price in advance. Also, be aware there are freelancers who are not legal taxis and who will charge whatever they think they can get. Look for taxis with a BAHAMA HOST sticker on the windshield. They are reliable, and their drivers are the best informed.

Town buses or jitneys ($1) run during the day from town to Lucaya and ($4) West End. However, as a cruise passenger with limited time, you are better off hiring a taxi or renting a car if you want to visit either end of the island.

Car Rentals: To rent a car with a credit card, you must be twenty-one years or older; without the card, twenty-five or older. Americans may use US driver's licenses for up to three months. Car rentals are available from several locations in town and at major hotels. When you have reserved a car in advance with Hertz or Avis, it will deliver your car free of charge to the port. Expect to pay $50 and up for a subcompact with unlimited mileage. Jeeps are available, too.

- Avis, call 352-7666
- Dollar Rent-A-Car, call 352-9325
- Econo Car & Bike Rental, call 351-6700
- Hertz, call 352-9250
- Thrifty, call 352-9308

And remember, Bahamians drive on the **LEFT**. You will need a map and a good sense of direction, because even new maps are not up-to-date. Do not hesitate to ask anyone for directions.

Information: The Tourist Information Centre has booths at Lucaya Cruise Facility (352-9651), the airport (352-2032), and offices in the International Bazaar. Booth hours: 8:30 A.M. to 5:00 P.M. Monday through Saturday. Office: 9:00 A.M. to 5:30 P.M. Monday through Friday.

In the United States contact Grand Bahamas Island Tourism Board, P.O. Box 22857, Fort Lauderdale, FL 33335; (954) 888-9293.

Emergency Numbers Medical Services: Rand Memorial Hospital; call 352-6735. **Police:** Freeport; call 919. **Ambulance:** Freeport; call 352-2689.

Mopeds/Bicycles: Inquire at the Tourist Information Office for rental locations. A valid driver's license and a helmet supplied by the rental agency are compulsory. Prices are about $30 per day. To repeat, driving is on the **LEFT**.

Grand Bahama Nature Tours (373-2485; 866-440-4542; www.grandbahamanaturetours.com) offers a guided bicycle tour that covers 20 miles in about five hours. It's an easy-paced ride to see Taino Beach, the dolphins at Sanctuary Bay, and the old settlement of Smith Point. A native snack at a seaside restaurant, a dip in the sea, or relaxing in a beach hammock are also included for $79.

Shopping: The **International Bazaar,** housing dozens of boutiques with merchandise from all over the world, set the standard for other tourist destinations when it first opened in the 1960s. It has since been expanded to hold about seventy-five shops where you can buy anything from $2 T-shirts to $2,000 emeralds. Among the familiar names are Colombian Emeralds, Fendi, and Little Switzerland. Other shopping centers in the Freeport area are Town Centre and Churchill Square.

Next to the International Bazaar, the **Perfume Factory**, which houses **Fragrance of the Bahamas,** is set in a replica of an old Bahamian mansion, where various scents for ladies and gents are made. Guides dressed in period costumes give visitors a tour and explain how the essences, made only from natural plants, are blended into perfumes and other products. There are six standard fragrances; you can also create your own, which will be officially registered in your name. Perfumes, lotions, and T-shirts are available for purchase. The fragrance Guanahani—the original name of San Salvador, where Columbus made his first landfall—was created in 1992 to mark the Quincentennial.

Port Lucaya, a waterside shopping, entertainment, and water sports complex in the heart of the Lucayan resort area, has more than forty stores, snack bars, and restaurants in attractive, colonial-style buildings. Celebration Circle, the entertainment center, features steel bands, reggae groups, and other entertainment.

Many of the best-known Nassau stores have outlets in Freeport and Lucaya. Generally, shops are open 9:30 A.M. to 5:00 P.M. weekdays. Most stay open at night on weekends. Oasis, which sells perfumes, toiletries, and jewelry, is open until 10:30 P.M. The Straw Market and pharmacies are open on Sunday.

Beaches and Water Sports: Grand Bahama has some of the finest beaches in the Bahamas. Among the best with hotels and facilities are Xanadu Beach, not far from the port, and Lucayan Beach, 11 miles east of the port. If you prefer an undeveloped beach with miles of sand all to yourself, head toward West End. Several minor roads near the Buccaneer lead to lovely beaches. The Lucayan National Park on the south coast is a drive of about thirty minutes from town. Grand Bahama Island also has terrific fishing, sailing, and windsurfing. All beachfront hotels have windsurfing equipment.

The island's facilities for scuba and snorkeling are not only the best in the Bahamas, but among the best in the world. It is home base for UNEXSO, the **Underwater Explorers Society** (Royal Palm Way, Freeport; 373-1244; 800-922-3483; www .unexso.com). Its facility, adjacent to Port Lucaya, offers eight levels of instruction and includes a 17-foot-deep diver training pool, outdoor bar and cafe, and pro shop. The facility also has a recompression chamber.

Introduction to diving has three phases: a lesson in the pool ($25); exploring the shallow reefs with a scuba instructor following the pool lesson ($60); and, after completing those two dives, completing the Shallow Water Scuba Plus, which involves diving 30 to 40 feet with the instructor ($79, including all equipment). A two-tank dive with all gear is $70. Shark dives are available for $89. Wreck and night dives for experienced divers are also available.

The Dolphin Experience: UNEXSO, the firm that operates the Dolphin Experience, has a pod of fourteen Atlantic bottlenose dolphins that live in Sanctuary Bay, where they are the star attraction of three visitor programs.

Close Encounters is a two-hour, hands-on learning experience in which guests are briefed on dolphin behavior before touching the friendly creatures as they swim by. You sit on the edge of the enclosure with only your feet in the water. Participants are picked up at Port Lucaya and ferried to Sanctuary Bay. Cost is $75 adult; $37.50 ages four to twelve; under four free. Other programs include Swim with Dolphins ($169), interaction in the water at the lagoon pen; and the new Open Ocean Dolphin Experience ($199), offered mornings daily. The participants are transported to the ocean, where they dive and swim with two dolphins at a time. Using their newly learned hand signals, participants have the dolphins performing as they interact.

Golf: The courses nearest the port are the pair of championship, PGA courses that have been closed for some time, and unfortunately, are not likely to open again in the near future as they are caught up in the litigation of the hotel complex to which they belong. Currently, the best courses are those in the Lucayan area, about 11 miles from the port, and described below. Cruise ships offering golf packages use these courses.

The Lucayan Course at Westin Grand Bahama Island Our Lucaya (373-1066 for tee times; 866-500-0277; www.starwoodhotels.com /grandbahama), designed by Dick Wilson, is tree-lined with doglegs and elevated greens. The Reef Course, laid out by the Robert Trent Jones II Group, is links style, featuring water on thirteen of its eighteen holes. Fees at both courses are $120; club rentals, $45 per set. A golf school here is operated by Jim McLean, five-time Ryder Cup team member and twice its captain.

The nine-hole course at **Fortune Hills Golf & Country Club** (373-4500) complements this luxurious country club community. Designed by Dick Wilson and Joe Lee, its challenging holes have the most expansive elevated greens in the Bahamas. Greens fees: $51 for eighteen holes; $35 for nine holes, including cart. Club rental: $10 to $15.

Some cruise lines have golf packages or will make arrangements for play for passengers. If not, you should call ahead for reservations. For cruise passengers who are planning to overnight here, some hotels have golf packages.

Horseback Riding: Pinetree Stables (Beachway Drive; 373-3600; www.pinetree-stables .com) offers two-hour guided trail rides at 9:00 A.M. and 11:30 A.M. daily. The trails wind through pine forests and rocky coppices and emerge onto the beach for an ocean splash. A two-hour tour costs $75 per person. The stable is located midway between Freeport and Port Lucaya. **H. Forbes Charter & Tours** (352-9311; www.forbescharter .com) offers two-hour guided rides daily (except Monday) at 9:00 and 11:30 A.M. for $65. The route passes the only castle on Grand Bahama and ends on the beach. **Trikk Pony Adventures** (374-4449; www.trikkpony.com) has a morning beach ride daily except Sunday and a sunset one on Saturday, 10:00 A.M. and 12:30 P.M. The cost is $80.

Tennis: Tennis, too, is popular and readily available at hotel courts convenient to the port. Rates are reasonable.

Sightseeing

In contrast to its high-living, high-stakes image, Freeport has several attractions that tell its history and highlight its tropical variety.

Lucayan National Park: Located 25 miles west of Freeport near the former US Army Missile Tracking Base, Lucayan National Park (352-5438; www.grand-bahama.com/lucayan.htm) is about a thirty-minute drive from downtown. The forty-acre

park, opened in 1985, is situated on land donated to the National Trust by the Grand Bahama Development Company and is composed of four different ecological zones. The park, designed by Freeport planner Peter Barratt, has a 1,000-foot-wide beach with some of the highest dunes on the island. Gold Rock Creek, which is bounded by extensive mangroves, flows through the park to the sea. Among the flora are coca plums, sea grapes, sea oats, and casuarinas. Another area has Ming trees, wild tamarind, mahogany, and cedar trees.

The park is also the entrance to one of the world's longest charted cave systems, but access to the caves is restricted to scientists and archaeologists who have permission from the National Trust. Lucayan Indian relics have been found inside the caverns.

There are footpaths and raised wooden walkways over the mangroves to the beach and a map on display at the car park. Further information is available from the Rand Nature Center. The area is popular with bird-watchers, but the main reason to visit this area of the island is the lovely, untouched beaches.

Rand Memorial Nature Center: (P.O. Box F-42441, Freeport; 352-5438; www.grand-bahama .com/rand.htm). Located 3 miles from the International Bazaar, the center, which is also the headquarters of the Bahamas National Trust, comprises one hundred acres of tropical plants, trees, birds, and butterflies and is home to hundreds of species of plants and approximately ninety-six species of birds. A preserve for the native pine forests that once covered the island, it contains many species endangered by the island's continuing development.

An hour-long walking tour along winding trails provides an opportunity to see and photograph tropical flora, including many species of wild orchids and a great variety of birds. At the end of the trail, surrounded by numerous flowering exotic plants, is a pond that is home to a small group of flamingos. Hours: 9:00 A.M. to 4:00 P.M. Monday through Friday. Admission: $5 adult; $3 ages five to twelve. The park is a prime birding location, and naturalists are on hand. A guided tour Monday through Friday at 10:00 A.M. combines Bahamian history and culture, flora, and bird-watching.

The Heritage Trail: (www.grand-bahama .com/naturetours.htm) Before 1955 the main transportation artery on Grand Bahama Island was the Old Freetown Road, a dirt path leading from Old Freetown in the east to Eight Mile Rock and other settlements in the west. After the development of Freeport began and a modern highway was built, the old road was abandoned. Eventually, nature did such a good job of reclaiming it that a stretch of the road near Freetown has become one of the island's main nature walks. Along the easy, 5-mile path, you can see more than thirty plant, eighteen bird, and seven butterfly species and the remains of the Hermitage, the oldest building intact on Grand Bahama, dating from 1901.

Adventure Tours: Several companies offer adventure and nature-oriented excursions. **Grand Bahama Nature Tours** (373-2485; 866-440-4542; www.grandbahamanaturetours.com) offers several nature tours. Old Freetown Trail, a 5-mile walk on the Heritage Trail, where a variety of bird life, vegetation, and butterflies can be observed, passes beaches, wetlands, coppices, and pine forest as well as a large inland cave, the home of barn owls. Hiking the Heritage Trail takes you on the path that early settlers walked, along the beautiful shoreline and through a pine forest. Stops occur at an inland blue hole and the ruins of one of the oldest settlements. A guide points out flora and fauna and interprets bush medicines along the way. Cost of the tour is $59. The Lucayan National Park Kayak & Cave Tour involves ninety minutes of moderate paddling in shallow waters; a guided nature walk through the park's diverse ecosystems, including the caves; and a stop at pristine Gold Rock Beach in Lucayan National Park for a light picnic lunch in a shady site, relaxation, and a swim. The cost is $79. Bird-watching and snorkeling are also available. All tours include lunch and refreshments, equipment, and admission to parks and attractions visited. Children's discounts are available on some tours.

Boat Excursions: Snorkeling trips, picnic trips, and sunset party cruises are available from **Pat & Diane Fantasia Tours** (373-8681; www.snorkeling bahamas.com), and Reef Tours (373-5880; www .bahamasvg.com/reeftours), all departing from Port

Lucaya. The latter also claims to have the largest glass-bottomed boat on the island. It departs daily from the Port Lucaya marina at 9:30 and 11:15 A.M. and 1:15 and 3:15 P.M. on reef cruises. $25 adult; $15 child (under five free). **Exotic Adventures** (374-2278; www.exoticadventuresbahamas.com) and **H. Forbes Charter & Tours** (352-9311; www .forbescharter.com) operate fishing (half day, $80 per person; $200 to $550 for up to four persons), snorkeling ($59 adult, including lunch; $39 child), sunset, and glass-bottomed boat excursions.

Seaworld Excursions (373-7863; www .superiorwatersports.com), a semi-submersible departing from Port Lucaya Marina, offers close encounters with marine life, viewed from inside the vessel. A marine expert gives commentary, while a crew member feeds the fish, bringing them close to the boat. A thirty-minute snorkeling session with gear provided is optional. The two-hour excursion departs daily at 9:30 and 11:30 A.M. and 1:30 P.M. $39 adult; $25 ages five through twelve; ages four and under free. This fee includes bus pickup and drop-off.

Other diversions include the **Hurricane Alley Bowling and Recreation** (East Sunrise Highway; 373-2197) featuring a twenty-four-lane bowling alley. Hours: 9:00 A.M. to 2:00 A.M. Monday through Saturday, noon to 2:00 A.M. Sunday. $5 adult; $3.50 child. The complex includes miniature golf, video games, and an ice-cream parlor.

Dining and Restaurants in Freeport

Like Nassau, Grand Bahama has a great variety of restaurants, including inexpensive ones specializing in Bahamian dishes. The International Bazaar, Port Lucaya, and large resorts also provide many choices.

Fatman's Nephew (Port Lucaya Marketplace; 373-8520) is among several eateries in the marketplace and offers patio dining on Bahamian specialties such as cracked conch. Popular in the Lucayan area is the **Stoned Crab** (Taino Beach; 373-1442; www.bahamasvg.com), which specializes in lobster and steaks.

On the more expensive side, but well worth it, is **Ferry House** (Pelican Bay Hotel, Port Lucaya; 373-1595), touted by locals as the best dining experience on the island. The elegant ambience at water's edge complements superb dishes, such as seared sea scallops with garlic and wild mushrooms or venison with butternut squash, all created by the Icelandic owner-chef. Open for lunch and dinner daily except Monday.

Bonefish Folley's Bar & Grill at Old Bahama Bay (West End; 350-6500; www.oldbahamabay .com), named for bonefishing legend Israel Rolle, serves dishes that use fresh local ingredients; Siboney conch chowder and lobster salad are favorites.

Every Wednesday evening a native fish fry dinner is held at Smith's Point, a small beachside settlement. Visitors dine on fresh seafood and can meet local residents. It's not an advertised event, but local taxi drivers know about it. The cost is about $10 per person.

Nightlife centers on the large hotels and casinos, but if you want to mix and mingle with Bahamians, Port Lucaya Marketplace has nightly entertainment on stage at the square, plus dancing—and it's free. Shenanigan's (373-4734), a lively Irish pub, is just behind the square. The Prop Room (on the beach behind the Isle of Capri Casino) offers big-screen sports, big drinks, singing waiters, and karaoke nightly.

A Drive Around Grand Bahama Island

To explore the less commercial side of Grand Bahama, a drive of 21 miles to West End will take you to the oldest settlements and some of the quieter corners of this surprising island.

If you are driving from the port or town, head west on Queens Highway to Eight Mile Rock, the largest Native settlement on the island, aptly named for the 8 miles or so of rocky shore on its south coast. The colorful village of brightly painted wooden houses was settled around 1830. The picturesque St. Stephens Anglican Church, built directly on the sea, dates from 1851.

Queens Highway continues to Seagrape, a tiny hamlet with a reputation for making the best bread in the Bahamas. As you near West End, you pass the saltwater Pelican Lake and Bootle Bay.

West End hugs the westernmost tip of Grand Bahama Island and is less than 60 speedboat miles from the Florida coast. It is the oldest settlement on the island and has had at least two fast but fleeting booms—during the American Civil War as a base for southerners running ammunition and supplies through the Yankee blockade to Confederate forces, and during Prohibition, when the likes of Al Capone found it a convenient shipping point for liquor from Europe.

After 1933, West End went back to being a sleepy fishing village, attracting such occasional deep-sea fishermen as Ernest Hemingway. Nothing else much happened until Billy Butlin of British resort fame built one of his holiday retreats, but it never had quite the success of its English seaside counterparts. It was followed by a Jack Tar Village, which also enjoyed a period of success before it closed. And now West End has gotten the biggest makeover ever, a multimillion-dollar resort and residential community on 150 acres that is expected to grow to more than 2,000 acres. Called Old Bahama Bay, it has been built by West End Resort Ltd. on the Jack Tar Resort site. The first phase included forty-nine privately owned hotel-condominiums for rental in nine low-rise beachfront buildings, and a seventy-two-slip deepwater marina, which is a port of entry. Pine Island, the residential community, has luxurious homes, each on an acre or more of land, and private docks for yachts up to 125 feet.

The road into town takes you by tiny wooden stalls beside mounds of conch shells where you can stop to watch one of the local fishermen prepare the day's catch for tomorrow's market. There's an old church built in 1893 as well as the Star Hotel (346-6207), the island's first, built in 1946. The rickety wooden building, no longer a hotel, got a new lease on life when it was renovated by the grandchildren of the original builder. At present it houses a bar and a restaurant serving local food.

On your return trip, stop by Sunset Village in Jones Town at Eight Mile Rock. It was originally one of the small shacks along that stretch of coast, but has grown in all directions, and is the weekend hot spot for lobster and great seafood, music and dancing—but if you linger too long, you are likely to miss your boat.

The Out Islands

The Other Bahamas—the hundreds of islands, islets, and cays that make up the Bahamas archipelago—are known as the Out Islands (meaning out beyond the main center of Nassau). They are the serene hideaways of our dreams, where endless miles of white- and pink-sand beaches are surrounded by gin-clear waters and where life is so laid-back, ten people make a crowd. Only about three dozen islands have permanent settlements.

No cruise lines offer year-round cruises, but several ships occasionally call at one or two locations, and most ships on three- and four-night Bahama cruises from Florida stop for the day at one of the typical uninhabited islands. These are leased from the Bahamas government for an extended period of time and outfitted with the facilities and amenities to give their passengers a comfortable and fun-filled day at the beach.

The Abacos: At the northern end of the Bahamas archipelago, a group of islands and cays is strung in boomerang fashion for 130 miles, enveloping the Sea of Abaco, whose sheltered waters offer some of the Bahamas's best sailing. Two main islands, Little Abaco and Great Abaco, are joined by a causeway.

Walker's Cay, a well-known fishing resort, lies off the north tip of Little Abaco. Hole in the Wall, at the south end of Great Abaco, was a strategic location throughout the eighteenth century for guarding the shipping lanes to Nassau.

Marsh Harbour, the capital and main hub of the Abacos, is the third largest town of the Bahamas and one of the main boat-chartering centers of the Caribbean. It has a resident population of about 1,000 and an airport. Its small resorts are operated by Native islanders or American and Canadian transplants. Guests dine on fresh fish and homemade island specialties, and enjoy lazy, sunny days sailing, snorkeling, windsurfing, or doing lots of nothing.

Wallys (on the main road at the edge of town; 367-2074) is a restaurant-bar in a pretty, attractively furnished pink villa with a veranda overlooking a flower-filled lawn and the sea. The popular bar is known for its special tropical drinks, and the restaurant serves lunch. There is also a boutique.

On nearby Elbow Cay, colonial Hope Town is one of many old settlements in the Bahamas that look like New England villages with palm trees. It is situated on a picture-postcard harbor complete with a candy-striped lighthouse and can be reached by ferry from Marsh Harbour. **Wyannie Malone Museum** (366-0293, www.hopetownmuseum .com), set in one of the island's oldest houses—it seems almost like a dollhouse, it's so small—is devoted to the island's history. In 1991 it won the American Express Heritage Award as an outstanding example of a small community's effort at preservation.

Of the Loyalists from New York who came in 1783 to join the English settlers living in the Abacos, some stayed at New Plymouth, another Cape Cod village in the tropics, on Green Turtle Cay. For many years it was the largest settlement and capital of the Abacos. In recent times the old fishing village has become something of an artist colony, whose members were attracted by its beauty and serenity and by two native sons—Alton Roland Lowe, a historian and one of the Bahamas's leading landscape artists, and James Mastin, an outstanding sculptor—who led the way.

The **Albert Lowe Museum** (367-4094), created by Alton Lowe in honor of his father, who was a noted carver of ship models, is devoted to the history of the Abacos and to shipbuilding. It occupies a pretty Victorian house on the main street, a short walk from the town dock. Lowe's paintings, most of which depict local island subjects and settings, and Mastin's works are on view, and prints are available for sale.

A few steps from the museum on the same street is the **Loyalist Memorial Sculpture Garden,** Mastin's contribution to the island. Opened in 1983 for the bicentennial of the island's Loyalist settlements, the bronze statues represent the people who shaped the history of the Bahamas down through the centuries, from the first settlers to the present. The busts are placed around a central monument of two women—one white, one black—representing the Loyalists, plantation owners who fled the American Revolution with their slaves and were the earliest settlers.

Almost as famous as the artists is **Blue Bee Bar** (365-4181), whose walls and ceiling are covered with thousands of business cards from around the world. Miss Emily, as Emily Cooper, the former proprietress, was affectionately known, is credited with creating the Goombay Smash, a famous tropical drink served in bars throughout the Bahamas—although this churchgoing lady was a teetotaler and never tasted her famous concoction. Now the bar and its traditions are carried on by her daughter. The town also has several tiny hotels situated in houses dating from the eighteenth century. These nestle between the neat white clapboard cottages trimmed with pink, blue, yellow, or green and set in flowering gardens. The neighboring island of Green Turtle Cay, another popular boating center, can be reached by small ferry.

Less than an hour's drive west of Marsh Harbour through forested land is Treasure Cay, where the 1973 movie *The Day of the Dolphin* with George C. Scott was filmed. Legend has it that seventeen Spanish treasure galleons sank here in 1595. Some have been found; exploration for the others continues. In 1962 two entrepreneurs developed a self-contained resort, Treasure Cay, on a 3½-mile, half-moon beach, which now is best known for its golf course.

Another island south of Marsh Harbour is Man-o-War Cay, famous for its boatbuilders who craft their vessels by hand. The cay has no cars, but in recent years progress has brought golf carts, which many of the American retirees who populate the island use to get around. One of Man-o-War Cay's enterprising Natives has turned the family's sail-making tradition into a prosperous cottage industry producing sturdy tote bags, hats, and a variety of other products that are particularly prized by visitors from yachts.

Andros: A thirty-minute flight west of Nassau will bring you to Andros, the largest island of the Bahamas and one of the least developed. The interior of the island is covered with pine forests interspersed with mangroves; other parts are mudflats or barren. Off the east coast of Andros lies the Barrier Reef, more than 100 miles long, the third largest in the world. Just beyond is the Tongue of the Ocean, a depression that plunges as deep as 6,000 feet at the north end. These natural phenomena attract divers and sportfishers from around the world. Andros also calls itself the bonefishing capital of the world. Among the resorts, **Small Hope Bay Lodge** (368-2015, 800-223-6961; www.small hope.com) at Fresh Creek was the first organized diving resort in the Bahamas.

Berry Islands: The group of about thirty islands with a total land area of only 14 square miles is located between New Providence (Nassau) and Grand Bahama Island (Freeport). Most are uninhabited, and several are popular stops for cruise ships whose passengers spend the day on "their" island, enjoying the beaches and swimming and snorkeling in clear water. Their lovely little harbors, coves, and protected waters make them popular with the yachting crowd.

The Biminis: South of Freeport where the Bahamas Banks meet the Gulf Stream are the Biminis, the Bahamian islands only 50 miles from Florida. Ernest Hemingway was a frequent caller, and his old haunt, the Compleat Angler, a wooden frame hotel and bar, displays his paintings and writings from 1931 to 1937. Adam Clayton Powell, the flamboyant Harlem minister and member of Congress, made Bimini his second home. Long before either of them, however, Ponce de León stopped here in his search for the Fountain of Youth. No less than four places commemorate his landing.

The group is divided into the North Biminis and South Biminis. They, along with Cat Cay, are among the prime gamefishing centers in the Western Hemisphere. Because of their proximity to the Gulf Stream, Bimini waters teem with sea life. Vestiges of old ships in Bahamian waters number in the hundreds. Among the most famous is the Sapona, which lies between South Bimini and Cat Cay. Built by Henry Ford around 1915, the ship served as a private club and is said to have been a rumrunner's storehouse in the 1920s until it was blown ashore by a hurricane in 1929.

The main settlement is Alicetown on North Bimini. You can walk or bike around most of the island in an hour or so. Although the island takes on something of a rowdy party atmosphere in the evening (the fishing crowd at one of its favorite bars), during the day it is a sleepy little place, pleasant for picnicking and lazing on the beach. The best beach is the mile stretch of sand opposite a Cape Cod–type cottage called the Anchorage, which Hemingway used as his setting for *Islands in the Sun.* Another pretty beach shaded with graceful pine trees lies north of town and is reached by a path at the end of the paved road to Bimini Bay. Its calm waters are delightful for swimming and snorkeling.

Cat Island: East of the Exumas lies Cat Island (not to be confused with Cat Cay). It is covered with forested, rolling hills that soar to the great height of 204 feet—the highest natural point in the Bahamas. Once prosperous with sugar plantations of the Loyalists who had fled the American Revolution, Cat Island is largely untouched today and is best known as the childhood home of actor Sidney Poitier. Its four tiny hotels and wide white beaches are made for ardent escapists.

Eleuthera: First-time visitors to the Other Bahamas often select Eleuthera because of its combination of faraway tranquility, the pretty setting of pastel-painted houses surrounded by gentle green hills, and its 300 years of history. It also has comfortable, unpretentious hotels, good dining and sports facilities, and more roads and transportation than the other islands. The island is famous for its pink-sand beaches.

Situated 60 miles east of Nassau, Eleuthera is a 110-mile skinny spine never more than 2 miles wide, except for splays at both ends. It has six official ports of call and three airports, with direct flights from Nassau, Freeport, Fort Lauderdale, and Miami.

Eleuthera has three of the Bahamas's oldest and prettiest settlements: Governor's Harbour, the main town near the center of the island and the hub of commercial activity, more than 300 years old; Dunmore Town on Harbour Island; and Spanish Wells.

Harbour Island, almost touching the northeastern tip of Eleuthera, is one of the most beautiful spots in the Bahamas and the site of Dunmore Town, its original capital and now a tranquil village of neat old houses and flower-filled lanes. A high green ridge dotted with pink and white colonial homes separates the seventeenth-century village

from a 3-mile beach of pink, powdery sand, whose color comes from the coral. The island has about a dozen small hotels.

Spanish Wells, located off the northern end of Eleuthera, is a popular fishing and yachting center. It gets its name from the Spaniards who came ashore here to replenish the freshwater supplies of their ships after making the long voyages between the Old and New Worlds.

The southern part of Eleuthera is slated for major development to create a new resort center that is low-key, tasteful, and ecosensitive, in line with the Bahamas's policy of encouraging development compatible with the environment.

Princess Cay: The "private island" used by Princess Cruises for most of its Caribbean itineraries is a recreational facility spread along a lovely beach at the southern tip of Eleuthera. Here Princess has developed excellent facilities for a day at the beach for its passengers, offering a wide range of water sports, beach games, guided nature walks, several bars, a boutique, small markets for local Bahamian crafts, and local entertainment. Lunch is served at a large pavilion to all passengers who choose to spend the day at the beach. Continuous tender service is provided by the line between the ship and the beach.

The Exumas: From 35 miles south of Nassau, the Exumas spread southeast over an area of 130 square miles. The group is particularly popular with the yachting set, for whom the variety of color and subtle shades of the waters around the Exumas have no equal. Snorkelers and divers sing their praises, too. The **Exuma Land and Sea Park** (359-1821) is a preserve accessible only by boat.

George Town, the capital, is a quiet village of 800 people and several small hotels. Across the bay is Stocking Island, whose lovely stretches of white-sand beach are rich with seashells. About a dozen resorts are dotted through the Exuma chain, as are hundreds of beaches and coves. This sea lover's mecca becomes busiest in April, when the islands host the annual Out Islands Regatta, the Bahamas's most prestigious sailing race. The luxury Four Seasons Resort Great Exuma at Emerald Bay was the chain's first Bahamas hotel and the Exumas' first luxury hotel and championship golf course.

Inagua: The Bahamas's third largest island is one of the least visited. Flamingos outnumber people 50,000 to 1,000. The 287-square-mile Inagua Park is the largest flamingo preserve in the Western Hemisphere. Union Creek National Park is a reserve for giant green turtles.

San Salvador: Situated east-southeast of Nassau and directly east of Cat Island, San Salvador is the island "where it all began," so to speak. Although the island had been neglected, it received a great deal of attention in 1992 when the Bahamas celebrated the Quincentennial as the site of Columbus's first landfall in the New World. The island has four monuments commemorating this event. (The landing site has been disputed as much as the landing!)

The New World Museum is in a renovated building that was originally constructed in the early nineteenth century and served until 1966 as a courthouse, a jail, and the commissioner's office. The building was restored by the Kiwanis Club of San Salvador with help from other service clubs and private groups. The exhibits are arranged in four groups: Columbus, 1492; the Lucayans, A.D. 600–1492; San Salvador, 1492–1838; and San Salvador in the late nineteenth and twentieth centuries. The Lucayan exhibit has a map that shows the forty-eight known Indian archaeological sites on San Salvador.

San Salvador has a Club Med, which the Bahamian government hoped would bring new life and tourism development to the island, but it hasn't happened yet. There is a small hotel, **Riding Rock Inn** (331-2631; www.ridingrock.com), near Cockburn Town, the main village. The island is prized by scuba enthusiasts because it is almost virgin territory. Both Club Med and the Riding Rock cater to divers.

Other Out Islands are being developed with small resorts, but perhaps the most significant will be Mayaguana, the least developed and most isolated of the island group. It's about to receive a multibillion-dollar investment, with an international airport scheduled to open by early 2008; a luxury resort, marina, villa and condominium development, and four nature reserves are slated to follow.

Transportation Serving the Out Islands

Airlines: Bahamasair (800-222-4262; www.bahamasair.com) serves all the airport centers of the Out Islands from Nassau. Same-day connections from US and Canadian gateways are available to Abaco, Andros, Bimini, Eleuthera, and Exuma. Several small airlines offer service to the main Out Islands from Florida.

Ferries: Bahamas Fast Ferry (323-2166; www.bahamasferries.com) offers interisland service among Nassau, Harbour Island, and North Eleuthera. The ferry is the first large-capacity luxury water service between Nassau and the Out Islands. The Bahamas Class Catamaran travels at about 40 knots, making the trip between Nassau and Harbour Island in about an hour and forty minutes.

Two scheduled daily round trips operate between Nassau and Harbour Island and North Eleuthera, and twice weekly between Nassau and Governor's Harbour. The air-conditioned ferry accommodates 177 passengers. Round-trip transportation costs $110 per person.

A one-day excursion, including a historical/cultural tour of Harbour Island, lunch, and a visit to the island's pink-sand beach, costs $149 per person. For information call Bahamas Fast Ferry.

Key West

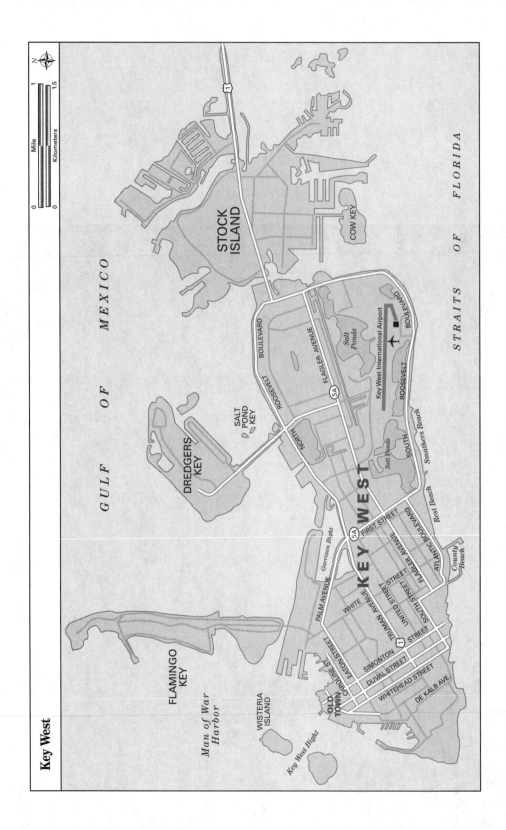

Key West

America's First Caribbean Island

Key West is a state of mind as much as a place. Earthy and stylish at the same time, America's southernmost town is one of the most delightful places in the world—one of a kind and infectious. Decades of writers, artists, and loads of eccentrics have made it that way—none more famous than author Ernest Hemingway, playwright Tennessee Williams, and nature artist John James Audubon. The first gave it his lust for living; the second, his flair for eccentricity; and the third, a cause for preservation. Combined, they set the stage for the theater that is Key West.

In recent years Key West has become one of cruising's most popular ports of call, visited by more than a dozen cruise ships at last count. And why not? It's one of the country's most interesting and charming towns—easy, convenient, and ideal for a day's visit. Cruise ships dock almost at the heart of Old Town, the oldest and most interesting part of Key West and within walking distance of major attractions, shops, and restaurants.

In the 1920s and 1930s, before Key West became a popular vacation destination, it barely qualified as a stopover on the way to Havana. Passengers in New York would board a train called the Havana Special and, on arrival in Key West, transfer from the train to their ship without leaving the pier for the overnight voyage to Cuba.

Key West began its transformation from a small, historic southern town to a major international resort in the 1950s and 1960s, attracting artists, writers, and people from the fashion world. But even with the changes, it kept its traditional resident communities: Cuban Americans (from the time of the Spanish-American War), blacks (who came even earlier as freemen, runaway slaves, and shipwreck survivors), and Conchs, longtime residents whose forebears came as traders, merchant sailors, wreckers, and fishers. (No one can say how many generations of living on the island it takes to be considered a Conch; the Old Island Restoration Foundation maintains that anyone born in the Keys is a Conch.)

In any case, the mix of artists and shrimpers, rednecks and blacks, yuppies and blue collars, gays and straights, writers, hippies, expatriates, and escapists from all over has given Key West an unusual combination of style and luxury and working-class simplicity (at least, until recently). Key Westers think of themselves as far removed from the Upper 48—and they are.

Key West has a long history of rags to riches. It was discovered by early Spanish explorers who, it is said, found piles of human bones on the island and called it Cayo Hueso (Island of Bones). History has not learned to whom these bones belonged, but the assumption is they were one of the Indian tribes, the Caloosa or Seminoles, who roamed the Keys.

Throughout the seventeenth and eighteenth centuries, Key West—indeed, all the Keys—was the lair of pirates who preyed on Spanish galleons laden with gold, silver, and gems from Mexico and South America that had to pass through these waters to return to Spain.

In 1822 the island was sold by a Spaniard to John Simonton, an American businessman, for $2,000, and the American flag was raised in the vicinity of Mallory Square the same year. Over the

At a Glance	
Antiquities	★
Art and Artists	★★★★
Beaches	★
Crafts	★★★
Cuisine	★★★
Dining/Restaurants	★★★
Entertainment	★★★
History	★★★★
Museums	★★★★
Nature	★★★★
Nightlife	★★★★
Scenery	★★
Shopping	★★★
Sightseeing	★★★★
Sports	★★★★
Transportation	★★★

next fifty years the population quadrupled to almost 3,000 and was made up of New England merchant seamen and white Bahamian traders, most of whom were engaged in the wrecking business—the very profitable enterprise of salvaging goods from ships that hit the reefs fronting the Keys. It was not uncommon for wreckers to cause such mishaps purposely by posting false signal lights for approaching ships during storms.

The construction of a lighthouse in the 1850s put a big dent in their business, and Key West had to wait for its next boom—first from sponging, then cigar making. Both were attributed to the influx of Cubans in the last quarter of the century. Once again the town flourished and was said to have been the richest town per capita in the country. But by the 1930s Key West was down on its luck to such an extent that 80 percent of the town's 12,000 people relied on public assistance.

World War II and the US Navy brought life back to Key West, but it was abandoned again after the war. President Truman visited in 1946 and continued to return frequently while he was chief executive, bringing the town a certain amount of attention. Hemingway had been living there since 1931, and Tennessee Williams came frequently in the 1940s, encouraging his literary friends to join him. By the late 1950s and for the next decade, investment filtered in slowly, but it was not until the 1980s—when Key West became fashionable and restoration of Old Town, which had started in the 1970s, was well under way—that real estate prices skyrocketed and the boom was on again.

Key West is small and easy to find your way around in, and it has something for everyone—historic sites enhanced by their colorful past, unusual architecture, and the famous writers and artists who lived and worked here; funky as well as smart shops, restaurants, bars, and entertainment; sports, including snorkeling and diving on the only coral reef offshore the continental United States; and, of course, the famous Key West sunsets, not to mention Key lime pie and margaritas.

Key West is both an island and a city, with a population of fewer than 50,000 residents that is swollen by more than a million tourists annually. Closer to Cuba than to Miami, Key West, with its graceful palms and masses of bougainvillea, its tropical climate, and easy-living ambience, seems as Caribbean as any of the islands bathed by that sea.

Key West will probably remind you of New Orleans in more ways than one. *Conch,* like the term *Creole* in New Orleans, refers to people, food, and a style of architecture. As you will quickly learn, the Conchs are proud of their name. In 1882 they even declared Key West the Conch Republic and seceded from the Union—but that's another story.

Local lore says the name *conch* (pronounced *konk)* comes from the seventeenth century, when the Eleuthran Adventurers, a group from Bermuda that had established a colony in the Bahamas, fled to Key West after the British tried to tax them, declaring they would "eat conchs" before paying taxes to the Crown. As enduring as the conch, some might muse, has been the legacy of piracy—reflected not only in real estate prices but also in the town's anything-goes attitude, relishing the unexpected and keeping rules only to break them.

Budget Planning

Key West is as expensive as you want to make it. Fortunately, your feet can get you around town to almost all the main attractions. There are bikes and mopeds for rent and public buses, as well as car rentals for those who want to get out of town. If you are on a tight budget, you should plan your sightseeing because the museums, historic homes, and other attractions charge admission—$5 to $10 for adults and half that amount for children. There are restaurants in every price range, and souvenirs from $5 T-shirts to $5,000 paintings.

Port Profile: Key West

Location/Embarkation: The port in Key West is located in the northwest corner of the island. Downtown, known as Old Town, stretches directly behind the dock to the south and east. Duval Street, the main thoroughfare of Old Key West, runs for about a mile from the dock to Southernmost Point, and in a bit of hyperbole is called the longest street in the world because it runs from the Gulf of Mexico to the Atlantic Ocean. Most cruise

Fast Facts

Population: Key West has about 50,000 permanent residents, and the population doubles or triples with the number of tourists at almost any time of the year, but particularly in winter.

Climate: Balmy weather almost year-round. Temperatures average 75°F in January and 82°F in summer. Short tropical rains come often in fall and spring but rarely last more than a few minutes.

Clothing: Tropical-casual. Seldom do men wear ties. A sweater or jacket is needed in the shade in winter and almost any time for air-conditioning.

Currency: US dollar. Traveler's checks and credit cards are widely accepted.

Customs Regulations: Cruise passengers are admitted without formalities (you're still in the United States), but it is wise to carry a passport, birth certificate, driver's license, or voter's registration card for identification.

Electricity: 110 volts, 60 cycles.

Language: English with a twang.

Postal Service: The post office is located on Whitehead and Fleming Streets, 5 blocks south of the pier.

Public Holidays: All US holidays, plus a few special local ones. (See Celebrations later in this chapter.)

Telephone Area Code: 305

Airlines: American/American Eagle, Cape Air (Continental Connection), Comair/Delta, Gulfstream, and USAir Express have frequent flights daily from Miami International.

Information: www.fla-keys.com
Key West Chamber of Commerce, 402 Wall Street/Mallory Square, Key West, FL 33040; 294-2587; (800) 527-8539. Hours: 8:30 A.M. to 5:00 P.M. Monday through Friday, 9:00 A.M. to 5:00 P.M. Saturday and Sunday. The office has maps, brochures, and information on self-guided walking tours.

Old Island Restoration Foundation, Hospitality House, Mallory Square, Box 689, Key West, FL 33041; 294-9501.

---

ships anchor at the piers fronting Old Town, but the megaliners dock at a newer facility on the west side of town, and their passengers are transported to Mallory Square by the Conch Train. (You are not allowed to walk it, even if you want to, as the area is under US Navy jurisdiction.) There's a third cruise ship dock at the Westin Marina behind the Westin Resort that some ships use; you can walk from here to Mallory Square as well.

Walk in any direction from Front Street or up Duval Street and you will find something of interest. It's hard to get lost: The center of town is only about 10 blocks square, laid out in a grid and easy to follow with maps available at the Key West Chamber of Commerce on Wall Street by Mallory Square.

Facilities: Key West has the feel of a tropical port with the added advantage of good transportation, communications, and technical facilities not always available in the Caribbean.

Local Transportation: Taxis are readily available, but you do not need them unless you have trouble walking. In that case, you might want to use public buses or take one of the town tours offered by the Conch Train or Old Town Trolley (see details under Shore Excursions). All major car rental companies are represented here. Because of the heavy demand during the peak winter season, you would be wise to make reservations from home through a rental company's 800 number before departing on your cruise.

Bikes and Scooters: Bikes and scooters are the best way to get around Key West. The island is only a mile wide, 7 miles long, and entirely flat. Rentals are available from the **Bike Shop** (1110 Truman Avenue at Varela Street; 294-1073) as well as **The Moped Hospital** (601 Truman Avenue, at Simonton Street; 866-296-1625; fax 305-292-7679; www.mopedhospital.com)—where all bikes are custom-made, specially geared with high handlebars, comfortable seats, and safety yellow baskets.

Also has bikes with baby seats and adult tricycles. All $12. Scooters rent for $35 for the day; those for two persons (carrying capacity of 550 pounds) are $55 per day. **Pirate Scooters** (401 Southard, at Whitehead Street; 295-0000; 877-PIRATE-6; www .piratescooters.com) offers shorter rentals for cruise ship passengers; call for price. **Paradise Scooters & Bikes** (430 Duval, at Whitehead Street; 292-6441; www.paradisescooterrentals .com) offers bikes at $12.90 for 9:00 A.M. to 4:30 P.M. rental; a single scooter will run you $42.63 for three hours or less, and a two-person model $64.13. The Web site has useful maps. **Barracuda Scooter Rentals** (1800 North Roosevelt Boulevard; 296-8007; www.barracudascooters.com) offers bikes for $12, scooters for $45 single, $75 double. The latter also has kayaks for half-day ($30) and full-day ($45) rentals, and offers three-hour kayak tours daily at 9:30 A.M. and 2:00 P.M.

Shore Excursions

Conch Tour Train (Mallory Square/Front Street; 294-5161; www.conchtourtrain.com). $27 adult; $13 ages four through twelve; 10 percent discount available for tickets bought on Internet. A leisurely hour-and-a-half orientation to Key West with running commentary by the driver-guide on dozens of sites en route. The train is made up of three or four open-sided cars pulled by a truck disguised as a caboose. With the tour ticket, you receive some discount coupons. Some driver-guides are better than others, adding interesting tidbits along the way; others sound like an endless recording, rattling off information too fast to understand or retain. (You can easily take the tour on your own; tours depart from the Conch Train's depot about every thirty minutes throughout the day. Hours: 9:00 A.M. to 4:30 P.M., daily year-round.)

Old Town Trolley (Mallory Square/Wall Street; 296-6688). $27 adult; $13 ages four through twelve. Trolley cars similar to those in San Francisco (except that they are motorized) have the same owners as the Conch Train and offer a similar tour—but with one important advantage. Passengers may get on and off the trolley at any of the ten stops along the route, making it a more useful vehicle for those who want to explore a particular

area of the town. (You can easily take the trolley on your own; tours depart about every thirty minutes 9 A.M. to 4:30 P.M. from the depot and, like the train, some guides are better than others.)

Conch Train/Trolley, Aquarium, and **Shipwreck Historeum:** Two and a half hours; $35 adult; $23 child. After an island trolley or train tour, participants visit Key West Aquarium for a self-guided tour of about forty-five minutes and the Shipwreck Historeum, where actors and exhibits bring to life the colorful history of Key West's wrecker days. (The Aquarium and Shipwreck Historeum, both by Mallory Square, can be visited on your own.)

Island City Strolls with Sharon Wells (294-0566; www.seekeywest.com) are offered on Tuesday, Wednesday, Thursday, and Saturday, each with a different focus, for a four-person minimum. The cost is $25 per person. Sharon Wells, a historian, photographer, and expert on Key West, writes and publishes *Walking & Biking Guide to Historic Key West,* a free periodical with fourteen illustrated, self-guided tours. The Web site has a wealth of information on tours and tips on planning your visit.

Key West Nature Bike Tour (inquire with Lloyd Mager, 294-1882; www.LloydsTropicalBike Tour.com). Mager leads a two-hour bike trip with a lesson in Key West history, architecture, and flora, daily except Monday, departing at 9:45 A.M. from Moped Hospital (601 Truman Avenue); call 294-1073 for a recorded message announcing the next tour. Cost: $35 per person, plus bike rental.

Pelican Path (Old Island Restoration Foundation, Hospitality House, Mallory Square; 294-9501). A carefully laid out, self-guided route leads past many of Key West's landmarks and famous old houses in Old Town. A folder with a good map of the route and brief descriptions of the houses, prepared by the Old Island Restoration Foundation, is available from its office. The few landmark houses open to the public charge admission. The tour is of particular interest to architecture and history buffs. The foundation also offers guided house and garden tours during the winter season, usually for about $10 per person.

Walking Tours (inquire with Denison Temple, 296-1866; fax 296-0922). Temple, a Key West resident, offers walking or biking tours with a focus on Key West history, architecture, or its literary highlights by appointment. Charges range from $15 to $20 per hour, depending on the number of participants. Tours usually last about one and a half hours. Another walking tour of historic Key West departs daily from the Key West Shipwreck Historeum (described later in this chapter), where information and tickets are available. Tours start at 10:00 A.M. and run about one and a half hours.

Catamaran Sailing and Snorkeling: Three hours; $45 adult; $24 child. A 65-foot catamaran sails to the continental United States' only living coral reef, which lies about 7 miles southeast of Key West. Snorkeling equipment, flotation devices, and instruction are included. The boat has changing facilities and freshwater showers. Complimentary soft drinks, beer, and wine are served. Children age eleven and under cannot participate in the snorkeling. Similar shore excursion sold by some ships, $45 to $50.

Coral Reef Glassbottom Boat: Several boats offer two- and three-hour excursions. The boat travels about 7 miles out to the only living coral reef in the continental United States for participants to see the colorful fish and dramatic corals. *Discovery,* operated by **Discovery Undersea Tours** (251 Margaret Street, Key West; 293-0099; 800-262-0099), is a catamaran with a specially fitted underwater viewing room and is wheelchair accessible. Departures are daily at 10:30 A.M. and 1:30 P.M. Cost: $35 adult; $15 child (under twelve) for a two-hour excursion; $89 and $69 for a three-and-a-half-hour one. Similar excursions are also available from Fury Water Adventures (400 Wall Street, Key West; 292-7260)

Key West Scuba: Three hours; $66. For certified divers, PADI five-star instructors offer a full range of services for diving on one of two sites: the Sambos, a collection of three shallow reefs 15 to 40 feet deep,1.5 to 2.5 miles apart and richly populated with reef fish; or an artificial reef formed by the 187-foot *Cayman Salvager,* sunk in 1985. Equipment is included. As a cruise ship shore excursion, four and a half hours, $75 including equipment. (See the Sports section later in this chapter.)

Back Country Kayaking: Two and a half hours; $49. A great experience for beginners or

experienced kayakers. After receiving instructions on paddling, you tour a cluster of mangroves with a guide and learn about flora, fauna, and folklore.

Seaplanes of Key West (Key West Airport; 294-0709; 800-950-2359; www.seaplanesofkeywest.com). Seaplanes fly to the Dry Tortugas and Fort Jefferson National Park, 70 miles into the Gulf of Mexico, where you can spot marine life, shipwrecks, and Mel Fisher's treasure site and enjoy swimming, snorkeling (free gear), bird-watching, and sightseeing.

Key West on Your Own

Key West, where a bit of Cape Cod meets New Orleans and mingles with the Caribbean, is a place to savor the atmosphere rather than to absorb the sun. There's no place quite like it. How you spend your time largely depends on your interests. There's historic Key West, architectural Key West, and literary Key West. There are forts, art galleries, museums, funky shops and chic boutiques, sidewalk cafes and legendary pubs, golf, diving, fishing, kayaking, and more. Indeed, Key West has more attractions and diversions than you could possibly handle in one day, but the one thing the island does not have is good beaches.

Key West's Historic District has more than 3,000 buildings constructed prior to 1900. Many are still privately owned by the families who built them; others have been made into stores, art galleries, inns, and museums and are windows onto the town's fascinating history and the people who have made it so special. Hemingway House, where

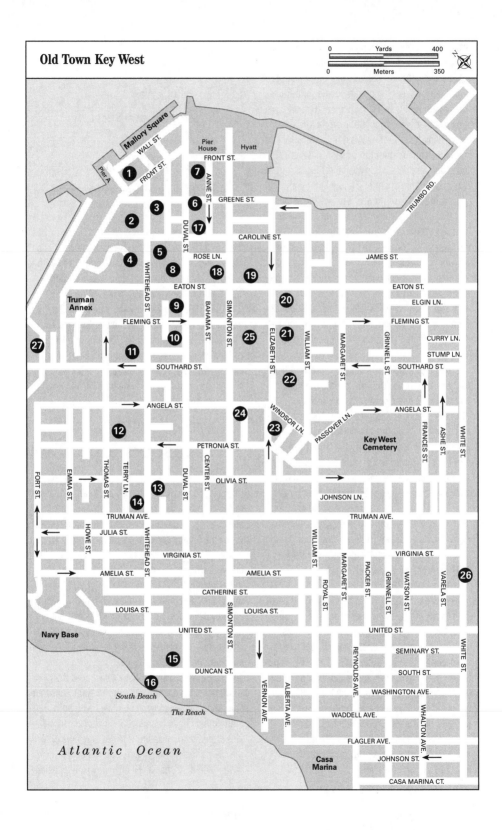

the author wrote *For Whom the Bell Tolls* and other masterpieces, is a National Historic Landmark. His favorite bars are still among the most popular spots in town.

For a quick overview, take a train or trolley tour, passing along tree-shaded streets lined with ginger-bread-trimmed houses and Victorian mansions. Then, to get the real feel of Key West, walk—*amble* is a better description—in Old Town. A stroll on Duval Street will help you measure the town's pulse. You can cross the entire island on Duval or Whitehead Street (a little over a mile) in thirty minutes, but then it can also take three hours. You will want to window-shop; stop at a bar or sidewalk cafe; chat with some of the town's friendly, funky characters; buy a souvenir or a work of art; and visit a museum or historic house. Stop by the Key West Chamber of Commerce or Hospitality House, both at Mallory Square, for maps and information.

Mallory Square and Vicinity

Mallory Square (1), on the island's northwest corner at the foot of Duval Street, a short walk from the pier, was the heart of Key West in the old days, and it's the center of activity for visitors today. The old buildings beside the square once quartered the trades (read: wrecking) that made Key West rich; now they house shops, restaurants, bars, and museums. You will need some imagination to picture the setting in seafaring days, as the square itself has been reduced to a small area by the sea where sunset devotees come to watch the nightly show. The rest is a parking lot.

On the east side of the square in a building dating from 1850 is the **Waterfront Playhouse** (294-5015), home of the Key West Players. On the west is **Hospitality House,** the headquarters of the Old Island Restoration Foundation, in a Conch house dating from the late nineteenth century. And behind it on Wall Street is the **Chamber of Commerce,** in a former warehouse. Wall, Front, White-head, Greene, and Duval Streets—with many of Old Town's main attractions—parallel or lead off the square. Most sightseeing excursions start from here.

Key West Aquarium (1) (1 Whitehead Street; 296-2051; www.keywestaquarium.com). Exhibits of Atlantic marine life are a hit with kids, especially watching sharks and turtles being fed by hand. Admission: $10 adult; $5 ages four to twelve; slightly less online; free for kids under four. Hours:

9:00 A.M. to 6:00 P.M. daily. Frequent guided tours between 11:00 A.M. and 4:30 P.M.

Key West Shipwreck Historeum (1) (Wall and Front Streets; 292-8990; www.keywestship wreckhistoreum.com). One of the island's newest museums offers an excellent presentation of the Keys' famous—and infamous—wrecking era with artifacts from the *Isaac Allerton,* said to have carried the richest manifest of any ship of its day when it went down in 1865. Key West's colorful history is brought to life by actors and exhibits that help viewers understand the times that revolved around shipping and the town that originally built its fortune rescuing survivors of shipwrecks and reaping rich rewards from the cargoes residents salvaged. The building has a 65-foot observation tower, similar to those used in olden days to spot ships and now offering visitors a great view of the harbor, Old Town, and its surroundings. Admission: $11 adult; $5 ages four through twelve. Hours: 9:45 A.M. to 5:00 P.M. daily. Presentations begin every twenty minutes; the last full presentation at 4:40 P.M. If you only have time for one historic museum, this would be the one to select.

On the corner at Front Street, the **Key West Art Center** is a nonprofit artist cooperative, housed in a late-nineteenth-century wooden structure that was used in the 1930s under the New Deal for the WPA Arts Project headquarters.

Next to the Aquarium, the **Clinton Square Market** was formerly a naval storehouse dating from 1861 and is now the town's oldest brick building. Today it houses a group of attractive specialty shops.

Key West Museum of Art and History (1) (281 Front Street; 295-6616; www.kwahs.com). Next to the market is the massive US Customs House, dating from 1891, said to be the only structure in Florida in Romanesque Revival style. Used for various government agencies over the century, it was put on the National Register of Historic Places in 1973 and renovated by the Key West Art and Historical Society as a museum. Opened in 1999 as the main repository for the island's art and history, this architectural gem houses interesting permanent collections and stages major touring exhibitions. Admission: $10 adult; $9 senior; $5 student; free for kids under six. Hours: 9:00 A.M. to 5:00 P.M. daily.

Front Street, as the name implies, fronted the harbor in olden days and was the main commercial street, with banks, trading offices, bars, and flophouses for merchant seamen. Apparently one of the most raucous, the **Havana-Madrid,** was a tavern and striptease joint; its namesake today is a seafood specialty restaurant at 410 Wall Street.

Mel Fisher's Maritime Heritage Museum (2) (200 Greene Street; 294-2633; www.melfisher .org; info@melfisher.org). A visit to this museum, with the discoveries by America's most noted shipwreck sleuth, Key West's own Mel Fisher, can turn anyone into a hopeful treasure hunter. In 1985, after many tries, Fisher found *Nuestra Senora de Atocha,* a seventeenth-century Spanish galleon that went down in 1622 only 45 miles west of Key West, with an estimated $400 million in gold and silver. On display is a copy of the ship's manifest, heavy gold crosses and chains, emeralds, coins, weapons, and other artifacts recovered from the sunken treasure. Much more is in storage and on the seabed, where it will stay. Other displays are from the *Santa Margarita,* another Spanish treasure ship. Admission: $10 adult; $5 ages six to twelve; free for kids five or younger. Hours: 8:30 A.M. to 5:00 P.M. weekdays; 9:30 A.M. to 5:00 P.M. weekends and holidays. Hours are often extended to accommodate seasonal needs and early/late cruise ship dockings. The museum is ADA-compliant and air-conditioned.

To the west of the museum is **Clinton Square,** with a small garden and gate leading to the Little White House, President Truman's winter retreat. The main entrance is farther south on Whitehead Street.

Key West Cigar Factory (306 Front Street, 3 Pirates Alley; www.keywestcigarfactory.com) is the last of a once major industry in Key West, brought here by Cubans in the late nineteenth century. In a setting of old equipment and furnishings that has not changed in a century, two people demonstrate the old method of hand rolling cigars. There are several other cigar stores in town; most now have their factories in the Dominican Republic.

Audubon House and Tropical Gardens (3) (205 Whitehead at Greene Street; 294-2116; 877-281-2473; www.audubonhouse.com). Built in 1830 for Capt. John H. Geiger, a skilled harbor pilot and master wrecker, the house is typical of Key West architecture of the period and is surrounded by lush gardens. When nature artist John James Audubon visited Key West in 1832 to hunt and sketch local birds, tradition has it that he stayed at Geiger's home, although there is apparently no historical record to substantiate the claim.

Nonetheless, more than a century later Key West native son and prominent Miami business-man Mitchell Wolfson acquired the Key West land-mark, restored it, and dedicated it as a public museum, to be named Audubon House. The restoration is credited with sparking a preservation trend in the mid-1970s, led by a pair of Old Town merchants who teamed up to renovate fifteen buildings along the 600 block of Duval Street. Today the downtown restoration is nearly com-plete, with the renovated buildings and homes housing smart boutiques, art galleries, restaurants, and pubs.

Audubon House, run by the Florida Audubon Society, has been elegantly furnished with antiques of the period. The original furnishings probably came from the salvaged cargo of wrecked ships, as was customary at the time, and would have origi-nated in far-flung places around the globe. Some of Audubon's most famous engravings, such as the roseate spoonbill, hang on the walls, and in the garden is the Geiger tree used as a background by Audubon for his engraving of the white-crowned pigeon, which he named the Key West pigeon; it was one of eighteen species new to Audubon. A fine collection of porcelain birds by Dorothy Doughty is also on display. The museum offers a videotape presentation of Audubon's *Birds of Florida.* The entrance is through the museum's store, where you can buy Audubon posters and books. Admission: $10 adult; $6.50 student; $5 ages six to twelve; free for kids five or younger. Hours: 9:30 A.M. to 5:00 P.M. daily. Tours are self-guided; the last tour is at 4:30 P.M.

Little White House (4) (111 Front Street; 294-9911). After his first visit in November 1946, Harry Truman became enamored of Key West and returned frequently throughout his presidency, mak-ing the estate his presidential vacation retreat. The house, built by the US Navy in 1890 for a naval commandant, is now a museum with Truman mem-orabilia. Admission: $10 adult; $5 ages twelve and

younger. Hours: 9:00 A.M. to 5:00 P.M. daily. A guided tour is given about every fifteen minutes.

Incidentally, the sign on the entrance gates at Whitehead and Caroline Streets is misleading, appearing to indicate that the white house imme-diately inside the gates was Truman's pad. It is naval officer quarters built in 1904. The Truman house is farther west.

The forty-four-acre Truman Annex extending south along Whitehead Street was part of the for-mer US Naval Base, bought some years ago by pri-vate developers who created a luxury residential and resort community. The Hilton Hotel, opened in early 1996, anchors the north end and has retail shops, restaurants, a deepwater marina, a beach club, and condos. The hotel faces Sunset Island (formerly known as Tank Island), which has beach facilities. Frequent ferry service is available from the hotel. Hyatt Hotels' first time-share venture is also there.

Florida Keys Eco-Discovery Center (809-4750; http://floridakeys.noaa.gov/eco_discovery .html), located on the waterfront at the end of Southard Street at Truman Annex, is Key West's newest attraction, having officially opened in January 2007. Incorporating 6,400 square feet of interactive exhibits, the center showcases the underwater and upland habitats that characterize the Keys, emphasizing North America's only living contiguous barrier coral reef, which parallels the Keys. Through interactive and touch-screen mod-ules, text and audio-video components, visitors can explore the region's mangrove, patch reef, seagrass, Dry Tortugas environments, and more. There's a walk-through version of the Aquarius Undersea Lab, the world's only operational under-water laboratory, located off Key Largo. The center is a cooperative effort of the National Oceanic and Atmospheric Administration's Florida Keys National Marine Sanctuary, the National Park Service, US Fish and Wildlife Service, and the South Florida Water Management District. Admis-sion is free. Hours: 9 A.M. to 4 P.M. Tuesday through Saturday.

USS *Mohawk* Coast Guard Cutter Memor-ial Museum (799-1143; www.ussmohawk.org), another new museum on the Truman Waterfront, has special appeal to military and history buffs. The museum is set in the USS *Mohawk*, believed to be the only remaining Coast Guard submarine chaser in existence. Built in 1934, the 165-foot-long historic ship was assigned North Atlantic escort operations in World War II. Regarded as the memorial ship of the Battle of the Atlantic, the vessel launched fourteen attacks against Nazi submarines and rescued hundreds of people at sea. Visitors can view the original radio room, bridge, galley, officers' staterooms, crew quarters, and weapons, as well as the sonar room where crew members listened for German submarines during the war. Future plans call for changing exhibitions of navy, Coast Guard, and veterans' history, as well as video recollections by former *Mohawk* crew members. Admission: $5 per person ($1 for veterans with identification). Hours: 10 A.M. to 5 P.M. Tuesday through Sunday.

As noted earlier, the gates on Whitehead Street face Caroline Street, an interesting block for detouring to Duval Street. Those with a keen interest in Key West's architecture or its literary and theatrical luminaries might prefer to continue on Caroline to the landmarks (17) to (25) on the map.

On the corner across from the Little White House gates is **Kelly's Caribbean Bar & Grill** (303 Whitehead Street; 293-9405; www.kellyskeywest .com), a garden restaurant in the former building of Aero-Marine Airways, which provided mail service between Key West and Havana in the 1920s. The building once occupied the site where Pier House is today, and it became the headquarters of Pan American World Airways after the airline launched its service to Havana in 1928, ushering in the new era of international passenger air travel. Kelly's belongs to actress Kelly McGillis of *Top Gun* and *Witness* fame.

Heritage House Museum and **Robert Frost Cottage (5)** (410 Caroline Street; 296-3573; www .heritagehousemuseum.org). Built about 1834—but it's not clear by whom—the house was owned by George Carey, a liquor merchant who expanded it in 1844 for his bride, adding the front rooms and porch. The house remained in the family for almost a century and was altered many times. In 1934 it

was bought by Jessie Porter Newton, one of the driving forces behind Key West's preservation efforts. She renovated the house and added a garden and swimming pool in place of the cookhouse and cistern, and another room (called the Chinese porch) decorated with Asian art and antiques. More recently she built a second house for herself, hidden in the trees at the rear of the property, and turned the old house into a museum brimming with furniture and collectibles from the four corners of the world.

Miss Jessie, as the guides refer to her, was a longtime friend of Robert Frost, who visited Key West frequently in the 1940s, staying first in a rental house at 707 Seminole Avenue and at Casa Marina until he took up semi-residence in the small, tin-roofed cottage at the rear of Miss Jessie's house, where he spent fourteen winters. Hours: 10:00 A.M. to 4:00 P.M. Monday through Saturday. Admission: $5 self-guided tour. Guided tours ($7) of the Heritage House are available, but the Frost cottage is not included as it is often used for literary meetings and seminars. A Robert Frost poetry reading and seminar is held in March. The gardens are often used for weddings.

On the corner of Caroline and Duval stands one of the town's largest houses, built in the last century for Dr. J. Y. Porter, Florida's first public health officer, credited with significant research on yellow fever. The building now houses several art galleries.

Duval Street

Key West's famous Duval Street, named for the first governor of the Florida territory, is the main drag of Old Town, awash with bars, shops, art galleries, and old houses with a slice of history at every address. The street from the north end at Mallory Square to the south end at the Southernmost House has been invaded by T-shirt and knick-knack shops, but happily there are plenty of other stores with attractive art, objets d'art, restaurants and sidewalk cafes, and clothing boutiques to make it interesting and easy to combine a shopping expedition with a stroll through history.

Sloppy Joe's (6) (201 Duval Street; www .sloppyjoes.com) was one of Hemingway's favorite haunts and is still a mecca for Hemingway fans. Owner Joe Russell, a Key West boatman, was immortalized by Hemingway as "Freddie" in *To Have and Have Not*. In 1937, when the rent on Russell's Greene Street location (the original site) was to be raised, Joe moved his bar to Duval Street in the middle of the night. Note the painting on the south wall by the bar; it shows a young Hemingway with a typewriter and Sloppy Joe wearing the crown of grapes and sitting at a table surrounded by friends—a rough bunch known as "The Mob." The painting was done by an artist in the WPA Arts Project.

When Hemingway left Key West to live in Cuba, he stored some of his belongings in a back room here. In 1962, after his death, Mary, Hemingway's last wife, discovered among those belongings the original manuscript of *A Farewell to Arms* and *To Have and Have Not*, and even some uncashed royalty checks.

The bar is full and noisy from morning to night, and no tourist to Key West would think a visit complete without a stop here. If you want a souvenir from the area's most famous bar, the adjoining T-shirt shop probably does as much business as the watering hole.

Pirate Soul Museum (7) (524 Front Street; 292-1113; www.piratesoul.com). Those fascinated with pirates can take a 1-block detour from Sloppy Joe's to one of Key West's newest museums. The collection includes authentic pirate artifacts along with interactive technology that enables viewers to take a historic adventure through the "Golden Age of Piracy" and learn about the infamous pirates of the period. Admission: $13.95 adult; $7.95 child, plus tax. Hours: 9:00 A.M. to 7:00 P.M. daily.

Wrecker's Museum/Oldest House (8) (322 Duval Street; 294-9502; www.oirf.org/museums). Built about 1829, it claims to be the oldest house in Key West and was the home of Capt. Francis B. Watlington, a merchant seaman and wrecker. Key West's piracy and wrecking days are described in pictures, old documents, and ship models; the furnishings reflect the family life of a sea captain of the time. The kitchen in the back is separate from the house, as was characteristic in those days. The building is now operated by the Old Island Restoration Foundation as a nonprofit museum. Among its

original furnishings, maritime artifacts, and items recovered from Keys waters, visitors will see an unusual miniature 1850-style dollhouse fashioned after the "Conch"-style houses of Key West and furnished in Colonial and mid-Victorian styles. There is also an interactive map showing the locations of shipwrecks along the Keys. Admission: $5 adult; $1 child. Hours: 10:00 A.M. to 4:00 P.M. daily.

St. Paul's Episcopal Church (9) (401 Duval Street). Begun in 1832, the present church is the fourth on the site. Among its many moments in history, it was seen in the film of Tennessee Williams's play *The Rose Tattoo.*

La Concha (9) (430 Duval Street; 296-2991; 800-745-2191). It's a Crown Plaza unlike any other in the chain. Opened in 1926 at a time when Key West—then a major port and link for tourists en route to Havana—needed a first-class hotel, La Concha quickly became the social center of the town. The seven-story building was—and still is—the tallest building in Key West, with fabulous newer features such as rooms adjoined by baths, hot and cold running water in all rooms, an elevator, telephone booths, a haberdashery, a bakery, and a bank.

Now listed on the National Register of Historic Places, the hotel has seen a great deal of history. Here in 1927, Juan Trippe, founding president of Pan American World Airways, formally announced the start of passenger service between Key West and Havana, launching international air travel. Hemingway, a guest and frequent patron of La Concha's Duval Street bar, included the hotel in his *To Have and Have Not*. And Williams wrote much of *A Streetcar Named Desire* while he was staying here in 1947.

The hotel's fortunes and misfortunes paralleled those of the town, and during the 1930s both fell on hard times. The hotel was sold and resold several times and suffered from hurricane damage and neglect. By the time Atlanta architect Richard Rauh was brought in to rescue it, the hotel had been badly vandalized and was boarded up. In 1986, after a multimillion-dollar renovation, the hotel reopened and quickly took its place once again as the belle of Duval.

Fast Buck Freddie's (10) (500 Duval Street; 294-2007; www.fastbuckfreddies.com) is Key

West's answer to Bloomingdale's. Those who are old enough to remember will immediately recognize the exterior as a former Kress Five & Dime store, built in 1913, but inside, it is a chic emporium. The building is shared with **Jimmy Buffett's Margaritaville,** the store and restaurant of Key West's most famous citizen (after Hemingway), who got his start here. And he does show up here from time to time.

There's now a second store, **Half-Buck Freddie's** (306 William Street, 294-2007). This discount outlet carries less expensive items.

San Carlos Opera House (10) (516 Duval Street). Restored in 1990, the building is the third on the site and has served the Cuban community since 1871, when the first structure was dedicated. It is used as a center for music, plays, and other cultural activities.

Ripley's Believe It or Not Odditorium (10) (108 Duval Street; 293-9694). The fun-house museum, based on the works and collection of Robert Ripley, is in its new home, across the street from its former one (the renovated Strand Theater, a former movie house with a fanciful facade built in the 1930s as one of the WPA projects to employ local artists and workers; it now houses a Walgreens, which operates a 24-hour pharmacy, 292-9833). Admission: $16.02 adult; $11 ages four through eleven. Hours: 10:00 A.M. to 11:00 P.M. daily.

If you continue south on Duval Street, the walk from Southard Street to the ocean becomes an art and shopping excursion more than a sightseeing one, as many of the best art galleries and boutiques are in these blocks.

*Alternatively, you could turn west on Southard and continue 1 block to Whitehead, where you will find the post office to your right and the **Monroe County Courthouse (11)** at Jackson Square to your left. The **Green Parrot Bar,** a watering hole popular with locals, has held down the corner of Whitehead and Southard since 1890. Straight ahead, Southard Street continues to **Fort Zachary Taylor (27).***

Blue Heaven (12) (Thomas and Petronia Streets). If it's lunchtime, you may want to detour another block south to Key West's most written-

about restaurant/art gallery in the heart of Bahama Village, the town's oldest black neighborhood.

Bahama Village historically was made up mostly of Bahamians and Cubans of African origin and has had various names—La Africana in the 1880s, Jungle Town in the 1950s and 1960s, and now Bahama Village. Indeed, a ceremonial arch with the Bahamian coat of arms mounted over Petronia Street at Duval proclaims it thus. The area is something of a hodgepodge architecturally and culturally, with tiny houses, narrow lanes, churches, funky art galleries, and men sitting under shade trees playing dominoes—a picture you're likely to see in any barrio south of Miami. Although some restoration has been done, enough of the neighborhood's character remains to get the feel of Key West in another era.

Blue Heaven, which dates from 1884, has had quite a past—as a pool hall, ice-cream parlor, dance hall, bordello, and artists' studios. Hemingway used to referee boxing matches in an outdoor arena under the Spanish lime tree, and young black boxers such as "Iron Baby" Roberts and "Battlin' Geech" Kermit Forbes sparred with him on Fridays. Apparently cockfights were frequent, too, as there's a "Rooster Graveyard" with tombstones intact in the northeast corner.

At the back of the outdoor restaurant, set under enormous shade trees and showers of bougainvillea, stands a water tower dating from about 1920; it was moved here from Little Torch Key, where it had been used for the men building the Flagler Railroad that once brought mainlanders to Key West on the Havana Special.

Oh, yes, the food. It's as eclectic as the setting, and quite good, and you can't beat the price. Several handsome roosters strut about underfoot, stopping from time to time to crow. But it's the fresh flowers on the tables in this chicken patch that's the pièce de résistance.

Hemingway Home and Museum (13) (907 Whitehead Street; 294-1136; www.hemingway home.com). The large house suggesting Spanish colonial design is set back from the street in lush tropical gardens. Built by a Connecticut merchant in 1851, it is now a National Historic Landmark and museum and one of Key West's most unusual structures. Constructed of native rock hewn from the grounds, the house has features unusual for Key West, such as arched windows with shutters and a second-floor wraparound veranda with an iron balustrade that would seem to fit better in New Orleans than Key West.

Hemingway bought the house in 1931 and added a swimming pool, the first in Key West. He lived here for two decades, during which he wrote many of his greatest works, including *For Whom the Bell Tolls, Death in the Afternoon, The Green Hills of Africa, Snows of Kilimanjaro, To Have and Have Not,* his play *The Fifth Column,* and many short stories. It was his most productive period, when he was idolized and imitated by writers the world over. The house was sold shortly before his death in 1961.

The gardens are beautiful, but the house is disappointing—sparsely furnished, with almost none of the furnishings having belonged to Hemingway except a collection of his childhood books in a glass case on the second floor and some family photographs. There are numerous cats, which tour guides say are descendants of Hemingway's cats, but that's questionable. Admission: $11 adult; $6 ages six through twelve. Hours: 9:00 A.M. to 5:00 P.M. daily. Guided tours start about every half hour.

Hemingway is said to have kept a rigorous schedule, up before sunrise and writing until noon in his study in the loft of the pool house, joined to the main house by a catwalk. He would spend the remainder of the day fishing with his friends and some local fishermen on his 40-foot boat, the *Pilar.*

Much of Hemingway's life was also centered at Sloppy Joe's, his favorite bar, originally located on Greene Street (see earlier description). There Key West's most famous writer had a reserved bar stool where he enjoyed his daily ration of booze. There, too, Hemingway saw for the first time Martha Gellhorn, whom he later married.

The bar is still there but is known as **Captain Tony's Saloon** (428 Greene Street; 294-1838). Although Tony Tarracino, the former owner and mayor of Key West, no longer owns it, the colorful bar, which claims to be the oldest in town, has changed little since Hemingway's day. The ceiling is covered with thousands of calling cards and almost as many bras, and a motley crew of loyal patrons occupy the bar stools, talking and vaguely listening to the entertainer plucking a guitar.

Key West Lighthouse (14) (937 Whitehead Street; 295-6616). Across the street from the Hemingway House, a 110-foot lighthouse, built in 1847, marked the water's edge in those days. It is still the best location for a panoramic view of Key West, with the Atlantic Ocean on the east and the Gulf of Mexico on the west. There are eighty-eight steps to the balcony and another ten steps to the light station.

The Lighthouse Military Museum, in a small building on the south side of the compound, has interesting exhibits of old military uniforms, ship models, and other seafaring paraphernalia. Admission: $10 adult; $9 senior; $5 student and child (under age six free). Hours: 9:30 A.M. to 4:15 P.M. daily.

Key West Butterfly & Nature Conservatory (15) (1316 Duval Street; 296-2988, 800-839-4647; www.keywestbutterfly.com). Walk through gardens filled with butterflies and colorful birds, flowers, and waterfalls. The facility has a learning center, gift shop, and gallery where original art work is available. Admission: $10 adult; $8.50 senior; $7.50 ages four through twelve; three and under free. Hours: 9:00 A.M. to 5:00 P.M. daily.

Truman Avenue, which you will cross when you continue south, is the southern terminus of US Highway 1.

Southernmost Point (16), a red, black, and yellow marker at the end of Whitehead Street, is a Key West landmark, establishing the spot as the most southerly in the continental United States. It also indicates that Cuba is 90 miles away. In the past a more portable sign—irresistible to souvenir hounds—was here until the townsfolk got fed up with having to replace it. They could hardly have thought up an uglier monument than the present one, yet no one passes here without stopping to take a picture.

As you will discover, all the surrounding streets have places claiming to be the "southernmost" hotel, motel, guesthouse, cafe, laundry, church, or whatever. Harris House, the large home occupying most of the block at South and Duval Streets, claims to be the **Southernmost House.** Built for a judge around 1905, it was a fashionable restaurant frequented by Tennessee Williams and his friends in the 1950s. It is now a private residence.

From here you can return via Duval Street and the art galleries, or, if you decide to skip the Southernmost Point, from the Hemingway House you could return to Duval as far as Angela Street and pick up the walk from Number (17) to (25) in reverse order.

Caroline Street and Beyond

For literary, theater, and architecture buffs, the streets east of Duval from Caroline to Angela have some of the finest houses in Key West. Most are private residences, but some have been converted to inns and stores, and many are the homes and haunts of famous writers, playwrights, and celebrities who have lived in Key West all or part of the year.

Curry Mansion Inn (17) (511 Caroline Street; 294-5349; 800-253-3466; www@currymansion .com). The elaborate Victorian house was built by Milton Curry, Florida's first millionaire, who made his fortune as a wrecker.

The rear of the house is part of the original structure built in 1855; the front part was added in 1899 when Curry married. The wide porch surrounding the house on three sides is one of its best features; the elegant design and details here and under the eaves are of special interest. The mansion was restored by the present owners, beginning in 1974, and includes the kitchen where the first Key lime pie is said to have been baked. The guest wing, added in 1989, houses the bed-and-breakfast inn, with fifteen rooms, each with private bath.

Among the many interesting features to note is the 1853 Chickering grand piano in the music room, which belonged to Henry James and came from his home in Newport. In a glass case in the library, you can see Ernest Hemingway's favorite big-game gun, a Westley Richards .577, with which he was often photographed. In the dining room, the gold-colored tableware is meant to suggest the original solid gold Tiffany service for twenty-four that Curry had made. Some pieces are on display at the Audubon House. Daily tours: $5. Hours: 10:00 A.M. to 5:00 P.M. daily.

Across the street (where there's a jewelry store) was the site of the **Tradewinds Club,** in which Tennessee Williams stayed.

Casa Antigua (18) (312 Simonton Street at the corner of Rose Lane) was Hemingway's first Key West pad and the place where he wrote most of *A Farewell to Arms.* Papa and his wife Pauline came to Key West in 1928 by ferry from Cuba after a voyage from France, having heard about the island from writer John Dos Passos, who joined them later. Key West's freewheeling atmosphere in 1929 is described by Dos Passos in his autobiography, *The Best of Times.* Casa Antigua was once an inn; now the large building is a private residence separated by a fabulous tropical garden and swimming pool from the owners' craft store, **Pelican Poop** (314 Simonton Street, 296-3887; www.peli canpoop.com), at the front. The gardens may be visited, but not the house.

Donkey Milk House (19) (613 Eaton Street; 296-1866). Built in the 1860s and occupied by the same family for more than 120 years, the house was saved from the Great Fire of 1886 by a US marshal who dynamited the nearby structures along Eaton Street. It is a good example of the architectural style known as Classical Revival in Key West and won an award in 1992 for its restoration.

There's a century-old Cuban rainwater vessel out front, now filled with plants; inside, the floors have Spanish tiles and hand-decorated ceilings dating from 1890. The owners live in the ten-room house filled with fine period furniture and open it to the public as a house museum. There is a small antiques shop on the first floor. Self-guided tours: $5; senior, $4. Hours: 10:00 A.M. to 5:00 P.M. daily.

Octagon House (20) (712 Eaton Street), a wood frame house built at the turn of the twentieth century by Richard Peacon, a grocery store owner, has been given its name because of its unusual multisided front. Angelo Donghia, one of the best-known interior decorators of the 1960s, bought the house in 1974 for $45,000 and renovated it. Six years later fashion designer Calvin Klein paid the princely sum of $975,000 for it—the highest amount ever paid for a Conch house up to that time. Now on the National Register of Historic Places, it recently sold for a reported $1 million.

On Peacon Lane, a small street facing the Octagon House, an abode at No. 328 is said to be the least altered of any Key West home. The kitchen in the rear is detached from the house, a precaution against fire seen in the design of houses in olden times. In the 1970s Henry Faulkner, an artist and every inch as much an eccentric as his friend Tennessee Williams, lived here with his goat, Alice, whom he often dressed up and took to parties. The house is now owned by the son of Bertolt Brecht.

Monroe County Public Library (21) (700 Fleming Street), in an art-deco-style building, houses a wonderful collection of old photographs, local historical documents, and genealogy records that researchers and other interested parties are welcome to use. The west side of the building opens onto a garden festooned with palms, acquired as a result of a benefactor who donated the money specifically for them.

Across the street, the twin Victorian houses (701 and 703 Fleming Street) with wraparound verandas were dilapidated when Jerry Herman of Broadway fame bought them in the early 1980s. After a superb two-year restoration, Herman sold the corner house and lived at the other. Herman's best-known hits were *Auntie Mame, Hello Dolly!,* and *La Cage aux Folles.*

Down the street, **Fausto's Food Palace** (522 Fleming Street) calls itself a social center and the town's oldest grocery store; and **Key West Island Bookstore** (513 Fleming Street) is the town's best for books about Key West and those by writers associated with the town.

Gingerbread House (22) (615 Elizabeth Street at Baker's Lane) has so much filigree trim it could be called the Wedding Cake House. The name would be appropriate because it was built in the 1880s by Benjamin Baker, a lumber-mill owner and builder, as a wedding present to his daughter. The house, which won a Preservation Award in 1995, was so well built that during a tornado in 1972 the structure was lifted 7 feet off its foundation but not damaged.

Around the corner the small, dark wood house at 709 Baker's Lane was the home of James Her-

lihy, author of *Midnight Cowboy* and *Blue Denim,* among others, in the late 1960s. He, too, was a good friend of Tennessee Williams. Note the stained-glass window above the front door.

Windsor Compound (23) (713–727 Windsor Lane). At several locations in Key West, groups of adjoining dilapidated houses have been renovated as residences for writers. The Windsor Compound has served as the winter residence for such important writers as 1993 poet laureate Richard Wilbur and Pulitzer Prize winner John Hersey, who wrote *A Bell for Adano* and *Hiroshima,* among others.

Farther along at Margaret and Angela Streets is the **Key West Cemetery,** where burials are in aboveground tombs, as in New Orleans. The cemetery is famous for some of the inscriptions on the tombstones; the one most often cited reads, I TOLD YOU I WAS SICK. Some of the deceased were buried with their pets. The gates close at sunset.

Burton House (24) (608 Angela Street). Philip Burton, a playwright, author, and Shakespearean scholar, served as headmaster at the Port Talbot School early in his career and became the foster parent of actor Richard Burton. The elder Burton bought the Key West cottage in 1974 and lived there until his death in 1995. Elizabeth Taylor was a frequent visitor.

Secret Garden (25) (1 Free School Lane; 294-0015). Immediately after 521 Simonton (across the street from the Heron Hotel) is Free School Lane, which leads to the entrance of Nancy Forrester's Secret Garden, the largest private tropical garden in Key West and jungle-thick with enormous trees, flowers, and birds. Hours: 10:00 A.M. to 5:00 P.M. daily. Admission: $6; private tour, $15 for a minimum of four people. Walking tours led by historian Sharon Wells and other guides depart from here daily at 10:00 A.M. Tours: $6 (294-8380).

Tennessee Williams House (26) (1431 Duncan Street). The famous playwright visited Key West for a few months in 1941, when he finished *Battle of Angels,* and returned frequently for visits. In 1951 he bought a modest house and had it moved from Bahama Street, a lane just east of Duval, to Duncan Street, about a mile to the east, for greater privacy. The one-story white frame cottage with red shutters was his home for three decades until his death in 1983. During those years he won two Pulitzers—for *A Streetcar Named Desire* and *Cat on a Hot Tin Roof*. Among the other plays he wrote here were *Night of the Iguana* and *The Rose Tattoo,* which was later filmed in Key West, with some of the scenes shot at Williams's house. The swimming pool has a mosaic tile rose tattoo on the pool floor.

Williams enjoyed playing the role of Key West's most famous celebrity during the 1950s and 1960s, appearing regularly at parties and bars and entertaining Gore Vidal, Truman Capote, and other famous friends. Williams, who was thirty years old when he first came to Key West, has been quoted as saying that he came because he "liked to swim and because Key West was the southernmost place in America."

Tennessee Williams Theatre (294-6232), at Florida Keys Community College on Stock Island, was built in Williams's honor. The center stages plays, dance, films, and concerts during the winter season.

Fort Zachary Taylor (27) (292-6713). On the southwestern end of the island (about a ten-minute bike ride from Mallory Square) stands a trapezoid-shaped fort, which was begun in 1854 and finished in 1875. During the Civil War it was controlled by Union forces who used it as a base for blockading Confederate ships. Buried under tons of sand and largely forgotten, it was restored in the 1960s, mainly through the efforts of historian Howard England. The fort has a large collection of Civil War artifacts. The grounds of the fort are a park with a large artificial beach and picnic areas, popular with families. Hours: 8:00 A.M. to sunset daily. Admission: $3. There's also a charge for bikes. Free tour of the fort at 2:00 P.M.

The Other Key West

Three miles from the pier and Mallory Square at the eastern end of the island along US 1 is another Key West, as different as the 150 years that separate them. A city bus connects the two, but unless you have a particular fondness for shopping centers, you need not bother.

East Martello (3501 South Roosevelt Boulevard, next to Key West International Airport). The historic brick-and-masonry Civil War fort is a National Historic Site. The East Martello Museum

and Art Gallery, located in the tower, holds a large collection of artifacts from the Keys and Key West. The second wing gallery features exhibitions that change monthly during the season. Admission: $6 adult; $5 senior; $3 student and child (under six free). Hours: 9:30 A.M. to 4:30 P.M. daily.

Thomas Riggs Wildlife Refuge (South Roosevelt Boulevard; 294-2116). Bird-watchers and nature lovers will find this spot to be a refuge away from the crowds. An observation platform provides views of Key West's historic salt ponds and a chance to see heron, ibis, osprey, and small wading birds. Phone ahead to be sure the reserve's gates are open.

Sports

Beaches: If you really prefer a day in the sun, Smathers Beach (South Roosevelt Boulevard) is a 3-mile stretch favored by sporty types. It's body-to-body during college spring break. Water sports equipment is available for rent. Higgs Beach (Atlantic Boulevard) is popular with gay men. There are shaded picnic tables and a snack stand.

Close to the port on the gulf, the Hyatt Key West has a postage-stamp beach and a pretty swimming pool. If you call in advance and plan to have lunch at its attractive restaurant, Nicola, you are not likely to be turned away for a swim.

Diving and Snorkeling: The water sports center at the Hyatt Key West arranges diving and snorkeling excursions. Key West Dive Center (877-243-2378; www.keywestdivecenter.com) has several departures convenient for cruise passengers at 10:00 A.M. and 1:30 P.M. for dives at two locations, for $90 with all equipment; $49 for snorkelers. Key West Pro Dive Shop (3128 North Roosevelt Boulevard; 296-3823; 800-426-0707) has daily excursions for snorkelers to advanced divers; instruction and equipment are available.

If you are not ready for diving but want something more than snorkeling, you might try Snuba, an apparatus attached to a boat that provides oxygen and greater range for swimming over the reef. Contact Snuba of Key West (Garrison Bight Marina, Palm Avenue; 292-4616; www.snuba keywest.com). There are three departures daily. Cost: $99 adult; $75 ages eight to twelve.

Fishing: Key West offers good deep-sea fishing in the Atlantic and bonefishing in the shallow-water backcountry on the north and west side of the Keys. Dozens of private sportfishing boats offer excursions on an individual or charter basis. Check out **Capt. Bill Wickers' Charter Boat** *Linda D* (City Marina; 296-9798; 800-299-9798; www.charter boatlindad.com), half-day charters $600, full-day charters $800; **Lucky Fleet** (Lands End Marina, Margaret Street; 800-292-3096; 294-7988; www .luckyfleet.com); or **The Galleon Marina** (619 Front Street; 292-1292; 800-544-3030; www .galleonresort.com), which has a water sports center. Half- and full-day charters are available. **Key West Fishing Club** (Garrison Bight Marina; 294-3618; www.keywestfishingclub.com) has guided fishing trips and charters. **The Saltwater Angler** (Hilton Resort & Marina; 296-0700; www.saltwater angler.com) offers professional guides for flats and offshore fishing; thirty licensed and insured boat captains. Half-day $400 to $700, depending on the type of fishing. Hours: 9:00 A.M. to 9:00 P.M. daily.

Golf Key West Resort Golf Course: (6450 East College Road; 294-5232). The eighteen-hole course (6,500 yards, par 70) is located on Stock Island, about 3 miles east of the pier. Greens fees: $42 to $52. Call for tee times, carts, and club rental information.

Kayaking/Nature in the Wild: The north/northwest side of the Keys, known as the backcountry, is a region of shallow flats and mangroves that, for the most part, lies along the north side of US 1. Not easily navigable or accessible to major boat traffic, the area is largely untraveled, unspoiled, and rich in plant and animal life. Kayaking is ideal for excursions here, and tours are available with guides eager to share their knowledge about the Keys' environment. Wildlife abounds; kayakers frequently spot roseate spoonbills, ospreys, great white herons, and even bald eagles. The flats support small lobsters, young reef fish, turtles, stingrays, and big predators such as sharks and barracudas. Guided kayaking excursions are available. **Outdoor Adventures** (5106 US 1, Stock Island; 295-9898; www.kayakthekeys.com) has a two-hour nature tour for $35; single kayak $35 half-

day, $75 adult, $55 child full day. Or **Adventures Charters & Tours of Key West** (296-0362; 888-817-0841; www.keywestadventures.com), which offers a two-and-a-half-hour nature kayak excursion ($35) daily at 10:00 A.M. and 2:00 P.M., and a full-day backcountry tour departing daily at 9:30 A.M. ($129, including lunch). **Sunset Watersports** (294-5500) offers two-and-a-half-hour boat excursions in the backcountry, departing at 9:00 A.M., noon, and 3:00 P.M. for $69 per person, two persons per boat. The company also offers kayaking and other water sports.

Dolphin Encounters: WILD About DOLPHINS, Inc. (P. O. Box 747, Key West, FL 33041; 294-5026; fax 292-1059; www.wildaboutdolphins .com) offers two four-hour excursions to the dolphin "playground" daily at 8:00 A.M. and 1:00 P.M. aboard the custom-designed vessel *Amazing Grace*, guided by Capt. Sheri Sullenger. Participants observe, swim or snorkel, and learn about wild dolphins in their natural habitat, as well as birds and other wildlife in the backcountry. Cost: $85 per person. Boat departs from Oceanside Marina (5950 Peninsular Avenue), a fifteen-minute taxi ride from downtown.

Sailing: Sebago Catamarans (328 Simonton Street; 292-5687; www.keywestsebago.com) offers catamaran sailing with snorkeling and kayaking. Excursions depart at 9:00 A.M. and 1:00 P.M. from Key West Heritage, at the end of William Street. Cost: $45. Discounts available on advance reservations. *Floridays* (744-8335; 888-733-5455), a 60-foot luxury sailboat, offers two snorkeling excursions daily, departing from the Hyatt Resort Hotel at 9:00 A.M. and 1:00 P.M. in winter, 9:30 A.M. and 2:00 P.M. in summer for $45; sunset, $35.

Shopping

Art and Antiquities: Key West has a lively art community and more than three dozen art galleries showing their works; most are on or near Duval Street and feature almost every kind of art. **Key West Art Center** (301 Front Street; 294-1241) is a nonprofit artist cooperative housed in a turn-of-the-twentieth-century structure where members, who must be local property owners, showcase their work.

Guild Hall Gallery (614 Duval Street; 296-6076; www.guildhallgallerykw.com) is a cooperative of local women artists. Gingerbread Square (1207 Duval Street; 296-8900; www.gingerbread squaregallery.com) is the oldest private gallery in Key West and represents many of the best artists. The Key West Art Gallery Association publishes a brochure with a map and brief descriptions of the specialty of each of its twenty-two members.

Candy, Coffee, and Wine: Jim Garrahy's Fudge Kitchen (Clinton Square) makes Key lime fudge, which you can watch being made in the afternoon and try a free sample, or buy a slice for about $10 a pound. Key West Candy Company (810 Duval Street; 292-1496) also has Key lime fudge. The Key West Winery (103 Simonton Street; 292-1717; www.thekeywestwinery.com) offers free wine tasting daily for its Key lime, mango, and other fruit wines, as well as Key lime and other products.

Clothing and Gifts: Bird in Hand (403 Front Street) features a great variety of crafts by local artists. Lilly Pulitzer (600 Front Street; 295-0995; www.lillypulitzer.com) is known for tropical resort wear. Jackie Arevalo (310 Duval Street; 292-3100; www.keywestbeadco.com) has custom-designed jewelry created by this Key West artist. Besame Mucho (315 Petronia Street; 294-1928; www.besamemucho.com) sells body care products and accessories. Kermit's Key Lime (200 Elizabeth Street; 296-0806; www.keylimeshop.com) sells Key lime sweets. Peppers of Key West (602 Greene Street; 295-0333; www.peppersofkeywest.com) has some 600 sauces from around the world. Purple-babydaddies Design Store (620 Duval Street; 292-7800; www.islandstylegalleries.com) sells funky, eclectic gifts, art, sculpture, jewelry, and other treasures from more than seventy-five artists. Club West Casual Wear (Clinton Square Market; 294-3864) has stylish, easy-to-wash cotton sportswear for great low prices.

Key West Aloe (Front Street; 800-445-2563) makes a full line of skin and body care products; Baskets, which is part of the store, makes up spice, candle, herb, and many other types of pretty gift baskets. Key West Island Bookstore (513 Flem-ing Street; 294-2904) has the best selection of books on Key West and its well-known writers. Arches (1208 Duval Street; 294-3771) specializes in African art and rugs, as well as furniture from Indonesia. Kindred Spirit (1204 Simonton Street; 296-1515; www.kindredspiritkeywest.com) is a bookstore-cum-tearoom.

Dining and Restaurants

Abbondanza (1208 Simonton Street; 292-1199). This moderately priced Italian restaurant, very popular with Key Westers, serves excellent food (huge portions) at reasonable prices in a very pleasant atmosphere.

Alice's Key West (1114 Duval Street; 292-5733; www.aliceskeywest.com) specializes in New American cuisine by famous chef Alice Wein-garten. Expensive.

Blue Heaven (729 Thomas Street; 296-8666; http://blueheavenkw.homestead.com) serves Caribbean and vegetarian soul food in an outdoor setting with huge shade trees overhead and roosters underfoot. (See No. 12 in the Key West on Your Own section for a description.) Inexpensive.

Cafe Marquesa (600 Fleming Street; 292-1244; www.marquesa.com) is one of Key West's top restaurants for sophisticated island fare in a chic setting. Dinner only. Moderately expensive.

Camille's Key West (1202 Simonton Street; 296-4811; www.camilleskeywest.com). A funky establishment that's been pure Key West for more than 20 years. Eclectic menus, posted on its Web site, change from time to time. Everything is cooked to order with freshest ingredients available. Moderate.

Croissants de France Bakery & Cafe (816 Duval Street; 294-2624) is a good place to take a break from sightseeing or shopping. Moderate.

El Siboney (900 Catherine Street; 296-4184) has won the hearts of locals for Cuban dishes, but we found only the black bean soup and price worth the long walk. Inexpensive.

Grand Café Key West (314 Duval Street; 292-4740; www.grandcafekeywest.com). Praised for its fresh seafood, steaks, and big martinis to be enjoyed in the courtyard or on wraparound porches while watching the passing Duval Street parade. Panini and sandwiches at lunch. Menus are posted on the Web site. Moderately expensive.

Hogfish Bar and Grill (6810 Front Street, 293-4041; www.hogfishbar.com). On Stock Island, the next island to Key West, this fun and funky eatery is totally old Key West in flavor. It may not be easy to find; ask locally for directions. The menu is mostly fresh fish; it's famous for its "KILLER" Hogfish sandwich. If you catch a fish, the restaurant will cook it for you.

Jimmy Buffett's Margaritaville Cafe (500 Duval Street; 292-1435; www.margaritaville.com). Enjoy "cheeseburgers in paradise" with a front-row seat on Duval for the passing parade. Music in the afternoon and evening. Moderate.

Louie's Backyard (700 Waddell Street; 294-1061) has been on everyone's favorites list for ages, no matter how disinterested the waiters are in providing good service. But then, there are great views of the Atlantic. Expensive.

Origami (1075 Duval Street; 294-0092). Often voted Best Sushi Bar by annual local award; other Japanese selections. Seating inside in air-conditioning or outside on the garden patio. Dinner only. Moderately expensive.

Pepe's Cafe & Steak House (806 Caroline Street; 294-7192) has served breakfast, lunch, and dinner for eons at surprisingly low prices. In season, Apalachicola Bay oysters are a specialty.

Pisces (1007 Simonton Street; 294-7100). Seafood is the specialty. Expensive.

Rooftop Cafe (308 Front Street; 294-2042; http://rooftopcafekeywest.com) in a pretty setting on the second floor overlooks Front Street and Mallory Square. The main dining room has sliding glass doors on three sides, left open for tropical breezes or closed for air-conditioned comfort. Its terrace is bordered by flowering plants and shaded by a large mahogany tree. Lunch is more brunch than lunch. Moderate.

Square One Restaurant (1075 Duval Street; 296-4300; www.squareonerestaurant.com). American cuisine and fresh seafood can be enjoyed in attractive surroundings. Lunch offers salads, sandwiches, and a few entrees; dinner is more ambitious. Menus are posted on its Web site. Being at the upper end of Duval, it's less crowded than restaurants closer to Mallory Square and the docks. Expensive.

Entertainment

After the sun goes down, Key West's nightlife lights up all over town with comedy and combos— rock, pop, reggae, soul, Cuban, country, and more. Key West even has its own brand of music— Conchtown rhythm, a mix of New Orleans jazz and calypso.

Unfortunately, cruise ships must leave their dock by 6:00 P.M.—that's part of the agreement the lines made with the city. But you don't have to miss out on all the fun, as some places, such as **Rick's** (208 Duval Street; 296-4890) and **Jimmy Buffett's Margaritaville Cafe** (500 Duval Street; 292-1435), get started with music in the afternoon, and others, such as **Sloppy Joe's** (201 Duval Street; 294-5717), never seem to stop.

The Bar at One Duval (1 Duval Street; 296-4600), a piano bar at the One Duval/Pier House usually presided over by Bobby Nesbitt—who has a way with Cole Porter—has a wide deck that's packed at sunset, and it's close enough to the pier that you could make a mad dash to your ship just before the gangway goes up.

Celebrations

January through April: Old Islands Days highlight the Keys' history and culture with Key West's House & Garden Tours, Art Fest, Literary Seminar, and others. A calendar of events is available from the chamber of commerce (Mallory Square/Wall Street).

April: A ten-day festival in late April celebrates the Conch Republic Independence, when in 1882 Key West declared war and seceded from the Union.

July: Hemingway Days is a week of activities to celebrate the birthday of Ernest Hemingway on July 21. The seven-day festival, rich in nostalgia for Hemingway buffs, includes Hemingway Look-Alike, short story, and story-telling contests; a writer's workshop and conference; a radio trivia quiz; and more.

October: Fantasy Fest, a ten-day event in late October embracing Halloween, is Key West's answer to New Orleans's Mardi Gras, with food fests, street fairs, concerts, an arts-and-crafts show, and more. You'll also find a Pretenders-in-Paradise Costume Contest, a Pet Masquerade and Parade, and other activities, capped by Saturday night's Twilight Fantasy Parade with fancy floats.

Sunsets

Key West abounds with wonders—both natural and created by people—but its famous sunset is something of both. Daily as sunset nears, islanders joined by tourists, young and old, arrive at Mallory Square pier. (Hotel desk clerks watch for the exact second the sun is to set and alert guests so they can go barreling down to see it.) Soon the place is alive with entertainment: jugglers here, tumblers there, foot-tapping music all around; a unicyclist wriggling free of a straitjacket; a gaily dressed young woman beating out a tune on a washboard. There is applause for not only the entertainers but the entire celebration. The applause grows louder when the Key West sun—that massive fireball symbolizing life—falls below the horizon.

Jamaica

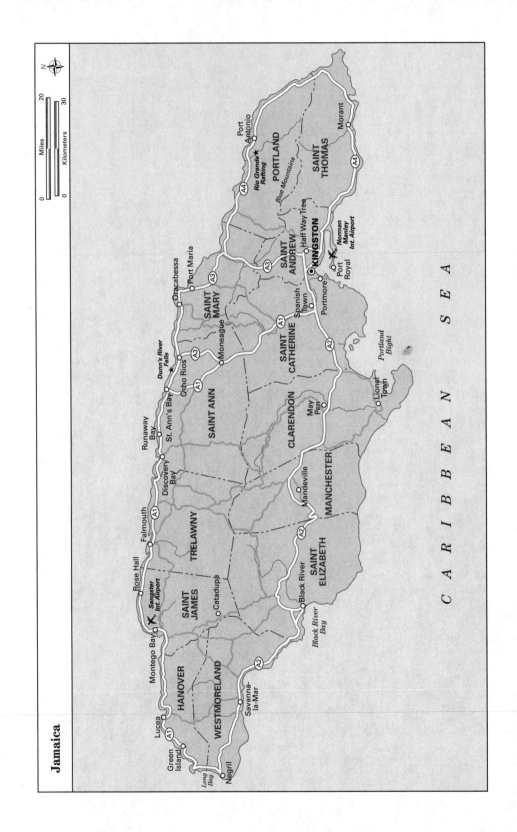

Jamaica

The Quintessence of the Tropics

How easy it is to fall in love with Jamaica! Awesome blue-green mountains frame its white-sand beaches and turquoise waters and cool the air of the tropical sun. Voluptuous hillsides decorated with brilliant flowers, forests alive with vivid birds, trees laden with exotic fruits, rushing waters, laughing children, gentle people whose voices lilt as though they were singing—these are the charms with which this Caribbean beauty seduces its admirers.

Jamaica, situated 90 miles south of Cuba and an hour and a half flying time from Miami, is the third largest island in the Caribbean and covers 4,411 square miles. Those who think of it simply as another Caribbean island are often surprised by their sense of being in a big country.

The impression comes in part from the thickly forested mountains, which rise to 7,402 feet at their peak and cut the north coast from the south. A further sense of space comes from the land's diversity and richness. More than 126 rivers flow down the mountainsides, and the tropical landscape nurtures 3,000 species of plants, including 600 unique to the island, and hundreds of birds. Indeed, Jamaica's name is derived from the ancient Arawak *Xaymaca*, meaning "land of wood and water."

A third, but more elusive, reason for Jamaica's aura of size is its distinctive culture, built layer upon layer from the Spaniards, who first plundered and victimized the original Arawak inhabitants, to the English, who colonized and exploited it, to the Africans and Asians, who worked the plantations or fled to freedom behind the mountains of the interior. Levantine traders, Christian missionaries, Rastafarian cultists, movie stars, polo players, novelists, Black Power advocates, Third World activists, and pop music superstars are all threads in its richly textured tapestry.

Jamaica's capital, Kingston, is situated on the south coast on one of the best natural harbors in the Caribbean. It is the commercial, cultural, and administrative center of the country, but not the tourist one. The tourist's Jamaica stretches more than 100 miles along the north coast from Negril on the west to Port Antonio on the east. It is dotted with resorts of all styles, where it's easy to be lazy under a bright Caribbean sun or active with tennis, golf, horseback riding, scuba diving, and a dozen other sports. More adventurous tourists climb the majestic Blue Mountains, camp along less traveled shores, and explore the river valleys and tiny villages of the interior. Near the coast, mountain streams rush headlong to the sea or converge in waterfalls under umbrellas of thick foliage and brilliant flowers—settings that are the quintessence of the tropics as visitors imagine them.

The Jamaican Discovery

Jamaica's history is as vivid as its landscape. It was first sighted by Christopher Columbus on his second voyage in 1494, whereupon its beauty led

At a Glance

Antiquities	★★
Architecture	★★★★
Art and Artists	★★★★
Beaches	★★★★★
Colonial Buildings	★★★
Crafts	★★
Cuisine	★★★
Culture	★★★★★
Dining/Restaurants	★★
Entertainment	★★
Forts	★★
History	★★★★
Monuments	★★
Museums	★★★★
Nature	★★★★★
Nightlife	★★
Scenery	★★★★★
Shopping/Duty-Free	★★
Sightseeing	★★★★★
Sports	★★★★★
Transportation	★★

him to describe it as "the fairest isle that eyes have seen" and to name it Santa Gloria. Unfortunately, the island was to become the scene of his most inglorious days.

On Columbus's fourth and final voyage, two of his ships were so badly damaged off the coast of Santa Gloria that he had to beach them at a protected cove that today is identified as St. Ann's Bay. Here Columbus spent a year awaiting rescue by other Spanish expeditioners in nearby Hispaniola. After his return to Spain, Columbus, having fought a long battle with the Spanish Crown to retain the land and titles promised him, was granted Jamaica as part of his family domain. To this day Columbus's heirs carry the title of El Marquis de Jamaica.

After Columbus's death in 1506, his son Diego became the governor of the Indies; from Santo Domingo he sent Juan de Esquivel, a former lieutenant of his father's, to Jamaica to establish a colony. Under him the town of Sevilla Nueva, or New Seville, was laid out in 1509, and other settlements were founded along the coast, particularly in the south, which the Spaniards found to be healthier. In 1523 they established Villa de la Vega, and twelve years later, abandoning New Seville, they moved their capital to the south coast. It was renamed St. Jago de la Vega; later, the English called it simply Spanish Town.

Arrival of the British

By 1655, when the British seized control of the island, the Spaniards had already annihilated the native Arawaks—estimated to have numbered between 60,000 and 100,000—through enslavement or disease and had replaced them with African slaves. The Spaniards fled to nearby Cuba, but their slaves took to the mountains and continued fighting; they became known as the Maroons, from the Spanish *cimarron*, wild. The British were unable to defeat them and finally made an agreement enabling the Maroons to stay in the mountains with a certain autonomy in exchange for peace.

Unfortunately, British rule was no better than Spanish. Rather, the island became the base for the most famous and infamous pirates of the century, who operated with the blessings of the Crown to such an extent that Henry Morgan, one of the most notorious, was actually knighted and made a lieutenant governor of Jamaica. Port Royal, on a spit of land west of Kingston airport, became such a scandalous pirate's port that it earned the title of "the wickedest city in Christendom."

From a pirates' lair, Jamaica became an eighteenth-century center of the Caribbean slave trade where, it is said, as many as a million Africans were sold to the owners of sugar plantations that had been developed throughout the region. The British also turned it into a sugar colony of enormous wealth.

The Road to Nationhood

By the nineteenth century Jamaica had become Britain's most important Caribbean colony, economically. Great plantations of sugar, tobacco, and indigo, and later bananas, created enormous wealth for their owners—often absentee landlords living splendidly in England. There were uprisings by slaves and rebellions by freedmen—the separate mulatto class that had resulted from the unions between white men and black women.

In 1834 slavery was finally abolished, but that was only the first battle. For the next century every attempt by the freed slaves to improve their lot and to have a voice in government was dealt with harshly by the British governors in charge. A naive effort led by a Baptist deacon and small farmer Paul Bogle in 1865 at Morant Bay met such vicious reprisals that the governor was recalled. Soon after, Jamaica was made a Crown Colony.

By the 1930s, after the Depression had taken its toll in Europe and the Americas, Jamaica's struggle for freedom and independence entered its last phase, bringing to the limelight two men whose influence is still felt today. Alexander Bustamante was a leader of the trade union movement, founder of the Jamaica Labour Party, and the first prime minister. Norman Manley, a prominent lawyer, was the founder of the People's National Party and father of the nationalist movement; he also served as premier. In 1944 Britain accepted a new constitution based on universal suffrage and in 1962 granted the country independence.

For almost a decade Jamaica enjoyed a honeymoon as the darling of the Caribbean for winter vacationers. Investment money poured in, and resorts mushroomed along the north coast. Bauxite, which is used to make aluminum, was found in commercial quantities, and its mining brought new wealth.

But in the 1970s the wave of unrest that had swept across America in the 1960s washed ashore in the Caribbean. Norman Manley's son Michael, who proved to be as charismatic as his father, sought to chart a new course, and Jamaica became the focal point of radical change. By then, too, the oil crisis and worldwide inflation were taking their toll. Before long Jamaica, in its search for identity and direction, had alienated most of its allies, frightened away potential investors, and mismanaged its wealth to the point of destitution.

By October 1980 Jamaicans concluded that their country's youthful excesses had gone far enough, and they voted in the government of Edward Seaga. Almost overnight the atmosphere changed; confidence was reestablished, and the American-born and Harvard-educated Seaga—with some help from his friends—got Jamaica back on track. In 1989 Manley was returned to power and, having by his own admission learned from past mistakes, steered the country on a more moderate, prudent course. Now his successors are continuing the task of building a new Jamaica.

Lasting Achievements

Although Jamaica's road to nationhood has hardly been filled with sunshine, the country radiates creativity and artistic fervor and can point to a long list of accomplishments by its multifaceted society. In addition to the quarter million slaves who were retained in Jamaica to work the sugar plantations, the colony was a trading center that attracted large numbers of Europeans and traders from the Mediterranean. After slavery was abolished, a new wave of Asians arrived as indentured workers. Thus over the centuries Jamaicans became a thorough mixture of races, nationalities, and cultures from which has grown one of the Caribbean's most dynamic societies, influential throughout the West Indies in music, dance, and art.

For starters, Jamaicans have enriched the English language and made it sing with a soft lilt. And they have made music. Reggae, one of the most influential rhythms on the pop scene today, was born in Jamaica. It, too, is a mixture of folk, soul, and rock. The annual reggae music festival attracts musicians and fans by the thousands from around the world. In the arts, Jamaica has its own national dance company, national theater, national pantomime troupe, national choral group, national art gallery, and national crafts institute.

In a country so rich with history and natural beauty, so full of fun and pleasures, it will be hard to decide what to do during your visit. You cannot see Jamaica in a day or even in a month, but if you take full advantage of your time in this extraordinary port of call, you will come away with some idea of why it enchanted even the most blasé of men like Noel Coward, beguiled suitors as different as Errol Flynn and Johnny Cash, and looms so large on the Caribbean landscape that only excessive images seem to capture the whole of it.

Budget Planning and Other Practical Tips

Jamaica is one of the Caribbean's best vacation buys. The favorable exchange rate means that many local goods, services, and dining experiences are excellent values. Some things, however, can be expensive; the pattern for what's cheap and what's expensive is uneven. As a rule, anything imported—wine, cars—is expensive because of steep import duties, but locally made products—rum, beer, crafts—are cheap.

Car rentals are expensive—starting at about US$70 for the smallest economy car, plus $10 to $15 per day for insurance. Driving is on the **LEFT.**

Taxis are expensive, but when shared with friends or other passengers, they are the best and most economical way to see the island. When you hire a taxi, you usually get a first-rate tour guide and raconteur who will enrich your visit with stories and pithy insights, especially if you enter into the spirit of the occasion with conversation that shows your interest in Jamaica.

Members of JUTA (Jamaica Union of Travellers Association) are trained drivers licensed by the government to transport visitors, and their rates are set by the government. There are also unmetered city taxis. When negotiating with a driver, be sure to agree on the price before you get

Population: Three million; 800,000 people live in Kingston and its surrounding metropolitan area.

Main Cities: Kingston, Montego Bay, Ocho Rios, Port Antonio, Mandeville, Negril.

Climate: Jamaica has no winter. Year-round, the temperature along the coast hovers around 80°F but can go as low as 70 to 75°F between December and March, and up to 90°F from July through September. The rainy seasons are May through June and September through October, with short tropical downpours. Cool breezes from the sea keep the days pleasant, and mountain regions can be chilly in winter months.

Clothing: Lightweight tropical clothing is best year-round, but beachwear, especially scanty bathing suits (on either sex!), is not acceptable anyplace but at beaches and beachside hotels. You should wear a shirt or cover-up while strolling in town. Jamaicans find a too-casual appearance offensive. In winter be sure to pack a light sweater or jacket as evenings, even on the coast, can be chilly.

Currency: Jamaican Dollar (JDS or JD$). The current exchange rate fluctuates around JD$68 to US$1. However, US currency is widely accepted, and major credit cards can be used in most hotels, shops, and restaurants.

Customs Regulations/Departure Tax: Cruise passengers who disembark in Jamaica and return to the United States by plane must pay a JD$1,000 or about US$17 departure tax plus a new US$10 fee for tourism improvements. Normally, the fee is included in your plane ticket. US Customs will confiscate any fruits, vegetables, or plants from Jamaica. The only exception is flowers sold in departure lounges at the airports that have been specially packaged by the Ministry of Agriculture.

Electricity: 110 to 120 volts; 50 cycles.

Entry Formalities: No visas for US and Canadian citizens; however, a US passport is required for US citizens as proof of citizenship to leave and to return to the United States. A valid driver's license is necessary for car rental identification.

Language: English is the official language and spoken with a melodic lilt that is sometimes difficult to understand. Jamaicans also have a patois, incomprehensible to foreigners, and their colorful speech is peppered with a plethora of words and idiomatic expressions dating from English settler days.

Postal Service: Every port has a conveniently located post office where you can buy colorful Jamaican stamps as souvenirs or mail postcards and letters. (You can also mail them from your ship.)

Public Holidays: January 1, New Year's Day; Ash Wednesday; Good Friday; Easter Monday; May 23, Labor Day; first Monday in August, Independence Day; third Monday in October, National Heroes Day; December 25, Christmas; December 26, Boxing Day.

Telephone Area Code: 876. Each of the main towns—Montego Bay, Ocho Rios, Kingston, et cetera—has one or more different prefixes (92, 93, 94, etc.) + five digits.

Time: Same as US Eastern Standard Time, but Jamaica does not switch to daylight saving time and is therefore one hour behind Eastern time from April through October.

Vaccination Requirement: None.

Airlines: *From the United States to Montego Bay and Kingston:* Air Jamaica, American, Continental, Delta, Northwest, Spirit Airlines, United Airlines, and USAirways. *From Canada:* Air Canada. *Intraisland:* International Airlink (www.intlairlink.com), TimAir Limited (www.timair.net), serves Montego Bay, Kingston Negril, Ocho Rios, and Port Antonio.

Airports: Sangster International Airport (952-3124); Norman Manley International Airport, (888-AIRPORT); www.mbjairport.com, www.manley-airport.com.jm.

Information: www.visitjamaica.com.

In the United States:

Jamaica Tourist Board: (800) 233-4582; info@visitjamaica-usa.com. Office: 5201 Lagoon Drive, Suite 670, Miami, FL 33126; (305) 665-0557; fax (305) 666-7239.

In Canada:

Toronto: 303 Eglinton Avenue East, Suite 200, Ontario M4P 1L3; (416) 482-7850; (800) 465-2624; fax (416) 482-1730; jtb@visitjamaica-ca.com.

In Port:

Kingston (main office): 64 Knutsford Boulevard, Kingston; (876) 929-9200; fax (876) 929-9375; info@visit jamaica.com.

Montego Bay: Cornwall Beach; (876) 952-4425; fax (876) 952-3587; Sangster Airport, 952-2462.

Port Antonio: City Centre Plaza; (876) 993-3051; fax (876) 993-2117.

into the vehicle. Don't be shy. Ask how much your intended time or tour will cost, and add a 10 percent tip at the end (if you have been pleased with the service).

Do not buy cheap crafts on impulse; look around first, as there are considerable differences in quality and variety. And don't be afraid to bargain with craftspeople; they expect it. As a strategy for bargaining: You will be amazed how fast the price drops when you start to walk away. And don't be intimidated by the large numbers of "higglers," as the women street vendors are known, that greet you. If you have no interest in buying, say a polite "No thank you, not today," and keep walking.

Eat in local restaurants featuring Jamaican cuisine, which is unusual, delicious, and reasonably priced. In contrast, meals and drinks at large resorts can be three times the cost of local restaurants. Wine and drinks of imported spirits are expensive. Bring plenty of film. It is very expensive in Jamaica—more than twice what you would pay at home—and often hard to find.

If the goal of exploring on your own is to have a closer look and touch of Jamaica than you can get from a tour bus, you might find these tourist dos and don'ts helpful:

- The Jamaicans are Jamaicans and very proud. Please don't refer to them as "the natives." Nor are they happy to have strangers shove cameras in their faces. If you want to take candid shots, be discreet. If you want a portrait, ask with a smile. It's easy to chat and make friends with Jamaicans. Some are delighted to have their pictures made; others do not like it. Some will ask to be paid for taking their picture, especially if they are dressed in costume.

- As important as a 10 percent tip may be, a "good morning," a "thank you," and a smile are valued even more. Older Jamaicans, particularly, are almost courtly in their manner, and they very much appreciate your courtesy. Jamaicans have a delightful sense of humor. You can often get rid of a Jamaican peddler with humor faster than with anger.

- Don't leave valuables unattended on the beach, and on crowded streets watch your handbag and

wallet as you would in any US city. Despite what you may have heard about ganja, the Jamaican marijuana, drugs are illegal in Jamaica. Foreigners are not immune from arrest and imprisonment if caught with drugs.

Crafts and Duty-Free Shopping

Jamaica has never been considered a mecca for serious shoppers, but there are some unusual buys, especially in certain crafts and food products. Items to buy fall into two categories: those produced on the island and duty-free imports, which can run up to 30 percent lower than US prices.

In Montego Bay the best shops are in the hotel district around Doctor's Cave and boutiques in deluxe hotels. Most in the city center are not worth your time, except for record stores. In Ocho Rios, there are several shopping plazas—Island Village (www.islandvillageja.com) next to the docks, Island Plaza, and Taj Mahal—less than a mile from the harbor. They have duty-free shops, souvenir stores, and clothing boutiques.

Art and Artists: The most outstanding and desirable Jamaican products are original paintings and sculpture by contemporary artists who do not mass-produce their work. The best have achieved international recognition and are a source of national pride to Jamaicans. Among the most respected names are the late Edna Manley, mother of former prime minister Michael Manley, noted for her sculpture; 1940s artists John Dunkley and Henry Daley; and the late Kapo, the best known of the intuitive artists.

To learn about current exhibitions during your visit, contact the Jamaica Tourist Board offices (see Fast Facts). The art galleries on the north coast selling original Jamaican art and sculpture include, in Montego Bay, Gallery of West Indian Art (11 Fairfield Road, Catherine Hall; 952-4547; www .galleryofwestindianart.com) whose owner and artist, the late Liz DeLisser, is credited with discovering the brilliant self-taught wood carvers of Bunkers Hill. They turn out an array of whimsical-looking animals, which they paint in the vibrant colors of Carnival, thus creating a new form of Jamaican intuitive art. In Ocho Rios, Harmony

Hall (Tower Isle, Highway A-3, 4 miles east of Ocho Rios; 974-2870) is one of the country's leading galleries, dedicated particularly to discovering and promoting promising young Jamaican artists. The largest number of galleries is in Kingston.

Books/Newspapers: US newspapers are available at hotel newsstands, usually a day late. Hotel shops are also the best places to find books on Jamaica and Jamaican cookbooks. In Ocho Rios, Bookland in the Island Village and several stores in Island Plaza and Taj Mahal carry books on Jamaica.

Clothing and Fabrics: Jamaica produces some attractive men's and women's tropical sportswear. Colorful silk-screened fabrics made into daywear and eveningwear can be found at better-quality boutiques in the shopping center at **Half Moon Club,** east of Montego Bay, and at **Couples Swept Away** resort in Negril. Jamaica has a crop of young designers creating bathing suits and resort and daywear for the country's young professionals.

Crafts: Shopping for Jamaican crafts and products can be fun if you are not deterred by insistent hawkers. A great deal of the straw work is similar to that found in many Caribbean markets. Other products, particularly spices, woodcraft, and dolls, are more distinctive. Prices are lower at markets and from street vendors than in shops, especially when you bargain, but the quality is generally better in hotel gift shops and specialty stores. The Montego Bay and Ocho Rios Craft Markets have almost identical merchandise, making up in quantity and cheap prices what they lack in quality. There are huge selections of straw hats, baskets, place mats, floor and beach mats; carved statues, animals, bookends, trays, bowls, and masks; and T-shirts of every description. For something different, locally made oils for the body by **Starfish** (901-7113; www.starfishoils.com) are available at its shop in the Island Village in Ocho Rios and in specialty shops and hotel gift shops.

The best wood products are fashioned from mahogany and mahoe, the national tree, a variegated hardwood with a blue tint. These are most attractive when they are combined with a variety of woods into such products as trays and jewelry boxes. In Montego Bay, the best workmanship can be found in products on sale in shops at the Half Moon Club Shopping Centre; in Ocho Rios, at **Harmony Hall** and **Coyaba Garden Gift Shop** (www.coyobagardens.com).

The most unusual woodcrafts to blossom are whimsical, brightly painted animals carved from wood. They started with the late Liz DeLisser, an artist and owner of the Gallery of West Indian Art in Montego Bay, who has been credited with discovering the brilliant, self-taught woodcarver Obed Palmer and a dozen other carvers in the Trelawney parish village of Bunkers Hill. The craftsmen turn out an array of whimsical-looking animals, from lions to doctor birds and parrots, and paint them in the colorful and unlikely colors of Carnival—a pink-whiskered lion with red or green dots, a blue alligator with orange and pink scales, and so on. The figures represent a new form of Jamaican intuitive art and are carved from Jamaican cedar, which resists cracking and termites but is easy to carve. The gallery, now operated by DeLisser's daughter, helped Palmer finance the workshop next to his home, and DeLisser added her colorful artistry, helping to make the animals enormously popular. Now they are produced for shops throughout Jamaica and in other Caribbean islands, and they have even been featured at Bloomingdale's in New York.

From mid-November to mid-December, crafts fairs and Christmas bazaars are held frequently and are good places to find unusual gifts for Christmas presents, such as savory jams and pickles, handmade dolls, aprons and some clothing, and original art at very reasonable prices.

Groceries: A variety of Jamaican food products make excellent gifts to take home. In supermarkets and hotel gift shops, you can find PickaPeppa, a delicious spicy sauce similar to a barbecue sauce; Hellfire, another savory sauce; local spices such as pimento (allspice), curry powder, ginger, and jerk seasoning; and jams and preserves.

Some labels to look for are Busha Browne and Walkerswood, for jars of chutney and spicy fruits. **Walkerswood** (800-827-0769; www.walkers wood.com) has an excellent and extensive range of products, from canned ackee to jerk seasoning to rundown sauce. Its community cooperative, located in picturesque Walkerswood in St. Ann near Ocho Rios, was begun two decades ago as a simple effort to provide employment for the villagers. Now it has grown into a multimillion-dollar enterprise employing more than one hundred people and exporting its products to the United States, Britain, the Caribbean, and South America. Recently the company completed a new factory and visitor center where you can have a guided tour of its gardens and factory, and learn how to use and purchase Walkerswood products. On-site cooking classes, lasting two to four hours, are available with advance arrangements. Jamaican coffees are among the world's finest; pure Blue Mountain coffee, however, is also the most expensive. Blends and other brands, including High Mountain, are less costly. They are priced most reasonably at grocery stores, but *not* at shopping centers or airport boutiques. In Montego Bay, **Wesgate Supermarket** is open daily, and another supermarket, **Bodue,** on the outskirts of town, near the port, is part of a new shopping center that also has a good pharmacy, Fortana.

Jewelry: Gemstone jewelry, including coral agate from Jamaican riverbeds, black coral, and other semiprecious stones in handwrought settings, is available at some crafts shops. However, workmanship and design are unsophisticated. Duty-free stores have gold, pearls, and famous-make watches, but do not expect any of it to compare to the selections found in ports famous for shopping, such as Nassau or St. Thomas.

Liquor and Liqueurs: Among the best local products are Jamaica's fine rums and liqueurs. Appleton and Myers rums are bargains at US$8 per bottle, as is Tia Maria, the country's famous coffee liqueur. Lesser-known flavors are Rumona, Sangster's Ortanique, Blue Mountain Coffee liqueur, and a wide range of fruit-based rums.

Perfumes and Toiletries: Parfums Jamaica (11 West Kings House Road, Kingston 10; www.parfums-jamaica.com) makes a variety of fragrances for men and women that are sold in hotel shops and specialty stores. They are nicely packaged, inexpensive, and make attractive gifts. So, too, are the soaps and herbal oils by Starfish and Blue Mountain Aromatics. Both are available in gift shops and specialty stores.

Duty-Free Shopping

Procedures for duty-free shopping in Jamaica permit you to take all purchases with you except liquor and tobacco products, which must be delivered in-bond to your ship. In case you are asked, you must be able to prove you are a visitor.

Duty-free stores offer the standard brands of perfumes, gold jewelry, china, and similar products available in other duty-free ports. Shops with the best and most attractive selections are found at large hotels and resorts, such as the shopping center at Half Moon Club in Montego Bay and **The Shoppes at Rose Hall** (953-9718; www.rosehall .com), a new development that will eventually showcase thirty-one luxury and boutique outlets and a java house stocked with Blue Mountain coffees. Some other stores you might visit are **Chulani, India House,** or **Presita** (City Center, Montego Bay; Taj Mahal, Ocho Rios) for cameras and electronic equipment; the **Royal Store** and **Indian Shop** (downtown Montego Bay and Ocho Rios shopping centers) for china and crystal; and the **Swiss Stores** (The Strip, Montego Bay; Island Village, Ocho Rios; The Mall, Kingston; www .swissstoresjamaica.com) for watches and fine jewelry.

Cuisine and Dining

Of all the islands you might visit during a Caribbean cruise, Jamaica is the one waiting for those with an inquisitive palate. The country's unusual and exotic national dishes are found no place else in the region. The taste of Jamaica is an experience that inspires the African expression *nyam,* meaning "to eat happily and heartily."

For a morning refreshment, pick an odd-looking fruit from a street vendor balancing her supply in a colorful basket on her head. (She will also be a wonderful portrait in your camera lens—especially when you please her by making a purchase.) Jamaica is a cornucopia of tropical fruits and vegetables: Ortanique (orange-tangerine hybrid), mango, soursop, star apple, and otaheite apple are a few of the delicious ones awaiting you.

The traditional breakfast dish is saltfish and ackee. Ackee is an unusual fruit that looks like a red pepper growing on a tree, but when ripe bursts open to reveal large black seeds covered with yellow lobes. The lobes are boiled and blended with onion, pepper, bacon, and salted cod. This mixture is often served with boiled green banana, johnnycakes (fried flour dumplings), and bammies (cassava cakes). The flavor and texture of ackee suggest scrambled eggs and blend well with the fish.

For lunch and dinner Jamaican soups are rich and bold enough to make a meal alone. The tastiest are pumpkin soup (hot or cold); red bean soup; and pepperpot, a hearty blend of callaloo (spinach-like greens), crab, pork, coconut milk, root vegetables such as yam, and seasonings. Callaloo, yams, yucca, or cassava are among the most common ingredients.

Among the most popular dishes are escovitched fish, snapper or small reef fish fried whole in a spicy sauce of onions, hot peppers, green peppers, and tomatoes; rundown, which is mackerel or salted cod boiled in coconut milk and eaten with a mush of onions and peppers; and stamp and go, crisp codfish fritters eaten with a meal or as finger food.

Jerk pork or jerk chicken is to Jamaica what barbecue is to Texas—only different. The meat is cooked slowly for hours over an open fire of the pimiento (allspice) tree wood, permeating the meat with the particular flavor. Jerking, as this method of preparation is known, was a specialty of the Port Antonio area, and thirty years ago there was only one jerk place on the entire north coast. Now they are everywhere—a testimony to this dish's great popularity with visitors and Jamaicans alike.

Seafood is plentiful in Jamaica, including local peppery shrimp from the Black River area, lobster, land crabs, and a variety of fish from grouper to wahoo. But of all the selections, smoked marlin is fabulous—more delicate and delicious than smoked salmon. Like jerk pork and chicken, it is cooked slowly over a pimiento wood fire, giving it an unusual flavor. This specialty frequently appears on restaurant menus; you can sometimes buy it packaged in deli shops and supermarkets.

For beverages, Jamaica's Red Stripe beer is the perfect complement to local cuisine. There's Dragon Stout, too, and a variety of liqueurs. Ting, a grapefruit juice soda, is wonderfully refreshing.

Sports and Entertainment

Jamaica has some of the best sports facilities in the Caribbean for golf, tennis, horseback riding, and aquatic adventures. If you have the time, you could hike through forests in the Blue Mountains, raft down the Rio Grande in Port Antonio, troll for blue marlin and other gamefish a few miles offshore, practice the equestrian arts at Chukka Cove at St. Ann's Bay, or kayak between Old Fort Bay and Dunn's River Falls.

If your cruise ship does not offer packages or make arrangements for your desired sport, you must do it yourself. A word of advice: Call ahead or ask your travel agent to make reservations in order to guarantee space. This is especially important during the peak season from December through April and particularly for golf, diving, and deep-sea fishing charters.

The three-leg blue marlin tournament—an event that showcases Jamaica as a premier marlin location—starts in early September with a five-day international meet sponsored by the Montego Bay Yacht Club; a second leg two weeks later in Ocho Rios; and a third in Port Antonio in early October. For spectator sports, cricket is king here and the national passion of many West Indians.

Nightlife, Cultural Events, and Festivals

Although there are no casinos (only slot machines in some hotels and entertainment centers) or glitzy cabaret shows in Jamaica, there is plenty of after-dark entertainment, from beach parties to concerts and special events featuring authentic Jamaican folkloric dancing, music, and local food. Most night spots do not open until 9:00 P.M. or really get going until midnight. To learn what's happening, check the tourist tabloids, distributed free at hotels and restaurants.

Several popular Jamaican evening events highlighting the indigenous culture are held in each of the major resort centers. In Ocho Rios beach clubs such as Mahogany Beach (walking distance from the port) and Reggae Beach (less than 4 miles) have entertainment on some evenings and weekends. Check locally. Island Village, an entertainment and shopping center next to the port in Ocho Rios, offers a variety of entertainment daily.

Jamaicans have a wonderful expression for "feeling happy and alive," which they sum up with one patois word: *irie.* Any event can turn into a festival, whether it's a long weekend during a public holiday or a gathering of friends for a special event. But in the true sense of festival, Jamaica's vibrant culture, lively spirit, and love of music are most visible and infectious during Carnival in April, Independence Week celebrations in August, and Junkanoo at Christmas.

Junkanoo is a sort of Carnival celebrated with lots of music, parties, and street parades highlighted by colorfully costumed participants, masked dancers, and musicians. It takes place between Christmas and the New Year and arises from the tradition during slavery when Christmas was the only day in the year the slaves were allowed to celebrate.

Carnival, which started in Jamaica in 1990 with guidance from experts who stage the famous Carnival in Trinidad, borrows the traditions from Trinidad but has acquired more of a Jamaican character with each passing year. The main venue is Kingston, with mini versions in the resort centers on the north coast. It is usually held in April.

The prelude to Independence Day in August starts in July with a monthlong agenda of Jamaica's best talent in the arts, including dance performances, art exhibits, culinary fairs, and concerts. The country's far-flung sons and daughters return en masse from overseas to celebrate, and visitors are encouraged to join in.

Annually in summer, the internationally famous Reggae Sumfest (www.reggaesumfest.com), featuring top local and foreign reggae artists, is held in the Montego Bay–Ocho Rios area. The five-day event is attended by thousands of music lovers from Jamaica and around the world.

Introduction to Montego Bay

Whether they arrive by cruise ship or by air, many visitors' first glimpse of Jamaica is Montego Bay, the country's second largest town and center of tourist development for five decades. Immediately behind the town and coast rise green-clad mountains with whitewashed houses and flowering gardens in the kind of setting that has earned Jamaica its lush, tropical image.

Even though MoBay, as it is known, looks new, the town was first developed two centuries ago as a port—one of several on the north coast—from which sugar was shipped to Europe and other markets. Something of its past is retained in restored old buildings that house attractive restaurants and shops and historic mansions that are museums or hotel centerpieces.

Freeport, where your ship docks, and the entire waterfront area from the pier to Doctor's Cave Beach are the result of government and private urban development on land reclaimed from the sea. In addition to giving Montego Bay a new harbor, this has restored and expanded the beach areas to as much as ten times their size three decades ago. The town of Montego Bay divides conveniently into two parts: the town center or western portion, which is the first part you reach coming into Montego Bay from the port, and the tourist district or eastern side.

The town center is the business district, which includes banks, professional offices, stores, and some historic landmarks as well as industrious street sales ladies, called higglers, who peddle their produce and products in the marketplace. Here, too, pushcart vendors sell snacks, cold drinks, and ice cream to the loudspeaker blare of reggae and calypso from streetside record shops. The scene might not be for everyone, but it certainly is Jamaican.

The eastern section of town (approximately a mile from the Montego Bay Craft Market at Market and Harbour Streets) comprises the original tourist area of older hotels, congenial meeting and eating spots, and a wide assortment of shops. If you want nothing more than a golden day on Doctor's Cave Beach and a chance to sample Jamaica's water sports, you won't have to travel any farther than this area of town. Most hotels and restaurants and dozens of shops and craft vendors are located along the main coastal arteries of Gloucester and Kent Avenues; a few are perched on the hillside overlooking the town. Hip Strip, as Gloucester Avenue is known, is where the action is in the evenings. Dining choices range from finger food sold by sidewalk vendors to continental fare at chic resorts. At the **Pork Pit,** now located in the hotel area known as the Strip, you can have your first adventure in Jamaican food by trying jerk pork or jerk chicken, a popular Jamaican specialty.

The touring area of Montego Bay and its nearby attractions covers a 40-mile coastal stretch between Falmouth, 23 miles to the east, and Tryall Golf and Beach Club, 15 miles west of the town. How far to travel and how much to see will largely depend on which attractions—grand plantation houses, lavish gardens, the beach, or sports—have the strongest appeal to you.

East of Montego Bay along a coastal road leading to Ocho Rios, there is a series of luxury beach resorts and two of the most splendid plantation houses or "great houses" in Jamaica, both dating from the eighteenth century. West from the pier for 10 to 12 miles, you come to the fashionable resorts of Round Hill and Tryall Golf and Beach Club, whose centerpiece is an eighteenth-century plantation house. Farther west, the road leads to Negril, famous for its 7-mile stretch of beach and laid-back lifestyle.

Port Profile: Montego Bay

Embarkation: The cruise ship dock is 3 miles west of downtown in the Freeport area of Montego Bay Harbor, a deepwater pier with eight berths for cruise ships and cargo ships. A fleet of JUTA (Jamaica Union of Travellers Association) cabs, mini buses, and other ground transportation is on hand to take passengers the short ride to town or on tour. A Jamaica Tourist Board information booth is in the terminal to assist visitors. There are phones, fax, postal service, Internet access, and shops. On the west side of the terminal building is the Montego Freeport in-bond shopping area, which has duty-free stores—that's why it's called "Freeport." Unfortunately, the shops have been

sorely neglected, and poor-quality merchandise is often covered in dust. It's hardly a wonder that clerks in these stores seem disinterested and half asleep. We have complained frequently to Jamaican tourism officials about the shops, and we keep being told that there is a master plan to renovate and upgrade the whole area. In the meantime, my advice: Don't hang around the port. Take a tour or go to the beach. The shopping is better elsewhere.

Local Transportation: Taxis: JUTA (Jamaica Union of Travellers Association), the government-licensed, government-approved fleet, is reliable and has something of a monopoly at the docks. Remember, you can share the cost of a taxi with up to three people. From the pier to MoBay city center costs US$3 per person; to Doctor's Cave Beach, US$4 per person; east to Half Moon Club, US$26; west to Tryall Golf and Beach Club, US$35 for one to four persons. A sign in the terminal building lists all prices of taxis and tours to major destinations. No public buses leave from the piers.

Car Rentals: Bargain Rent-A-Car (800-348-5398; www.avis.com.ja), **Budget** (952-3838; www.budgetjamaica.com), **Elite Car Rental/Hertz** (952-4250; hertzja@cwjamaica.com), and **Island Car Rental** (929-5875; 866-978-5335; www.island carrentals.com) offer reasonable rates by Jamaican standards and have pickup service at the port if you call. As an example of prices, Island Car Rental in Montego Bay charges for a subcompact, standard shift, US$70; automatic, US$75; air-conditioned, US$80. Rates include unlimited mileage and insurance, which is compulsory. If you do not have a major credit card, you must leave a large deposit.

Major rental companies are located at Sangster International Airport, east of town (about 5 miles from the pier). If you want to rent from one of them, it is better to go directly to its airport office. Although the companies have pickup service at the pier when you reserve in advance, there could be a long wait, as rental companies are inclined to deal with their airport traffic first. Remember, driving is on the **LEFT.** It is imperative that you be an experienced driver. Jamaican drivers go slightly mad behind the wheel of a car and think the entire road is theirs—blind curves and all!

Emergency Numbers: Medical Services: Dial 110 or Cornwall Regional Hospital, 952-5100. **Police Department:** Call 119. **Ambulance:** Call 110.

Information: The Jamaica Tourist Board's main office at Cornwall Beach (952-4425) has extremely courteous and helpful staff and literature on local tours and attractions.

Montego Bay Shore Excursions

Cruise ships offer passengers many tour options and often have reduced rates for children. We have selected the most interesting, unique-to-Jamaica tours or those designed for a special interest. These excursions can be taken on your own by hiring a taxi or renting a car or by going on a tour. The choice between taking an organized tour and following independent travel should not be based on cost but on preference. Descriptions of places visited are given elsewhere in the chapter. The following prices are based on JUTA's published fees and may vary by a few dollars from one tour company to another.

Great House Tour: Four hours; US$25 per hour for one to four persons by car. Cruise ship shore excursion, US$42 for three hours. This half-day trip combines a tour of Montego Bay, a drive east of town passing Half Moon and Rose Hall Resort & Country Club, and a visit to the beautifully restored eighteenth-century Rose Hall Great House.

Scuba Diving: Three-hour resort course for noncertified divers; US$75 to $100, includes equipment and instruction at a hotel pool, followed by an open-water dive with an instructor. For certified divers, MoBay has good licensed dive operators. You may need to make your own arrangements in advance, although more cruise ships are offering diving excursions. Most morning trips are four-hour, two-tank dives that depart between 8:30 and 9:00; afternoon trips are two-hour, one-tank dives that leave at 2:00.

Martha Brae River Rafting: Four hours; US$45 per person. Cruise ship excursion, US$69 to $80 including transportation. Four miles upstream on the Martha Brae River, 23 miles east of Montego Bay, you board a 15-foot bamboo raft, skillfully maneuvered by a Jamaican helmsman, for a relaxing hour's meander downstream through lush riverside vegetation.

Negril Beach Tour: Eight hours; US$30 to $50 per person. A one-and-a-half-hour motorcoach drive west of Montego Bay through some of Jamaica's loveliest coastline to Negril, famous for its 7-mile beach of Caribbean beauty. The tour is for those who have visited Jamaica before and have never been to Negril. Cruise ship excursion US$59 to $79 with lunch.

Semi-submersible: One hour; US$60 per person. See the Montego Bay Marine Park description in the Sports section later in this chapter.

Golf: See the Sports section later in the chapter. As a cruise ship shore excursion, golfing at Half Moon, 12 miles east of Montego Bay, is US$90 for nine holes; $150 for eighteen holes, nonguests.

Day Cruises: Up to four hours; about US$40 to $60 per person. Cruises depart from Pier One Marina (Howard Cook Highway) and include reef snorkeling, light lunch, and drinks.

Horseback Riding and Swim: Three hours; US$69 to $80 per person. A mountain-to-sea adventure, riding through old sugar estates to the Caribbean Sea for a ride in the water. Cruise ship tour US$99.

Canopy Excursions: See the description under A Drive West of Montego Bay later in this chapter.

Biking: See Sports later in the chapter for companies offering biking tours and rentals.

Montego Bay on Your Own

A Walk Around Montego Bay

Montego Bay is not a walker's joy in the way Nassau and Old San Juan are, as there is little of its historic past left to see. Yet the old town is not without interest, particularly for people-watchers. Start with a brief taxi tour of Montego Bay to decide which part of town, if any, to explore on foot. Montego Bay is a maze of streets, particularly in the area of Fort and Gloucester Streets, and can be confusing. Fort Street turns into Queen's Drive and curves up a hill to inland hotels and restaurants overlooking the bay. It's not a walk but a hike, and it's hard going under the warm Jamaican sun. We don't suggest it.

Fort Montego: At the roundabout on Harbour Drive (1 block south of Howard Cook Highway) at the base of Miranda Hill are the ruins of Fort Montego, built in 1752, which still has three of its original seventeen cannons pointed seaward. To the south, all roads merge into St. James Street (sometimes shown on maps as Barnett Street), the main road through downtown that leads to Sam Sharpe Square, the town square.

Sam Sharpe Square: The square, a miniature version of the Parade in Kingston, is named for Jamaican hero Sam Sharpe, who was hanged by the British for leading a slave revolt in 1831. It has become traditional in recent years for candidates for national political office to launch their campaigns here. The square is centered on a white-painted, bronze fountain dating from the early 1900s. On the south side, a tableau of five bronze statues by Jamaican sculptor Kay Sullivan depicts Sharpe, Bible in hand, preaching to his followers. At the southeast corner, a very small eighteenth-century building called "the Cage" was once a prison for runaway slaves. It now houses a travel agency.

The Town House: Church Street, which crosses St. James Street on the west of the square, has two fine old buildings. The Town House is a Georgian structure built as a private residence in 1765 by David Morgan, a wealthy merchant. It has been a church manse, a Masonic Lodge, a warehouse, and a lawyer's office, and it served as Montego Bay's first synagogue.

St. James Parish Church: Across from the Town House is the beautifully restored St. James Parish Church, established in 1782, which contains ornate monuments erected by wealthy sugar barons. Several nearby streets have nice old balconied houses, which may be interesting to photograph.

Georgian Court: Another block south, at 2 Orange Street, are two restored eighteenth-century town houses connected by a courtyard.

One block east at Union Street you can turn south to the City Center, a group of duty-free shops with a limited but well-priced selection of standard goods and souvenir shops with low-quality merchandise. Unless you are an incurable shopper, your time can be better spent elsewhere. One exception is record stores that carry reggae and other West Indian recordings.

Montego Bay Crafts Market: You should return to the foot of Market Street and the Crafts Market. You can easily spend an hour or so poking around the dozens of crafts stalls and haggling with vendors, but you will quickly discover that most of the stalls sell the same merchandise, and unfortunately very little is of high quality. The stall keepers will vie insistently for your attention, but do not feel under any pressure to buy. Here you can have a tropical-print shirt tailored in a few hours. There is a refreshment stand with shaded tables where you can take a break from your walk.

Walter Fletcher Beach: East of the market, Walter Fletcher Beach, a large public park, has good facilities, tennis courts, and clean, protected waters. Entrance fee: US$5 adult; $3 child. Aqua-Sol Theme Park (979-9447; www.aquasoljamaica.com) is the concessionaire that operates the water sports and other facilities here. The Fish restaurant anchors the east end of the beach.

A Drive Around Montego Bay

A taxi tour of Montego Bay and its environs should be about US$75 to $100 for a half day or US$150 for a full day for up to four people. Agree on the price before you depart.

Richmond Hill: To get your bearings, Richmond Hill Inn offers a splendid panoramic view of Montego Bay. You will come back down from that lofty perch along Union Street through the downtown marketplace area. Before turning onto Gloucester Avenue to continue to the eastern beach and hotel strip, you pass the sprawling Montego Bay Crafts Market.

Doctor's Cave Beach: One mile east on Gloucester Avenue, a main thoroughfare, brings you to Doctor's Cave Beach, the heart of the tourist area. It's the prettiest beach in the MoBay area. There are a bar and snack counter, water sports, changing facilities, Internet cafe, and entertainment. There is a small entrance fee. A short distance beyond is Cornwall Beach, where the Tourist Board's office is located. It, too, is a nice beach with facilities and water sports.

A Drive East of Montego Bay

Golf, Great Houses, and Rafting

If you rent a car rather than hire a taxi and guide, you should familiarize yourself with a good map first. Maps published by the Jamaica Tourist Board are available from the board's information offices. Be especially careful when driving through busy town streets. The pedestrian is always right. And remember, driving is on the **LEFT.**

Heading east on Gloucester Avenue, you must turn right onto Sunset Street, which will lead you to a series of roundabouts and Sangster International Airport. The road that passes the airport is the main coastal road, A-1. Two miles beyond the airport, the highway passes several resorts in the Rose Hall area and a cluster of duty-free shops and other stores selling low-quality goods. The Rose Hall Resort & Country Club reopened in November 2007 after a comprehensive renovation. Farther along you pass the Holiday Inn Sunspree Resort, where **Resort Divers** (953-9699; www.resortdivers .com), the main dive operation of the area, is based.

Half Moon Beach: After another mile or so, you reach the **Half Moon Club,** one of the leading hotels in the Caribbean. It is set on 400 acres of landscaped gardens fronting a mile-long beach—the prettiest and longest in the area—and has an eighteen-hole championship golf course and one of the largest tennis complexes in Jamaica. The **Seagrape Terrace** is popular for lunch, and there's a delightful bar by the beach. The **Sugar Mill,** another restaurant, overlooks the golf course. Half Moon's shopping complex, adjacent to the east end of the property, has sophisticated boutiques and duty-free shops. Most of the hotel's sports and restaurant facilities are available to nonguests and day visitors with prior arrangements. Reservations are also essential because the hotel enjoys a very high occupancy year-round.

Rose Hall Great House (953-2323; fax 953-2160; www.imexpages.com/rosehall). About halfway between Half Moon Beach and Rose Hall Resort & Country Club is Jamaica's most famous plantation house, Rose Hall Great House, a restored mansion with a majestic setting on a hillside overlooking the sea. Built around 1770 by John Palmer when he was the queen's representative for the Parish of St. James, the mansion was acquired in the 1960s by American millionaire John Rollins, a former lieutenant governor of Delaware, in the purchase of a huge tract of land for development. The plantation house was partially damaged in the 1831 slave uprising and unoccupied for more than a century, and it was a ruin when Rollins acquired it. He spent several million dollars to restore it as a museum and furnish it with art and antiques to re-create the grandeur of an eighteenth-century plantation house.

Named for Palmer's first wife, Rose, the mansion is even better known for the legends that surround his fourth wife and last mistress of the house, Annie, although there is little foundation for them in fact. Known as the White Witch of Rose Hall, Annie Palmer, whose ghost was said to haunt the estate after her murder by an unknown hand in 1833, was a beautiful English woman tutored in the black arts by a Haitian priestess. According to the legend, she poisoned one husband, strangled another, murdered a third, and handed out similar fates to a gaggle of lovers (often picked from among her slaves) before meeting her end—and she was only twenty-nine years old! Admission: US$20 adult; $10 child under twelve with a tour by

colonial-costumed guides, who embellish the stories of the haunted house with some imagination of their own. Hours: 9:00 A.M. to 6:00 P.M. daily; the last tour is at 5:15 P.M.

Nearby, the 427-room **Ritz-Carlton Rose Hall Resort & Country Club** has an eighteen-hole championship golf course designed by Robert von Hegge—the White Witch—a full-service spa and fitness center, and six restaurants and lounges, among other facilities.

Cinnamon Hill: Another side road past Rose Hall and the walled burial plot of the Moulton Barrett family leads to Cinnamon Hill Great House, the home of relatives of English poet Elizabeth Barrett Browning. The Barrett family was one of the largest plantation owners in Jamaica. The house

has been restored and belonged to the late American country-and-western star Johnny Cash, who visited Jamaica frequently. It is not open to the public, but golfers who play the Wyndham Rose Hall golf course pass the mansion on the fourteenth hole.

Greenwood Great House (953-1077; www.greenwoodgreathouse.com). Continuing east on Highway A-1, 4 miles past Rose Hall Resort & Country Club and White Witch Riding Stables, a turnoff on the right leads to another Barrett mansion, occupied continuously since it was built in the late 1700s by Sir Richard Barrett, a cousin of the English poet. In the 1980s it was restored and furnished with antiques by its present occupants and owners, Bob and Ann Betton. The most interesting aspect of the house is the Bettons' collection of antique musical instruments. Several pieces of furniture belonged to the original Barrett owners. From the second-floor balcony there is a spectacular view of the north coast as far as Discovery Bay, 35 miles away. There is a bar in the former kitchen and a gift shop. Outside in the garden is a collection of old carriages. Admission: US$12 adult; $6 child, includes a tour. Hours: 9:00 A.M. to 6:00 P.M. daily.

Although these are the most famous historic houses, the north coast of Jamaica has a wealth of lovely old homes and historic buildings. In her book *Jamaican Houses: A Vanishing Legacy*, artist Anghelen Arrington Phillips includes fine sketches of forty such structures.

Falmouth: Built as the capital of Trelawny Parish at the height of the area's sugar-growing prosperity, Falmouth, 23 miles east of MoBay, has a significant group of historic structures dating from the late eighteenth century. Today, the town is part of the National Trust and preserves Jamaica's Georgian heritage. The most significant buildings are on Market Street west of Water Square. The **post office** is a particularly well-proportioned structure with fine details, and the brick house at 21 Duke Street is considered the best example of the early Georgian style. Falmouth has been used several times as a movie set.

Jamaica's newest attraction, the Outameni Experience, which was launched in September 2007, is an interactive journey through 500 years of Jamaican history and culture. Located in Trelawny, the attraction, eleven years in the making, is the concept of Jamaican film producer, Lennie Little-White.

Martha Brae River (954-5168; www.jamaica rafting.com). Falmouth is near the Martha Brae River, the town's water source and the venue for a river-rafting excursion. Signs on the highway point to the turnoff to the **Rafter's Village,** 4 miles upriver, where the raft trip begins. There are a restaurant, bar, swimming pool, and boutique. The raft trip operates from 9:00 A.M. to 4:00 P.M. and takes one and a half hours. You are driven back to the village at the end of the trip. Cost: US$45 for two people. A similar rafting trip, Mountain Rafting at Lethe, costs $45.

A Drive West of Montego Bay

Natural and Man-Made Splendors

Rocklands Bird Sanctuary (952-2009) From the pier, the drive west on Highway A-1 takes less than two hours to Negril. A detour at Reading goes to the Rocklands Bird Sanctuary and Feeding Station, home to large numbers of hummingbirds and many other bird species. The hummingbird species known locally as the "doctor bird" is Jamaica's national bird. The sanctuary is open from 2:00 to 5:00 P.M. Call in advance to be sure it's open. At feeding time—3:30 P.M.—you can have the tiny birds eating out of your hand. Admission: US$10 includes a guided tour along a nature trail.

Beyond Reading, you pass some elegant homes, many owned by foreigners who winter in Jamaica. The road crosses the Great River, where visitors can enjoy river rafting by day and, in the evening, a torchlit cruise upriver to a landing for a Jamaican dinner and entertainment. During the summer months, after heavy rains, the excursion does not operate. To inquire, call 952-5047.

At Reading, too, the road to Anchovy leads to Montpelier Plantation, where **Chukka Caribbean Adventures** (888-424-8552; www.chukkacaribbean .com) offers canopy excursions similar to those in Costa Rica and built by the company that created the concept. The excursions use a harness system of pulleys mounted in the trees that enables participants (supervised by experienced guides) to fly up to 1,000 feet between platforms high in the trees. Cost: US$80 per person. Try it! It's really fun.

Round Hill: After crossing the parish boundary into Hanover at the Great River, you will see the entrance to Round Hill Hotel marked by gateposts. Set on a small peninsula of ninety-eight acres in beautifully terraced gardens overlooking a private beach, the resort is one of the most exclusive and expensive in Jamaica. It was developed in 1953 by Jamaican entrepreneur and later director of tourism John Pringle with a group of investors who included Noel Coward and Oscar Hammerstein. Hugging the cove in stair-step fashion are the villas, each built to the design of its owner and most with private pools and gardens festooned with brilliant flowers.

Tryall Golf and Beach Club: Four miles farther west is the magnificent 2,200-acre sprawl of Tryall Golf and Beach Club, created in a fashion similar to Round Hill. The main house, an eighteenth-century estate house, and forty-three palatial private villas are perched on a hillside. The rolling terrain of its eighteen-hole championship golf course, with an aqueduct and nineteenth-century waterwheel, serves as a backdrop for the villas, while flowering gardens, the Montego Bay coast, and the sea provide picture-window views. In addition to the wealthy homeowners who come for the winter season, both resorts have long attracted an array of international luminaries and celebrities.

Kenilworth: Beyond Sandy Bay to the west is the Kenilworth Estate, the finest sugar estate ruins in Jamaica. The factory buildings, impressive stone structures with Palladian windows and arched doorways, lie a mile south of the main road.

Lucea: Another 25 miles west is Lucea, once the main port and center of life for this corner of Jamaica during the heyday of the sugar plantations. Today it is an agricultural center for banana cultivation and molasses production. The town has several historic buildings, the most significant of which is the early-nineteenth-century **Courthouse.** In the restoration the cupola was redesigned and enlarged to fit the clock, whose face measures almost 5 feet. As the story goes, the clock was shipped to Jamaica by mistake and had been intended for the island of St. Lucia, 1,000 miles away!

Negril: Hotels and tourist facilities have been added to Negril in large numbers since it was discovered by the flower children of the 1960s when it was a small village. However, its natural beauty has been saved somewhat because no building can be constructed higher than the tallest tree. Negril is particularly popular for scuba diving and windsurfing; you'll also find also tennis, horseback riding, and an eighteen-hole golf course. The nearby region is full of lore and legend dating from the sixteenth and seventeenth centuries, when this coast was a pirates' haven. The new road from Montego Bay to Negril has cut driving time to about an hour and twenty minutes, depending on the traffic; this makes an easy day excursion for cruise passengers.

Other Sightseeing Options

The following tours depart daily from Montego Bay and cost about US$50 to $60. To join one, you need to contact the Jamaica Tourist Board in advance of your cruise to make arrangements, as most pick up participants at hotels by 8:30 A.M. In some cases passengers with prior arrangements can be picked up at the port. Alternatively, you can hire a taxi and tour on your own.

Barnett Estate (Bellefield Great House) (952-2382; fax 952-6342; www.bellefieldgreathouse .com). In the hills behind Montego Bay is the 3,000-acre Barnett Estate, with an eighteenth-century great house, the former home of the Kerr-Jarrett family and now a museum, and **Bellfield 1794,** an open-air restaurant in the plantation's old sugar mill. In the rustic setting with music by a calypso band, guests can enjoy tropical drinks and dine on Jamaican and European specialties. The 200-year-old estate, which has been owned by the Kerr-Jarretts for more than eleven generations, is still a working plantation producing sugarcane, bananas, mangoes, papayas, and coconuts. The great house, which has been renovated to reflect plantation life in the eighteenth and nineteenth centuries, has a dining room, master bedroom, nursery, study, boudoir, and parlor furnished with family heirlooms and mannequins depicting the Kerr family. The "Real Taste of Jamaica" tour includes a tour of the great house and gardens, buffet lunch, and live music by a traditional mento band.

Appleton Estate Tour (963-9215). Formerly a train dubbed the Catadupa Choo Choo, the excursion is now taken by a bus that travels south of Montego Bay, 40 miles deep into the mountains to the Cockpit Country, which was once the region of the Maroons, the runaway slaves and freedmen who fought the British to a truce that allowed them self-government. At the Appleton Rum factory, a guided tour concludes in the tasting room where many different products can be sampled by those over twenty-one years old. The excursion is US$59 adult; $37 ages twelve and under booked through the cruise line. If you travel to St. Elizabeth on your own, the factory tour is $15. Hours: 9:00 A.M. to 3:30 P.M. Monday through Saturday.

Seaford Town: In 1835, 532 Germans from Hanover and Weserbergland arrived in Jamaica as indentured laborers. Of the group, 251 were to form the township of Seaford, a 500-acre plot given by Lord Seaford from his 10,000-acre estate. After emancipating the slaves, the British colonial government made a policy of bringing European peasants to the island, ostensibly to create thriving communities that would act as both models and employers for the former slaves. But in fact, the new immigrants were to populate the countryside with whites and help keep the peace. The scheme was never a success, and the people who suffered most were the immigrants who had been lured to the tropics by promises of land and a new life in Paradise.

In Seaford Town disease, malnutrition, and migration to the United States reduced the population to one hundred within three years. Originally the settlers were to be given title to the land after five years; it took fifteen. Nonetheless, in the next 150 years the survivors scraped out a small living as farmers and became completely integrated into the mountain life of Jamaica. Among those in the first group was a teacher and minister who taught the children to read and write and began a church, which gave the settlement a sense of community that continues today.

In 1978 a minister, Father Francis, completed the **Seaford Town Historical Mini-Museum,** which tells the story of the immigrants and traces each of the family trees. In the same year, St. Boniface Industrial Training Centre was opened with the help of the German and Jamaican governments and German Catholic church. The center is a trade school for more than one hundred boys and girls from throughout Jamaica. Mission Medical Project, opened in 1981, provides a doctor and nurse for the area; a health center was added in 1984.

YS Falls (634-2454; www.ysfalls.com). Located in the hills behind Montego Bay, about halfway to Black River on the south coast, the beautiful waterfall cascades 120 feet in several stages into the YS River and is the centerpiece of a newly developed nature park situated on a 2,000-acre estate. There are food and picnic facilities and river swimming. **Chukka Caribbean Adventures** (www.chukkacaribbean.com) operates a three-stage canopy tour over the falls; the cost is $30. A stop here is now included on some cruise ship shore excursions. Open daily except Monday and holidays.

Hilton High Day (952-3343; www.jamaica hiltontour.com). A visit to Seaford Town is one of the stops on the tour offered by Hilton Plantation, which is situated on forty tropical hillside acres about 20 miles south of Montego Bay near Catadupa and Seaford Town. The excursion is organized by Norma Hilton Stanley, who returned to her native Jamaica after many years of living in the United States and has a genuine desire to show visitors the "real" Jamaica.

The trip leaves Montego Bay at 8:30 A.M. (passengers with prior arrangements are picked up from the cruise ship pier) for a drive up the mountainside to Mrs. Stanley's home, where you enjoy a Jamaican breakfast and a tour of the grounds with an explanation of tropical fruits, vegetables, trees, and flowers. It continues with a visit to Seaford and concludes with a Jamaican lunch at the homey retreat. The food is fresh and grown on the land and includes roast pig, the main dish of the luncheon. The tour returns by a different route through the Cockpit Country and is back in Montego Bay by 3:30 P.M. The Plantation Tour, including round-trip transportation and two meals, costs $52 when booked directly. Tour days: Tuesday, Wednesday, Friday, and Sunday. Those arriving at the countryside on their own can have lunch and the Hilton Plantation tour for US$25 per person.

In recent years a dozen or more similar plantation tours have become available—different ones offered by various cruise lines. For example, **Croydon Plantation** (six hours; US$69 adult; US$55 child; 979-8267; www.croydonplantation.com) is offered by Princess Cruises, and **Lethe Plantation** (four hours; US$54) is offered by Holland America Cruises.

Meet-the-People: The Jamaica Tourist Board has a Meet-the-People program through which visitors have the opportunity to spend time with a Jamaican host or hostess with whom they may share a common interest. It gives visitors a close look at the lifestyles and culture of the country. You can ask to participate at the Tourist Board's Montego Bay office at Cornwall Beach or sign up online at www.visitjamaica.com/meetthepeople. To ensure that someone with your particular interest is available, contact the US office of the Jamaica Tourist Board nearest you in advance.

Restaurants

Marguerites, Margaritaville, and **The Blue Beat** (Gloucester Avenue; 952-4777; www.margaritaville caribbean.com). Long MoBay's most popular restaurants, Marguerites has indoor/outdoor terrace dining overlooking the sea and fabulous cuisine for dinner only. Seafood is the specialty, but there are many other selections of creative, Caribbean-inspired dishes, pastas, and great desserts. It's a bit pricey for Jamaica, but worth it.

The second restaurant, Margaritaville, is open day and night and has several levels: One houses a casual, moderately priced sports bar serving sandwiches and snacks and a boutique; another features an open-air disco with live entertainment; and on the top level you'll find a wild-ride slide that winds three stories down to the sea. Margaritaville is also a stop on the semi-submersible, which takes passengers on excursions in the Montego Bay Marine Park.

Now there's a third member: The Blue Beat, a martini bar and jazz club by the same owners and located next door to the restaurant. The multimillion-dollar Blue Beat, with state-of-the-art lighting and sound equipment, features live jazz for four hours nightly, hosting established musicians as well as new talent.

The Groovy Grouper Beach Bar & Grill (Gloucester Avenue; 954-8287; www.groovygrouper .com) serves good local cuisine with an emphasis on seafood on the decks by the beach. Moderate.

Guangzhou (39 Gloucester Avenue; 952-6200) is a Chinese restaurant with a typical large selection of good Cantonese cuisine. Inexpensive.

Horizon (Ritz-Carlton Rose Hall; 800-241-3333; www.ritzcarlton.com). The top member of five restaurants at the hotel serves Jamaican-Asian fusion cuisine created by a Jamaican chef. The plantation-style decor in aqua and rose provides a cheerful atmosphere for the restaurant, which is made up of one large and two small rooms and an outdoor patio. Expensive.

Juici Patties (36 St. James Street; 979-3733; www.jucipatties.com). This islandwide chain is known for inexpensive Jamaican turnovers—the Jamaican version of meat or cheese patties.

The Pelican (Gloucester Avenue; 952-3171), the longtime favorite for Jamaican specialties, remodeled its interior with fancier decor and increased prices, but it's clean, comfortable, and convenient. Moderately expensive.

Scotchie's (east of the airport, near Holiday Inn) is an open-air barbecue pit serving some of Jamaica's best jerk meats and fish. Jerk, cooked slowly on a wood fire all morning, is ready by 1:00 P.M. and can be eaten here or carried out. Inexpensive.

Sports

Beaches/Swimming: The most popular beach in town is **Doctor's Cave Beach,** 3 miles east of the cruise ship dock. It has water sports concessions, shops, an Internet cafe, and a snack bar. There are changing areas and showers. A small entrance fee is required.

AquaSol Theme Park (979-9447, www.aqua soljamaica.com), at Walter Fletcher Park, is the closest-to-port good beach with clean, protected waters and water sports. An open secret is the nude beach at **Sunset Beach Resort & Spa** (979-8800; www.sunsetbeachresort.com), near the cruise ship dock. It's a private beach for the hotel's guests, but if you inquire at the front desk and ask to have lunch and use of the beach, you normally will receive permission.

Also at the Sunset Beach Resort & Spa is the Pirate's Paradise Water Park, opened in 2006. There are two 40-foot-high shooting waterslides, a 40-foot-high Pirate's Plank Bridge, Blackbeard's Lazy River, and Buccaneer Beach. Admission: US$60 for those over age eleven.

The **Sugar Mill Falls Water Park** (953-2650, www.rosehallresort.com) features waterfalls, a 280-foot thrill slide, lagoons, a lazy river, and three terraced pools. In the jungle garden you'll find a rope-and-wood suspension bridge, faux rock formations, and replicas of the aqueducts of the former Rose Hall Plantation. The park provides a variety of entertainment, including "dive-in" movies, live music, activities, and games as well as poolside food service at two swim-up bars. Admission: US$55 adult; US$35 child. In Negril the five-acre **Kool Runnings Water Park** (957-5400; www.kool runnings.com) features ten waterslides, an interactive children's play area, and a lazy river ride as well as three restaurants a juice bar, and a sports bar. More attractions are planned, including a rock wall and go-kart racing. Admission: US$28 adult; $20 senior (sixty-five-plus); $19 child (under 48 inches); under two are free. Hours: 11:00 A.M. to 7:00 P.M. Tuesday through Sunday; closed in September.

Boating: For day sails, snorkeling cruises, and boat charters, contact **Pier One** (Howard Cook Highway, opposite Craft Market; 952-2452; www .pieronejamaica.com). The *Calico* (940-4465; www.calicopiratecruises.com), a pirate ship, offers daily cruises at 10:00 A.M. with stops for snorkeling in the Marine Park. Cost: US$60.

Fishing: A half-day deep-sea fishing charter, with bait and tackle provided, for blue marlin, tuna, dolphin, and wahoo costs US$400 to $460; full day $780 to $800. Contact **No Problem Charter** (381-3229; fax 971-5601. Cruise ships can arrange charters. Cost: US$149 per person, for a minimum of four people for a four-hour excursion. A half-day fly and light-tackle fishing for tarpon, snook, barracuda, and dorado costs US$380. Contact **Salty Angler Fishing Charters** (863-1599; www.fly fishingjamaica.com)

Golf: For beauty, variety, and challenge, it would be hard for anyplace in the Caribbean to surpass golfing in Jamaica. There are courses within reach of major tourist centers, but for serious golfers Montego Bay, with five championship courses, is the undisputed headquarters. Call for starting times. All locations have clubhouses, restaurant-bars, and pro shops with clubs for rent.

East of MoBay, in the Rose Hall area, the eighteen-hole championship layout by Robert Trent Jones at **Half Moon Club** (7,143 yards, par 72; 953-3105; www.halfmoon.com) is characterized by lush, green rolling hills overlooking the sea. It has putting greens, a practice range, a pro shop, and a clubhouse restaurant. Greens fees: US$70 for nine holes; $130 for eighteen holes in summer and

US$90 and $150 in the winter for nonguests; cart fees are $25 and $35.

Cinnamon Hill Golf Course (6,930 yards, par 71; 953-2650; 800-822-4200; www.rosehall.com), the most unusual course, was rebuilt by well-known golf architect Robert von Hagge. The front nine stretch over gentle hills by the sea, but the back nine climb up and around steep hills and are as interesting as they are difficult. The fifteenth hole has a waterfall as its backdrop; the ninth and sixteenth holes are laid out around the ruins of an eighteenth-century aqueduct; and the fourteenth plays alongside Cinnamon Hill Great House, the home of the late singer Johnny Cash. Greens fees: US$125 for eighteen holes. Club rental $35.

The Ritz-Carlton Rose Hall White Witch Golf Course (6,859 yards, par 71; 800-241-3333; www.ritzcarlton.com) is Jamaica's newest eighteen-hole championship layout. Named for the famed storybook *The White Witch of Rosehall* by Herbert G. de Lesser, the course was designed by Robert von Hagge and Associates. It stretches across more than 200 acres of lush rolling countryside, with sixteen holes embracing views of the Caribbean Sea. The clubhouse has a pro shop, men's and ladies' locker rooms, and a popular open-air restaurant with a 1,700-square-foot veranda that takes in a fabulous view of the greens, the ocean, and the mountains. Greens fees: US$179 for eighteen holes for hotel guests and $199 for nonguests.

About 12 miles west of the pier, the eighteen-hole championship course of Tryall Golf and Beach Club (6,680 yards, par 72; 956-5660; www.tryall club.com) is considered the island's best, in terms of layout, play, and scenery. Greens fees: US$125; cart for two $27; caddie $15 for nine holes, $30 for eighteen holes plus tip. The course is often closed to nonguests in winter; inquire in advance of your cruise.

Horseback Riding: Available by reservation at the Half Moon Equestrian Centre (Half Moon Club; 953-2286; www.horebackridingjamaica.com) The Beach Ride starts with a ride through the Half Moon property and includes a deep swim on horseback. It is scheduled at 7:00 A.M. and 4:00 P.M. and costs $60. Riders must be over eight years old and under 230 pounds. There's also a tour at 9:00 A.M.

---

on the Mount Zion Trail through the countryside and Rose Hall Estate, about one and a half hours from the stable. The cost is US$40; riders must be over twelve years old. **Chukka Caribbean Adventures** (953-5619; www.chukkacaribbean.com) offers Horseback Ride 'N Swim, a three-hour tour of the countryside with panoramic coastline views, ending with a swim in the sea on horseback. Cost is US$69. Riders must be over six years old and under 250 pounds. In Negril, **Rhodes Hall Plantation** (957-6883; www.rhodesresort.com) offers two horseback-riding experiences. The forty-five-minute Mountain Ride (US$50) passes by a crocodile reserve, while the Mountain and Beach Ride (US$60), approximately two hours, ends with a deep ocean swim on horseback. Call ahead for reservations. Hours: Sunday through Friday, with rides at 8:30, 9:30, and 10:30 A.M., as well as 1:30 and 2:30 P.M.

Montego Bay Marine Park: A 15.3-square-kilometer shoreline preserve on the east side of Montego Bay is Jamaica's first Marine National Park. The preserve is home to mangroves, seagrass beds, and coral reefs and boasts some of the greatest coral diversity in the western Atlantic. In recent years these marine habitats have been severely disturbed by increased tourism, overfishing, and pollution. The marine sanctuary, together with the Blue Mountain National Park, is part of a project financed in part by aid from the United States.

Those who do not dive can enjoy the marine park from the comfort of a semi-submersible, available as a cruise ship shore excursion. If your ship doesn't offer it, inquire at **MoBay UnderSea Tours** (940-4465; www.mobayunderseatours.com). The boat to the sub leaves from Pier One at 11:00 A.M. and 1:30 P.M. except Wednesday. The excursion over the reefs is about an hour and costs $60.

Snorkeling/Scuba: The shallow reefs and drop-offs of Jamaica's north coast offer good diving over unusual underwater sites whose highlights are tunnels, crevasses, mini walls, and what Jacques Cousteau once called "some of the most dramatic sponge life in the Caribbean." Each dive operator has different names for the sites selected. *Do not* dive or snorkel with "freelance" guides soliciting business along the beach. Use only established operators, where you must show your certification card or take a scuba resort course before you can don tanks. **Resort Divers** (Rose Hall Resort & Country Club; 953-9699; www.resortdivers.com) is a PADI operator with shops in six locations on the north shore; it handles beginners and novices as well as certified divers. An introductory course is US$90; one-tank dive $45; two tank $80, including equipment. Snorkeling costs about $30 per trip with equipment.

Tennis: There are public courts downtown at Walter Fletcher Beach; otherwise, the courts available to cruise passengers are located at hotels. Most hotels in Jamaica do not charge their guests for the use of courts and give hotel guests preference over visitors, who must pay a fee. You should make arrangements in advance, particularly in high season.

Half Moon Club (Rose Hall area; 953-2211) has one of the finest facilities in the Caribbean, with thirteen courts, a fully equipped pro shop, and a resident pro. You must write in advance or call for court time; prices vary by season for nonguests. The hotel also has four squash courts; rental equipment is available.

Windsurfing: You will find the sport at all beachfront resorts on the north coast including **Captain's Watersports** (Half Moon Club, 953-2211) Cost: $30 per hour. Hours: 8:00 A.M. to 4:30 P.M. daily.

Introduction to Ocho Rios

By design and a great deal of help from nature, Ochi, as Ocho Rios is called locally, is a town created for Jamaican tourists as much as foreign ones. Situated on one of the widest, prettiest beaches on the north coast, Ocho Rios, a former fishing village, is said to take its name, meaning "eight rivers" in Spanish, from an English corruption of the town's Spanish name, Las Chorreras, "the waterfalls." There are waterfalls in town near the pier, and Dunn's River Falls, a dramatic cascade of 600 feet, is only a few miles away.

Ocho Rios is centrally located on the north coast within easy reach of three completely different faces of Jamaica, which is one reason for its popularity as a cruise port. In a radius of 20 miles, the beach-trimmed shore is punctuated by tiny fishing villages between major resorts, while the interior behind the coast is dotted with tourist-free small towns and hillside hamlets where Jamaicans earn a simple living from the land.

Separating the tourist coast of the north and the Jamaican's Jamaica of the south are the awesome Blue Mountains, where the famous coffee grows and where the wild forests are home to hundreds of exotic birds and butterflies, tropical plants, and flowers—many unique to Jamaica. The main highway over the towering mountains leads to Kingston, the capital and heart of the country's business, government, and cultural life.

Ocho Rios's location at the center of many varied attractions enables it to offer so many choices that you may have difficulty deciding among them. For water sports enthusiasts, boating, fishing, waterskiing, windsurfing, scuba diving, and snorkeling are all available at the public beach next to the pier from concessioners licensed by the Jamaica Tourist Board. For shoppers, there are crafts markets, boutiques with locally made clothing and other products, duty-free shops, and supermarkets for Jamaican spices, coffee, and other local goods.

For serious explorers, Ocho Rios's attractions stretch from Port Maria on the east to Discovery Bay on the west. Hidden in the hills behind the coast are exquisite gardens, bird sanctuaries, and working plantations of citrus, bananas, mangoes, and a host of other tropical fruits. The lush landscape and its natural beauty are the features that appeal most to visitors and easily convince them that Ocho Rios deserves its title as the Garden of Jamaica.

Port Profile: Ocho Rios

Embarkation: The cruise ship dock and Reynolds Pier (both used by cruise ships) are located on the western side of the town's public beach, anchored at the east end by the Sunset Jamaica Grande Resort and on the west by Island Village, an entertainment and shopping complex, at the cruise passenger exit. A Jamaica Tourist Board representative is on the pier to assist visitors. There is a bank on the pier, but you really do not need to exchange money. US dollars are accepted everywhere.

Upon exiting the terminal building, you will find fleets of taxis and tour buses awaiting cruise passengers. Those who are not on an organized tour will be bombarded by taxi drivers who want to be their guide for a tour. Prices are supposed to be set by the taxi association, but do not hesitate to bargain. If you don't want a taxi or tour, just smile, say "No, thank you," and keep walking. In addition to the facilities of Island Village next to the port, more public telephones, shops, restaurants, and the Jamaica Tourist Board office are in the Ocean Village Shopping Center on Main Street, a ½-mile walk east of the pier. Adjacent to the center is the Ocho Rios Crafts Market.

Local Transportation: Taxis: JUTA (Jamaica Union of Travellers Association) is the government-licensed, government-approved fleet, which sets and publishes rates that most companies follow. Remember, in Jamaica you hire the taxi and can share the costs with up to three other people. A taxi from the pier or Main Street to one of the nearby posh hotels, such as Jamaica Inn, is about US$10 one way.

Buses: There are no public buses from the piers. Jamaica has an intracity bus service between Ocho Rios and Montego Bay, but it is seldom used by tourists. Given the limited time most ships are in port, you are better advised to hire a taxi, especially if you have others with whom to share the cost.

Car Rentals: There are two problems with renting a car in Jamaica. First, Jamaicans pay extremely high import duties on cars and parts—thus car rentals are expensive. As an example, Island Car Rental charges US$70 for a subcompact with standard shift; US$75 for an automatic; and US$80 with air-conditioning; rates include unlimited mileage and compulsory insurance. Second, in high season there often aren't enough cars to meet the demands of hotel guests; day visitors may find no cars available.

Car rental firms in Ocho Rios have pickup service at the port if you have made reservations in advance, but do not be surprised if your car is not on hand for your arrival. If not, go directly to the rental office, as you could waste a great deal of time waiting for your car to show up. Two area firms are **Island Car Rental** (929-5875; 866-978-5335; www.islandcarrentals.com) and **Budget Rent A Car** (15 Milford Road, 974-1288; www.budgetjamaica.com).

Emergency Numbers: Medical Services: Tourist Board Courtesy Unit, 974-2570. **Police** Department: Call 119. **Ambulance:** Dial 110.

Ocho Rios Shore Excursions

The following tours are those most frequently offered by cruise ships and local travel agencies. They can also be arranged with a taxi driver-guide. Descriptions of the attractions are given later in the section. Tour length and prices vary from one tour company to another; those here are examples only.

Ocho Rios Highlights Tour: Four hours; US$45. Tour combines the area's main mountain and garden attractions: Fern Gully; Shaw Park Gardens or Coyaba River Gardens; and Dunn's River Falls, Jamaica's most famous natural attraction, where you can climb a waterfall and enjoy lunch and a superb look at Jamaica's lush flora. A three-hour version, US$35, is sometimes available. Because it's the single most popular tour in Jamaica, you will do your visiting in a crowd. Bathing suit and sneakers are a must.

Prospect Park Plantation Tour: Three and a half hours; US$40 (other plantations are toured as well). Journey by jitney (or horseback) through citrus groves and forests on a guided tour of a 1,000-acre working estate. An ideal tour to get the feel of Jamaica in the short time. (See the description later in this chapter.) When combined with Dunn's River Falls, cost is about US$50; as a shore excursion, $82.

Scuba Diving: Four hours; US$50 one tank; $75 two tanks. Divers must have certification cards. You can sometimes reduce the cost of rentals by bringing your own mask, fins, and snorkel. Trips usually depart at 9:00 A.M. for four hours and 2:00 P.M. for two hours. (See Sports later in this section.)

Art, Literary Gems, and Nature: Three to four hours. Several lesser-known attractions east of town make an interesting tour for those on their own. Harmony Hall (www.harmonyhall.com), an art gallery in a pretty colonial manor house near Ocho Rios, and Noel Coward's modest hilltop retreat Firefly are among those included. Nearby is the James Bond Beach Club (975-3663; www.island jamaica.com), a beach and entertainment facility with water sports and a restaurant that's open Tuesday through Sunday. There is an entrance fee.

Dolphin Cove: Set in four tropical acres at a natural cove next to the turnoff for Dunn's River Falls, Dolphin Cove offers three programs: Touch Encounter for US$67, Swim Encounter for US$129, and Swim with Dolphins for US$195. To simply browse through the lovely surroundings and see the dolphins costs $45 adult; $30 child under sixteen. Hours: 8:30 A.M. to 5:30 P.M. daily. (See Dolphin Cove later in this section.)

Kayaking: Three and a half hours; US$69 adult; $48 ages twelve and older. Excursions between Old Fort Bay, west of Ocho Rios, and Dunn's River Falls are available as a shore excursion that includes climbing the falls and transfer from the port.

Biking: Mountain-to-sea biking excursions are available from several companies for about US$60 per person. (See Sports later in this section.)

Tubing: Floating down the White River in a rubber tube is one of Jamaica's most popular excursions. The cost is US$60 adult; $48 ages six and older. (See White River Valley later in this section.)

Dogsledding: Two tours at Chukka Farm (888-424-8552; www.jamaicadogsled.com), home to the Jamaica Dogsled Team, include one-on-one interaction with the team dogs and either a demonstration or a 2½-mile ride. All the dogs are rescues from local animal shelters and have been professionally trained. A fully rigged ride with fourteen dogs costs $180; a demonstration is considerably less.

Learn to Cook Jamaican: Walkerswood Caribbean Foods (800-827-0769; 876-917-2318; tours@walkerswood.com), a community cooperative in a mountainside village about 25 minutes from Ocho Rios, makes a range of products from sorrel chutney to jerk seasoning. You can have a forty-five-minute guided tour of its gardens and learn how to use the herbs, dine at its clubhouse, visit its new multimillion-dollar factory and visitor center, and purchase Walkerswood products. Or, with advance arrangements, you can take a cooking class and learn to make some Jamaican dishes. Classes generally last three hours, and Chef Dennis will tailor yours to your interest.

Ocho Rios on Your Own

Be prepared! Cruise ship arrivals turn this town into a beehive of excitement. Like many Caribbean ports, Ocho Rios has a street-fair atmosphere when cruise ships are in port. Everyone in Ocho Rios—or so it seems—will be on hand along the main road to welcome you and try to persuade you not to leave town without taking their tour or buying their necklace, doll, hat, or the hundred other souvenirs they want to sell you.

Taxi drivers, mini bus tour operators, higglers, and crafts peddlers all jockey for the best positions to get your attention. Just smile and keep walking. If you can enter into the spirit of the affair, you can have fun, try your hand at bargaining, take some great pictures, and come away with attractive souvenirs at cheap prices. Some visitors find this exuberant salesmanship intimidating and others say it's simply irritating, but if you deal with such encounters as sport, you will quickly get the knack of enjoying Ocho Rios.

A note of warning: Ocho Rios has worked hard in the past several years to clean up its act. The great majority of entrepreneurs are warm, friendly, and trusting people, but as in ports anywhere in the world, there are hustlers among them not to be trusted and definitely *not* to be hired as guides. *Do not* go off by yourself in a rented car or on foot with anyone wanting to "show you a special place." They are hustlers posing as guides and could leave you stranded and cashless or worse. Licensed guides and taxis are just that—licensed. Authorized driver-guides wait near the pier, dressed in uniforms with the company logo clearly visible on their shirts. Anywhere else, you should ask to see their credentials. If you have any doubt about a

guide, you need only ask him to step into the Tourist Board Office with you. Or, if you feel you are being harassed, don't hesitate to ask a police officer for assistance.

The Tourist Board maintains a "Courtesy Corps" of men and women specially trained to help tourists; they have the powers of arrest, if that should be necessary. You can recognize them by their uniforms: black trousers, green shirts, and yellow lanyards—the colors of Jamaica's flag.

Meet-the-People: For a close-up look at the lifestyles and culture of Jamaica, the Tourist Board has a Meet-the-People program through which visitors can spend time with a Jamaican host with whom they may share a common interest. You can ask to participate at the Tourist Board's Ocho Rios office, Ocean Village; however, to ensure someone is available with your particular interest, contact the US office of the Jamaica Tourist Board nearest you in advance.

A Walk Around Ocho Rios

Downtown Ocho Rios, except as a place for browsing through shops and crafts stalls or sampling local restaurants, does not merit a walkabout. Your time can be better spent enjoying the beach and water sports or on excursions to interesting attractions in outlying areas.

Island Village: Designed to resemble a small Jamaican village, the complex is something of a theme park, entertainment and sports center, and shopping mall in one. Located next to the cruise ship pier and built primarily for cruise ship passengers, Island Village (www.islandjamaica.com) is the brainchild of Chris Blackwell, who is credited with Bob Marley's success. Island Village is intended to showcase the best of Jamaica. Entrance is free, but some attractions have charges.

The first pavilion (admission US$15) holds the first museum devoted to reggae, Reggae-Xplosion, with interactive displays of its history and best-known artists, and a branch of the National Gallery of Jamaica, with works by Jamaica's finest artists on display. The building also has the country's first digital cinema.

At the center of the complex is the Village Stage and Village Green, an outdoor concert venue with a capacity for 3,000 people where a variety of free, local, and international musical performances, as well as other cultural events, can be enjoyed daily. Other attractions include a casino, video games arcade with pool tables, and Internet cafe (US$4 for thirty minutes).

From here, walkways lead to colorful cottages housing stores, restaurants, bars, and attractions. There are duty-free stores for jewelry, perfume, cigars, and liquor, and specialty shops, such as Bookland, Cool Gear, and Island Trading Hemp Hut; Starfish Oils for Jamaican incense, candles, and toiletries; and others for Jamaican art, crafts, spices, and jams.

The ice-cream parlor specializes in tropical flavors; Veranda Blue cafe in Blue Mountain coffee; and Island Grill in Jamaican jerk selections. There's a photo shop, a Massage Hut with such treatments as "Soul Satisfaction" and "Hot Thighs" costing from US$20 for twenty minutes to $60 for an hour, and a salon for hair braiding and fancy nails.

Jimmy Buffett's Margaritaville (675-8813; 888-VILLAGE; www.islandjamaica.com), serving drinks and snacks, is Action Central all day long. Behind the restaurant is a small, white-sand beach with water sports. Basic entry is US$3, but for $15 you have use of equipment for snorkeling, kayaking, pedal biking, and more.

Probably the best thing about Island Village is that it has improved the port area with a clean, orderly complex and thus enhanced cruise passengers' first impression of Jamaica by all but eliminating the rush of vendors that in the past many passengers found so distasteful.

On Main Street, if you turn east (with the traffic), a five-minute walk will bring you to the Ocean Village Shopping Center and Crafts Market, and the public beach. Five minutes more brings you to the Sunset Jamaica Grande Resort, where there are shops, restaurants, and sports facilities. If you turn west at Island Village, you could walk about a mile to Dunn's River Falls and Dolphin Cove.

West of Ocho Rios

Fern Gully: Highway A-3 (a road perpendicular to A-1, the main coastal highway) is the main artery south of town. It winds through an old riverbed bordered by hundreds of species of fern. The lacy branches of the giant ferns and lush vegetation form a natural canopy over the highway, cooling and refreshing the air. The gully is also the first 3 miles of the road to Kingston, the capital of Jamaica.

Shaw Park Gardens (974-2723; www.shawparkgardens.com). Watch for the turnoff to Shaw Park Botanical Gardens and Bird Sanctuary, where you will need at least an hour to tour the pretty grounds and enjoy the spectacular view of Ocho Rios. The variety of indigenous flowers, trees, shrubs, and rushing streams and waterfalls makes this a popular photo stop as well. Guided tours every day between 8:00 A.M. and 4:00 P.M. Admission: US$10. Refreshments are available.

Coyaba River Garden and Museum (974-6235; www.coyabagardens.com). A garden 1 mile from Ocho Rios, at 420 feet, is named for the Arawak word meaning "paradise." The museum displays pre-Columbian artifacts and exhibits covering the island's history. There are walkways for strolling through the gardens to enjoy natural waterfalls, a gift shop featuring local products, and an art gallery. Admission: US$5 adult; $2.50 child, which includes tour and welcome drink. Hours: 8:00 A.M. to 5:00 P.M. daily.

Dunn's River Falls (974-2857; www.dunnsriverfallsja.com). The magnificent waterfall gushes from lush, wooded limestone cliffs along the inland ridge and cascades 600 feet over a series of natural stone steps to the sea. Surefooted tourists climb the rocks—in bathing suits—fighting the rushing water like salmon beating upstream. You can climb with or without an official guide. We strongly recommend a guide. The rocks are very slick, and the water torrents powerful enough to knock you off balance. Daily tours to the falls are available from all of Jamaica's main towns, including Kingston. Hence the falls are frequently crowded with visitors from not only cruise ships but hotels as well. The later in the day you go, the less crowded the area is likely to be. Admission: US$15 adult; $12 child. Hours: 8:30 A.M. to 5:00 P.M. daily.

The prettiest part of the falls, known as Laughing Waters, is private property where some scenes from the James Bond movies *Dr. No* and *Live and Let Die* were shot.

Dolphin Cove (974-5335; www.dolphincove jamaica.com). Located across the road from Dunn's River Falls, Dolphin Cove is set on a lush hillside by the sea and offers three programs. Swim with Dolphins, US$195, provides a close, one-to-one encounter as you swim and frolic with a group of dolphins, including the chance for a foot push or dorsal pull. Swim Encounter, US$129, allows you to swim in the deep for thirty minutes with one dolphin. Touch Encounter, US$67, offers landlubbers and children a chance to learn about dolphins and touch and enjoy their company.

Program times: 9:30 and 11:30 A.M.; 1:30 and 3:30 P.M. Reservations are required, and because the number of participants in the swim programs (you must be able to swim) is limited, you would be wise to book ahead.

Included in the entrance fee (US$45 adult; $30 child under sixteen for those not participating in a dolphin program) is a nature walk through the tropical landscape, where you see birds, tropical fish, reptiles, flowers, and dolphins at play. Kayaks and mini boats are available to explore the scenic coastline. Recently the facility added a stingray encounter program similar to the dolphin one.

Discovery Bay: West of Dunn's River Falls are three small villages that had big moments in Jamaica's history. Until excavations at St. Ann's Bay (1 mile west of the falls) in the 1980s raised doubts, Discovery Bay (15 miles west) was traditionally marked as the site where Christopher

Columbus first sighted Jamaica in 1494. The event is commemorated in a seaside monument and memorial park, built by Kaiser Aluminum, the principal company that once mined Jamaica's bauxite. The park has a sugar-refining display—a reminder of Jamaica's plantation economy for most of its colonial history.

On Columbus's fourth voyage in 1503, two of his ships were damaged beyond repair and were beached on Jamaica's north shore. Columbus spent a year on the island awaiting rescue—thus giving Jamaica the unique status as the only place in the New World where the great explorer lived.

New Seville: After Columbus's death in 1506, his son Diego came to the New World as governor of the Indies and from Santo Domingo sent Juan de Esquivel, a former lieutenant of Columbus's, to Jamaica to establish a colony. Under him the town of Sevilla la Nueva, or New Seville, was laid out in 1509. It served as the capital of the Jamaica colony until 1534, when it was abandoned for the new capital of St. Jago de la Vega (present-day Spanish Town) on the south coast. Excavations near the village of St. Ann's Bay uncovered the remains of a settlement and church dating from the fifteenth and sixteenth centuries; scholars have identified it as New Seville. Although silt from the sea and adjacent river has altered the shoreline in the intervening five centuries, authorities established the authenticity of the site from artifacts found in the excavations.

Seville Great House: About a mile from the site on a hillside is Seville Great House (972-2191; www.jnht.com), a nineteenth-century plantation house; nearby, an Arawak site has also been excavated. It is but one of more than 200 Arawak sites identified in Jamaica. History has recorded that Diego Columbus was the first in a long list of European explorers who succeeded in annihilating the Arawaks within fifty years of Columbus's arrival. Little remains to help scholars reconstruct Native life at the time the Europeans arrived or to understand the commingling of the two cultures. Admission: US$4 adult; $2 child. Hours: 9:00 A.M. to 5:00 P.M. daily.

Cranbrook Flower Forest (770-8071, www .cranbrookff.com). Just west of St. Ann's Bay is 120 acres set by a gentle flowing river with tropical vegetation and gardens. Here guests enjoy nature walks, birding, swimming, volleyball, croquet, and horseback riding. There is a museum of local history and a gift shop in an old sugar mill. Admission and garden tour: US$10 adult; $5 child. Hours: 9:00 A.M. to 5:00 P.M. daily.

East of Ocho Rios

East from town, Main Street becomes Highway A-3 and passes some of the area's best resorts in ravishingly beautiful settings. If your ship is in port on a Sunday and you are more in the mood for elegance than exploration, you should treat yourself to the luncheon buffet—complete with white-gloved waiters—on the terrace of the **Royal Plantation Resort** (876 974-5601; www.royalplantation.com) overlooking the tropical gardens and beach. But then, Jamaica has many settings equally as beautiful. You need several return visits to see them all.

Prospect Plantation (994-1058 www.pros pectplantation.com). Near the White River, a clearly marked road leads inland 1 mile to a working plantation and wooded estate covering 1,000 acres. Here you will see a great variety of tropical trees, shrubs, and flora typical of Jamaica and the Caribbean, and—unlike so many other locations—species here are labeled. The guides, too, are knowledgeable and make tours interesting and enjoyable, stopping along the way for scenic views of the coast, a lookout over the heavily forested ravine through which the White River flows, and a lane of trees planted by such famous visitors as Winston Churchill, Noel Coward, and Charlie Chaplin. The tour in a jitney leaves the tour center at 10:30 A.M., 2:00 P.M., and 3:30 P.M. weekdays; Sunday, 11:00 A.M., 1:30 P.M., and 3:00 P.M. Cost: US$32 adult; $15 child twelve and under; price includes drink and fruit sample. There is also hiking and horseback riding as well as a bar and shop for locally made products.

Harmony Hall (974-2870; www.harmonyhall .com). Beyond White River (4 miles east of Ocho Rios), Harmony Hall is a handsomely restored nineteenth-century great house of a small pimiento (all-spice) plantation, which now houses a fine-art gallery and **Toscanini** (975-4785), the area's leading restaurant, featuring seafood as well as Italian

cuisine for lunch and dinner. It is open daily, except Monday. The gallery (open 10:00 A.M. to 6:00 P.M. daily, closed in September) specializes in top Jamaican art and sculpture, quality crafts, antiques, and old prints. All works on display are for sale. The 1886 Victorian structure has its original stonework; its new gingerbread trim and balustrade were designed by a batik artist and produced on the property by local artisans. The art gallery has a representative collection of contemporary artists, including Jamaican primitives or intuitives, as they are called, and other young artists whom the gallery owner, Annabella Proudlock, herself an artist, encourages through frequent expositions year-round. Harmony Hall is particularly interesting for those who have not visited Kingston, where the National Museum of Art and major galleries are.

The gallery has a collection of prints and gifts mounted with miniature copies of prints by English artist Jonathan Routh from his popular book *Jamaican Holiday: The Secret Life of Queen Victoria*. There are also prints by the late Australian artist Colin Garland, who lived in Jamaica for more than thirty years and taught in the Ocho Rios area. Garland's paintings were so deeply influenced by his Jamaican environment that he was looked upon as a local artist and included among the Jamaican artists in the National Collection.

Farther east, Rio Nuevo is the spot where the British finalized their claim to Jamaica by routing the last of the Spanish forces from a stockade at the river's mouth. A small monument marks the battle site.

White River Valley (917-3373; www.wrvja .com). One of the newest attractions in the Ocho Rios area is an adventure park 7 miles east of town at the hamlet of Cascade. Set in the valley on 300 woodland acres, the park straddles the cool river waters that run for a mile through the property. Here, in this picture of serenity, you can spend the day enjoying river tubing, mountain biking, horseback riding, hiking, and picnicking.

At the entrance is a manicured "village green" surrounded by stands of bamboo, lime and guava trees, and red ginger lilies, heliconia, and other tropical flora beside some colorful cottages of local style. They house the park offices, a juice bar, a coffee bar, a souvenir shop, changing rooms and toilet facilities, horse stables, and a restaurant with an outdoor veranda where you can dine on janga, a spicy soup made from crayfish fresh from the river, and other Jamaican specialties.

The most popular sport—river tubing—begins at the old Spanish Bridge, said to have been built by the Spaniards more than 400 years ago. Here guides instruct you on maneuvering the tubes and lead you throughout the excursion, never losing sight of their charges. The watery ride of about forty-five minutes ends downriver at an embankment with small thatched huts where you can picnic and where transportation awaits to take you back to the village square. Along the way you can enjoy the tropical scenery lining the riverbanks—if you dare take your eyes off the swift-moving river.

The entrance fee, which is waived with the purchase of an excursion, is US$10. Sports range from hiking with a guide for US$65 to river tubing, kayaking, biking, or horseback riding for US$60 (www.chukkacaribbean.com).

Goldeneye: At the next town, Oracabessa, a small lane leads to the beach and to Goldeneye Estate (975-3354; www.islandoutpost.com), the haunt of Ian Fleming, the author of thirteen James Bond novels. Fleming spent winters here from 1946 until his death in 1964, often keeping company with his friend Noel Coward, whose home is farther east. The estate is now privately owned by Jamaica's most successful music promoter, Christopher Blackwell, who is credited with helping to launch reggae superstar Bob Marley and others. The luxury villa is now a very expensive boutique hotel and anchors a seventy-acre beach resort community and the James Bond Club, a beach and entertainment facility with water sports and a restaurant.

Firefly (424-5359; www.islandoutpost.com). Farther east, a small sign directs you to turn south off Highway A-3 and up a winding hillside road, past modest homes and through lush vegetation to a lane lined with towering hardwood trees. At the end on a hillside overlooking Port Maria is Firefly, the cottage and refuge of playwright Noel Coward. The modest bachelor pad was donated to the country by his estate after his death in 1973. First renovated by the Jamaica National Trust and opened as a museum in 1985, it was leased in 1993 by Christopher Blackwell, who made extensive renovations, reopening it as a museum evoking its glamorous heyday of the 1950s, when the songwriter and wit entertained his friends—all the most famous stars and celebrities of his day.

Coward is buried, as he had requested, in the far northwest corner of the garden beneath a simple marble slab, protected by a white wrought-iron gazebo. The site was his favorite evening roost to watch the sunset and sip his brandy and ginger. The view from here is one of the finest panoramas in the tropics. Also on the property is a small limestone building, said to have been the perch of the seventeenth-century pirate Henry Morgan, the first to discover the site—apparently as an ideal lookout for preying on Spanish galleons. That's before he became governor of Jamaica and was knighted! Firefly is used for weddings and special events to augment the museum's income, but this is Blackwell's ode to Jamaica—a labor of love and some nostalgia: Blackwell's uncle had sold the land for Firefly to Coward, and his mother was a longtime friend of the playwright. Admission: US$10 adult, US$5 child. Hours: 9:00 A.M. to 5:00 P.M., closed Friday and Sunday.

East of Ocho Rios is the beautiful small town of Port Antonio. Even if you have a full day to explore the route east of Ocho Rios, you will not have time to see Port Antonio unless you eliminate most of your sightseeing en route, which we would not recommend. Occasionally, Port Antonio is a port of call.

Restaurants

Almond Tree (Hibiscus Lodge, 83 Main Street; 974-2813) has good local and continental selections, particularly seafood and soups, in a delightful setting of several terraces that spill down the cliffside overlooking the sea. The daily lunch specials are a good value. The smoked marlin is fabulous. Lunch noon to 2:30 P.M.; dinner 6:00 to 9:30 P.M. Moderate.

Coconuts on the Bay (Fisherman's Point; 795-0064), an Ocho Rios standby, has a new location by the cruise ship pier. It serves soups, salads, sandwiches, wraps, and a variety of seafood, steaks, and Jamaican specialties. Inexpensive.

Ocho Rios Jerk Centre (Town Center; 974-2549) is an open-air restaurant and bar, popular for jerk. Inexpensive.

Passage to India (Sony's Plaza, second floor, 50 Main Street; 795-3182) serves good, authentic Indian cuisine. Moderate.

The Ruins (Da Costa Drive; 974-8888; www.ruinsjamaica.com), extensively restored by the owners, serves Asian and Jamaican dishes at lunch and Mediterranean and Jamaican cuisine at dinner, in a romantic outdoor setting amid tropical gardens and a natural waterfall. Moderate.

Scotchies (Highway A-1, St. Ann's Bay; 876-794-9457). This new outdoor garden restaurant, across from Draux Hall polo grounds, specializes in jerk pork, chicken, and fish, as well as other popular Jamaican dishes, cooked on grills as close to the original method as to be found and in a delightful setting. It's about 5 miles from the cruise port, but worth the trip. Inexpensive.

Spring Garden Cafe (Ocho Rios Bypass Road; 795-3149). Specializes in seafood, offering a variety of preparations for conch, crab, lobster, and shrimp as well as vegetarian dishes. Situated on a quiet knoll about a mile from the noisy crowd of town, it has inside and outside seating and ample parking space. Moderate.

Toscanini (Harmony Hall; 975-4785) is the top restaurant in Ocho Rios, offering excellent Italian food made from fresh ingredients in an attractive setting. Open for lunch and dinner; closed Monday and September. Reservations recommended. Moderately expensive.

White River Ranch Bar Restaurant (974-6932), on the edge of Ocho Rios in an open shed, serves home-cooked local specialties such as steamed fish, chicken and chips, and fried rice. Inexpensive.

Sports

Beaches: Within sight of the cruise ship dock upon arrival in Ocho Rios is the public beach, one grand strand of white sand curving from Turtle Beach Towers Apartments to the Sunset Jamaica Grande. It is complete with water sports facilities, refreshment stands, and hordes of independent vendors eager to sell you anything from wood carvings to hair braiding.

More appealing is **Reggae Beach,** a ½-mile stretch in a quiet cove with a pretty natural setting 3½ miles east of town. Heave Ho Charters sells cruises on its catamarans and by land or water taxi to Reggae Beach on some cruise ships. Independent visitors are welcome for an admission fee of US$5, including one drink. The snack bar serves Jamaican dishes; lifeguards, first aid, changing rooms, and showers are available. It's not likely to be the quiet hideaway of the past, but it should still be a hassle-free beach with no vendors.

Mahogany Beach, a small beach in a cove with a small stream surrounded by low cliffs, is less than a mile east of town, a twenty-minute walk. A lifeguard is on duty, and security is provided day and night. The hassle-free beach is maintained throughout the day. The clear water, less than 6 feet deep, is ideal for novice swimmers. Water sports are available. There are showers and bathrooms, chairs and umbrellas. No admission charge, except Friday night and special events. The grill and bar has television and music. Hours: 9:00 A.M. until the last person leaves.

Biking: Mountain biking and combinations of biking and river swimming have become popular enough to be offered as cruise ship excursions. If you want to do it on your own, the excursions are offered by **Chukka Caribbean Adventures** (953-5619; 877-4-CHUKKA; www.chukkacaribbean.com), US$60 adult; $48 ages twelve and under, includes refreshments. **Blue Mountain Bicycle Tours** (15–16 Santa Maria Plaza, 121 Main Street, Ocho Rios; 876-974-7075; www.bmtoursja.com) offers guided downhill rides on mountain bikes Tuesday through Saturday for US$93 adult; $65 ages twelve and under, including transfers, brunch, lunch, and equipment. Nonbikers can be accommodated on the tour.

Boating: Heave Ho (180 Main Street; 974-5367; www.heaveho.net) has large catamarans for charter for ten or more people to go sailing and snorkeling, with drinks and barbecue lunch.

Canopy Excursions (877-424-8552; 888-424-8552; www.chukkacaribbean.com). A facility at

Cranbrook Flower Forest in the hills near Ocho Rios enables you to swing high above the treetops in a harness pulled on horizontal traverse cables, similar to those in Costa Rica.

Deep-Sea Fishing: Available at **Watersports Enterprise** (974-2151). Rates for boats with crew are US$350 to $420 per half day, including bait and tackle for marlin and other deepwater gamefish.

Golf: In Ocho Rios, **Sandals Golf & Country Club** (6,600 yards, par 70; 974-0119; www.sandals.com), which belongs to the all-inclusive chain Sandals, is an eighteen-hole course a few miles east of town. Greens fees: US$50; carts $40; caddie $17; club rental $12. At Runaway Bay, the course belonging to **SuperClubs Runaway Bay Golf Club** (800-467-8737; 876-973-7319; www.superclubs.com/golf) charges US$80 for eighteen holes, $50 nine holes; cart $35 and $23; club rental $14; caddie $16 and $11. Phone in advance for tee times, especially during peak season, December to April.

Horseback Riding: Chukka Cove Farm Equestrian Center (877-4-CHUKKA; www.chukka caribbean.com) is a full-scale operation with facilities for serious and recreational riders. The center offers tours through historic sugar plantations with a bareback swim ($73) as well as mountain trekking ($60). The farm also stages shows and polo tournaments throughout the year. **Prospect Plantation Stable,** 2 miles east of Ocho Rios, offers one- and two-hour treks through a working plantation. To reserve, call 994-1373 or contact Watersports Enterprise (Sunset Jamaica Grande). Another stable, **Hooves Limited** (972-0905; fax 972-9204; www.hoovesjamaica.com), offers guided tours through the countryside on well-trained horses. Its Rain Forest River Ride is for experienced riders. It starts at 1,800 feet, stops for a swim under a waterfall, continues along the river, and makes a second stop for another swim. Four and a half hours, US$100. Open 9:00 A.M. to 5:00 P.M. daily.

Polo: Regular polo matches are played at Chukka Cove (St. Ann's Bay) and at **Drax Hall Polo Field** (5 miles west of Ocho Rios). Chukka

Cove offers lessons at various times of the year, but to play in a match a visitor would need to phone (972-2506) or write ahead (P.O. Box 160, Ocho Rios) and include credentials information.

Scuba Diving: Good shallow reefs, tunnels, archways, and drop-offs close to shore make scuba diving interesting in Ocho Rios. Resort courses are available for beginners; boat dive trips require that participants have certification cards. **Resort Divers** (www.resortdivers.com) is a PADI operator headquartered in Ocho Rios. An introductory course is US$90; one-tank dive US$40; two-tank $75, including tanks and weights. Other water sports operators are found at the Sunset Jamaica Grande Hotel.

Tennis: Courts within walking distance of the pier are at the **Sunset Jamaica Grande,** which has four courts. Nonguest fees are US$8 per hour. Use of courts is subject to availability, and since it is a large hotel, the likelihood of finding a free court is not in your favor.

Windsurfing and Other Sports: Watersports Enterprise at the Sunset Jamaica Grande can arrange almost any activity you want. Windsurfing costs US$30 per hour; waterskiing US$30 per half hour.

Port Antonio

In the extravagantly beautiful tropical setting of this old port, it is easy to believe that if there is an Eden on this earth, you have found it. You will not be the first to have made this discovery, and you will be in very good company. Yet, despite the steady flock of admirers—all eager to help—Port Antonio always seems to be on the verge of a new day that never comes.

Port Antonio is the place where Jamaica's tourism began. In 1871 a Yankee skipper by the name of Lorenzo Dow Baker sailed out of Port Antonio with a cargo of bananas—introduced by the Spaniards three centuries earlier. When he sold them in Boston, he made such a killing, he returned to Jamaica, bought land, planted bananas, and began shipping the fruit to markets in the United States and Europe. From that enterprise grew the

United Fruit Company, whose name was synonymous with bananas—not to mention banana republics—for most of the twentieth century.

But Baker did not deal in bananas only. The ships that took the bananas north brought tourists south. They stayed at Baker's inn, the Titchfield Hotel, described in an 1898 guidebook as a "novel hotel admirably adapted to a hot climate."

Mitchell's Folly: The next Yank to fall under Port Antonio's spell was quite eccentric. Alfred Mitchell, a wealthy mining engineer, built a sixty-room palace for his child bride, a Tiffany heiress. As the story goes, the palatial mansion was painted white, white flowers filled the gardens, white birds flitted about the grounds, white horses filled the stables, and white monkeys played on an islet at the shore. But his wife refused to live in the fabled retreat, and it became—you guessed it—a white elephant.

In building the mansion, salt water had been used to mix the mortar, and as the salt ate away at the stone, the mansion crumbled. It became known as Mitchell's Folly, although Mitchell lived here until he died in 1912. Today, it is a melancholy ruin that looks like the ideal set for a Greek tragedy.

Flynn Estate: Over the years many others who came to Port Antonio were intoxicated by its beauty, but none as much as matinee idol Errol Flynn. Some say Jamaica was his only lasting love affair. Flynn happened onto Port Antonio in the late 1940s while cruising the Caribbean on his yacht, the *Zacca.* A sudden storm forced him to change course and head for the nearest shelter. When he saw the twin-harbored port, he apparently was so taken with it that he bought Navy Island, an islet at the entrance to the harbor; the Titchfield Hotel; and 2,000 acres of a coconut plantation and cattle ranch. He then set out to create his Eden. But the famous actor died before he could realize the dream house and the other projects he had in mind. His widow, Patrice Wymore, still lives on the estate, which is now a working plantation.

Rafting on the Rio Grande (993-5778). Errol Flynn left another legacy that will never die. Rafting on the Rio Grande had been a Port Antonio pastime since 1911, when Simon Grant, a United Fruit Company representative, got the idea after watching bananas being towed by raft downstream to the docks for loading onto ships. But it was Flynn who popularized the pastime by launching the first rafters' race.

Today the excursion on the Rio Grande is one of Port Antonio's leading tourist attractions. The trip starts about 8 miles upstream at Berrydale, where passengers board a 30-foot-long bamboo raft that seats two. With the Blue Mountains towering in the background, a skilled and experienced helmsman guides the raft at a leisurely pace for two to three hours down the Rio Grande while you enjoy the river's tropical setting. You can also stop for a swim.

Along the way you see cattle grazing, children playing, mothers laundering, birds darting about, and banana groves and wild orchids growing in profusion. The serenity makes it easy for anyone to fall in love with Jamaica all over again. Cost is US$45 per person for two and a half hours.

Blue Lagoon: Six miles east of Port Antonio is the Blue Lagoon, which many Jamaica devotees call the most beautiful spot on the island. Well, maybe. Local folks claim the Blue Lagoon is bottomless; others say it's been measured to be 185 feet deep. It is fed by freshwater springs, one of which has the power to increase virility, according to local lore. After a long controversy over conservation, Blue Lagoon reopened in 1995; it has a restaurant and organized water sports. The small admission charge is deducted from the meal check when you dine at the restaurant. At San San Bay next to Blue Lagoon is Princess Island, a honeymoon gift of Prince Sadruddin Khan to Nina von Thyssen. And down the road another millionaire built Dragon Bay, a resort, now owned by the Sandals group.

The Castle: Perhaps the most curious story of all is about the Castle, situated on a rocky promontory next to the Trident Hotel. In 1979 a German baroness, Elizabeth Siglindy Stephan von Stephanie, began building an enormous structure complete with turrets that might have a duplicate on the Rhine. Then, as abruptly as construction had begun, it stopped, and the baroness vanished. The owner of the Trident Hotel completed the structure as a private mansion for use in conjunction with the hotel. Ah, but the story does not end. In 1988 the baroness returned and built the Jamaica Palace, a hotel directly across the bay from the Castle. Less imposing, perhaps, but no less grand, the hotel is furnished with antiques, crystal chandeliers, and splendid Oriental carpets. Among its many bizarre features are round beds with navy-blue satin bedspreads and a swimming pool in the shape of Jamaica, which has a full view of the Castle.

Touring Port Antonio

Port Facilities: If you arrive in Port Antonio by sea, you will sail into the **Errol Flynn Marina at Port Antonio** (715-6044; www.themarinaatport antonio.com), a mega-yacht facility in the protected West Harbour. The full-service marina, which can take boats up to 350 feet, is an official port of entry with 24-hour customs and immigration services and security. The harbor also has a cruise ship terminal, information center, gift shop, restaurant, bar, swimming pool, and a pretty white-sand beach.

The town of Port Antonio is very small and can be seen in a few minutes' walk. The most interesting sights are out of town and too far away for walking. The easiest way to see the area is on a tour that begins with a harbor cruise, followed by a ride to Athenry and a grand view of Port Antonio; a stop at San San Beach for a swim; and last, a visit to Somerset Falls. A guided tour can be arranged through the Jamaica Tourist Board office in Port Antonio (993-3051) or **Joanna's Port Antonio Tour** (831-8434; www.portantoniotours.netfirms). The tour can include any of the Port Antonio attractions previously described.

A popular attraction at the port is **Norma's at the Marina** (993-9510) restaurant, which serves refined Jamaican cuisine. It's owned by well-known restaurateur Norma Shirley, who also operates Norma's facilities in Kingston, Negril, and Miami. Closed Monday. Expensive.

Valley Hikes: Eco-adventures around Port Antonio and the Blue Mountains can be arranged in advance of your cruise through **Unique Destinations** (401-647-4730 or 213-431-1571; 993-3881) or **Hotel Mocking Bird Hill** in Port Antonio (993-7267; www.hotelmockingbirdhill.com). **Valley Hikes** (993-3085; valleyhikes@cwjamaica.com) is a cooperative effort of Port Antonio hotels to promote and protect the diverse environment in the Rio Grande Valley, the Blue and John Crow Mountains National Park. The excursions are led by trained guides from the region who know the vegetation and wildlife as well as herbal medicines used here for generations.

The ecotours offer hiking through the lush valley and mountains on maintained trails that parallel rivers and lead to old banana plantations, little-known streams, and hidden waterfalls. They range from easy, light adventures to moderately challenging and strenuous ones. For history buffs there are tours into the Land-of-Look-Behind and Maroon Country, a meeting with the Colonel (chief of the Maroons, descendants of escaped Spanish slaves), and trails to tiny mountain villages.

In addition to hiking tours and trail maintenance, the award-winning organization works closely with the Portland Environment Protection Association (PEPA), the first nongovernmental environmental group in Jamaica, which operates PEP Clubs—youth educational programs. It holds seminars and can arrange a buffet luncheon and folklore show with mento (the forerunner of reggae) and calypso music, a tour of Foxes Caves from which the Foxes River springs, river rafting down the Rio Grande, and a four-hour horseback ride along the Say River. Rates range from US$15–$65 for day hikes to US$185 for the three-day hikes and include all food, rafting, horseback riding, and folkloric entertainment.

Kingston

Jamaica's capital, a city of more than 800,000 people, is the hemisphere's largest English-speaking city south of Miami. It is the commercial, political, administrative, and cultural center of Jamaica but is largely ignored by tourists. The much-maligned capital is neither the dangerous den nor the ugly duckling that publicity has made it. Indeed, the city enjoys a rather spectacular setting by the sea on the world's seventh-largest natural harbor, with the lofty Blue Mountains in the background.

The capital is the headquarters of Jamaica's theater, music, dance, and art, but the opportunity to enjoy the best talent is a matter of timing. The National Pantomime Theatre performs January through March; the Jamaica Folk Singers, March through April; the University Dance Society, May; and the National Dance Theatre, July through August. Many also have mini sessions during the Christmas and New Year period.

Plays written by Jamaicans are presented year-round at the Ward Theatre, one of the oldest theaters in the Western Hemisphere; at the University of the West Indies' Creative Arts Centre; and at other playhouses in Kingston. The Cultural Training Center near the Pegasus Hotel in New Kingston has a year-round schedule of music, dance, and art exhibits and other cultural activities.

National Gallery of Art (12 Ocean Boulevard; 922-1561; www.galleryjamaica.com). The gallery's collection represents Jamaica's most important native artists from the nineteenth century to the present as well as foreign artists who have worked here. One room is devoted entirely to the works of the late Kapo, Jamaica's leading primitive artist, known particularly for his sculpture. One of the museum's most outstanding collections is of works by Edna Manley, the wife of the first prime minister and the mother of Michael Manley. Her sculpture *Negro Awakened* is considered one of the most significant works in the body of Caribbean art. Admission: US$2. Hours: 10:00 A.M. to 4:30 P.M. Tuesday through Thursday; 10:00 A.M. to 4:00 P.M. Friday; 10:00 A.M. to 3:00 P.M. Saturday.

Institute of Jamaica (12–16 East Street; 922-0620; www.instituteofjamaica.org.jm). Founded in 1879 and similar in scope to the Smithsonian Institution, the Institute of Jamaica is an umbrella organization with wide-ranging responsibilities for the Jamaica National Trust Commission, which has identified hundreds of old buildings, churches, houses, and other structures for preservation and oversees archaeological excavations. The institute's West Indian Reference Library chronicles Jamaican and Caribbean political, social, and economic developments and maintains the world's largest collection of books, articles, and prints on the West Indies. It also maintains the Natural History Museum, which collects and studies the flora and fauna of Jamaica, including hundreds of species unique to the Caribbean.

Devon House (26 Hope Road, Kingston 10; 929-6602; www.devonhousejamaica.com). With the opening of the National Gallery in 1984, Devon House, a beautifully restored nineteenth-century mansion of Jamaica's first black millionaire, was made into a museum and a showplace for Jamaican crafts. Admission: adult US$5, child $3. The coach house of the Devon estate was converted into an attractive restaurant, the **Grog Shoppe** (960-9730), serving light lunches and Jamaican dishes; other buildings house shops for Jamaican products, a bakery, a smoke shop, an ice-cream parlor, and displays of musical instruments. Devon House's restaurant, **Norma's on the Terrace** (26 Hope Road; 929-6602), is under the watchful eye of Norma Shirley, Jamaica's best-known restaurateur, who also has restaurants in Negril, Port Antonio, and Miami. It offers a light fare and Caribbean specialties in a pretty setting overlooking the gardens. Moderately expensive.

Bob Marley Museum (56 Hope Road; 927-9152; www.bobmarley-foundation.com), the former home of the famous reggae superstar, now houses a collection of Marley memorabilia, photos, and news clips reflecting his life and career, including the studio where he recorded many of his hits. A twenty-minute video of his best-known concerts is shown. Admission: US$10. Hours: 9:30 A.M. to 5:00 P.M. Monday through Saturday.

Port Royal: Jamaica's past is as well represented as its creative present at two important sites within easy reach of the capital. Port Royal, on a spit of land west of Kingston airport, was Jamaica's infamous pirates' port in the seventeenth century. It was destroyed in 1692 when an earthquake caused 90 percent of the town and its legendary treasures to sink into the sea. Although several excavations were attempted in the 1800s, the first organized work was conducted by the National Geographic Society, the Smithsonian, and the Institute of Jamaica in 1959 and again in 1968 by the National Trust. More recently, after several years' restoration work, Port Royal has been made into a park and museum. Another ambitious project calls for excavating Port Royal's underwater ruins.

Spanish Town: Located 12 miles west of Kingston is the town founded in 1523 by Diego Columbus as Villa de la Vega; it was renamed

St. Jago de la Vega when it became the capital in 1534. The town was destroyed by the English after they seized Jamaica in 1655. They built their own town on the same site but continued to call it Spanish Town. Today the cathedral on the site of the previous Spanish one is the oldest Anglican church in the New World. Tombstones on the church floor date from the seventeenth century. Government buildings on the town square and a few private houses on the adjacent side streets date from the eighteenth and nineteenth centuries. Recently, the Spanish Town Historic Foundation launched an effort to entice private individuals and investors to restore historic homes and buildings and to preserve the town's historic character and make it a "living" museum.

Blue Mountain National Park: The main highway between Ocho Rios and Kingston is a scenic drive of 54 miles over the mountains. A narrow, winding, and even more scenic road passes through the heart of the Blue Mountains between Newcastle and Buff Bay. The 193,000-acre Blue Mountains and John Crow Mountains National Park, located in these rugged mountains, contains some of the most diverse tropical rain forests in the world. Its peaks and valleys are home to seven distinct forest communities and to the endemic swallowtail butterfly, the world's second largest butterfly. Old logging roads and trails provide nature lovers with some of the most beautiful and interesting hiking in the Caribbean. A night hike during full moon up Blue Mountain's peak, arriving at over 7,500 feet in time for the sunrise, is one of the great outdoor experiences of all times.

The Cayman Islands

The Cayman Islands

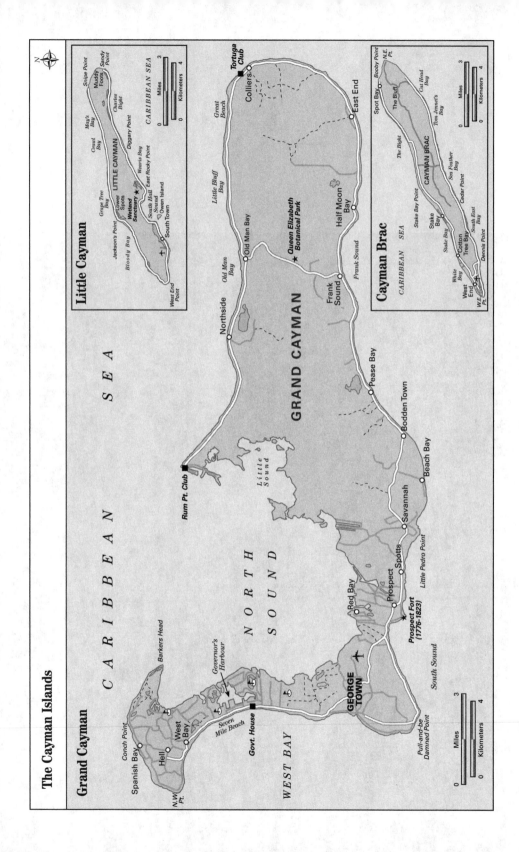

Grand Cayman

CARIBBEAN SEA

N.W. Pt.
Conch Point
Spanish Bay
Hell
West Bay
Barkers Head
WEST BAY
Seven Mile Beach
Governor's Harbour
Govt. House
NORTH SOUND
GEORGE TOWN
South Sound
Pull-and-be Damned Point
Red Bay
Prospect
Spotts
Little Pedro Point
Prospect Fort (1776-1823)
Savannah
Beach Bay
Bodden Town
Pease Bay
Little Sound
Rum Pt. Club
Northside
Old Man Bay
Frank Sound
Queen Elizabeth Botanical Park
Half Moon Bay
Little Bluff Bay
Great Beach
Colliers
East End
GRAND CAYMAN
Tortuga Club

Miles 3
Kilometers 4

Little Cayman

CARIBBEAN SEA

Snipe Point
Muddy Foots
Sandy Point
Charles Bight
Digarry Point
May's Bay
Great Bay
Wearis Bay
East Rocky Point
Grape Tree Bay
LITTLE CAYMAN
Lower Spots
South Hall
Wetland Sanctuary
Queen Island
South Town
Jackson's Point
Bloody Bay
West End Point

0 Miles 3
0 Kilometers 4

Cayman Brac

CARIBBEAN SEA

Spot Bay
Booby Point
N.E. Pt.
The Bluff
Cut Head Bay
Tom Jrmett's Bay
The Bight
Sea Feather Bay
CAYMAN BRAC
Stake Bay Point
Stake Bay
Cotton Tree Bay
Cedar Point
Stake Bay
White Bay
West End
W.E. Pt.
Dennis Point
South East Bay

0 Miles 3
0 Kilometers 4

N

The Diver's Mount Everest

The history of the British Crown Colony of the Cayman Islands might be called the tale of the turtles and the pirates. The Cayman Islands were discovered by Columbus in 1503 on his fourth voyage when a chance wind blew the great explorer's ship off course and thrust it onto "two very small islands full of tortoises," which led Columbus to dub them Las Tortugas. On later maps the islands were shown as Caimanas, a Carib Indian name for the marine crocodile. Sir Francis Drake also called them Caymanas when he arrived to claim them for Britain in 1586. That's when the pirates came, too.

At the close of the sixteenth century and for the next hundred years, the Cayman Islands became a favorite hiding place for Blackbeard, Henry Morgan, Neal Walker, and other pirates (including the infamous women Anne Bonny and Mary Read), buccaneers, privateers, and the whole corps of sea captains and adventurers who preyed on Spanish galleons laden with treasures from Mexico and the Spanish Main.

(When one of these entrepreneurs was a dashing corsair like Drake and had the blessing of the Crown, he went down in history as a swashbuckler or privateer, but if he had a reputation like Edward Teach, better known as Blackbeard, history more accurately called him a pirate—the most notorious scoundrel of his day.)

Whether because of the pirates or the turtles, little effort was made to colonize the islands, and as late as the early nineteenth century fewer than 1,500 people lived here. In 1863, as part of the territory under the British governor of Jamaica, the Cayman Islands became a Crown Colony. But it did not become a separate entity until a century later, when Jamaica got its independence in 1962.

Situated 480 miles south of Miami and about 200 miles from Cuba and Jamaica, the Caymans are made up of three islands: the 22-mile Grand Cayman, with the capital and major port of call, George Town; Cayman Brac, 12 square miles of untamed tropics 86 miles to the northeast of the capital; and Little Cayman, the smallest of the trio, 5 miles from the western end of Cayman Brac.

Today's residents have taken both the turtles and the pirates to heart. A turtle dressed as a pirate has become the emblem of the islands' airline, Cayman Airways. Sea turtles, which are on the endangered species list, are bred at the world's first sea turtle farm at the rate of 20,000 a year. Local menus feature turtle steak and turtle soup. The pirates turn up once a year to reclaim their lair during Pirates Week, the Caymans' Carnival, usually held in late October.

Cynics might also note that the turtle-paced islands are still an ideal place to stash away a treasure or two. As a tax-free haven and offshore banking center, they are favored especially by the fast-track world of international finance. Thanks to their commerce, the Cayman Islands have the best communications, the lowest unemployment, and the highest standard of living in the Caribbean.

Yet of all the Caymans' assets, the most appealing and enduring is the gift of nature—magnificent beaches and spectacular coral gardens and marine life, often less than 100 yards from shore

At a Glance

Antiquities	★
Art and Artists	★★
Beaches	★★★★★
Colonial Buildings	★★
Cuisine	★★
Culture	★
Dining/Restaurants	★★★
Entertainment	★
History	★
Museums	★
Nature	★★★★★
Nightlife	★
Scenery	★★
Shopping	★
Sightseeing	★★
Sports	★★★★★
Transportation	★★

Fast Facts

Population: The Cayman Islands were settled by deserters from Oliver Cromwell's army, shipwrecked sailors, pirates, and freed slaves. To this day the racial and ethnic mix of the original settlers is reflected in the 40,000 people who inhabit the three islands, 90 percent of whom live on Grand Cayman. Intermarriage has made the Cayman Islands one of the most well-integrated societies in the Western Hemisphere.

Main Town: George Town.

Government: Great Britain got Jamaica and the Cayman Islands from Spain in the Treaty of Madrid in 1670. The Caymans were a dependency of Jamaica until 1961. The following year, after the failure of the short-lived West Indies Federation, Jamaica became independent, but the Caymans chose to remain a British Overseas Territory, self-governing in all internal affairs but administered by a governor appointed by Great Britain.

Climate: The western Caribbean is noted for calm, balmy weather. Temperatures average 75°F in January and 86°F in summer, and there are many more sunny days than elsewhere in the area. Short tropical rains often catch you by surprise, particularly in fall and spring, but they rarely last more than a few minutes.

Clothing: Tropic-casual is right in style here. Lightweight suits are appropriate for those transacting business. A sweater may be needed on cloudy days in the winter.

Currency: The Cayman Island dollar, called the "CI" locally, is tied to the US dollar at a set rate of CI$1.25 to US$1. One hundred US dollars equals 80 CI dollars, when you exchange cash, and equals 82 CI dollars for checks. However, you do not have to exchange dollars: US currency, traveler's checks, and credit cards are widely accepted.

Entry Formalities: US government regulations now require all US citizens traveling by air to have a passport to leave and to enter the United States; the same will be required of those traveling by sea after January 1, 2009. The departure tax is US$25, which is normally included in your air ticket.

Electricity: 110 volts, 60 cycles, as in the United States.

Language: English, but with a lilt all its own, a delightful mixture of West Indian and Scottish brogue.

Postal Service: Air mail to the United States takes four to ten days for delivery. In George Town, post offices are located at the end of Cardinal Avenue 2 blocks from the pier and in the West Shore Plaza on West Bay Road (Seven Mile Beach). Both are open 8:30 A.M. to 3:30 P.M. Monday through Friday.

Public Holidays: January 1, New Year's Day; annual Agricultural Fair; Ash Wednesday; Good Friday; Easter Monday; May, Discovery Day; mid-June, Queen's Birthday; July, Constitution Day; November, Remembrance Day; December 25, Christmas Day; December 26, Boxing Day.

Telephone Area Code: 345. When calling from the United States, add "94" in front of the five-digit local number: 1-345-94 + local number. Special direct phones to call the United States are available at the dock and other selected locations where cruise passengers disembark.

Vaccination Requirement: None.

Airlines: Cayman Airways (1-800-4-CAYMAN, www.caymanairways .com), the national carrier, has daily flights to Grand Cayman from Miami. It also operates flights from Houston, Fort Lauderdale, Tampa, and Atlanta to Grand Cayman, and in June 2007 began nonstop service to New York JFK. Others flying to Grand Cayman are Air Canada, Air Jamaica, American Airlines, Continental, Delta, USAirways, and Northwest in the winter season. Island Air provides service from Grand Cayman to Little Cayman and Cayman Brac.

Information: www.caymanislands .ky; www.divecayman.ky.

In the United States:

Cayman Island Tourist Offices:

Chicago: 1 Lincoln Centre, 18 West 140 Butterfield Road, Suite 920, Oakbrook Terrace, IL 60181; (630) 705-0650; fax (630) 705-1383.

Houston: 2 Memorial City Plaza, 820 Gessner, Suite 1335, TX 77024; (713) 461-1317; fax (713) 461-7409.

Miami: Trenton Building, 8300 Northwest Fifty-third Street, Suite 103, FL 33166; (305) 599-9033; fax (305) 599-3766.

New York: 3 Park Avenue, Thirty-ninth floor, New York, NY 10016; (212) 889-9009; fax (212) 889-9125.

In Canada:

Earl B. Smith, Travel Marketing Consultants, 234 Eglinton Avenue East, No. 306, Toronto, Ontario, Canada M4P 1K5; (416) 485-1550; (800) 263-5805; fax (416) 485-7578.

In Grand Cayman:

Regatta Business Park, Leeward Two, West Bay Road, P.O. Box 67, George Town, Cayman Islands, KY1-1102, British West Indies; (345) 949-0623; fax (345) 949-4035.

Cayman Islands National Trust, Eastern Avenue; (345) 949-0121; fax (345) 947-7494; www.nationaltrust.org.ky.

and in water so clear that visibility of 200 feet is not unusual. As a further incentive to divers, there are 350 shipwrecks recorded in these waters— apparently, not all of the pirates made it in and out of the tricky waters of their hideaway. Then, too, not all the wrecks were accidents. Some ships, it is said, were lured onto the reefs by islanders who plundered the wrecks as a means of livelihood.

In addition to their banks and beaches, the Cayman Islands offer many other attractions, including three golf courses, one of which features the "short" ball developed by golfing great Jack Nicklaus.

Budget Planning

That there are no taxes in the Cayman Islands would at first seem to be a blessing. As we all know, however, there is no free lunch, either, and the government supports itself with a steep customs duty on everything brought into the islands. The duties run from 15 to 27 percent on the cost of all imports, including shipping charges to bring goods into the islands. As always, these prices are passed on to the consumer, making just about everything you buy expensive, with the exception of a limited number of local products and duty-free items. You should always review the prices of taxis, restaurants, and anything else you buy to avoid any unwelcome surprises.

Fortunately, your feet can get you around George Town easily enough. If you are taking a taxi any distance, consider sharing with some fellow passengers. A moped costs about US$25 a day including helmet and permit, with an additional charge of $5 for insurance and driver's permit, and bikes $10 to $15; a car rental runs US$42 and up a day, with $7.50 fee for driver's permit for visitors, easily given upon presentation of a valid US driver's license. All are a convenient means of transportation.

If you are watching your budget, mini buses operate frequently along West Bay Road to all the beaches and can be picked up at bus stop signs en route. The fare is CI$1.50 to CI$4, depending on destination, and can be paid in US currency.

Port Profile: Grand Cayman

Location/Embarkation: George Town, the Caymans' capital and port of call, is located on the west side of Grand Cayman. It is perhaps not what you would expect of a Caribbean port. Downtown George Town, which stretches east directly behind the harbor, looks more like a metropolitan banking and financial center than the capital of a Caribbean island. That's not surprising when you learn that more than 500 banks from more than sixty countries, 1,895 entities registered or licensed as mutual funds, and approximately 35,000 other companies are doing business here. The Cayman Islands is now the fifth largest financial center in the world. Little wonder it is called the Switzerland of the Caribbean.

Cruise ships cannot dock in George Town; rather they anchor just outside the harbor and tender passengers to a dock at the center of town. You can hardly get lost as the center of town is only 3 blocks wide and 3 blocks deep, clean and neat, filled primarily with shoppers and businesspeople.

Occasionally when the sea is rough, cruise ships anchor on the south end of the island at Spotts Landing, about 6 miles from George Town. There is a welcome/information center here, and taxis are on hand to take passengers to the town center or on tour.

Facilities: While George Town may not have the "feel" of a typical tropical port, this center of international finance demands and gets the most efficient transportation, communications, and technical facilities available in the Caribbean. As soon as you get off your tender, there is a special phone available for making calls to the United States, and you can charge the call to a credit card number. Public phones, which almost always work in George Town for local calls, are available, but you will need Caymanian coins or local phone cards to use them. Tourist information booths are located at both the north and south cruise ship terminals.

Walk straight ahead across North Church Street down Cardinal Avenue and you will find most of the shopping. (US dollars are acceptable everywhere.) If you don't plan to leave George

Town by taxi or tour, everything you need in port is within a few hundred yards of the town dock. Your ability to come and go between ship and shore is restricted only by the tender schedule.

Internet Access: As with most Caribbean ports, Internet access facilities have mushroomed. Ask at the tourist information booths at the cruise terminal for facilities nearest the port. On Seven Mile Beach there are Internet facilities at **Cafe del Sol** (Marquee Cinema Shopping Centre, 2 miles north of George Town; 946-2233; www.cafedelsol .ky); and **PD's Pub** (Galleria Plaza, West Bay Road, 3 miles north of George Town; 949-7144). Three blocks up on Shedden Road (directly in front of the cruise ship docks) there are two Internet cafes: **Coffee & Bites** (Bodmer Building; 945-4892) and **Geeks Internet** (Elizabethan Square).

Local Transportation: Taxis are available at the dock whenever there is a ship in port. There are taxi stands in town and near the public beach at Seven Mile Beach on West Bay Road. The drivers speak English, although their lilting accent and their tendency to speak softly take some getting used to. There are no meters, and the rates tend to be high by US standards. Be sure to confirm the rate before you get in the taxi, and be sure, also, that you and your driver understand whether the amount is Cayman Islands or US dollars. As an

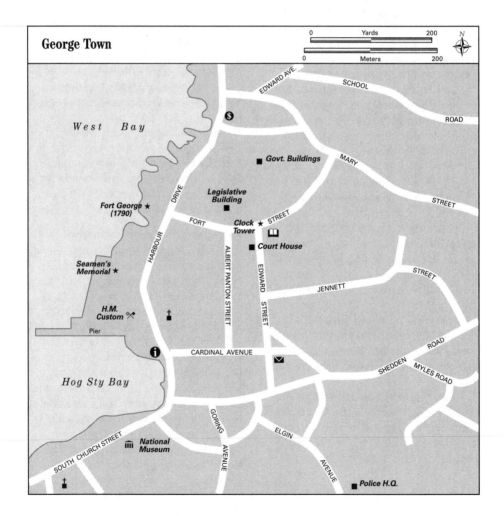

George Town

example, the fare from the dock to a hotel on Seven Mile Beach costs about US$16 for up to four people, or US$3 to $4 for a seat in a taxi van.

A word of caution: Traffic congestion on Grand Cayman can be terrible, especially along West Bay Road and in town on busy cruise ship days, when it moves at a turtle's pace during the lunch hour (noon to 1:30 P.M.) and around 3:00 P.M. when passengers are heading back to their ships. Be sure to allow yourself at least double the normal driving time during these peak hours. Also, a *mandatory* seat belt law was introduced in 1998 that requires both drivers and passengers in all vehicles to wear seat belts. Driving is on the **LEFT.**

Buses: In 1998 Grand Cayman inaugurated its first official public transportation system of small buses (sixteen-passenger is average), which run every half hour or hour (depending on the route) Monday through Friday from 7:00 A.M. until midnight from downtown George Town to outer districts. The buses are privately owned but government-licensed and operate on routes with fixed fares ranging from CI$1.50 to $4 one way along main routes. All licensed buses have blue-and-white license plates and color-coded stickers that identify the route they follow. The central depot is behind the public library on Edward Street, about 2 blocks from the cruise ship piers. Even so, you might find it more efficient, when your time is limited, to take a taxi or, if you are planning to tour the island, to rent a car.

Car Rental: Driving is on the **LEFT.** Several car rental companies on Grand Cayman offer excellent service. For a car, expect to pay about CI$37.50 a day and up, with unlimited mileage (without insurance); for gas, about CI$4.30 per imperial gallon. You will also need a valid driver's license from home and a visitor's driving permit, which costs US$7.50 and is obtained at the time you sign out the car.

You would be wise to make reservations from home before departing on your cruise. Most car rental companies have toll-free 800 numbers. Car rental companies will deliver cars anywhere on the island, including the town dock. For information call **Andy's Rent a Car** (Seven Mile Beach; 949-8111;

fax 949-8385; www.andys.ky), **Avis Cico** (near airport; 949-2468; 800-331-1084; fax 949-7127; www.aviscayman.com), **Budget Rent A Car** (949-5605; 800-527-0700; www.budgetcayman.com), **Coconut Car Rentals** (Crew Road; 945-4377; 800-941-4562; www.coconutcarrentals.com), or **Hertz** (Industrial Park; 949-2280; 800-654-3131; www.hertzcaribbean.com).

Ferries: Regular ferry service to Rum Point was suspended after Hurricane Ivan in 2005; instead you will need to go by car or the shuttle-van service for US$25 per person round trip.

Shore Excursions

If you prefer an easy walk with a little shopping, you can stroll about the center of George Town in only a few blocks. The national museum's gift shop, only a few feet from the dock, has an excellent brochure for a self-guided walk of historic George Town. On the other hand, to really see Grand Cayman and get the feel of the Caymans, you will need to get out of town to see the island and its fabulous beaches, get out on the sea to enjoy its lovely waters, or get under the sea to enjoy nature's spectacular show. Whichever you choose, you will need transportation.

You can easily negotiate with a taxi driver for a tour of Grand Cayman along West Bay Road to the Turtle Farm or a spin around the island to East End. However, unless you are sharing the cost with friends, that could be expensive. Expect to pay US$75 or more for a half-day excursion.

There are several tours available that will give you a good look at Grand Cayman's shoreside attractions. Among the agencies providing sightseeing are **AA Transportation and Sightseeing Tours** (949-7222; www.islanddrivers.com), **Reality Tours** (947-7200), **Majestic Tours** (949-7773; www.majestic-tours.com), and **Tropicana Tours** (949-0944; www.tropicana-tours.com).

The first three of the following tours are those most frequently available on cruise ships. The other options are offered by some lines; if your line does not offer them, you will need to make arrangements in advance through your travel agent or on your own. Recently we found great discrepancy between prices available from local tour companies and sports operators and those being offered by some cruise ships. Prices are US dollars unless specified otherwise.

George Town/West Bay: Two and a half hours; $37.50. The tour briefly visits downtown George Town's shopping district and continues along Seven Mile Beach to West Bay, with stops at Turtle Farm, Tortuga Rum Cake Factory and Duty Free Shop, and Hell to send postcards. You can be dropped off at the beach or returned to town for shopping. A longer version adds lunch at the beach and time for a swim.

Atlantis Submarine (949-7700; 866-546-7820; 800-887-8573; www.atlantisadventures.com). For a close look at Grand Cayman's famous reefs, cruise 150 feet below the surface in the new forty-eight-passenger *Atlantis XI* submarine. (See Unusual Dive Opportunities for Nondivers at the end of this chapter.) Atlantis Expeditions, $79 adult; $49 child four to twelve and over 36 inches tall; $69 for ages thirteen through seventeen.

Stingray City/Island Tour: Three hours; $50 to $57 ($70 adult as a cruise ship shore excursion). For the thrill of a lifetime, try swimming and snorkeling with a dozen or so stingrays. (See Scuba Diving/Snorkeling later in this chapter for a description.) The boat departs from the northwest side of North Sound or other locations. In addition to snorkel excursions, there are glass-bottomed boat trips combined with an island tour for $37 and one-tank dives for certified divers at $45 to $65. Stingray City Charters (949-9200) or Bayside

Watersports (949-3200; fax 949-3700) welcome advance reservations from cruise passengers.

Seaworld Explorer **Semi-Submersible:** One hour; $34 adult; $19 ages twelve and thirteen. Float in a semi-submersible with large glass windows at 5 feet below the surface of the water to see the reefs, fish, and shipwrecks near the cruise ship pier. *Nautilus* **Undersea Tour** (945-1355) offers a similar excursion in a submersible that has the advantage of a viewing area with wall-to-wall windows ($49 adult; $34 child as a cruise ship shore excursion).

Golf: Britannia Golf Course (www.britannia villas.net/golf.aspx), or the Links. (See the Sports section for fees.) The Greg Norman–designed course at the Ritz Carlton debuted in 2006; it is only open to hotel guests and residence owners.

Scuba Diving: Beginning resort course, $75 to $120. One-tank dive, $40 to $60; two-tank dive, $65 to $85. Snorkeling trips, $30 to $35. (See Sports section for information.)

Grand Cayman on Your Own

George Town's nickname, the Switzerland of the Caribbean, refers not only to its major position as a financial center for offshore banking and insurance, but also to a certain Swiss-like efficiency, cleanliness, and businesslike attitude. Although the best of Grand Cayman is out of town, you might want to take a walk in the immediate area before you leave the dock.

Cayman Islands National Museum (949-8368; www.museum.ky). This museum opened in 1990 in the Old Courts Building, which dates from the 1830s. The courthouse/jail has served as a public library, bank, church, and local social center. A good example of Cayman-type architecture, the building won an American Express Preservation Award. Although it is an important tourist attraction, the air-conditioned museum was created mainly to give the local population a place to preserve its natural and cultural history.

Exhibits, some with dioramas, highlight the islands' important events. The ground floor is devoted to exhibits on the Caymans' natural historical and marine life; the second floor has historical and cultural displays. Admission: CI$5 adult; $3 child. Hours: 9:00 A.M. to 5:00 P.M. Monday through Friday; 10:00 A.M. to 4:00 P.M. Saturday. The section holding the gift shop was once a jail. The shop is open, but the museum remains closed after the hurricane in 2005. There is a snack bar with local food.

Cardinal D's Park (949-8855). East of the National Trust House on Courts Road off Eastern Avenue is a nature park with a collection of animals typical of the Caribbean, including blue iguanas, turtles, Grand Cayman parrots, agoutis, and more than sixty species of exotic birds. There are miniature ponies and a petting zoo. Developed by Heath Hill, a local businessman, the facility works with the National Trust to ensure the proper care of its animals. Admission: CI$5 adult; $2.50 child. Hours: 10:00 A.M. to 6:00 P.M. Monday through Friday; noon to 6:00 P.M. Saturday and Sunday. The park has not reopened since the hurricane in 2005.

The Butterfly Farm (946-3411; www.the butterflyfarm.com). Located on Lawrence Avenue, east of West Bay Road, the attraction, opened in 2003, offers guided tours of its tropical garden, resplendent with butterflies from around the world. Admission: US$15 adult; $9 child twelve and under. Hours: 8:30 A.M. to 4:00 P.M. daily.

Driving Tour of Grand Cayman

*Driving is on the **LEFT**.*

Although Grand Cayman is only 22 miles long and about 8 miles wide, you will need to leave yourself plenty of time if you plan to tour the entire island. Unlike many Caribbean ports of call where the road goes around the island, Grand Cayman does not have a loop road encircling it. Rather, the island is shaped something like a boomerang; roads go either to the west side or the east side of the island. You will need to backtrack from any extended drive in either direction to return to town and your ship.

From your starting point at George Town, with a good map in hand (available at the Tourist Office and in bookstores), you have two choices. First, you can follow North Church Street to West Bay Road, the island's main north–south artery along Seven

Mile Beach. This plan takes you into the West Bay section, a peninsula that borders the North Sound and contains the vast majority of the island's hotels and condo developments, the Turtle Farm, most restaurants, the island's best beaches, water sports and fishing centers, tennis courts, and golf courses. All the roads in West Bay feed back to West Bay Road, which leads directly into George Town and the harbor. Permitting a reasonable amount of sightseeing time, you can tour West Bay in two hours.

As a second option, you can head south on South Church Street, which leads out of town into rural Grand Cayman to Bodden Town and East End. Eventually, the drive will take you to Rum Point, on the northwestern tip. This tour requires three to four hours or longer if you stop along the way to enjoy the sights, picnic, and swim.

To make both the west-side and east-side drives, you need a minimum of six hours going even at a fast clip. Remember, with each tour you will have to double back to George Town, so plan to turn back when you have used up half of your allotted time.

Also, stick to the main coast road. It adds a few more miles to your trip, but the route is far more scenic, easier to follow, and will bring you directly back to the harbor without any turnoffs. There are shortcuts through the middle of town to or from the harbor, but do not use them if you are unfamiliar with George Town. Traffic is heavy, and you could get lost quickly on the twisting roads, particularly when you are concentrating on staying left while at the same time trying to follow a map.

Finally, be aware of roundabouts on many main roads; they can be confusing. You must yield to traffic entering from the right. Familiarize yourself with the traffic flow and proceed carefully.

To the West End

For the western drive, head north from the harbor toward West Bay and along the famed Seven Mile Beach. For the next few miles, you will be traveling straight north with the beach on the left (west), past the hotels and luxury condominiums that line both sides of the road.

Golf Club and Government House: Some points of interest to note are the Britannia Golf Club (which features the Jack Nicklaus short-ball course and lies across the road from the former Hyatt Hotel); the public beach; and Government House, the residence of the governor, also near the public beach. The Links at Safe Haven, an eighteen-hole championship, par-72 golf course, is located farther north. Also in this area is the Ritz Carlton Hotel and its Greg Norman–designed golf course.

Farther along at West Bay is a new area called Camana Bay, which has been ten years in the planning. First to open is Cayman National Bank, to be followed by restaurants, shops, a six-screen cinema, and sixty-two terrace apartments overlooking the waterfront in the first phase. Expected to open in 2008 is Restaurant Row—which will have six new places to dine and a calendar of events from outdoor concerts to farmers' markets—and water sports at the center's harbor.

Boatswain's Beach/Turtle Farm: After several miles you will come to a fork in the road; the road on the left takes you directly to the Boatswain's Beach/Turtle Farm (825 Northwest Point Road; 949-3894; www.boatswainbeach.ky). Here at the world's first sea turtle farm, which is also a research station, you will be able to observe turtles in their breeding ponds at various stages of development; you can even pick up one from the water for a photograph. Some grow as long as 4 feet and weigh up to 600 pounds. The farm breeds turtles—at the rate of about 20,000 per year—to help restock the waters of countries around the world as well as for commercial purposes.

In 2006 the Turtle Farm underwent a major $45 million expansion and is now located directly across the road from its former location in the new thirty-acre marine theme park called Boatwain's Beach. The park has a large saltwater lagoon where visitors can swim with marine life; a predator tank; a nature trail; a free-flight Caribbean Bird Aviary; a Caymanian Heritage Street with artisans and craftspeople; a restaurant featuring contemporary Caymanian cuisine; and state-of-the-art research and educational facilities focusing on the conservation of sea turtles. Cost: Wet package (includes all features), $75 adult; $35 ages two through twelve; dry package, $50 adult; $25 child.

We must warn you that tortoiseshell and other turtle products are not allowed into the United States, because these animals are still on the endangered species list. For information write Cayman Turtle Farm, Box 812, West Bay, Grand Cayman; or phone 949-3893. Hours: 9:00 A.M. to 5:00 P.M. daily.

Hell: You can take a detour to Hell (949-6999; www.tab.ky). By following the right fork, the road will take you away from the tourist areas and into the residential sections of West Bay. Follow the signs to Hell, which was given its name because of the area's dramatic and ominous coral and limestone formations known as ironshore, a dominant feature of part of the Cayman shore. HELL postmarks on your postcards—and, of course, HELL T-shirts—are the main industries here. This unusual attraction was given its name in the 1930s and its post office in 1962. In 1986 Hell got a face-lift that added a boardwalk with better access for viewing the rocks, as well as crafts shops, plants, and a new post office.

North Sound/Stingray City: Across the mouth of North Sound is a barrier reef, and just inside is one of the Caribbean's most unusual sites, dubbed Stingray City. In only 4 to 15 feet of water, divers and snorkelers can touch, feed, and photograph a dozen or more friendly southern Atlantic stingrays. These creatures look prehistoric and frightening, but they are actually very gentle, with skin as soft as velvet.

To the East End

For the second option to the south and eastern parts of the island, South Church Street will take you along the manicured residential areas of the South Sound, around the town, and along South Sound Road, which borders the sea on one side and edges mangroves and ponds on the other—all popular locations for bird-watching. The Caymans, because of their location on the migratory routes among North, Central, and South America, are visited by a large number of bird species in fall and spring. There are, in addition, endemic species. The road turns inland for a short distance before reaching the village of Savannah.

Pedro St. James Historic Site (947-3329; www.pedrostjames.ky). In 1991 the Cayman Islands government bought the historic Pedro Castle to restore as a national landmark and develop as a tourist attraction under the supervision of the National Historic Sites Committee. Built in 1780 by William Eden as a private residence called St. James, the ruins were the oldest standing structure in the Cayman Islands and were constructed from coral rocks common in that area. The most important recorded event here was a meeting on December 5, 1831, establishing the country's first elected legislature.

Along with its historical significance, the 7.65-acre site has one of the most scenic and tranquil locations on Grand Cayman's rugged south coast. It lies on Pedro Bluff, a limestone ridge that rises 20 feet from the sea and supports a variety of native flowering plants and shrubs, including the silver thatch palm, a plant that has had an important role in the islands' crafts and heritage. Comprehensive research on the site's history, restoration of the structure, and landscaping were part of the committee's work that went into making the site a national park.

Completed in October 1998, after seven years and $7.5 million, the complex includes a three-story house in nineteenth-century style and other buildings and a $1.5 million visitor center with a multimedia theater featuring a twenty-four-minute video on Pedro St. James and Cayman history. Other facilities include a resource center, gift shop, wedding gazebo, and cafe.

The Pedro St. James Great House, designated as the Cayman Islands' first national historic landmark, is a historically accurate restoration with every detail reflecting authentic building techniques of early-nineteenth-century Caribbean great houses—from rough-hewn timber beams and wooden pegs to a gabled framework. Other period features include mahogany floors and staircases, wide-beam wooden ceilings, stone walls, outside wooden louvered shutters, and mahogany doors.

The first floor houses the jail, storerooms, kitchen, and pantry. The second level is a dining room, courtroom, and veranda, and the upper level is the living quarters. Furnishings combine original nineteenth-century mahogany antiques and reproductions. A bake oven and outdoor kitchen are re-creations of the original estate.

An early-twentieth-century Cayman-style cottage and a traditional hundred-year-old Cayman wattle-and-daub home were added to enhance the site's educational value.

Pedro St. James, with its lovely seaside setting, is a popular venue for weddings and social events. The grounds have been landscaped as a tropical park with native trees and plants, as well as traditional gardens representative of a small early-nineteenth-century West Indian plantation. Interpretative displays and signs allow self-guided tours; guides also are available. Admission: US$10 adult; free for ages twelve and younger. Hours: 8:30 A.M. to 5:00 P.M. daily; presentations are on the hour, the first at 10:00 A.M., the last at 4:00 P.M.

Bodden Town: After Savannah the main road turns back out again to the small village of Bodden Town, once the capital of Grand Cayman. Here you will get a glimpse of a different Caymanian lifestyle—one that depends on the sea and land for survival. There are caves here that legend says were once pirate hideouts.

After another 6 miles, you will see the Lighthouse Restaurant on the right. Use this as a checkpoint to find Frank Sound Road just beyond to the left. If your time is limited, you can use this cross-island highway to drive from the south coast to the north side of the island and trim about an hour off your trip. The cross-island highway passes the entrance to the botanic park.

Queen Elizabeth II Botanic Park (947-9462; www.botanic-park.ky). Since 1991 the National Trust of the Cayman Islands has been developing this nature park to preserve the islands' natural environment and wildlife, provide a place for local people to enjoy their natural heritage, and create an attraction for ecotourists. The park, situated on a sixty-acre tract of woodland, was donated to the government by a private owner. As much as 80 percent of the parkland is being preserved as native woodlands with signposted walkways and interpretive displays. A nature walk bordering the heart of the area was completed in 1993, and the park was officially opened the following year by Queen Elizabeth II, for whom it is named.

Some areas have been developed as display gardens to showcase vegetation native to the Cayman Islands. An estimated 40 percent of the plants endemic to the Caymans are found in this area, and more species of native flora are being added. The largest garden and main tourist attraction is the Heritage Garden, a historically oriented display of the plants raised by the local population over the years and their uses.

The area is a habitat for the Caymans' two subspecies of Cuban parrots and Grand Cayman's endemic blue iguana, an endangered species estimated to number fewer than fifty in the wild. The park has a captive breeding program under way for the iguana. There is a wedding gazebo set in pretty landscaped gardens—popular with islanders and visitors alike—a visitor center, and gift shop. Admission: US$7.50 adult; $5 ages six through twelve; free for ages five and younger.

Mastic Trail: A 200-year-old pedestrian path that once linked the north and south coasts of Grand Cayman is now a hiking trail that links Caymanians with their past and introduces visitors to the island's rich natural history. The 2-mile trail, developed by the Cayman Islands National Trust, passes through primary dry evergreen forest, now rare throughout the Caribbean, and is amazing for its variety. You can have something of a look at the land as it might have been when Columbus first came upon the Cayman Islands. Named for the massive mastic tree, the trail passes karst pinnacles, mangrove swamps, and ancient woodlands and has a variety of birds. Until recently, much of the flora was unidentified and unrecorded.

The original path was cut into the woodlands in the north by settlers in search of timber to build ships and export hardwoods such as mahogany and West Indian cedar. About the same time, farmers on the south coast cut a path north, clearing land to grow fruit trees and graze cattle. This part of the trail runs past mango and tamarind trees, as well as through buttonwood swamps. It also includes a short, old causeway across a mangrove swamp, which demonstrates the great effort required by the settlers to harvest the timber.

By reservation only the National Trust offers guided nature walks of two hours in small groups with a trained guide who meets you at the southern trailhead (off Frank Sound Road), normally starting at 9:00 A.M. on Wednesday and once a month on Saturday. Soft drinks and transport back to the southern trailhead at the end of the walk are provided. The price is CI$20 (US$25) per person.

Since cruise ships usually do not arrive in time for the scheduled departure, you will need to arrange in advance for your round-trip transportation and rendezvous with the guide. Phone or fax 949-0121 Monday through Friday between 10:00 A.M. and 3:00 P.M. The Mastic Trail walk is not suitable for children ages five and younger, the elderly, or persons with physical handicaps or conditions that might require emergency medical assistance.

East End: If you continue straight ahead along the coast instead of turning onto Frank Sound Road, you will soon come to East End, which is the name for both the area and one of the most historically authentic Caymanian villages, where you can have a look at Grand Cayman's past. The shipwreck lying at the fringe of the reef is the remains of the *Ridgefield*, a US cargo vessel that went aground in 1961 during the Bay of Pigs operation—a reminder that the Caymans are located only 200 miles south of Cuba.

As you round the eastern end of the island, you pass Morritt's Tortuga Club and the Reef Resort, two sprawling time-share hotels. They are just beyond where the road bends west onto the Queen's Highway. Several rare species of bird are found only here.

Old Man Bay: Continuing west along Queen's Highway about 5 miles, you will come to Old Man Bay and the northern terminus of Frank Sound Road, the north–south artery connecting the shores of the eastern peninsula. Your fastest way back to George Town, if you are short on time, is to turn left (south) and go back to South Sound Road, which will take you into George Town.

Rum Point: If you continue straight ahead to Rum Point, overlooking North Sound, you come to one of the island's nicest stretches of sand, second only to Seven Mile Beach; in winter it's the site of the island's most spectacular sunsets. Stingray City is just off the coast, although you can't get there from here. At Rum Point there is a snack bar with tree-shaded picnic tables where lunch is served. **Red Sail Sports,** the water sports operator, has a complete facility on the beach and is open daily. To return to George Town from here, you must retrace your route to Frank Sound Road and turn right (south). At South Sound Road, turn right (west) again. Along the way you will come to two forks in the road en route to town. If you hug the coast, always taking the left road at these forks, you will minimize the risk of getting lost on your way back into town.

Shopping

Grand Cayman is not known as a major shopping island. Heavy import duties make most items rather expensive, but duty-free shopping on a limited number of items, such as liquor, jewelry, and luxury products, offers good buys. Cayman Sea Salt is a popular gift. The quality of native art and handicrafts is good, but the supply is limited. The prosperity of the Caymans is reflected in a general appetite for imported high-tech consumer goods. Not surprisingly, Caymanian youth gravitate toward high-paying, skilled jobs and unfortunately show little interest in learning the traditional crafts and artistic skills of the islands. The best of Cayman's artisans are not being replaced, and native art and handicrafts have suffered as a result.

A word of caution: Those highly polished turtle shells and other turtle products for sale in Grand Cayman *cannot* be imported into the United States. Such products, even when produced on a commercial farm, are prohibited because the sea turtle is on the endangered species list. US Customs will confiscate these items upon your return, and you may be subject to a fine.

Antiques Artifacts: (Harbour Drive; 949-2442; www.artifacts.com.ky) has prints, maps, coins, silver, and other interesting pieces mainly from England. The most popular antiques are authentic gold and silver coins set into jewelry by local artisans.

Art and Artists: Several shops, all within walking distance of the harbor, are worth visiting in George Town. **Pure Art Gallery** (South Church Street; 949-9133; pureart@candw.ky) is an art lover's dream. If you had to select only one place on the island to shop, this would be the best choice. Even if you do not plan to buy, you will enjoy a visit to see the array. The gallery is set in a charming old Cayman cottage where every nook and cranny is filled with art as well as the usual crafts, herbs, and spices. Most of the items are locally made or come from other Caribbean islands, and all reflect

high quality and creativity. Among the crafts are the popular birdhouses by Charlie Ebanks.

Kennedy Fine Art Gallery (West Shore Center, West Bay Road; 949-8077; kgallery@candw.ky) stocks local and foreign artists who spend time in the Caymans.

Heritage Crafts (Soto Freeport Building, second floor; 945-6041). Traditional Caymanian baskets and other woven items are a particularly good buy. Made from thatched palm fibers of a strong species that grows in the Caymans, these baskets are tough and durable. **Cayman Islands National Gallery** (Harbour Place, South Church Street, 945-811; www.nationalgallery.org.ky) is a new, small gallery focused on contemporary local and international art and has changing exhibits.

Island Glass Blowing (189 North Church Street; 946-1483; islandglassblowing@candw.ky). At Cayman's only glassblowing studio, you can watch daily demonstrations while experienced glassblowers shape, blow, and form pieces from hot molten glass. Stingrays, turtles, dolphins, fish, plates, vases, and bowls are some of the items available. **The Craft Market** (waterfront corner of South Church Street and Boilers Road). A short walk from the cruise ship dock in George Town, vendors in an outdoor venue offer locally made items of leather, thatch, wood, and shell, as well as Cayman Sea Salt and samples of traditional Caymanian food. **Cayman Sea Salt** (943-7258; www.caymanseasalt.com) can also be found at island gift and grocery stores.

China/Crystal: Fine duty-free shops are within an easy walk of the harbor. English crystal and china are specialties. The prices are good, and the selection is wide. **Kirk Freeport Center** (Albert Panton Street, Bayshore Mall; 949-7477; www.kirk freeport.net) and **Waterford/Wedgwood Gallery** (Cardinal Avenue; 949-7477) have the best selections of duty-free china and crystal. **Duty Free Stores** (at the harborside Anchorage Center) have excellent selections of perfumes and designer items such as watches.

Clothing: Generally most clothing items are imported from the United States, and the selection is limited. Resortwear is plentiful—but at resort prices. One of the most attractive shops is

Shellections (Waterfront Centre, Church Street; 945-1023), which is a vision in pastels and flowers with hand-painted resortwear for the whole family. There are dresses, summer garden-party hats, painted shirts and dresses, jewelry, and jewelry boxes.

Along Edward Street, just north of Cardinal Avenue, **Tropical L'Attitude** (Butterfield Place, Edward Street; 945-1233; fax: 945-1237) and **Aqua World Duty-Free Mall** (Merrendale Drive; 946-9219) have batik and colorful island fashions. Tropical L'Attitude is one of the twenty-two shops filling the four-story shopping mall on Grand Cayman's harborfront, next to the Hard Rock Cafe. It's painted yellow, blue, and red—you can't miss it.

Jewelry: You will see black coral jewelry advertised, but the Cayman Islands prohibited its harvest in 1986, when they passed marine conservation laws. The coral you see is mostly from Asia. Those who care about the environment will have trouble understanding the logic in the Caymans' protecting their own coral but allowing that from other countries to be sold in local stores. If you buy it, you only encourage the practice.

Some of the most attractive ancient coin jewelry is found at **24-K-Mon Jewelers** (Fort Street; 949-1499); a certificate of authenticity accompanies all purchases. The store also has delightful gold jewelry with sea themes, including stingrays, scuba divers, dolphins, and more.

Many of the waterfront buildings along Harbour Drive have been renovated, giving the downtown an attractive face-lift, splashed with bright Caribbean colors. Among the stand-alone stores is **Colombian Emeralds** (Harbour Drive; 949-8808; sheal@colombianemeralds.com; www.dutyfree .com). On Cardinal Avenue, directly in front of the docks, you will find **Cartier Boutique** (949-7477), along with the **Kirk Freeport Center** (Bayshore Mall; 949-7477; www.kirkfreeport.net) and **Caymania Duty Free** (949-7972), one of the oldest establishments.

Liquor: With nearly US$28 per gallon duty on alcohol coming into the Cayman Islands, liquor is no bargain for local residents. However, cruise passengers can buy duty-free liquor in-bond at Tortuga Rum Company outlets (seventeen retail outlets,

including four in town and at the Turtle Farm and its headquarters, which are stops on tours). Be sure to order a few hours in advance. Liquor is delivered in-bond to your ship. You can't take it with you. There are no locally made rums or other spirits as on many Caribbean islands. Tortuga rum cake is by far the best buy in Grand Cayman, available at **Tortuga Rum** (South Church Street; 949-6322; www.tortugarums.com) and all the company's other outlets. Tortuga Rum now has six flavors of rum cake and a growing line of products from coffee to gourmet sauces. It is a delicious rum-soaked pound cake that's so popular, the company even has offices in Miami (877-486-7884) for fans to order from. Tortuga Rum Company's modern, spacious headquarters and bakery is often a stop on island tours. Free samples are available. Here you can buy Tortuga products as well as liquor that will be delivered to your ship. The larger bakery is better able to handle the volume of cakes—5,000 a day—using a century-old recipe. They are sold vacuum-packed.

Another great souvenir is *Tortuga Rum Fever and Caribbean Party Cookbook,* with more than 400 rum drinks, island dishes, and humorous tidbits of rum and island history, written by Cayman Islands resident Barbara Currie Dailey. The book is available at all Tortuga Rum outlets, in shops islandwide, and online.

Dining and Restaurants

In the last few years, the range and quality of restaurants on Grand Cayman has widened considerably. The bad news about dining in Grand Cayman is that it tends to be expensive. Again, the need to import most ingredients, high labor costs, and a steep duty on imported items keep the prices high. Expect to pay US$50 or more per person with wine in an expensive restaurant.

Native Caymanian cooking emphasizes seafood. Fish served in Grand Cayman's top restaurants is usually ocean-fresh and prepared well. Turtle steak is a national delicacy, which, if properly prepared, can be good. Turtle has a taste best described as a cross between chicken and veal. However, the supply of turtle meat is limited, and it can be hard to find in local restaurants.

Abanks Watersports and Paradise Bar and Grill (just south of George Town on the sea; 945-1444). Known locally as Paradise Restaurant, it's a casual bar and cafe with great burgers, daily specials, and some island dishes. You can rent snorkeling equipment here for US$10 for mask, snorkel, and fins and enjoy Devil's Grotto, then dry off, have lunch in your bathing suit, and go back to splash some more. The restaurant is open daily from 7:00 A.M. to 10:00 P.M.; the water sports shop is open based on cruise ship arrivals. Moderate.

Cracked Conch by the Sea (West Bay, next to the Turtle Farm; 945-5217; www.crackedconch.com.ky). This well-known restaurant changed ownership in 2006 and was totally redesigned and upgraded by its new owners. It specializes in local dishes and seafood. A spacious outdoor terrace and bar 15 feet above the ironshore coast and sea offers panoramic views and spectacular sunsets. Expensive.

Grand Old House (South Church Street; 949-9333; www.grandoldhouse.com) was the first of Grand Cayman's elegant restaurants. It is located in a turn-of-the-twentieth-century plantation house and serves seafood and continental cuisine with a distinct West Indian touch. Expensive.

My Bar (Sunset House, South Church Street; 949-7111; www.sunsethouse.com). The thatched-roof restaurant of this thirty-plus-year institution is popular with local folks, from English bankers to taxi drivers, for its chummy atmosphere overlooking the sea. Fish-and-chips, snacks, sandwiches, and daily drink specials. Inexpensive lunch. Don't miss **Cathy Church's Underwater Photo Center** (949-7415; 607-330-3504; www.cathychurch.com) on the premises, where you will see a gallery of underwater photography by one of the world's top photographers.

Ritz-Carlton Grand Cayman (Seven-Mile Beach/West Bay; 815-6851; www.ritzcarlton.com) has six restaurants and bars offering tradition and novelty: Periwinkle by Eric Ripert (of New York's Le Bernardin) is an open-air eatery for seafood, grill selections, and homemade pastas; Bar Jack provides light fare poolside; Sushi and Wine Lounge offers sake martinis and forty wines by the glass, in addition to sushi, sashimi, and Japanese green teas; Silver Palm serves a traditional English tea

and fifty-six wines by the glass. 7 Prime Cuts & Sunsets, the haute cuisine venue, is only open for dinner. All are expensive.

The Wharf (Seven Mile Beach; 949-2231; www.wharf.ky), with its pretty setting of white-washed gazebos stepping down to the water's edge, is one of the island's most popular restaurants. The menu offers an interesting variety of creative fish and meat dishes. Moderately expensive.

Sports

Beach/Swimming: There is but one beach on Grand Cayman worthy of your time. Seven Mile Beach runs north of George Town for—yes, 7 miles. It is one of the best anywhere in the Caribbean. The crest of white powdery sand edged by tall Australian pines slopes gently into a waveless turquoise sea. There are other beaches on Grand Cayman, but for cruise passengers with a limited amount of time, we recommend Seven Mile, a ten-minute taxi ride from the harbor.

For active water sports, head for any of the water sports centers on Seven Mile Beach or **Red Sail Sports** (www.redsailcayman.com) at the Westin Casuarina Resort, where every imaginable type of equipment is available for rent. On the other hand, if you prefer a quiet spot of sand with little to do but swim and sun, have the driver take you farther down the road to the public beach. When you are ready to return to George Town and the ship, walk to the Westin Hotel nearby, where you can pick up a taxi.

Another choice spot is the **Royal Palms Beach Bar** (945-6358; www.reefgrill.com), located on one of the last undeveloped parts of Seven Mile Beach (on the old Royal Palms site) and an ideal place to enjoy the beach. You'll find volleyball, lounge chairs, a full beach bar, and a casual grill/restaurant. There may be a small admission fee.

Boating: You have a choice of several small sailing craft from Sunfish to Hobie cats; there's also a 60-foot catamaran with crew available for charter. Day sailors and Hobie cats rent for about US$30, and kayaks $15 to $20. **Stingray City Charters** (949-9200; www.stingraycitycharters.com) and **Kirk Sea Tours** (949-7278; www.kirkseatours.com)

offer daily guided snorkeling excursions to Stingray City and a variety of water sports, including Snuba, and welcome advance reservations from cruise passengers. Stingray City Charters tours depart at 9:30 A.M. and 1:30 P.M. Cost: US$39 adult (seven-day advance purchase, US$35.10); half price ages four through eleven; free to those three and under.

Deep-Sea Fishing: You cannot find a more perfect spot than the Cayman Islands for deep-sea fishing. It's a passion here, and just about every type of boat is available. The waters are noted for marlin, yellowfin tuna, wahoo, mahimahi, and barracuda.

All equipment is available for rental, from smaller boats to fully equipped charters for deep-sea fishing. The latter range from US$600 for up to four people for a half day, $900 full day; on up to $900 for up to eight people for a half day, $1,600 full day, depending on the boat. A list of charter boat operators is available in the Tourism Department's booklet *Cayman Islands Travel Planner*. Among them are **Bayside Watersports** (949-3200; www.baysidewatersports.com) and **Black Princess Charters** (949-0400; www.fishgrand cayman.com).

The annual **Cayman Islands International Fishing Tournament** (www.fishcayman.com), which runs for a week in April, offering more than US$50,000 in prizes, is now the top sportfishing event in the Cayman Islands. For information contact the Cayman Islands Department of Tourism at 949-7099.

Golf: Grand Cayman has three golf courses. The first of its kind, **Britannia Golf Club** (949-8020; www.britanniagolfclub.com), was designed by Jack Nicklaus as a regulation nine-hole course overlapped by a special short-ball eighteen-hole course, now known as Cayman Golf. The course is located about a ten-minute taxi ride from the harbor. All equipment is available. The eighteen-hole Cayman course costs US$150 for non-hotel-guests from November 1 through April 30; $100 May 1 through October 31. The regulation nine-hole course costs US$90 November 1 through April 30; $70 May 1 through October 31. As a cruise ship shore excursion, about US$175. Club rentals $20 for nine holes, $40 for eighteen. Reservations are necessary

and can be made by calling 745-4653. The new Blue Tip, nine-hole course at the Ritz-Carlton (815-6500; www.ritzcarlton.com) was designed by Greg Norman. Five long par-fours into the trade winds make this course a challenge. It is open to hotel guest and residence owners only.

The Links (345-949-5988; www.safehaven.ky /links.htm) is an eighteen-hole championship course in the West End at Safehaven, a 280-acre resort and residential development. The course (6,605 yards, par 71) was designed by Roy Case to suggest the old Scottish coastal courses. The clubhouse has a restaurant-bar, pro shop, and changing facilities. Rates are US $40 for nine holes and US $70 for eighteen holes for nonmembers; tee times may be booked 24 hours in advance. *Note:* The Links does not yet have golf carts, so golfers must walk the course. A limited number of rental clubs area available on a first come, first serve basis for US $35 per set. The course has been renovated and upgraded with new greens and turf and is open Monday, Thursday, Friday; tee-off times begin at 8:00 A.M., weekends at 7:30 A.M. In December 2007, Ritz Carlton, Grand Cayman, announced the creation of North Sound Club and acquired the Safe Haven property which, with the cooperation of Greg Norman's Great Shark Enterprises, will merge the golf course with Ritz-Carlton's Blue Tip course. The plan also calls for new practice facilities, putting course, club house with pro shop, dining facilities, and private primary and vacation homes. No timetable was announced.

Horseback Riding: Pampered Ponies (945-2262; www.ponies.ky) offers guided trail rides and beach rides, including sunset rides for all levels, on trained horses imported from the United States; US$75 for a ninety-minute ride. Cruise passengers must call in advance for reservations. Other options are **Horseback in Paradise with Nicki** (Barkers Beach, West Bay; 945-5839; www.caymanhorse riding.com) and **The Equestrian Centre** (949-7360), a riding school that specializes in English riding lessons for ages seven and older.

Scuba Diving/Snorkeling: The Cayman Islands, which have been called the Mount Everest of Diving, are considered by many scuba divers to have the best waters in the Caribbean for diving and snorkeling. If you are a certified diver (and can prove it with current PADI, NAUI, or YMCA C-Card), you should certainly put diving the Cayman Islands at the top of your priority list.

Although there are dives to be made from shore and even shipwrecks right at George Town Harbor, the particularly interesting features of Cayman diving are gigantic corals, canyons, and walls in areas that you must take a boat to reach. In some places there are freestanding coral heads of 30 feet or more in height and many caves to explore. The Cayman Islands' coast and waters are protected by a marine park created in 1986 and have more than 280 permanent mooring positions off the three islands.

One of the most popular snorkeling and dive sites is just south of George Town harbor near Eden Rocks. It is a complex system of underwater tunnels connecting coral heads in 40 feet of water and rising to within 5 feet of the surface. Fish life, too, is abundant, with schools of yellowtail snapper, blue tangs, and an occasional moray eel and stingray. North of George Town are fine shallow reefs and good drop-offs; at East End and along the south shore to South West Point, the highlight is shallow elkhorn coral reefs that crown labyrinths of limestone caves and grottos housing grouper and giant blue parrotfish.

Because Grand Cayman's North Sound is, in effect, a marine estuary, fish life is abundant. The 20 miles or so of North Wall, off Rum Point, offer great wall diving, with craggy fissures and cuts predominating in certain areas. Circular chimneys that drop 30 to 50 feet and then open out into the ocean are commonplace. However, do not have your heart set on going to one particular place, or you could be disappointed. Dive operators choose the dive sites, and they base their choices on the weather and currents and on the level of experience of the participants.

The Cayman Islands' Department of Tourism's publications and the Web site www.divecayman.ky have maps and a list of the Caymans' three dozen or more dive operators, with their addresses, phone numbers, services, equipment, prices, and other pertinent information.

Most cruise ships calling at Grand Cayman offer dive packages, but they are often more than double the price than if you make arrangements directly with local operators. We recommend you call or write from home for a reservation before leaving on your cruise, particularly during the winter season. When you arrive you will have to get yourself to the dive operator by taxi. Timing is very important—most dive trips depart at 9:00 A.M.

Eden Rock Diving Center (on the south side of George Town, within sight of the port; 949-7243; www.edenrockdive.com). This PADI training facility and underwater photo center has one of Grand Cayman's top shore-diving facilities. Its proximity to the dock makes it ideal for snorkelers and certified divers (must show C-Card), who can rent diving equipment and tanks and underwater cameras right there and do a shallow dive on spectacular Devil's Grotto and Eden Rock, Cayman's most famous shore dives. You can also reserve a two-tank boat dive for US$80 to $100 per person by booking online in advance—e-mail edenrock@candw.ky. The boat leaves at 9:00 A.M. and returns by 1:30 P.M.

Other excellent dive operators include **Don Foster's Dive Grand Cayman** (949-5679; 800-833-4837; www.donfosters.com) where a one-tank dive costs $55, a two-tank dive $85, and Stingray snorkeling, $35; as well as **DIVETECH/Turtle Reef Divers** (949-1700; fax 949-1701; www.divetech .com), the dive shop at the Cracked Conch, which is open daily from 8:00 A.M. to 8:00 P.M. and offers easy access to a sponge-encrusted mini wall beginning at 30 feet, only 200 yards offshore.

Stingray City—as the site has been dubbed—is just inside the barrier reef that protects North Sound and is one of the most unusual sites in the Caribbean. Here, in water never more than 15 feet deep, divers and snorkelers can see, touch, and photograph two dozen or more friendly stingrays inhabiting the area. This unusual fish has eyes on top of its body, has a wing span of up to 5 feet, and looks like a ship from outer space as it glides gracefully through the water. When purchased directly from a local operator, the going rate for a snorkeling excursion to Stingray City ranges from US$30 to $57 ($49 as a cruise ship excursion) and $45 to $50 for a dive ($74 as a cruise ship excursion). **Stingray City Charters** (949-9200) and **Kirk Sea Tours** (Queen's Court; 949-7278) welcome requests for advance arrangements from cruise passengers. Stingray City trips go either to the original deep site used by divers and snorkelers or to the Sand Bar, which is shallower.

Windsurfing/Kayaking: The calm waters along Seven Mile Beach are a good place to learn to windsurf; most resorts have equipment. For greater challenge, the northeast coast is one of the main windsurfing locations. **Cayman Windsurfing** (947-7492) has rentals (US$35 per hour) and an introductory lesson ($45). It also has kayaks for rent. **Cayman Kayaks** (345-926-4467; www.cayman kayaks.com) is an adventure tour company offering a range of guided kayak tours in the Rum Point and Cayman Kai area.

Unusual Dive Opportunities for Nondivers

For those who are not divers, Grand Cayman offers several extraordinary opportunities to see the underwater world. The *Atlantis,* a submarine designed specifically for recreational undersea travel, can dive to a depth of 150 feet. The 50-foot-long ship holds forty-six people and a two-member crew; it boasts one extra-large window in front and eight large viewports along the sides, from which passengers can see nature's display. The ship makes day and night dives along the famous Cayman Wall, where divers normally swim at 40 to 90 feet. The ship is air-conditioned, and all its systems are duplicated to ensure safety. A surface vessel travels with the submarine and is in constant contact by underwater telephone or VHF radio.

Passengers go by motor launch, which leaves about every hour from 9:00 A.M. throughout the day from George Town Harbor, for a ten-minute ride to the *Atlantis* boarding point. The dive itself is about one hour along the wall to a depth of 90 to 150 feet and is accompanied by a guide who gives a running commentary on the various fish and coral.

Atlantis Expeditions, US$79 adult; $49 child twelve or younger and over 36 inches tall; $69 ages thirteen to seventeen; those three years old and younger are not admitted. You should buy this as a ship's shore excursion, as the price is the same when bought directly. *Seaworld Explorer,* a semi-submersible operated by Atlantis, and *Nautilus* (945-1355), a similar semi-submersible but offering better viewing, are less expensive alternatives.

Entertainment/Nightlife

Cruise ships seldom remain in port in the evening, but if yours does you will find clubs with live entertainment, a comedy club, discos, and even a karaoke bar. The island's famous band, the Barefoot Man, plays everything from calypso to pop at the Reef Resort (East End) three nights weekly. You can also catch the Coconuts Comedy Club at **Legendz Bar** (945-5288) in Cayman Falls Plaza and other venues. The **Harquail Theatre** (West Bay Road; 949-5477) is used for a variety of cultural events and stage performances.

Festivals and Celebrations

High on the list of unique entertainment in Grand Cayman is the annual **Pirates Week Festival** (949-5859; www.piratesweekfestival.com) in late October. In celebration of its history as a pirate lair, the whole island is transformed into a pirate encampment complete with a mock invasion of George Town, parades, pageants, parties, and the crowning of a pirate queen. If you happen to land here during Pirates Week, be ready to be swept up into the fun and frolic. The **Batabano Festival** (949-7121; www.caymancarnival.com) in May is the more traditional Carnival. **Cayfest** (949-5477; www.artscayman.org), the Caymans' celebration of the arts, runs for several weeks in April.

The Mexican Caribbean

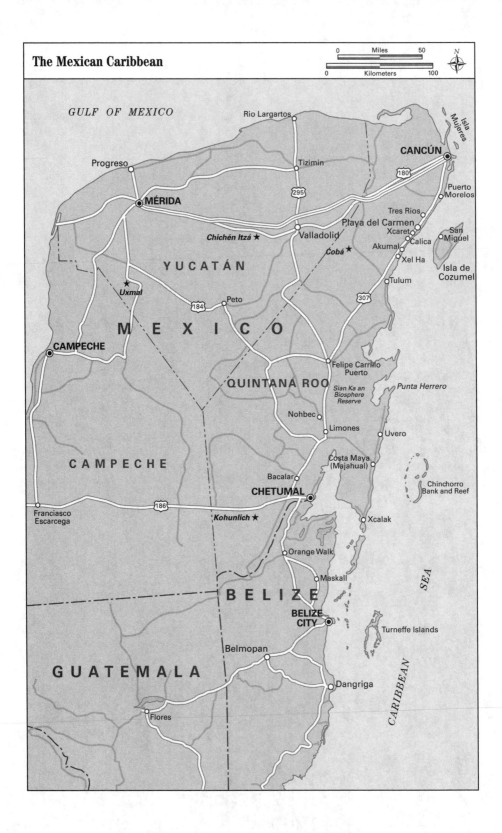

The Mexican Caribbean

GULF OF MEXICO

Rio Largartos

Isla Mujeres

CANCÚN

Progreso

Tizimin

Puerto
Morelos

MÉRIDA

295

180

Tres Rios

Playa del Carmen

Chichén Itzá ★

Valladolid

Xcaret

San
Miguel

Calica

Cobá ★

Akumal

Xel Ha

Y U C A T Á N

Isla de
Cozumel

Tulum

★
Uxmal

Peto

184

M E X I C O

307

CAMPECHE

Felipe Carrillo
Puerto

QUINTANA ROO

Punta Herrero

Sian Ka an
Biosphere
Reserve

Nohbec

Uvero

Limones

C A M P E C H E

Costa Maya
(Majahual)

Chinchorro
Bank and Reef

Bacalar

CHETUMAL

186

Franciasco
Escarcega

Kohunlich ★

Xcalak

Orange Walk

Maskall

SEA

B E L I Z E

**BELIZE
CITY**

Turneffe Islands

Belmopan

G U A T E M A L A

Dangriga

CARIBBEAN

Flores

Miles
0   50

Kilometers
0   100

N

Where the Past Meets the Present

The Mexican Caribbean is one of the oldest, most historic regions of Mexico and one of its newest, most popular vacation resorts. It is best known by the names of the two most developed islands, Cancún and Cozumel, famous for their lovely beaches and magnificent water rich in coral gardens and marine life.

Both islands are located on the tip of the Yucatán Peninsula at the easternmost extreme of Mexico, where the Caribbean Sea meets the waters of the Gulf of Mexico. Cancún is connected to the mainland by roads and bridges and seems more like an extension of the mainland than an island. Cozumel is located about 10 miles off the coast, directly east of the port of Playa del Carmen, about 40 miles south of Cancún.

Cancún bills itself as the first resort of the computer age. The site was nothing more than a sandbar in 1973 when it was selected by computer analysis as the best place to start Mexico's long-range development of its coast. Today it is an international playground with glamorous resorts and restaurants, golf, tennis, and a full complement of water sports.

Cozumel, too, has come into its own as a resort since the 1980s, with an array of hotels, restaurants, and sporting activity, but the island was put on the tourist map even earlier by scuba divers. It has been a prime location for diving for more than forty years. These days it's as popular with shoppers as with divers. Yet for all their up-to-the-minute fun and facilities, both resorts are part of a land whose history stretches back more than 1,000 years before the arrival of Columbus.

Before Columbus and Cortés

Long before the discovery of America by Columbus and the conquest of Mexico by Cortés, there were civilizations throughout the Americas—the Inca, the Aztec, the Maya—that reached great heights of culture and achievement. One of them, the Maya, dominated the region of the Yucatán from about the first to the twelfth century A.D. Today the remnants of their civilization are among Mexico's most important antiquities. At its height the Mayan domain comprised an area extending roughly 550 miles north to south and 350 miles east to west. This included the present states of Yucatán, Campeche, and Quintana Roo in Mexico, as well as Belize, Guatemala, and Honduras. By the time the Spaniards conquered Mexico in the early sixteenth century, the Mayan culture had already declined, and many of the towns had been abandoned. Why this happened is one of the many mysteries about the Mayas confronting archaeologists.

Indeed, Mayas are almost synonymous with mystery. They stepped into history seemingly from nowhere, spawned a civilization that lasted 1,500 years, and disappeared almost as suddenly as they came. Archaeological evidence shows that the Mayas established cities with as many as 50,000 inhabitants, constructed stone pyramids seventeen stories high and palaces of a hundred rooms or more, chiseled massive sculpture, and painted detailed murals and friezes that can still be seen on their magnificent temples and pyramids throughout the Yucatán.

The Mayas had a complex written language, charted the revolution of the sun and the planets in

At a Glance

Antiquities	★★★★★
Archaeology	★★★★★
Art and Artists	★★
Beaches	★★★★★
Crafts	★★★★★
Cuisine	★★★
Dining/Restaurants	★★★
Entertainment	★★★
History	★★★★★
Museums	★★
Nightlife	★★★★
Scenery	★★
Shopping	★★★★
Sightseeing	★★★★
Sports	★★★★★
Transportation	★★

Main Towns: Cancún, 572,973; Playa del Carmen/Calica, 200,000; Chetumal/Costa Maya, 200,000; San Miguel (Cozumel), 70,000.

Climate: Consistently warm, around 80°F year-round, and dry.

Clothing: Casual and comfortable summer sportswear for day and only a little less casual for evening.

Currency: The unit of currency is the Mexican peso, written with a $ dollar sign or as MXP, meaning "Mexican peso." In January 1993 the government introduced a new peso, dropping the last three zeros on the old peso. The new peso is represented by N$ to distinguish it from the old peso. Now, US$1 equals about N$10 instead of 10,000 pesos. Banks are open 9:00 A.M. to 1:30 P.M. Monday through Friday.

Because of the fluctuation in the peso, we have included very few prices in this chapter. Those that are included are provided for readers' planning purposes. None is likely to be precisely accurate at the time of your visit, but we hope they are close enough to be useful.

Customs Regulations: If you disembark in Mexico to return to the United States by plane, there is a departure tax of US$20 or 200 pesos; cash only.

Electricity: AC 60, 110 volts.

Entry Formalities: Normally visitors need tourist cards to enter Mexico. These formalities are handled by the cruise lines. However, you should have your passport with you for identification, and you will need a driver's license and a major credit card to rent a car.

Language: Spanish. English is spoken at hotels and most, but not all, shops.

Postal Service: The post office in Cozumel is located at the corner of Calle 7 Sur and Avenida Rafael Melgar (known as the Malecon).

Telephone Area Code: Mexico, 52; Cancún, 998; Cozumel, 987. From the United States dial 011-52+998 and the local, seven-digit number for Cancún, or 987 and the local, five-digit number for Cozumel. Cancún has expanded its phone numbers, generally with the addition of an 8 as a prefix to the local number, but not all printed matter reflects the change. If you have trouble connecting, try adding an 8 in front of the local number.

Time: Cancún, Playa del Carmen, and Cozumel lie in the Central Standard time zone.

Vaccination Requirements: None.

Airlines: *From the United States:* American, Continental, Delta, Mexicana, Northwest, and United. *From Canada:* AirCanada and Mexicana. *Between Cozumel/Cancún/Mérida:* Click Mexicana. *Between Cancún and Chetumal:* Click Mexicana, Aviacsa Consorcio.

Information: www.visitmexico .com For information on Cancún, call (888) 401-3880 or visit www.cancun.info. For updates on the Riviera Maya (Playa Del Carmen, Tulum, Akumal, Puerto Morelos), call (877) 7GOMAYA (746-6292) or log on to www.rivieramaya.com.

In the United States, Mexican Government Tourism Offices:

New York: 400 Madison Avenue, Suite 11C, NY 10017; (212) 308-2110; (800) 446-3942; fax 308-9060; newyork@visitmexico.com.

Chicago: 225 North Michigan Avenue, Suite 1850, IL 60601; (312) 228-0517, ext. 14; fax (312) 228-0515.

Houston: 4507 San Jacinto, Suite 308, TX 77004; (713) 772-2581; fax (713) 772-6058; houston@visitmexico.com.

Los Angeles: 1880 Century Park East, Suite 511, CA 90067; (310) 282-9112, ext. 23; fax (310) 282-9116; losangeles@visitmexico.com.

Miami: 5975 Sunset Drive, Suite 305, South Miami, FL 33143; (786) 621-2909; (786) 621-2907; miami@visitmexico.com.

In Canada, Mexican Government Tourism Offices:

Montreal: 1 Place Ville Marie No. 1931, Quebec, H3B 2C3; (514) 871-1103; fax (514) 871-3825.

Toronto: 2 Bloor Street West, Suite 1502, Ontario, M4W 3E2; (416) 925-0704; fax (416) 925-6061.

Vancouver: 999 West Hastings Street, No. 1110; British Columbia, V6C 2W2; (604) 669-2845; fax (604) 669-3498.

their observatories, calculated great mathematical sums, developed a calendar more accurate than the one we use today, practiced brain surgery, composed music, and wrote books (destroyed by zealous Spanish priests). And what makes the Mayas all the more remarkable is that they gained these achievements without benefit of the wheel, the plow, or other aids usually associated with an advanced civilization.

Archaeologists estimate that less than 10 percent of the Mayan cities have been found. The best known of the archaeology sites today are Chichén Itzá, about 70 miles from Mérida, the capital of the Yucatán near the northwest coast; Uxmal, 35 miles south of Mérida; and Tulum and Cobá, about 35 miles from Playa del Carmen on the east coast.

The combination of superb sports and modern facilities, Mexican crafts, cuisine, and proximity to some of the most important archaeological sites in the Western Hemisphere has made the Mexican Caribbean resorts popular as ports of call.

Budget Planning

Mexico is one of today's best travel bargains, but you may not see the benefit as a cruise passenger because the Mexican Caribbean is a tourist resort area where prices tend to be higher than in the interior of the country.

If you are on a budget, stay away from fancy bars and restaurants, particularly in resort hotels. You will do best eating at places that specialize in Mexican fare, drinking local Mexican drinks, and dealing directly with tour companies and dive operators. You do have the alternative of good public transportation in Cancún, particularly if you speak Spanish.

Shore Excursions

Generalizations about shore excursions for Cozumel, Cancún, and Playa del Carmen/Calica are difficult because there is little consistency in cruise ship arrivals and departures, in the ports they use, or in price. Some ships arrive early in the morning and leave in the afternoon about sunset; others arrive in Cozumel, where they remain through all or most of the next day while passengers make their

excursions to the mainland by ferry, plane, or hydrofoil. A few call at Cozumel only or Playa del Carmen or Calica only, while even fewer make stops at both Playa del Carmen or Calica and Cozumel or dock directly at Cancún.

As for prices, to take only one example, the Tulum/Xel-Ha tour varies from an overpriced US$80 to $105 for a three-hour excursion from Playa del Carmen, to a moderate $55 to $68 for five to six hours from Cozumel, to a low price of $40 to $45 for seven hours from Cancún—all for the same tour.

Adding to the confusion in terms of planning your day in port is the listing in some brochures of Cozumel and Cancún or Playa del Carmen and Calica as though they were one port. Playa del Carmen is on the mainland, about 10 miles directly west of Cozumel island and 40 miles south of Cancún. Calica is 5 miles south of Playa del Carmen. More often than not when a ship's itinerary is shown as Cozumel/Playa del Carmen, the ship stops in Cozumel only. To reach the mainland, you must go and return via a thirty-minute ferry ride from Cozumel to Playa del Carmen for the excursion to Tulum. Or, on your own, you can take a fifteen-minute plane ride from the Cozumel airport to Cancún or a thirty-minute plane ride to Chichén Itzá. There are "fast" or "express" ferries—hydrofoils—between Cozumel and Playa del Carmen, which depart about every one to two hours during the day from the main pier in town and take thirty minutes.

Out of the three dozen or so cruise ships on regular Western Caribbean cruises, the majority's itineraries read Playa del Carmen/Cozumel. That means the ship anchors at Playa del Carmen long enough for passengers to disembark for their excursions, and then the ship continues to Cozumel. Passengers return to their waiting ships in Cozumel by ferry.

You should study the cruise line's brochure carefully, if you are interested in visiting a locale such as Chichén Itzá. If a particular attraction or site is not offered as a shore excursion on the cruise line's Web site, ask your travel agent to obtain the information you need in advance of your cruise. Some cruise lines offer a Chichén Itzá excursion; otherwise you must make your own arrangements, and knowing which port or ports your ship visits is essential to your planning. Another caution when making independent arrangements: Some excursions do not operate daily, except in high season (from mid-December to mid-April).

The following tours are described elsewhere in this chapter. The order of priority is based on our experience, but you should be guided by your personal interest in making a selection. When shore excursions run longer than four hours, a box lunch will be provided by your ship.

We are happy to report that in the past several years, cruise lines have made significant additions of interesting and innovative excursions in Cozumel, Playa del Carmen, and Costa Maya. They range from hiking, rock climbing, kayaking, and fly fishing to classes in Mayan cooking and an adventure tour by Segway.

Note to photographers: At all archaeological sites, a charge of US$8 or $10 is levied by the Mexican government for video cameras.

Prices in the following three regional sections are in US dollars. Those given here are merely guidelines, as they vary from cruise line to cruise line and are subject to change.

Cozumel

Chichén Itzá Air Tour: Five to six hours; $230 and up. Arrangements can be made through local tour companies. Some ships offer an eleven-hour overland Chichén Itzá tour from Cozumel for $79 to $98, but this requires a round-trip ferry ride to Playa del Carmen, where the bus departs and returns. For those who can afford it, the difference for the air tour is worth the price.

Robinson Crusoe Boat Excursion: Full day; $45 with drinks; $65 with lunch. The boat sails along the leeward coast to a secluded cove for swimming, snorkeling over the reefs, and a seafood lunch. The trip is usually sold aboard ship as a half-day excursion with lunch for $72 to $77; or party cruise on a boat for 200 people, which is not recommended unless you want this kind of atmosphere, for $59.

Cozumel Diving: $50 to $76 for a one-tank dive; $60 to $80, two-tank dive. The best dive sites are an hour from Cozumel; boats depart between 8:00 and 9:00 A.M. (See the Sports section for details.) As a cruise ship shore excursion, a half-day dive trip will cost $80 to $120; for snorkeling, $35 to $55, depending on the ship. Some ships offer a two-hour dive course for beginners at $95 to $130.

If you are ready to venture beyond snorkeling but not sure about scuba diving, Snuba (two hours, $69) might be the answer. It's a combination of snorkeling and scuba diving—well, almost. Instead of donning cumbersome scuba diving equipment, you are tethered to a boat wearing an apparatus that provides a mask and oxygen. After a brief orientation by the divemaster in shallow water, where you try out your skills and build your confidence, you go to deeper water (15 to 18 feet) to spend twenty-five minutes viewing some of Cozumel's famous underwater world. *Note:* Participants must be at least twelve years old and meet certain medical requirements.

Island Tour: Three and a half hours; $36 to $40. Tour the island by bus, visit Mayan ruins, stop for a swim at a coral beach on the windward side, visit National Marine Park at Chankanaab Lagoon, and shop in San Miguel. As a cruise ship excursion, the cost ranges from $40 to $60 for adults, depending on the ship.

Jeep Safari: Four hours; $75 to $89 per person (four persons per jeep). Many cruise lines offer a wilderness/beach excursion by self-drive jeep that is to be avoided. You travel caravan-style on a very rough dirt and sand path through the jungle to a beautiful beach on the east side of the island that's too rough for swimming. Buffet lunch is served. The excursion is a big rip-off; you can rent a similar jeep for $50 for the full day, tour the entire island on your own, at your own pace, have a safe swim at a west coast beach and a great lunch in town, or picnic by the beach for less than $20 per person. The total for four persons would be about $130, instead of the cruise line's $300 to $348 intake. Some cruise lines have different versions of jeep safaris. For example, there's "Dune Buggy and Snorkel," which costs about $90 per person. It, too, can be done on your own for considerably less.

Cozumel by Horseback: Three and a half hours; $80 to $89. Most ships offer a safari by horseback, starting from a ranch in the heart of the island. After a briefing by an English-speaking guide, you are assigned a horse suited to your riding ability and experience. The ride follows trails in the wilderness and takes in ancient Mayan ruins. **Adventure Naturales** (phone/fax 011-52-987-872-1628; US 1-858-366-4632; http://aventurasnatural ascozumel.com) offers two-hour rides at 9:00 A.M. and 3:00 P.M. with bilingual guides for $35; minimum age ten and older, maximum weight 275 pounds. The company also offers bike tours, sailing, and other excursions.

Atlantis **Submarine:** One and a half hours; $79 adult; $45 child ($99 and $49 through a cruise line). The forty-eight-passenger submarine offers nondivers a chance to see what all the excitement is about since Cozumel is one of the top dive destinations in the world. The air-conditioned vessel has 2-foot-wide windows from which to view coral and marine life at depths of up to 100 feet along the second longest reef in the world. Passengers are picked up from their ship either by water ferry or bus and taken to the starting point. Bring your camera.

Dolphin Royal Swim: One hour; $139 ($165 as a cruise ship excursion). Swim with dolphins at Chankanaab National Marine Park, available four times daily. For details see the Chankanaab Park section later in this chapter, or log on to www .dolphindiscovery.com.

Playa Mia Beach Day: $19 adult; $14 ages three through twelve. ($39 for one hour; $75 for five hours as a cruise ship excursion.) Spend the day at a beach club 10 miles south of town (you are likely to find others from your ship there, too). You'll find a bar, beach, pool, lounge chairs, floats, kayaks, and other nonmotorized water toys, as well as organized beach activities. The activities desk

has a welcome packet of information about the facilities and their use.

Playa del Carmen or Calica

Tulum and Xel-Ha Lagoon: Three hours, $68; or five to six hours, $95 to $102 (returning by ferry to Cozumel to rejoin your ship). The tour includes a visit to the archaeological site of Tulum and a swim and refreshments at the lagoon. Take your snorkel gear and towel. Instead of Xel-Ha, some tours stop at Xcaret, a nature reserve and recreational park a few miles south of Playa del Carmen. The cost will be considerably higher in this case.

Snorkeling Excursion: Three hours; $49. Snorkeling at Akumal Bay and Yalku, a spring-fed saltwater lagoon.

Chichén Itzá Tour: Nine hours; $98 to $115. An all-day trip by air-conditioned motorcoach to the Yucatán's most important antiquity site. You can easily go on your own by taxi for about $200 for up to four persons.

Sian Ka'an: Full day; $70 to $80 from Playa del Carmen, including bus transportation, breakfast, and lunch. The largest nature preserve in Mexico, made up of low tropical forest, wetland and mangroves, and coastal and marine environments, stretches 100 miles south of Tulum. It was declared a Biosphere Reserve in 1986 and part of UNESCO's World Heritage List. (See the description later in this chapter.) Some excursions also include a hike to Muyil, an important Maya antiquity site.

Xcaret: $53 adult; $27 child, entrance fee; sports are extra. The privately owned, 180-acre nature theme park is 5 miles down the coast from Playa del Carmen and about a mile before Calica. It has nature trails, horseback riding, a beach, Mayan ruins, a lagoon and underwater tunnels that snorkelers and divers can explore, dolphins, an aviary, a butterfly attraction, museum, folkloric entertainment, and more. Brightly colored Xcaret buses depart regularly from Cancún, Playa del Carmen, and Calica. Xcaret is also sold as a shore excursion. (See the Xcaret section later in the chapter.)

Jeep Safari: Five hours; $83. Venture by jeep with a driver-guide through the wilderness south of Playa del Carmen to Aktun Chen, a cave with stalactites, stalagmites, and an underground lake known to ancient Mayans but rediscovered only recently. Next is the beautiful beach at Xpu-Ha, where you can swim and relax while lunch, Mayan style, is prepared for you on an open grill.

Cancún City and Shopping Tour: Three to four hours; $35. Tour of Cancún City and the Hotel Zone, with stops at the town market or shopping plazas. Rather than an organized tour, some cruise ships provide a shuttle from port to Cancún for $20; other ships offer a five-hour trip for $45, including a box lunch. Some packages also include swimming at a beach in Cancún.

Golf: Playacar, the eighteen-hole championship golf course, is part of the Playacar Resort next to Playa del Carmen. Some ships have golf packages with this club or with several other new golf courses on the north side of Playa del Carmen; otherwise, you will need to make arrangements on your own. (See the Sports section later in this chapter.)

Cancún

Chichén Itzá Tour: Full-day; standard tour $65 adult, $39 child; deluxe $85 and $51. The all-day excursion is by air-conditioned motorcoach to the archaeological site, 125 miles west of Cancún. It is available from Cancún Vista (998-887-3414; fax 998-892-3967; www.cancunvista.com/travel), which also offers a wide range of tours in the Cancún/Riviera Maya area.

Isla Mujeres Day Excursion: Full day; $59 adult; $39.50 child. A day sail to the Island of Women, 4 miles north of Cancún, includes snorkeling at Garrafon Reef, a marine shelter, and a seafood lunch at the beach. It leaves between 9:00 and 10:00 A.M. and returns at 4:00 or 4:30 P.M. daily. An advantage of some cruise ship excursions is that they bring you back directly to your ship. The Dolphin Experience available in Cancún is actually at Isla de Mujeres. To swim with dolphins, the cost is $99.

Jeep Adventure: Full day; adult $120; child $79. Excursion departs Cancún at 8:00 A.M. and returns at 5:00 P.M. It visits the corridor south of Cancún with a stop at the Crocodile Farm and zoo, a jungle tour on hidden trails, snorkeling, swimming at a beach and lagoon, horseback riding, and a lunch. For information, contact Cancún Vista

Tours (800-860-5917; www.cancunvista.com). A canopy zip line option can also be added to the tour for $135 adult; $94 child.

Golf: Cancún Golf Club (Pok Ta Pok Golf Club, 998-883-0871), designed by Robert Trent Jones, in the heart of the Hotel Zone, has a restaurant, a pro shop, showers, a swimming pool, and tennis courts. Open 6:00 A.M. to 6:00 P.M. Another eighteen-hole championship course is part of the Hilton Hotel. Some ships have golf packages with the course; otherwise you will need to make arrangements on your own through the hotel. (See the Sports section for information and fees.)

Horseback Riding: Four hours; $56 plus $15 transportation fee ($89 as a cruise excursion). A forty-five-minute bus ride across the Yucatán countryside takes you to Rancho Viejo Loma Bonita near Cancún, where you take a horse based on your riding experience and receive instructions on riding a western saddle. A guide escorts you on a leisurely ride along a trail to the Caribbean Sea, where you can ride bareback into the ocean waves. Beverages are served at the ranch. *Note:* You ride at your own risk. For those on their own, a ranch shuttle bus departs from Kukulcan Plaza daily at 8:00 A.M. and 1:30 P.M. and returns at 1:00 P.M. and 6:30 P.M. Cancún Vista offers rides daily at 8:00, 10:30, and 11:30 A.M. with a dip in the sea. At the end participants can enjoy a game of donkey polo and lunch.

Snorkeling: Daily, three hours at 1:00 P.M.; $44.90 includes national park pass. Manta Divers (Kukulcan Boulevard, km 6.5; 998-849-4050; www.mantadivers.com) has a wide range of programs covering Cancún and Riviera Maya.

Cozumel

Port Profile: Cozumel
www.islacozumel.com.mx; www.cozumelparks.org.mx/eng/ parks

Embarkation: Some cruise ships dock at the pier in front of San Miguel, the island's only town. Others dock at the SSA Pier (formerly known as International Pier), about 2 miles south of San Miguel, or Puerta Maya (being reconstructed after a 2005 hurricane to reopen in 2008) farther south.

Passengers are allowed to go to and come from their ships freely provided they show the identity card issued to them by their cruise ship. There are ample taxis going constantly between the port and town. Be sure to set the price with the driver before you get in the car. The current price is US$5 for the car for up to four passengers from the Punta Langosta Pier and $6 from the SSA Pier and SSA Shopping Plaza.

Cozumel is an easy place to be on your own. You can walk the entire length of the Malecon, the main street fronting the sea, in thirty minutes—but you will probably need two hours, as you are likely to stop in shops along the way. Shopping is the town's main attraction. For those interested in diving, the main dive operators are located at the south end of town on the Malecon. Don't bother to change your dollars to pesos; every place in Cozumel accepts US dollars.

Local Transportation: Taxis provide local transportation and can be found easily on the Malecon. From SSA Pier at the south end of town to the town center costs about US$6 for up to four persons. Always ask the price in advance, and if you think it is too high, do not hesitate to bargain. This is particularly true when you hire a taxi for a few hours to tour around the island. The price could range from US$40 to $70 for four hours, depending on your ability to bargain and the driver's eagerness for your business. To phone for a taxi: 872-0236.

Car Rental: Avis, Budget, Hertz, and several local car rental agencies are located on the Malecon or its side streets. Cars and jeeps range from US$45 to $65 for day rate, 8:00 A.M. to 8:00 P.M. Insurance can add another US$25. You will not need a car unless you want to tour the island on your own.

Motorscooters and Bicycles: Motorscooters or mopeds rent for about US$25 per day at several locations on the Malecon and Avenida 5 Sur, one street east of the waterfront, and on several side streets in between. They are the most popular means of transportation as the island is very flat and distances are not great. **Rentadora Cozumel** (Hotel Flores, 10A, Avenida Sur No. 172, Cozumel; 872-1120; 872-1429) and **Aguila** (Avenida

Rafael E. Melgar No. 685, between Calle 3 and 5 Sur; 875-0729; fax 872-3285) rent mopeds for $25; bikes, $10; and Volkswagen cars, $45. They are open from 8:00 A.M. to 8:00 P.M. Be aware that when several cruise ships are in port at one time, bikes, scooters, and cars are likely to be in short supply. You can try reserving ahead, but there's no guarantee it will work.

Ferry Service: (872-1588; email@cruceros martimos.com.mx). Regular ferries and the Water Jet Mexico depart almost every hour from 5:00 A.M. to 10:00 P.M. from the dock in San Miguel for Playa del Carmen. Cost: N$110 (US$10.50) adult, N$60 (US$5.50) child.

Air Transportation: The airport is located 1 mile north of San Miguel. Flights to Cancún Airport (12 miles south of Cancún) leave about every two hours during the day. There are also flights directly to Chichén Itzá and Mérida. Inquire from AeroMexico (287-1860) or Mexicana (872-0157; 800-502-2000), which have offices in San Miguel on the Malecon.

Cozumel Past and Present

The island of Cozumel was the first place in Mexico discovered by Hernando Cortés, the Spanish conqueror, who used it as a staging area for his first expedition to the mainland in 1518.

The island, 30 miles long and 10 miles wide, was also the first of the Yucatán's islands to be discovered by scuba divers who came—as early as the 1950s—to enjoy the world's second longest underwater reef (only Australia's Great Barrier Reef is longer). In the intervening years the divers were joined by deep-sea fishermen, boating enthusiasts, and beachcombers trying to keep one pace ahead of the crowd. But by the 1980s, with an international airport, a host of new hotels, and up to a dozen cruise ships making regular calls, the crowds had come, too.

In antiquity, according to local legend, Cozumel was something of a Garden of Eden from which the gods departed to populate the mainland. Even up to the time of the Spaniards, it was considered a sacred place. Remnants of temples and artifacts used in religious rites have been found throughout the island.

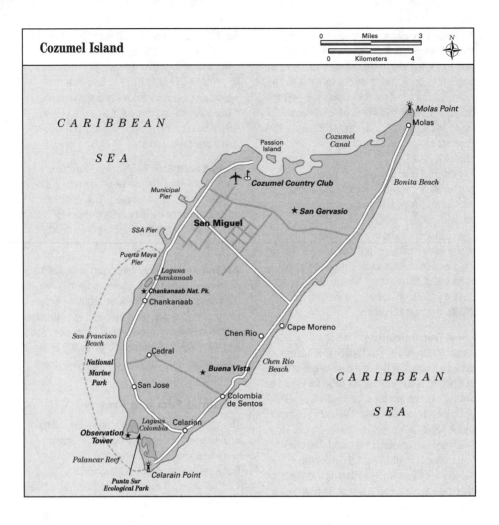

Cozumel Island

0 Miles 3
0 Kilometers 4

N

CARIBBEAN

SEA

Molas Point
Molas

Passion
Island

Cozumel
Canal

Cozumel Country Club

Bonita Beach

Municipal
Pier

★ San Gervasio

SSA Pier

San Miguel

Puerta Maya
Pier

Laguna
Chankanaab

★ Chankanaab Nat. Pk.
○ Chankanaab

San Francisco
Beach

Chen Rio ○

○ Cape Moreno

National
Marine
Park

○ Cedral

★ Buena Vista

Chen Rio
Beach

CARIBBEAN

○ San Jose

○ Colombia
de Sentos

SEA

Laguna
Colombia

Celarian

Observation ★
Tower

Palancar Reef

Celarain Point

Punta Sur
Ecological Park

In the days of the Spanish Main, the coves and inlets of Cozumel became favorite hideouts for pirates, including the infamous Henry Morgan and Jean Lafitte, who preyed on Spanish treasure ships as they passed en route from Spain's gold- and silver-rich colonies in South America to the mother country.

It seems, however, that many pirates' ships never made it home safely; there are dozens of old wrecks in these waters, and more are being found all the time. Today they are part of the rich treasures for divers to explore in Cozumel's underwater wonder world. It is not unusual for them to find real treasures as well.

In the waters surrounding Cozumel, more than two dozen reefs have been named and charted for diving. The south shore of the island alone has a dozen dive sites. The best known is Palancar Reef, which lies about a mile off the south shore and stretches for a distance of 3 miles. Here visibility ranges from 150 to 200 feet. The reef is considered by experts to be one of the most spectacular in the Caribbean for its coral formation.

In the early 1970s—and none too soon—the government introduced strict laws to halt the destruction and exploitation of the reefs. The protected waters lie from the SSA Pier south for 20 miles to Punta Celerain on the south coast. In 1996 the Mexican government created a national marine park, including the beaches, from Paradise Reef (next to the SSA Pier) to Chiqueros Point on the southeast coast. Chankanaab National Park, a marine park on the coast about 5 miles south of San Miguel, has nature trails and is popular for swimming and snorkeling.

Diving and the marine life are only part of Cozumel's diversions. Bird-watchers and naturalists have almost as much to enjoy on land as divers do in the sea. Only about a third of Cozumel is inhabited; the rest of the island has a wild, natural landscape barely touched by development. Cozumel's plants and trees are unusual, even for the Caribbean, and scampering about the undergrowth are lots of weird little creatures, including a 3-foot-long iguana that looks like a miniature dinosaur.

It is easy to explore the island by car or jeep; there is a coastal road around about two-thirds of it. At the excellent museum in town, you can learn about the island's natural environment and diversity. A visit is highly recommended, as it will help you plan your sightseeing. There is also an archaeological park that can give you a brief look at Mexico's pre-Columbian civilizations and Cozumel's flora.

San Miguel, the island's port and only town, was a sleepy little village with a World War II airstrip when tourism began in the 1970s. Over the years it grew and prospered, but it didn't really take shape until the 1980s with its growth as a cruise port.

The main plaza is closed to traffic and designed as a pedestrian mall with shops and handicrafts markets. The wide, flower-bedecked street along the waterfront, Avenida Rafael Melgar, is better known as the Malecon. Here you will find the museum, dive shops, jewelry shops, clothing boutiques, pretty open-air restaurants overlooking the sea, lively bars with mariachi music, and more souvenir and T-shirt shops than you would ever want to see.

San Miguel is laid out in a grid with streets, or calles, running east–west for more than 30 blocks, with those *norte,* north, having even numbers and those *sur,* south of the plaza, having odd numbers. They are crossed by north–south streets called *avenidas* (avenues). These are numbered in incre-

ments of five and carry the suffix *norte* or *sur*—Avenida 5 Sur, Avenida 10 Sur, Avenida 15 Sur, and so on—indicating that the avenue is north or south of Avenida Benito Juarez and the plaza.

The waterfront street, Avenida Rafael Melgar, commonly known as the Malecon, is the main drag of the town and has the most fashionable stores. Since these stores pay a premium for their location, their prices are sometimes higher than the stores on streets farther inland from the waterfront. As Cozumel's tourism has boomed, many new shops have opened on side streets and on those deeper into the town. It pays to shop around. You can also find plenty of Internet cafes. **The Calling Station** (Melgar and Calle 3 Sur) has the best prices of any port in the Caribbean—US$1 for thirty minutes and US$2 for sixty minutes. The store also offers telephone, fax, and postal services.

Museum of Cozumel: Museo de la Isla de Cozumel (Rafael Melgar Avenue, between avenues 4 and 6 norte; 872-1545), which opened in 1987, is a wonderful museum and the best place to start your acquaintance with the island of Cozumel. Comprehensive exhibits utilize relief maps and dioramas to describe the natural environment, including its history of land and sea formations and wildlife; others depict the history of the Mayas and the arrival of the Spaniards. In the center of the building is a table map that lights up when you press the name of a particular location so you can easily and quickly find places you might want to visit. The museum is situated in a lovely old Colonial-style house. On the first floor is a book and gift shop; on the second, a veranda restaurant overlooking the Caribbean Sea. Here, too, you can buy a ticket to three of the main historic sites. Admission: $3; children under eight years old free. Hours: 9:00 A.M. to 5:00 P.M. daily.

San Gervasio: For those not visiting Mayan antiquities on the mainland, San Gervasio is an interesting site, easily reached from the Cross Island Road, with ruins dating from A.D. 300 to 1500. Usually there is an English-speaking guide at the site. Hours: 7:00 A.M. to 4:00 P.M. Admission: $5; children under eleven free.

Discover Mexico (½ mile south of the SSA Pier; www.discovermexico.org) is Cozumel's newest attraction, a cultural theme park where visitors can learn about Mexico and experience the country's amazing history and culture. Admission: $14 adult; $9 child. Hours: 8:00 A.M. to 6:00 P.M. Monday through Saturday.

Chankanaab National Marine Park (987-872-0914; www.cozumelparks.com.mx). On the coast 5 miles south of San Miguel, the park was built around a natural lagoon that is home to more than sixty species of fish. A nature trail through the botanical gardens showcases more than 400 species of native trees and plants and another 350 from twenty-two tropical countries, and a museum displays shells and information about marine life. A Mayan house with a garden is meant to demonstrate traditional building and farming techniques. A small archaeological park with reproductions of statues, stelae (inscribed stone slabs), and other artifacts represents the different periods and civilizations in Mexico's ancient history. The marine park has a beachside restaurant, La Laguna, and a beach with palapa umbrellas for refuge from the strong sun. The reefs in front of the beach are popular for snorkeling; equipment is available for rent from dive shops in the vicinity. There are restrooms, dressing rooms, and a gift shop. Admission: US$16 adult; $8 ages three through eleven. Hours: 7:00 A.M. to 5:00 P.M.

Dolphin Royal Swim (987-26604/5/6/7; www.dolphindiscovery.com). Swims with dolphins in Chankanaab National Marine Park are offered daily at 10:00 A.M., noon, and 1:00, 2:00, and 3:30 P.M. The price, which includes a thirty-minute educational program and a thirty-minute swim, is US$139 per person. Participants must be eight years or older. Swimmers start by watching an educational video and getting instruction from the professional trainers before their swim with the dolphins. For the first twenty minutes in the water, participants work with the dolphins and trainers to perform specific exercises. The final ten minutes, they are free to swim with the dolphins under the trainers' supervision. Dolphin Encounter, $88 adult, $74.50 child, does not have a swim.

Punta Sur Ecological Park (987-22940). Cozumel's newest nature preserve, which was three years and US$1.5 million in the making by the Parks and Museum Foundation of Cozumel, opened in 1999. The 247-acre park, whose goal is to promote conservation of the island's flora and fauna, is located on the southern end of the island in an area known as the Colombia Lagoon and encompasses mangroves, white-sand beaches, and reef formations.

At the information center visitors can watch a twenty-minute video on the park's ecosystems, birds and wildlife, and marine life. Here, too, visitors can rent electric bikes (US$5 per hour) to explore Punta Sur on their own. An Ecobus circles the park continuously for transportation from site to site.

The reserve has a 30-foot-high observation tower and a dedicated snorkeling and beach recreation area. Snorkeling equipment can be rented for US$5. Between May and September snorkelers might see sea turtles that arrive here to nest. At Punta Sur's South Point Camp, a sea turtle research and protection center, visitors learn about turtles and their nesting season.

The observation tower offers great views of the lagoon and mangroves and is an ideal perch for bird-watching, which is best between November and March. Cozumel's bird population includes several species of herons, ibises, frigates, and flamingos, among others.

Punta Sur also offers learning sessions by appointment, each organized by an instructor who teaches with lectures, videos, and field experience. The cost is US$25 per person; children ages seven and younger are free. For reservations call 987-20914 or 987-20093; www.cozumelparks.org.mx.

The park's other amenities include a recreation area, kayaks, volleyball nets, palapa umbrellas for shade, a restaurant, a snack bar, and a souvenir shop. There is a museum and El Caracol, ruins of an ancient Mayan structure. Admission: US$10 per person; ages seven and younger free. Punta Sur is open 8:00 A.M. to 6:00 P.M. daily.

Shopping

For many passengers Cozumel's top attraction has been shopping. Mexico has wonderful crafts. Unfortunately, crafts are no longer the inexpensive bargains they were in the past—but they are still fun gifts to take home. The best buys are colorful papier-mâché decorations, dolls, birds, and animals; Christmas tree decorations; brightly colored straw place mats; hammocks; leather handbags and sandals; cotton dresses, skirts, and blouses for women and shirts for men; silver plates, pitchers, and dishes; silver jewelry (fine-quality work is not cheap, however); copper plates and cooking utensils; clay and ceramic dishes; toys; handwoven tapestries; colorful paintings on bark; and more.

Larger stores tend to carry some of all these crafts. Quality and workmanship vary a great deal, so look around before you buy and don't hesitate to bargain. Cozumel is a free port, but we have not found the usual duty-free items such as perfume to be particularly good buys. You'll probably do as well aboard your ship. Many stores are open from 9:00 A.M. to 9:00 P.M. Using cash rather than credit cards can sometimes get you up to a 20 percent discount.

When you step off the cruise ship pier, a few blocks south of San Miguel's main square, you will see Punta Langosta, a two-story, open-air shopping mall connected directly to the pier by an elevated walkway with stores with such familiar names as Versace and Colombian Emeralds. It may be tempting to linger here, but more interesting shops crammed full of Mexican products await you farther up the street.

When the reconstruction is completed at Puerto Maya, 2 miles south of town, you will walk directly into an attractive shopping plaza designed to resemble a Mayan village. It has many of the same shops found in town on the Malecon. Puerto Maya was built by Carnival Cruise Lines; once the work is done, all its ships will dock here.

Art and Artists: Regrettably, hurricanes in 2004 and 2007 drove away many of the artists and art shops we have visited in the past. One remaining is Studio One (25 Avenida 25 Sur, No. 981 between Calle 13 and 15, Cozumel, Quintana Roo 77600; 872-2659; www.studioonecozumel.com; Jennifer@studioonecozumel.com). It is the gallery of artist Gordon Gilcrest and his wife, Jennifer, both American transplants who have lived in Cozumel many years. Gilcrest's forte is sketches inspired by Maya and other pre-Columbian antiquity sites and motifs, but with an artist's eye and talent that make them more than reproductions.

Clothing: On the Malecon, the new **Pirana** (Rafael Melgar, near Calle 2) has cotton sportswear with prices a little high for Cozumel; nearby is **Ron Jon Surf Shop** (Melgar at Calle 4 Norte) for beachwear. **Miro** (on the Malecon south of the Plaza and at the International Plaza) features distinctive sportswear with stylized toucans in bright primary colors.

There are so many souvenir and T-shirt shops, it's hard to distinguish any; they stock similar merchandise. Look before you buy. The streets behind the Malecon and east of the Plaza are better places to look for typical, inexpensive Mexican cotton dresses with appliqué, and caftans. **Unicornio** (Avenida 5A Sur, No. 2) has a vast array at reasonable prices. The store also stocks a variety of crafts.

Crafts: Viva Mexico (on the Malecon; 872-5466) has a large selection of Mexican crafts and clothing and offers performances by colorfully costumed folkloric dancers five times a day. All the docks feature arrays of Mexican crafts, toys, resort clothes, and accessories. Take a look to see what's available, but wait until you get to town to buy.

Los Cinco Soles (Avenida Rafael Melgar 27, north end of the Malecon, 872-0132; www.loscinco soles.com) is Cozumel's best crafts store, with a vast selection of quality products generally a cut above the others. The well-established shop belongs to Sharon Welch de Morales, an American transplant, and her husband, Francisco. Our advice is to walk as far as this store before you buy anything. You will have passed many similar shops and gotten an idea of prices. Los Cinco Soles, set in a series of Colonial-style houses, features a large collection of silver jewelry and clothing by Mexican designers.

Los Cinco Soles also stocks handsome and unusual pottery that has leather, wooden beads, or cotton cord incorporated into the design. Made in Mexico City, and known as Rainbow Clay, this collection of pottery uses ancient techniques but molded into modern shapes for vases, bowls, and plates. The clay is gathered, cleaned, and then given its form and decorated using only natural adornments. Thus, the potters say, every piece of pottery takes its soul from Mother Earth.

At the rear of the store is a courtyard cafe, **Pancho's Backyard**, one of the best restaurants in town for margaritas and Mexican fare.

Gifts and Jewelry: For top-quality modern jewelry inspired by traditional Mexican art, take a look at the work of **Tanya Moss** (Punta Langosta Mall and on the Malecon at Calle 2 Norte), an American who learned her craft while attending college in Mexico City. Her jewelry uses Mexican gold, sterling silver, and turquoise, along with semiprecious stones, and is very expensive.

As Cozumel has grown in popularity as a cruise ship destination, the number of jewelry shops, such as those of Diamond International, has mushroomed. Most are on the Malecon, and all will be after your business with claims of bargains and other incentives. As we have cautioned throughout this guide, don't be taken in by the sales pitch. Any expensive purchase should come with appropriate guarantees.

Household Accessories: The pottery from Pueblo, Jalisco, Guadalajara, and the other main centers throughout Mexico can be found in crafts stores. Also look for papier-mâché fruits and vegetables; these inexpensive, fun souvenirs can make attractive table centerpieces.

Manuel Azueta (Avenida 5 and Calle 4 Norte) has hammocks made to order. **Los Cinco Soles** (Avenida Rafael Melgar 27, north end of the Malecon) has some of everything—household gifts, clothes, accessories, leather, jewelry (including reproductions of ancient pieces in museums), silver, and more. One of the stores in its complex, **Mi Casa,** sells furniture and other household items and has a branch store on the Malecon at Calle 3 Sur.

Leather: If you are in the market for fancy boots or other leather items, **Roger's Boots** (Avenida Melgar) is known for belts, handbags, wallets, and other leather goods decorated with elaborate tooling. Its boots come in alligator, armadillo, ostrich, frog, and, of course, cowhide. The store also has jackets, hats, and accessories. Prices are moderately expensive, but don't hesitate to bargain.

Liquor/Cigars/Candy/Food: Mexico produces some excellent spirits. Kahlúa is a delicious

Mexican liqueur made from coffee. Tequila is the distillation of the agave plant and the basic ingredient of the margarita, Mexico's potent answer to a daiquiri. These and other spirits are available at liquor stores on the plaza and the first and second streets east of the waterfront. The **Havana Club Cigars** store (Avenida Melgar at Calle 10 Norte) is located in the Forum Shops mall at the north end of the Malecon; so, too, is **The Belgium Chocolate Factory.**

Not liquor but liquid: Bottled vanilla is a popular souvenir; Los Cincos Soles says it's numero uno with visitors to its stores. But remember, all liquids must be packed in your checked luggage when you go through security to board your plane home from your cruise.

Dining and Restaurants

Carlos 'n Charlie's (Melgar at Punta Langosta Mall, 869-1646; www.carlosandcharlies.com) is a branch of the famous chain in Mexico City. (The equally famous Señor Frog's is next door.) Carlos 'n Charlie's seems to be a must-do on every cruise passenger's list. Music never stops. Some find it great, wild fun with customers, having drunk enough margaritas, dancing on the tables; others discover it to be a boisterous bore.

Guidos (2 blocks north of the ferry pier, between Calle 6 and Calle 8; 872-0546; www .guidoscozumel.com), set in an outdoor garden profuse with bougainvillea, serves seafood and oven-fired pizzas, its specialty. Locals say it's the best Italian cuisine in town. There's also a reasonably priced wine list. Hours: 11:00 A.M. to 11:00 P.M. Monday through Saturday. Moderate.

La Cocay (Calle 8 between Ave. 10 and Ave. 15; 872-5533) is popular with local residents and especially divers, for good food at good prices and in a great atmosphere inside in air-conditioning or outdoors. Lunch starts at 1:00 P.M.

La Laguna (Chankanaab National Park; 872-0747) serves a light lunch with a view of the Caribbean and mariachi music. Moderate.

La Lobsteria (Avenida 5 Sur and Calle 7), one long block in from Melgar Street behind Punta Langosta Mall, is situated in an old Mayan house. It offers fresh lobster and shrimp and fresh fish—

simply but well prepared to be enjoyed in easygoing atmosphere. Lobster tails tagged with prices are kept on ice; you choose one and it's cooked for you. Hours: 4:00 to 11:00 P.M. Monday through Saturday. No credit cards. Expensive.

Less expensive, **Costa Brava,** one block in from the Malecon fronting on Calle 7 Sur, has the best lobster and seafood and the biggest, best margaritas we've found in Cozumel.

Las Palmeras (on the Malecon, across from the ferry dock; 872-0532) may never win a Michelin star, but it's a classic of a Mexican restaurant catering to tourists, with lively music, generous drinks, and lots of food. Moderately expensive.

Pancho's Backyard (Los Cinco Soles, Avenida Rafael Melgar 27; 872-2124) is an attractive courtyard cafe serving nouvelle Mexican cuisine and light Mexican specialties for lunch and dinner. It's known for its "Awesome Margaritas." Moderate.

All Sports Bar (Avenida 5 Norte 2; 872-1199) is a restaurant-bar with television screens for viewing satellite-delivered US and other sporting events. The decor comprises pennants and polo shirts of every college and major-league team you can imagine, and the food is sort of Tex-Mex. Moderate.

And on the Malecon there's also a **Hard Rock Cafe** that's open until 1:00 A.M.; **Jimmy Buffett's Margaritaville,** where you'll want a pair of earplugs to withstand the noise; **Pizza Hut** and on its second floor, **Chi** (Chinese-Asian fusion cuisine); and **Fat Tuesday** on the main square.

Nightlife

At present and probably until Puerto Maya is completed and there's more cruise ship docking space, most ships leave Cozumel by 6:00 P.M.

Cozumel's nightlife centers on hotels and a few of the discos in town. As in towns all over Mexico, restaurants frequently have musical entertainment—guitars, mariachis, or the like. Some ships bring local folk dancers and mariachis aboard ship to perform.

If your ship remains in port for the evening, one of the shore excursions sold will probably be a nightclub show with flamenco dancers and mariachis at one of the hotels. If not, check the **Fiesta**

Americana Sol Caribe Hotel (near the International Pier), which usually has the best show in town.

The **Mexican Folkloric Ballet** performs at the Cabanas del Caribe Hotel on Thursday at 7:30 P.M. and at the Mayan Plaza Hotel on Saturday at 7:00 P.M.

For the disco scene, make your way to **Neptuno's** on the Malecon at the south end of town or **Scaramouche,** a short walk south of the ferry dock in town. There's even karaoke, at **Laser Karaoke,** about a mile south of town. Some beach clubs also have nightlife.

Sports

Beaches/Swimming: Cozumel's water is so spectacular, you may want to do nothing more than spend a day on the beach. The nearest one is Sol Caribe Beach, next to the International Pier. Better beaches, about 5 miles from the pier, are San Francisco Beach and Palancar Beach on the south shore. Passion Island, offshore, north of San Miguel, is a popular destination for boat day trips. Almost all hotels, except those in the center of town, are on the water.

By law, all Cozumel beaches are required to be open to the public. Even so, some are more desirable and accessible than others. The beaches on the west side of the island are safe for swimming; those on the east side, however, no matter how beautiful, are too dangerous for anything more than your toes. For convenience, it's probably best to use one with a "beach club" where there are showers and changing rooms and a restaurant or bar.

Among the newest, most stylish and sophisticated is **Playa Uvas** (Carretera Sur, km 8.5; 876-1104) about 5 miles south of town. It's Cozumel's answer to Nikki Beach (of South Beach fame) with similar white daybeds around the pool and by the beach. There are showers, lockers, a dive shop, kayak rentals, and free snorkel gear. In the evening it becomes a nightclub and serves dinner to midnight. **Mr. Sancho's Beach Club** (Carretera Sur, km 15; 876-1629, www.mrsanchos.com), about 9 miles south of town, is the polar opposite—crowded with partygoers, beach lovers, screaming kids, and locals on Sunday. It has showers, lockers, and a thirty-person hot tub, and its restaurant offers a tequila seminar at lunchtime—no joke!

Deep-Sea Fishing: Cozumel is one of the prime gamefishing areas of the Caribbean, particularly noted for sailfish, blue marlin, white marlin, tuna, dolphin, wahoo, shark, and barracuda, as well as bonefish in quiet lagoons and hidden bays. Boat charters can be arranged through **Dive Cozumel** (Avenida Rosado Salas, No. 85, and Fifth Avenue, P.O. Box 165, Cozumel; 872-4567; 866-319-2649; www.divecozumel.net) or local boat operators and range from US$400 for a half day to $500 or more for a full day, depending on the time of the year and the type of fish. Cozumel has a special fishing resort, **Sol Pez Maya** (P.O. Box 9, Cozumel; 872-0072; fax 872-1599), or contact **Club Abrigo Nautico de Cozumel** (872-1024), Cozumel's fishing headquarters at Puerto de Abrigo, north of town near the airport.

Golf: Cozumel's first golf course, a Jack Nicklaus–designed eighteen-hole championship layout (6,847 yards, par 72), and the Cozumel Country Club clubhouse opened in 2001. Located on the island's north end across from the Sol Mela Paradisus Cozumel resort, about a fifteen-minute drive from the pier, the facility is managed by Clubs Corporation of America.

The course incorporates the natural landscape in its design, with fairways built around native trees, mangroves, and wetlands to preserve ecologically sensitive areas. The greens consist of hybrid Bermuda turf. Greens fees are US$149 per person for eighteen holes including shared cart ($175 as a cruise ship excursion). An online package for green fees, clubs, balls is $179; $139 without clubs. Tee times are available in advance. There is a practice range, and the clubhouse has a fully stocked pro shop and a snack bar. Call (987) 872-9570; fax (987) 872-9590.

The course is part of a golf community development. In conjunction with Sand Dollar Sports, a local tour operator, the club offers excursions for cruise passengers (minimum of two, maximum of twelve people) who are met portside, transported to the club, and given a guided tour, beverage, and souvenir (and probably a sales pitch, too). **Cozumel Country Club** (Carretera Costera Norte, km 6.5

Interior Casa Club, Cozumel, Quintana Roo 77600; 872-9570; fax 872-9590; www.cozumelcountryclub.com.mx).

Horseback Riding: Rancho Buenvista (872-1537; www.buenavistaranch.com) offers half-day riding tours Monday through Saturday, including transportation and accompanied by bilingual guides.

Snorkeling and Scuba: When you've come to one of the world's prime scuba diving locations, you will certainly want to include a dive here if you are a certified diver. The island is surrounded by two dozen or more reefs; those off the south/southwest shore offer the best diving and are now protected by the national marine park created in 1996. Cozumel has both reefs close to shore and drop-offs farther out at sea.

There is diving from the beach at several locations within walking distance of the International Pier. **Paraiso Reef North** is about 200 yards off Sol Caribe Beach in depths of 30 to 50 feet, with visibility up to 100 feet. **La Ceiba Reef and Plane Wreck**, in front of La Ceiba Hotel, next to the pier, has an underwater trail designed by marine ecologist George Lewbel. The trail was created by Pancho Morales, former owner of La Ceiba Hotel and current proprietor of Los Cinco Soles. It starts at the plane, sunk for the filming of a movie, and continues along the reef for 120 yards with signs explaining various types of corals and sponges. The location is popular for cruise ship dive excursions. **Paraiso Reef South** is a continuation of the same reef and is rich in fish life. It is particularly popular for night dives.

Continuing south, the next group of reefs is in the **Chankanaab Lagoon** area. Close to shore are huge coral heads, and along the shoreline are caves that go back under the shore. These can be reached from the beach; the area can be enjoyed by snorkelers as well. The reef is farther out and reached by a boat.

Between Punta Tormentos and Punta Tunich, just before San Francisco Beach, is **Tormentos Reef,** popular with photographers for its coral heads, sea fans, and abundant fish. **Yocab Reef,** at a depth of about 30 feet, is a good location for beginning divers. **San Francisco Reef,** situated about ½ mile directly in front of San Francisco Bay, is popular for its abundant fish.

Palancar Reef, the best known, lies about a mile off the south shore and stretches for 3 miles with visibility up to 200 feet. The variety of formations is the attraction. Here the wall is sloping, rather than a sharp drop-off, and starts about 50 feet down. It is a maze of canyons, tunnels, and caves. The south end has enormous coral pinnacles spiraling up to 60 feet or more. **Maracaibo Reef,** off the southwestern tip of the island, is the most challenging for experienced divers.

If a scuba or snorkeling package is not available on your cruise ship, you will find a dozen dive operators on the main street at the east end of the town. You should contact them in advance and plan to get to them early; most morning dive trips leave by 9:00 or 9:30 A.M. You must show a certification card before going out on a boat or renting tanks. Each offers regularly scheduled half- and full-day dive packages, and prices are very competitive. Many US dive specialists can make your arrangements in Cozumel as well as most other locations in the Caribbean.

A typical day consists of two dives on different reefs and lunch on a beach. The first dive is usually about 60 to 80 feet or more depending on your level of experience, and the second, shallower dive is about 40 feet. The exact location of the dives is determined by the divemaster on each boat, depending on weather conditions, currents, and the like.

Among Cozumel operators are **Caribbean Divers** (Calle 3 Sur, P.O. Box 191, Cozumel; 872-1080; www.caribbeandiverscozumel.com) and **Dive Cozumel** (Avenida Rosado Salas, No. 85, and Fifth Avenue, P.O. Box 165, Cozumel; 872-4567; 866-319-2649; www.divecozumel.net). **Aqua Safari** (Avenida Rafael Melgar 1 Sur; 872-0101; www.aquasafari.com) offers a two-tank dive for US$60, plus equipment rental.

Servicios de Seguridad Sub-Aquatica (Calle 5 Sur-21b; 872-2387; VHF 16 and 21) is a professionally operated recompression center. It is open from 8:00 A.M. to 8:00 P.M. and can be reached at other times by radio.

Tennis: Presidente Hotel, an Intercontinental hotel about 1 mile south of the International Pier, has three courts, and there are courts at the Fiesta Americana Sol Caribe, Cozumel Caribe, and Plaza Azul hotels. You should contact the hotels in advance to request permission to play.

Windsurfing/Kiteboarding: Windsurfing is available at beachside hotels for about US$20. Like most places in the Caribbean, the sport of kiteboarding has come to Cozumel, too. In fact, Mexico's own Olympic champion, **Raul de Lille** (987-103-6711; www.kitecozumel.com), introduced the sport to Cozumel and became its first certified instructor. He offers instruction and tours, but he's not cheap—US$125 per hour for minimum of three hours for private one-on-one instruction, or $500 per day. If you have a pal to take lessons with you, it's $300 each. Also check out www.cozumel kiteboarding.com or contact **Adrian Angulo Romero,** Puro Mar Surf-Kite Co & Bikini Shop, Fifth Avenue at Third Street; 876-1558; adrian @cozumelkiteboarding.com.

Riviera Maya
www.rivieramaya.com

The 100-mile stretch of Caribbean coast south of Cancún Airport to the border of the Sian Ka'an Biosphere Reserve, south of Tulum, is now officially known as the Riviera Maya. It boasts more than five dozen megaresorts and a host of smaller ones, most built only since the mid-1990s.

Playa del Carmen/Calica

Situated 10 miles directly west of Cozumel and equidistant between Cancún on the north and Tulum, a major Mayan temple complex, on the south, Playa del Carmen is the main port of the coast and the gateway to the Yucatán Peninsula for cruise ships. Its growth from a minuscule fishing village to a major town was the start of the development of the Riviera Maya.

A word of caution: Some cruise line brochures leave the impression Cozumel/Playa del Carmen or Calica are one locale. They are not. Some ships stop only in Cozumel. You must take a thirty-minute ferry ride to Playa del Carmen or a fifteen-minute flight to Cancún to reach the mainland. Other ships stop in Playa del Carmen only long enough to disembark passengers taking the ship's shore excursions and continue on to Cozumel.

Those who want to be on their own will find ample services in Playa del Carmen for tours, car rental, and taxis. If you have arrived from Cozumel or plan to return to your ship there, you should try to time your return via ferry either before or after the rush of passengers returning from shore excursions.

When passengers arrive in Playa del Carmen, they find a lively town with many changes, starting with a much-improved pier and shaded waiting area. On the south side of the pier is Señor Frog's, a member of the Mexican restaurant chain, and several beachside hotels—Continental Plaza and Playacar, among others, and the Playacar Golf Course.

On the north side is the public beach, with small hotels and beach clubs, and the main part of town beginning at Fifth Avenue, a north–south pedestrian street lined with shops, restaurants, small hotels, travel companies, dive shops, car rental agencies, and other tourist services. It is intersected about midpoint by Avenida Juarez, the town's main thoroughfare, a short walk from the pier.

Directly in front of the pier, a lane lined with tourist shops leads to Fifth Avenue. Next to the kiosk where tickets for the Cozumel ferry are sold, you are likely to find Ricardo waiting to rent you a Hondo Elite scooter (US$28, including gas, insurance, and helmet). Ten steps away is **Camelot Tours** (873-2967), which offers popular excursions at reasonable prices and has an Internet cafe.

Next door is a large convenience store selling Kahlúa, the famous Mexican coffee liqueur, and bottles of vanilla, another popular souvenir. There's also a drugstore next to the office for Xcaret, the popular nature theme park (morning bus departures hourly, Monday through Friday, US$50), and **Budget Rent a Car** (US$45 for small cars to $99 for jeeps, including insurance and taxes).

Even with Playa del Carmen's growth, it has more Mexican character than Cancún. The action is on the beach during the day—you can even have a massage there—and at the restaurants, bars, and sidewalk cafes of Fifth Avenue in the evening. (Calica information appears later in this chapter.)

Restaurants

Ajua Maya (Calle 4, off Fifth Avenue; 873-2523; 818-581-4075; www.ajuamaya.com). According to owners Brenda and Jorge Alfaro, the name is pronounced *ahhhhh—who—ahhhhhh ma-ya*—which gives you a sense of this restaurant that's a tequila bar, grill house, and Latin club in one, as serious about food as it is about fun. Nightly, there's live Latin music and dancing waiters. The menu ranges from lobster and seafood, to USDA Angus steaks and New York cheesecake, to Mayan and Mexican cuisine, including nineteenth-century French-influenced mestizo cuisine. Ajua Maya also does weddings and fiestas, and can provide a personal chef for the day.

Alux (Avenida Juarez, Mza 12, Colonia Ejidal; 984-80-32936; www.aluxlounge.net). This restaurant is sited in a cave (specifically a cenote—a sinkhole sacred to the ancient Maya) and lit by candles; you can tour the cave before dining. The exotic menu includes salmon carpaccio, vegetables a la tiramisu, and clams Chilean style. Open 7:00 P.M. to 2:00 A.M. Tuesday through Friday, with live music nightly. Expensive.

Del Sol (Alhambra Hotel, on the beach; 984-80-30057) has delicious fresh fish. Moderate.

Gaia (Fifth Avenue and Calle 28) is a new Moroccan restaurant that gets high marks. Moderate.

La Casa del Agua (Fifth Avenue and Second Street, upstairs; 984-803-0232; www.lacasadel agua.com). Decorated with wood and Mexican artifacts, with a fountain as part of the decor, the restaurant offers diverse entrees, such as stuffed avocado with shrimp and Yucatán seviche, in a romantic atmosphere and great service. Moderately expensive.

La Cueva del Chango (Calle 38, between Av. 5 and the beach; 984-116-3179), a restaurant-bar, is laid-back and cool and a favorite of local residents. Built with wood and natural stone in a jungle garden setting, it's complete with waterfalls, fishponds, monkeys, and birds flying about. Lunch and dinner menus have a wide selection of Mexican dishes, fresh fish, salads, fruits, and homemade bread and tortillas. There's also a selection of Mexican wines. Moderate.

La Parrilla (Fifth Avenue and North Eighth Street; 988-48193) serves steaks and Mexican specialties. Moderately expensive

Makkeroni (Calle 4 between Tenth and Fifteenth) is a small eatery serving great pizza and authentic Italian dishes. Moderate.

Yaxche (North Eighth Street; 873-2502; www.mayacuisine.com) serves the most authentic Mayan cuisine in Playa del Carmen, if not the Yucatán, at reasonable prices. Be sure to have Mayan coffee—it's quite a show being made.

North of Playa del Carmen/Cancún

The region north of Playa del Carmen has a great deal of interesting sightseeing. Along with outstanding Mayan archaeological sites, there are caves, underground rivers, cenotes (sacred sinkholes), nature parks, and new opportunities for adventure sports, including kayaking, biking, trekking, and bird-watching, as well as two new golf courses. If your ship offers an excursion to Chichén Itzá and you have any interest in history and archaeology, you should put this tour at the top of your priority list. If you do rent a car, there are also several important sites of antiquity within a short drive from the pier. Be sure to have a full tank of gas before starting out: Gas stations on the byways are few and far between. Taxis are readily available at reasonable prices.

The main highway (No. 307) between Playa del Carmen and Cancún is an excellent four-lane parkway that runs as straight as an arrow about a mile or so inland from the sea until just south of Cancún. The stretch from Playa del Carmen has been developed with so many small hotels, big resorts, and attractions that's it's hard to keep track. To reach most of them, you need to turn off the main road and head toward the sea. (Mileages indicated are measured from Playa del Carmen.)

Mayakoba (3 miles): Directly north of Playa del Carmen is a large hotel and villa resort development. It features the first two of five hotels to be built—the Fairmont Mayakoba and the Rosewood Mayakoba (opening February 2008)—and the El Camaleon Golf Course, designed by Greg Norman, as its centerpieces. The golf course is open to non-

hotel-guests. Greens fees for eighteen holes are $126, May through October; and $158, November through April. After 1:30 P.M., the rates drop to $75 and $94, respectively. For tee times: 984-206-3088. El Camaleon is the home of the PGA Tour in Mexico and has a clubhouse as well as a full-service golf shop with carts, clubs, and shoes for rent. There are showers and lockers, an open-air casual restaurant for breakfast and lunch, and an Argentinean steak house overlooking the eighteenth hole for dinner.

Playa Xcalacoco (7 miles) is home to The Tides Riviera Maya (984-877-3000), a member of the Kor Hotels group and one of the most luxurious resorts on the coast. Punta Bete (11 miles) is about a 3-mile drive from the highway through typical Yucatán dry brush jungle and banana trees to a rustic, palm-fringed 3 miles of white-sand beach, popular for swimming and snorkeling. La Posada del Capitán Lafitte (998-873-0214) is a modest, attractive beachside resort with a pool, showers, and a restaurant overlooking miles of beautiful, reef-protected white sand. Snorkeling on the reef is available.

Tres Rios (12 miles). The former nature park here has closed. The owners are developing the area as a resort with several hotels and recreational facilities.

Playa Maroma (14 miles) (987-28200). The turnoff at kilometer 51 leads to Maroma Beach Hotel and Spa, a small, upscale resort that has received a great deal of publicity for the celebrities it attracts. Small groups of four or six people are welcome to have lunch and swim. It's ideal for those who want to get away from the crowds. Call or fax in advance.

Playa Paraiso (18 miles) has a huge resort complex that includes five Iberostar hotels: Iberostar Paraiso del Mar, Iberostar Paraiso Beach, Iberostar Paraiso Lindo, Iberostar Paraiso Maya, and the new Iberostar Grand Hotel Paraiso (877-2847; www.iberostar.com) and its 18-hole Peter Dye–designed golf course (golfparaiso@iberostar.com.mx), which is open to the public. Greens fee: $190. It has a full-service pro shop, club and shoe rentals, men's and women's lockers and showers, and a restaurant.

Puerto Morelos (22 miles) is the oldest port in Mexico. The quiet fishing village, with inexpensive beachfront restaurants where you can enjoy the day's catch, had been bypassed by developers until now. The port is being developed, and a few cruise ships are beginning to call here. The area between Morelos and Cancún has also undergone intense resort development in the last three years.

Selvatica, a Yucatan adventure company based in Puerto Morelos, offers a Canopy Tour through the jungle that consists of eleven zip lines, mountain biking, and swimming in a cenote. This and other Selvatica tours depart from Puerto Morelos, Cancun Hotel Zone, Playa del Carman, and Playacar. Prices and details are available by visiting the company's Web site at www.selvatica.com.mx or by contacting the Selvatica Mexico office (998-847-4581; reservations: 1-866-552-8825).

At the turnoff for Puerto Morelos on the main highway is the 150-acre **Dr. Alfredo Barrera Marin Botanical Garden** (835-0440), which features flora of the Yucatán region. It has a small archaeological site and nature trails through thick, dry forest. The park is maintained by the Quintana Roo State Research Center. There's a small admission fee There's also a gasoline station here.

Crococún and Palancar Aquarium (24 miles). Crococún, a crocodile farm, has several species of crocodiles ranging in age from one to twenty-five years. There are also spider monkeys, Mexican raccoons, and other species native to the Yucatán. There is a small admission fee; a guide is available for an extra tip. Next door is the Palancar Aquarium, named for the reef that lies off the coast of Cozumel. The aquarium has exhibits on all aspects of the region's marine environment.

Beyond Puerto Morelos, 15 miles from Cancún, is the luxury, all-suite **Paraiso de la Bonita Resort** nestled in 14 acres of landscaped gardens and mangroves. The architecture is meant to capture the essence of Mayan culture with open courtyards, fountains, and reflecting pools. The spacious suites are furnished with antiques that have been collected from around the world; each suite has a private terrace facing the sea. There is also a 24,000-square-foot spa.

Cancún
www.cancun.info

Cancún came out of a computer. Well, almost.

In the late 1960s, when the Mexican government set out to develop the country's coastal regions for tourism, researchers fed a pile of data about climate, water, land, history, and the like into their computers to find the ideal area in which to begin. All the positive signs pointed to a 14-mile sliver of land off the northeastern Yucatán coast on the Caribbean Sea, known as Cancún.

Most people's response was "Can-who?" And understandably. Cancún was little more than a sandbar, and the eastern zone of the Yucatán was an uninhabited jungle. There were no roads, no water, no electricity, and only about 120 people living there.

Today Cancún has almost two hundred hotels in all categories, with such well-known names as Hyatt and Ritz-Carlton. There are approximately 500 restaurants, large shopping centers, native markets, four eighteen-hole golf courses, a convention center, a wide range of sports and entertainment facilities, and a town of almost 600,000 people.

A hotel/resort zone was created on the island of Cancún, and the commercial district was placed on the mainland. The hotel area's strict zoning prohibits garish signs and buildings over nine stories. There is frequent bus transportation between the island and town, and the international airport is 12 miles away.

The island of Cancún has the shape of the number 7 and is connected at both ends to the mainland by bridges. The long side of the island faces the Caribbean on the east and the Nichupté Lagoon on the west. Most resorts are located along the beach on the road heading north to Punta Cancún.

Cancún's flat terrain, which might surprise those who have traveled elsewhere in Mexico, and the Yucatán jungle bear no resemblance whatever to the tropical lushness of Jamaica or the Eastern Caribbean. On the contrary, the jungle is thick, low brush—miles and miles of it.

The Beaches: What Cancún lacks in verdant tropical splendor is more than made up for in its beaches and water. Cancún has the most beautiful beaches we've seen anywhere in the world (and we've seen a lot of beach!). What makes them so spectacular is both the color and the quality of the sand and water. The powder-fine, blinding white sand looks as though it would scorch your feet, but it is actually cool to the touch. That the sand, which is coral and limestone in origin, is very porous accounts for this unusual characteristic and was one of the determining factors in the computer's selection of Cancún. The intense, deep blue-green color of the water is marvel enough, but when you step into it, you will discover it has an unusual silken quality.

That's the good news. The bad news is that some parts of the coast have a strong undertow.

Warning signs are posted, but many tourists do not take them seriously. Never go far from shore, and never swim where someone on shore cannot see you. The water of the lagoon and the north shore of Cancún island are considered the safest places. Hotels have swimming pools.

Hotel Zone: Hotels—many of which are fabulous architectural creations—line the beach for 14 miles, from Club Med and the huge Hilton Resort and Golf Club on the south to the Fiesta Americana and El Presidente InterContinental on the north. Most of the hotels tend to be self-contained resorts with their own sports and entertainment, which is helpful for cruise passengers with limited time because they can select one and stay. But if

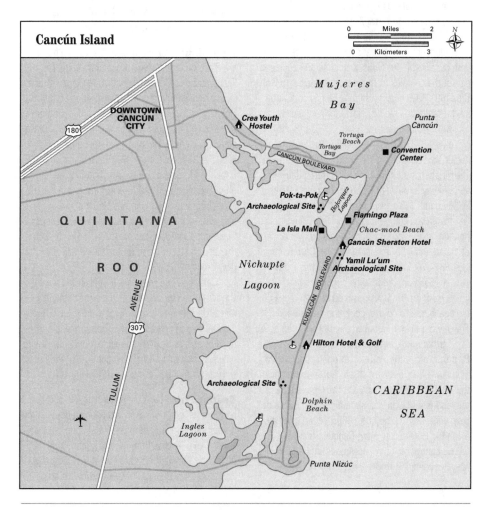

you want to check out the scene at another hotel, it takes more effort than a simple stroll down the beach. A paved pedestrian walkway, the *ciclopista,* winds through the northern part of the Hotel Zone and is a pleasant walk for those who want to have a look at some of Cancún's beautiful hotels.

Sports and Attractions: In addition to the water sports facilities at hotels, the Hotel Zone has many water sports centers where you can find equipment for snorkeling, scuba diving, and fishing. Most major resorts have tennis courts. Windsurfing is best at Bahía de Mujeres. (Most of the Cancún shore excursions detailed earlier in this chapter can be taken on your own.)

Cancún Golf Club at Pok-ta-Pok (988-883-1230; fax 883-3358; www.cancungolfclub.com) is on a series of islands in the lagoon, connected by road to the Cancún Hotel Zone. The course is open from 6:00 A.M. to 6:00 P.M. The cost is US$105 to $150, depending on the season, for eighteen holes with cart; US$40 for clubs. A second golf course is part of the complex at the **Hilton Resort and Golf Club** (881-8000 or www.hiltoncancun.com). Rates are for eighteen holes, US$199 for nonguests.

Rancho Loma Bonita (km 49, near Puerto Morelos; 887-5423; www.lomabonita.com) offers horseback riding along the beach or jungle trekking. The ninety-minute tour, which is offered daily, is followed by a Mexican lunch at the ranch. Rates: US$69 adult; $55 ages six through twelve.

When you come into Cancún from Playa del Carmen, as most cruise passengers do, you arrive at the south end of the island where **Club Med** (984-881-8200) is located. The resort has a day pass for $55 per person, which includes lunch, a guided tour (at 10:00 A.M. or 6:00 P.M.), and use of the beach, tennis courts, pool, and water sports. The day pass can be booked directly with the hotel.

Farther north, beyond the Holiday Inn, **Dolphin Beach** is a beautiful stretch of open beach. Hard as it may be to imagine, all of Cancún looked like this only four decades ago. On the lagoon side of the road is a Mayan archaeological site, **Ruins del Rey,** uncovered in the late 1980s. About midway along the Hotel Zone is the Cancún Sheraton, whose central building is designed in the form of a Mayan pyramid; it fronts a magnificent beach.

Yamil Lu'um: The Sheraton obliges you with its own Mayan ruin, Yamil Lu'um, a small temple complex on a mound next to the hotel. One of the temples contained an impression of a Mayan footprint, which is now exhibited in the Cancún Archaeological Museum. The **Melia Cancún,** topped with a glass pyramid, has one of the most dramatic lobbies of the hotel group.

Convention Center: At the north end of the island at Punta Cancún is the Convention Center (www.cancuncenter.com), within easy walking distance of many hotels and several of the largest shopping plazas. The center was the venue for the first economic summit, attended by President Ronald Reagan in 1981; the Miss Universe Contest in 1988; and many other major events. The center's showpiece is a tower that rivals Paris's Eiffel Tower in height. The center is also the home of the Museum of Anthropology and History of Cancún.

Shopping: Among the largest shopping malls are Plaza Caracol (www.caracolplaza.com), La Fiesta at Punta Cancún, La Isla, and Plaza Kukulcán (www.kukulcanplaza.com), about midpoint in the Hotel Zone. Luxury Avenue is a boutique mall in Kukulcan Plaza, which brings together in one place some of the most famous international brands, including Vuitton, Cartier, Salvatore Ferragamo, Ermenegildo Zegna, Fendi, and more. Incidentally, all of Quintana Roo—the easternmost province of Mexico, in which Cancún and Cozumel are located—is a duty-free zone. Generally, business hours are 10:00 A.M. to 1:00 P.M. and 4:00 to 8:00 P.M. Not all stores close for the siesta, nor do downtown markets.

Cancún City: From Punta Cancún to Cancún City, the commercial center on the mainland, is 6 miles. Cancún City is a completely new town that is gradually acquiring character. There are wide, tree-lined streets and parks, and an outdoor market with typical Mexican crafts of cheaper quality and price than those found in the large shopping plazas.

Restaurants: Cancún has as many as 500 restaurants, and new ones are opening daily. Some restaurants convenient to the Hotel Zone are **Captain's Cove** (across from the Mayaland Hotel; 885-0016) and **Lorenzillo's Live Lobster House** (Hotel Zone, km 10.5; 883-1254; www.lorenzillos.com), with romantic settings overlooking the lagoon. Both serve seafood and are moderately expensive.

Carlos 'n Charlie's (Forum by the Sea, Boulevard Kukulcan km 8.5; 883-4468; www.carlosandcharlies.com) is a moderately priced member of a famous Mexico City chain specializing in seafood.

Glazz (La Isla Shopping Village, Boulevard Kukulcan, km 12.5; 883-1881). A posh restaurant and bar with incredible decor that has been called "South Beach Miami meets Indonesian chic." Moderately expensive.

Jimmy Buffett's Margaritaville Cancún (Flamingo Plaza, Boulevard Kukulcan, km 11.5; 885-2375; www.margaritaville.com.mx), located in Cancún's popular Flamingo Plaza, offers the usual familiar fare—cheeseburgers, nachos, and of course, margaritas. Moderate.

La Fisheria (Plaza Caracol shopping center; 883-1395) is the place to go for delicious fresh seafood, moderately priced.

Labna (Margaritas Street 29, downtown Cancún, 892-3056; www.labna.com). Yucatecan specialties. Moderate.

Locanda Paolo (Avenue Bonampak 145 at corner of Jurel Street, downtown Cancún; 887-2627; www.locandapaolo.com) is an owner-chef-operated restaurant that gets high marks from Cancún residents for its Italian cuisine. Moderate.

Salute! Cancún (Boulevard Kukulcan, km 11.5; 881-5556; www.salute.com.mx), with a wide terrace for great views of the Nichupté Lagoon, especially at sunset, is a new eatery offering a wide range of Mediterranean and other cuisines including seafood, sushi, steaks, pasta, carpaccio, and daily specials, along with an extensive wine list that includes Mexican wines. Branch in Playa del Carmen. Expensive.

For specialties of the Yucatán, **Los Almendros** (across from the bullfight ring; 884-0807; www.losalmendros.com.mx) is open from noon to 11:00 P.M. **Maria Bonita** (km 9.5, next to the Camino Real Hotel; 883-1730), set in a large Mexican hacienda, offers a great variety of classic dishes from around Mexico, along with mariachi music.

If you hunger for a Big Mac, McDonald's has eight locations. For pizza, there seems to be a pizzeria on every corner; and for a juicy steak, there's an Outback Steakhouse.

Entertainment: Cancún is famous for its nightlife and has the variety to suit almost everyone. Unfortunately, most cruise ships leave by sunset, and Cancún's nightlife doesn't even begin to flicker until after 10:00 P.M. If you are here in the evening, however, you can learn what is happening from one of the free local publications, *Cancún Tips* or *Caribbean News.*

There are Planet Hollywood, Hard Rock Cafe, and rock, jazz, salsa, and reggae bars galore. A popular nighttime activity is lobby bar-hopping. The lobbies are often architectural masterpieces, and many feature live musical entertainment from classical guitar to jazz. But Cancún is also known for its discos, which do not open until 10:00 P.M. and don't really get going until midnight or later.

Bullfights are staged at the stadium, **Plaza de Toros Cancún** (Avenida Banampak, Lote 1; 884-5629), on Wednesday at 3:30 P.M. The cost is US$45 adult; child under twelve is admitted free.

Transportation: Taxis are available at all Cancún hotels, and there is frequent bus service between the Cancún resorts and Cancún City. There are car rental offices at major hotels, in the plaza of the Convention Center, and in Cancún City. Budget Rent A Car (Alquiladora Montejo S.A., Avenida Tulum 214; 884-6955) has American, European, and Japanese cars that cost from US$60 to $80 per day, depending on the model. Generally, car rentals in Cancún are overpriced—about double the prices in the United States or even those in Cozumel. It is important to compare the terms as well as prices of rentals.

If you plan to spend the day exploring on your own, you should either rent a car or moped or hire a taxi with a driver—distances are too great for walking. Bus stops, marked PARADA, are conveniently located throughout the Hotel Zone and in the downtown area; the fare is 6.5 pesos. "Turicun" buses are air-conditioned and more plush.

Useful Numbers: Tourism Office: Call 884-6531. **Police:** Dial 884-1109. **American Hospital:** Call 884-6133. **Red Cross:** Call 065.

Isla Mujeres

Four miles off the north coast of Cancún is Isla Mujeres, the Island of Women, so named by the

Spaniards because of the large number of erotic terra-cotta female idols they found when they landed there in 1517. A Mayan temple, believed to have been dedicated to the goddess of childbirth and weaving, suggests it was a sanctuary.

Today the 5-mile-long island, where life is even more carefree and casual than on Cancún, is noted for its scuba diving and snorkeling and good seafood restaurants. During the summer (June 15 through September 1, and strictly regulated) whale sharks in their natural habitat can been sighted (www.islawhalesharks.com); the cost is $125. Dolphin Discovery, located in the heart of the island, offers the 45-minute Encounter for $79 adult; $69 child. Like Cancún, Isla Mujeres has been transformed and now has a population of 15,000. The island is a duty-free port, too.

Day trips to Isla Mujeres depart from the marina next to El Presidente InterContinental at 10:30 A.M. and return at 4:00 P.M. A similar excursion leaves from the Playa Linda dock at 9:30 A.M. The price (about US$65) includes snorkeling on El Garrafon Reef and a seafood lunch. Fast water taxis make the trip to Isla Mujeres from Puerto Juarez or Punta Sam in about twenty minutes. Cost is US$8 for the boat. Ferries leave frequently throughout the day.

Contoy Island

Approximately 15 miles north of Cancún is Contoy Island, a national bird sanctuary and nature preserve scalloped with pretty beaches. Only 2 miles long and less than ½ mile wide, Contoy is the Cancún of three decades ago. The island is home to about a hundred species of birds, including frigate birds, pelicans, cormorants, flamingos, and herons.

Until recently the island had been closed to the public because of careless use; it has now reopened, but under more controlled conditions. The boat trip to Contoy (about US$40 round trip), with a stop for snorkeling en route, takes two hours. Normally day excursions depart daily.

South of Playa del Carmen

An excellent road, Highway 307, runs directly south from Playa del Carmen and Calica to the Belize border, about 150 miles away. Along the way are many places that you may find more rewarding to visit than Cancún. The choice depends upon your personal interests. In addition to organized tours available aboard ship and car rentals and taxis that can be arranged in port, there are public buses from Playa del Carmen to Tulum town. From there you will need to walk a few hundred yards to the temple complex. If you rent a car or hire a taxi, you can combine snorkeling at Xel-Ha or Akumal with sightseeing at Tulum.

Highway 307 runs slightly inland, and because the land is so flat you cannot see the sea from the road. Instead you drive through low, thick brush, which is, frankly, boring from a scenic point of view. (For the following, mileage is indicated from Playa del Carmen.)

Playacar: Next to Playa del Carmen is one of the most extensive resort developments on the Riviera Maya. It is made up of a dozen all-inclusive resorts, running south one after the other along the beach, along with private homes and condominiums, and **Club de Golf** (873-4960; 800-635-1836; www.palaceresorts.com), an eighteen-hole championship golf course, which is open to the public. Designed by Robert von Hagge, the course (7,202 yards, par 72) has gently sloping hillsides, rock formations, roller-coaster greens, indigenous flora, and wide fairways. It offers a driving range, practice area, putting green and green-side bunker areas, pro shop with Callaway and Titleist equipment and merchandise, qualified staff, and restaurant, the 19th Hole. Greens fees include food and beverages: US$180 with shared cart; $120 after 2:00 P.M. Junior to age twelve $90. Club rentals: $30 steel, $50 graphite. Lessons: $45 per hour. The entrance to the golf club is on the main highway, about a mile south of Playa del Carmen. Round-trip transportation to the course US$20.

Xcaret (pronounced *ish-ca-ret*; 984-871-5200; www.xcaret.com) is a privately owned, 200-acre nature, archaeological, and recreational theme park 5 miles south of Playa del Carmen and next door to the port of Calica. The site was once an important Mayan commercial port and a ceremonial center where Mayas from all over the peninsula came to purify themselves in the sacred waters of the cenotes (large, natural sinkholes in the limestone that pockmark the Yucatán). The Maya believed the rain god lived in the cenotes and provided the water for their crops.

Xcaret, the Mayan word for "paradise," has nature trails, an aviary, botanical gardens, a museum, recently excavated Mayan ruins, a beach, underwater tunnels for snorkelers and divers to explore, and two huge cenotes, where you can snorkel in water so clear, you hardly need a mask. The park offers horseback riding and a three-hour dive course, but the most popular and unusual experience is a float down an underground river. There are restaurants, lockers, and thatched umbrellas and chairs for refuge from the bright sun.

The park also has a **Dolphin Encounter** (998-206-3304; www.delphinusworld.com) The one-hour Swim with Dolphin Primax offers fifty minutes of interaction with the dolphins, including submarine visualization. The thirty-minute Swim with Dolphins is US$80 and includes a free pair of swimming goggles. Reservations can be made online. Xcaret is ideal for families, offering something for everyone, regardless of age. The entrance fee is a steep US$53.10 adult, $26.55 ages five through twelve, but worth it if you plan to spend the day. Horseback riding, diving, and snorkel equipment cost extra. Hours: 8:30 A.M. to 10:00 P.M. (As a full-day cruise ship shore excursion, $94 adult; $75 child.) Xcaret's Web site provide details of packages and other information.

Calica (5 miles): South of Playa del Carmen and adjacent to Xcaret is another gateway to the Yucatán, developed primarily as an industrial/commercial port by private investors; cruise ship docking facilities were added later. Calica's protected mooring facilities are its main advantage, enabling cruise ships to dock and remain in port for the entire day—the principal reason cruise lines use it. Its proximity to Xcaret is another advantage. In fact, cruise itineraries that list Xcaret as a port of call most likely dock at Calica. The port facilities include a small restaurant and bar, crafts shop, restrooms, telephone for international calling, and taxi stand, but Calica is not a place to linger. Like Playa del Carmen, it has the advantage of being about an hour's drive from either Cancún or Tulum. Taxis are plentiful; prices to all the major sites of interest are posted at the dispatcher's kiosk.

Paamul: A short road about 12 miles south of the Xcaret turnoff leads to a bay with a rocky beach that is popular for beachcombing and watching bird life. (Some giant sea turtles come ashore in summer to lay their eggs.) Paamul now has a dive resort, where the dive shop offers snorkeling trips for US$25. The north side of the area is a protected area and will not be developed.

Puerto Aventuras (16 miles) (www.puerto aventuras.com) is a 766-acre development with a large marina and yacht club, a beach club, a tennis club, a PADI dive center, a gym, two hotels and ten condominium buildings, residential homes, nine restaurants, five snack bars, six bars, a golf course, a shopping complex, a disco, a bird sanctuary, a dolphin aquarium, the CEDAM Nautical Museum, and an archaeological site. It has been designed to retain 65 percent of the area as green space in a natural, parklike setting. If you want to spend the day here and play golf, you should make the arrangements in advance, but you will most likely have to listen to a real estate sales pitch somewhere along the way.

Kantenah Beach: Farther along, at Kantenah Beach, you can find facilities that make it a good stop for beach lovers—a palapa or thatched-roof restaurant, hammocks rocking in the breeze, volleyball nets, showers, and restrooms.

Bay of Akumal: Sheltered by one of the longest coral reefs in the Western Hemisphere, the Bay of Akumal, 4 miles south of Puerto Aventuras, has seen tremendous development since the early 1990s: fifty hotels, large and small; dive shops; seven restaurants; grocery stores; and more. The beaches are beautiful, and the snorkeling, diving, fishing, and windsurfing are among Mexico's best. Divers can enjoy some of the Caribbean's finest coral reefs, plus the wreck of an eighteenth-century Spanish galleon. You can also explore the surrounding countryside by bike or horseback.

Akumal has seven entrances off the main highway, each leading to a different group of resorts. **Hotel Club Akumal Caribe** (www.hotelakumal caribe.com), one of the oldest resorts on the bay, welcomes day visitors. You can enjoy the beach, and snorkel gear is available for rent. Snorkeling packages sold on cruise ships often use this location. The **Akumal Dive Shop** (www.akumal.com)

offers a deep dive every morning at 9:30 A.M., and 40- to 60-foot dives at 11:30 A.M. and 2:30 P.M. Single-tank dives are $50; a two-dive package is $70. Freshwater cavern tours are $75 for two or more divers, and $95 for a private tour. Divers must be open-water-certified.

Yalku: A small lagoon on the north side of Akumal, Yalku is full of fish so tame, you can have them eating out of your hands. Your tour guide will tell you to bring some bread along so you can watch the fish swarm in to feed. It's great for picture taking.

Xcacel: In another 5 miles or so is a major turtle nesting site.

Aktun-Chen: A road west of the coast between Akumal and Xcacel leads to a 988-acre tropical park with trails where visitors might spot local wildlife, such as deer and monkeys, and three caves with an underground river. The main cave, which is more than 600 yards long, has paths and is illuminated. Visitors see stalactites and stalagmites formed more than five million years ago. Hours: 9:00 A.M. to 5:00 P.M. daily (to 7:00 P.M. in summer). Guided tours are offered throughout the day for US$24 adult; $13 ages three through ten (www.aktunchen.com)

Xel-Ha (32 miles): Farther south is Xel-Ha (www.xel-ha.com; 998-898-1900), set amid tropical forest. It is an ecological park with an incredible natural aquarium and a network of inlets, lagoons, cenotes, and underground rivers. Here the water is so clear, you don't need a mask to see the fish. It is also a popular swimming and snorkeling spot. Cruise ship shore excursions to Tulum often stop here for passengers to have a swim; some include a picnic lunch. There are trails for hiking, or you can swim with the dolphins or explore the park by floating down the waterways in oversize inner tubes. About a mile away, there are Mayan ruins, with murals of birds and jaguars, and a cenote, which attracts wildlife. Visitors have also reported seeing jaguars. Admission: Daily, basic fee US$39 adult; $15 ages five through eleven, plus tax; under five free. All-inclusive day package (beverage, towels, lockers, snorkel gear, food) $59 adult; $42 child. A cruise ship excursion combining Xel-Ha and Tulum costs US$124 to $140 adult, $75 to $80 child; the Dolphin Swim (998-883-3293) runs $89.

Tulum
www.tulum.com

The walled city of Tulum, about 36 miles (less than an hour's drive) from Playa del Carmen, is perched on a cliff overlooking the Caribbean. It is the only known walled city built by the Mayas on the coast. Tulum and other towns of the Yucatán were once connected by an elaborate road system, which is still visible in some sections.

In 1518 a Spanish expedition exploring the Yucatán coast prior to Cortés's conquest of Mexico sighted Tulum. One of its members later wrote, "We saw in the distance a town so large the city of Seville could not be better or larger."

Tulum was one of many coastal towns and temple sites that continued for some time after the Spanish conquest, but for how long we do not know. By the mid-nineteenth century, when Tulum was "rediscovered," most of the former Mayan sites were buried under the growth of the Yucatán jungle—and still are.

When compared with Chichén Itzá or Uxmal, the ruins of Tulum are not grand, but they are interesting. The site dates from about A.D. 700 to 1000, the post-Classic period after the Mayan civilization had reached its peak, and shows the influence of the Toltecs, who conquered the Yucatán in the tenth century.

Originally named Zama, "the dawn," because it faced east to the sea, Tulum sits dramatically on cliffs 40 feet above the Caribbean and was protected by the reefs from invasion by way of the sea. The other three sides had walls more than 6 feet thick and varying in height from 4 to 19 feet. There were five entrances; today's entrance is on the west.

The site is dominated by El Castillo, the Castle, the name the Spaniards always gave to the central grand structure of a temple complex. The view of the sea from the top of the castle is lovely. After passing through the entrance and walking directly east, you will see a group of buildings—the Temple of the Frescos on the south and the Great Palace on the north. Directly in front is the Castle, approached by a long series of steps. The first level was the dance platform for religious observances.

The Temple of the Frescos is the best preserved and most interesting structure at the site because it still has remnants of the murals that once covered the walls of all the buildings in the complex.

On the east side of the Castle is the Temple of the Descending God, so called because, in the band of decoration over the doorway, the figure of the god is pointed toward the ground. The symbol appears in the Castle ornamentation and else-where and is said to represent the bee god of the Mayans. The cultivation of bees was important to the ancient Mexicans, because honey served as their sweetener; they had no sugar.

On the west side of the Castle is the Temple of the Initial Series, which takes its name from the method by which Mayan dates were calculated.

The archaeological site is open from 8:00 A.M. to 5:00 P.M. daily. The once-remote ruins of Tulum are now reached by a four-lane highway, and shops line the way near the entrance. From the parking lot, a tram provides transportation to the site for those who do not care to walk the ¼-mile distance. Entrance fee is US$3.50; $3 for video camera use. Guides are available. Booklets are available for purchase at the site as well. When you visit on a cruise ship excursion, an English-speaking guide is provided.

If you are traveling on your own, you might want to include a stop at jungle-chic **La Zebra** (998-112-3260; www.lazebratulum.com), Tulum's hip beach cantina and tequila bar, which is run by California beach transplant Heather Froeming, manager, and Mexico City native Lina Avila and her sisters—all experienced in the serious tequila and home cooking they serve.

Sian Ka'an
www.siankaan.org

A vast region covering 2,026 square miles (or 1.3 million acres) of a peninsula and coastal waters, stretching 100 miles south of Tulum down the Caribbean coast, Sian Ka'an was declared a Bios-phere Reserve in 1986 and added to UNESCO's World Heritage List. The largest nature preserve in Mexico, it is made up of one-third tropical forest, one-third wetland and mangroves, and one-third coastal and marine environments. It's inhabited by jaguar, margay, cougar, puma, lynx, ocelot, monkey, manatee, tapir, and white-tailed deer, as well as

340 species of birds. It's also rich in flora, with more than 1,200 plant species. Part of the reserve is the barrier reef fronting the Yucatán, which forms part of the world's second longest reef, stretching south to Honduras. Scattered throughout the reef are cays, or islets, that provide nesting grounds for thousands of water birds, including such rare species as the jabiru stork and roseate spoonbill, and four species of endangered sea turtles.

The reserve consists of three parts where envi-ronmental conservation and sustainable develop-ment are working together: a Buffer Zone, where fishing, tourism activity, and agriculture are permit-ted under certain guidelines; a Gathering Zone, reserved strictly for local people to hunt, fish, gather food, and build; and a Core Zone, account-ing for 80 percent of the area, where only scientific research is allowed. The region is dotted with archaeological sites, some of which are 20,000 years old. The area can be visited with advance arrangements through the **Friends of Sian Ka'an Association** (Plaza America, Cobá No. 5, Third Floor, No. 48-50, Cancún; 998-884-9583; fax 998-887-3080), which is a private, nonprofit conserva-tion organization promoting national and international support for the reserve and managing certain projects under the authority of SEDUE (Sec-retary of Urban Development and Ecology).

The association offers an all-day tour escorted by a naturalist guide, with bird-watching and snor-keling in a cenote. The cost is US$68 per person, including bus transportation, lunch, and contribution to the reserve's upkeep. The tour is limited to six people. During the winter peak season, you need to make reservations at least one month in advance; during the off-season, reservations should be made two to three weeks ahead of time. With advance arrangements, the association's tour bus will pick up cruise passengers at the ferry dock in Playa del Carmen about 8:30 A.M. and return about 4:00 P.M. The tour includes a three-hour boat ride through the coastal lagoons and lunch at Anna y José, a rustic seaside inn. Excursions are also provided by local tour companies that specialize in adventure travel, such as Eco-Colors (www.ecotravelmexico.com) and Alltournative (www.alltournative.com).

West of Playa del Carmen

Cobá

The archaeological site of Cobá is 25 miles inland from Tulum. More extensive than Chichén Itzá, Cobá covers 10 square miles with an estimated 6,500 structures. The area is dominated by a building known as the Church, which stands ten stories high. Two miles away is Nohoch Mul, the largest pyramid found in the Yucatán, rising 120 steps to the top at an incline that is almost perpendicular.

Little of the huge site has been excavated, and scholars do not yet know its origin, except to establish that it is older than Tulum. Recent excavations have led archaeologists to question whether Cobá belonged to a civilization even earlier than the Maya. Since some parts of Cobá date from the Classic period (after A.D. 600), it is assumed that the Mayas inhabited the site. However, pre-Classical remnants have been found, indicating that the area was occupied prior to the period of the Mayas. Someday, when more excavations have been completed and further information is available, Cobá will likely be as important an archaeological site for visitors to the Yucatán as Chichén Itzá.

Getting to Inland Archaeological Sites

To visit Chichén Itzá, you should take the shore excursion by air or motorcoach, as the case may be, if offered by your cruise line. If not, and your cruise ship remains in port long enough to make the trip, ask your travel agent to book your arrangements in advance—there probably won't be enough time upon your arrival in port to do so. Excursions leave early in order to maximize time at the site.

There are several alternatives. First, some ships remain in Cozumel overnight or until late in the day, enabling passengers to make the full-day excursion to Chichén Itzá by air. (See the Shore Excursions section earlier in this chapter.) Second, when a cruise ship visits both Cozumel and Cancún/Playa del Carmen, it may be possible to leave the ship in one port and rejoin it in another on the same day.

Highway 180 leads to Chichén Itzá and Mérida from either Cancún or Playa del Carmen; the drive takes about two and a half hours. The drive from Chichén Itzá to Mérida is 70 miles or one and a half hours; from Mérida to Uxmal is 35 miles (about an hour). Flights from Cozumel to Cancún take twenty minutes and operate about every two hours throughout the day. There are also flights from Cozumel and Cancún to Chichén Itzá and Mérida. Excursions from Cozumel by air fly directly to Chichén Itzá. Occasionally a cruise ship will call at Progreso, the port for Mérida.

Chichén Itzá

The most important site of antiquity in the Yucatán, Chichén Itzá (pronounced *che-cha-neat-za*) was recently named one of the "New Seven Wonders of the World" by a mail and online vote of a hundred million people from around the world. The site is 125 miles west of Cancún and Playa del Carmen on Highway 180, the road to Mérida. The city was originally founded in A.D. 432 but abandoned in 608. It was settled again in 960 and prospered until about 1200.

Today the site covers an area of about 6 square miles. One part has the great pyramids and temples of the Maya; another was built by their successors, the Toltec, who invaded the Yucatán in the tenth century. The Toltec, a fierce tribe from Tula in central Mexico, brought with them their belief in Kukulcan, the man-god represented as the plumed serpent, and introduced the practice of human sacrifice to the Maya.

El Castillo: The first major excavations were undertaken by Carnegie Tech over a period of twenty years. The site is dominated by El Castillo, a giant pyramid eighteen stories high. An interior tunnel leads into a tiny throne room where you see a red jaguar shaped into a bench and set with jade eyes and turquoise mosaics. It is thought to be a throne. Jade is not native to the Yucatán, so its use here is one more question in the Mayan puzzle.

The Castle is a calendar in three dimensions. On each of the four sides, ninety-one steps lead to the top; these, along with the upper platform, correspond to the 365 days of the year. On each side of the stairways there are nine terraces representing the two seasons; combined, they correspond to the eighteen months of the Mayan year. The steps are about 6 inches wide and rise at least a foot each. The climb is steep, but worthwhile. From the top the Yucatán jungle stretches as far as the eye can see.

At the equinoxes in March and September, the light and shadow on the steps cast a zigzag pattern from the temple on top of the pyramid to the sculptured snake's head at the bottom of the stairs: The pattern looks like the undulating body of a serpent. For the Mayas, the sight represented the return of Kukulcan and heralded the change of season.

The building is so perfectly constructed acoustically that you can clap your hands at its base and hear the echo ripple up each step, and then project itself to listeners standing hundreds of yards away across the giant open courtyard the Castle once dominated.

Temple of the Warriors: The Temple of the Warriors has intricate carving and 1,000 columns.

Ball Court: The 650-foot-long Ball Court is another acoustic wonder: A person standing at one end talking in a normal voice can be heard at the far end. The court was the setting for a ritual game known as pok-a-pok, said to resemble basketball or soccer and played with a hard rubber ball about the size of a baseball. The rules dictated that when the ball was put through a high stone hoop at the side of the court, the game was over. Only the knee, foot, or elbow (but not the hands) could be used. The games sometimes lasted three or four days, and then the defeated captain was conducted to an adjoining ceremonial platform where he forfeited his head to the victors' swords.

New research has led scholars to believe the opponents in this game were prisoners—perhaps of a rival city-state or tribe who may have been Mayan themselves—forced to participate as a final humiliation. The bloodletting at the end of the match was, apparently, a basic element of Mayan life associated with major events such as birth and death. Human sacrifices had mystical meanings we cannot quite fathom, intended to connect the natural and supernatural worlds. (Such scholarly explanations, of course, do not make the knowledge of such brutality any less revolting, but before we condemn the Mayas, it is good to remember that Roman gladiators were little better.)

Another puzzle: No one has discovered what the Maya did with their dead. Human bones have been discovered in only a few of the ruins, a fact that alludes to human sacrifice. Scholars believe that the practice of human sacrifice was introduced into Mayan rites by the Toltec.

Ceremonial Well: A raised ceremonial road leads to the giant ceremonial well, measuring 350 feet long, 150 feet wide, and 60 feet deep, with sinister-looking greenish black water. A sinkhole in limestone known as a cenote, it was once the focal point of the Mayas' religious rites where, annually, thousands of people gathered to pray to Chaac, the rain god, who was believed to live in the well and provide water for the crops.

During the ceremony a young maiden clad in precious jewels was fed to the god. These young virgins were trained by the priests to accept their own sacrifice as the high point of the group's religious life. Weighted down with gold and silver ornaments, they quickly drowned, becoming brides of the rain god and ensuring good crops in the coming season. Knowledge of the events has been pieced together from carvings on the sides of temples and the thousands of silver, gold, jade, and bone relics recovered from the well.

In other ceremonies at the well, captives were painted blue and thrown into the water at dawn to appease the angry gods. If by noon they were still swimming, the priests would pull them out and worship them for the rest of their lives in the belief that they had been to the other world and come back.

Chac Mool: At Chichén Itzá and elsewhere you will frequently see statues of the ceremonial Chac Mool, a partially reclining stone figure that seems almost whimsical—until you learns that his belly was used to receive the heart of the sacrifice during the temple rites.

There is an entrance fee to the antiquity site. Temple rubbings are available at local shops, as are books, literature, postcards, Mexican crafts, and souvenirs.

Between Chichén Itzá and Uxmal, there are several lesser-known Mayan sites, such as **Izamal,** noted for its yellow facades and its new light-and-sound show; **Oxkintok,** which has trilevel labyrinths; and **Ek-Balam,** where there is a new rest area with tourist services and rappelling into a cenote. However, unless you have visited both

Chichén Itzá and Uxmal in the past, you will not have time in a day's visit to take in these sites, too.

Uxmal

The structures of Uxmal are considered the finest pre-Columbian relics in Mexico. Located 35 miles south of Mérida (about an hour's drive), Uxmal (pronounced *oosh-mal*) is pure Maya without the Toltec overlay. It is built of yellowish stone rather than the gray material that gives Chichén Itzá such a sober, forbidding appearance. The site dates from about A.D. 600 and was inhabited for about 800 years. As many as 250,000 people lived in a 4½-square-mile area around the government and religious center, which was filled with magnificent buildings.

Palace of the Governors: The massive, ornately decorated Palace of the Governors, constructed with more than 20,000 cut stones, covers five acres. It is built on an elevated terrace that measures 600 feet by 500 feet. The 320-foot facade has lovely filigree of detailed bas-relief, all the more remarkable when you remember that the Mayas did not have metal tools with which to work.

Pyramid of the Magician: Another imposing structure is the Pyramid of the Magician, also known as the House of the Dwarf, with 118 steep steps leading to the top. According to legend, the pyramid was built on the site of the house of a sorceress who grieved because she had no children. Finally she hatched an egg, and from it came a small child who grew up to be a dwarf. When he was fully grown, she urged him to challenge the Mayan ruler, who in turn condemned him to death unless he could build a house higher than any other in one night. And he did.

Nunnery: The Nunnery, named by the Spaniards, was not a nunnery but part of a quadrangle of four temples that surrounded a courtyard. It is noteworthy for its bas-relief carvings and arches. During the sound-and-light show, presented nightly in Spanish and in English, audiences sit in this area to watch the show.

Recently a group of authorities on Mayan civilization were reported to have found the key to deciphering the glyphs on some Mayan temples. If this news is true, it may mean that we can at last begin to unlock the mysteries of the Mayas and answer many of the questions that have puzzled us for so long.

Costa Maya
www.puertocostamaya.com

Note to readers: In August 2007 Hurricane Dean was a Category Five storm when it slammed Costa Maya and Chetumal and caused extensive damage to the area. Cruise lines estimate that it will be late spring or summer 2008 before their ships will be able to call again at Costa Maya.

Costa Maya, a new port on Western Caribbean itineraries, is much more than a place to dock ships. It is a broad concept and a major development intended to open up southern Quintana Roo, a part of Mexico mostly unknown to tourists. (Quintana Roo, Mexico's newest state and the same state in which Cancún and Cozumel are located, is one of three states that make up the Yucatán Peninsula.)

Located in the southeastern corner of the peninsula, almost to the Belize border, *Costa Maya* is the name of both a port complex and an 80-mile finger of land with Caribbean-washed white-sand beaches, jungle-thick scrub, and mangroves running from Punta Herrero—a fishing village on the shores of Espiritu Santo Bay on the south side of the Sian Ka'an Biosphere Reserve—to Xcalak at the southern tip, and only a forty-five-minute ferry ride from Ambergris Caye in the barrier reef off Belize.

Chances are you will not find Costa Maya on a map, but you may find Majahual (or Mahahual) midway along the coast. The tiny fishing village is the location of the port and the nucleus of the Costa Maya development. Roads, added only in December 2000, run north and south of the port, edging the mangroves and leading to small hotels and hamlets. There is also a small airport. Electricity came in January 2001. The new infrastructure is some of the US$100 million investment being made here by Fonatur, the quasi-governmental agency that developed Cancún.

The port and the yet-to-be-developed coast are only part of the story about Costa Maya. The region behind the coast is equally compelling and full of

Costa Maya

delightful surprises, starting with Chetumal, the pretty capital of the state of Quintana Roo, and its attractions, as well as the prodigious Mayan antiquities—as many as 800 sites—in the surrounding area. Add to this a 30-mile-long lagoon with boating, kayaking, and fishing; seven cenotes for swimming and diving; a tropical jungle alive with birds and wildlife; and two of the most unusual hotels in Mexico, and you can understand why Costa Maya is being called the next Cancún—but with a difference: the promise of low-impact, ecologically sensitive development.

Port Profile: Costa Maya

The first phase of the port of Costa Maya, representing an investment of N$21 million and built by PTM (Promociones Turisticas Mahahual), began operation in February 2001. The second phase is seeing the creation of New Majahual, a community for 20,000 people, and at the same time, excavation and restoration of dozens of Mayan sites and inland attractions. Beyond the planned expansion of the port facility, new roads, an airstrip, and a hotel are being added. The Costa Maya airport is served by Aerocosta and Aeroprinco nineteen-seater aircraft.

Costa Maya is unusual in many ways. First, the builders went to the major cruise lines and asked, "What do you want or need at the port?"—and they listened! Arriving cruise passengers are not likely to be aware of this, but Royal Caribbean, Princess, and Carnival, among others, have been advising PTM almost every step of the way.

The port's design incorporates aspects of Mexico's history—Mayan, Spanish, and modern—in its architecture and facilities, beginning with the terminal entrance, which replicates the facade of a Mayan temple with a high pointed arch. Passengers who do not want to walk can ride the short distance from their ship to the terminal entrance in Disney-style trams pulled by a caboose.

Beyond, they will enter a large plaza framed on the seaside with three huge palapas whose high, pointed thatched roofs are an expression of indigenous houses seen in villages throughout the Yucatán. The first two palapas are devoted to crafts; the third houses a restaurant serving Mayan dishes and lobster. On the far side of the plaza is a large swimming pool with a swim-up bar. And beyond the pool you'll find an amphitheater, where performances of Mexican folklore are staged at intervals throughout the day, and another restaurant overlooking the sea.

Around the colonnaded perimeter of the plaza are modern shops, mostly branches of jewelry, clothing, ceramics, and silver stores based in Cancún and Cozumel. At the center of the complex is a bell tower, a typical Spanish feature of every town and village in Mexico. The bell tower marks the exit where passengers will find taxis and other services, and sightseeing buses waiting to take them on tours.

On the north side of the port is a small private beach club with a restaurant and bar. The port has an agreement with the club for passengers to use these facilities for a small fee. However, most passengers are likely to want to explore other beach areas north and south of the port.

At **Uvero,** about 15 miles north of the port, a former naval marina was converted by PTM into a beach club for cruise passengers. It has a restaurant, bar, palapas, and water sports. The area is a natural habitat of dolphins. Recently the Dolphin Dream Experience, a joint venture with the ecopark Xcaret, opened. The tour, led by bilingual naturalists, gives visitors the opportunity to swim with and learn about dolphins in their natural habitat.

Before the new development began, **Xcalak,** a settlement at the south end of the coast, was merely a spot for divers to pass on their way to Chinchorro Bank, the atoll 18 miles offshore. Now Xcalak has begun to develop, too, with rustic beachfront bungalows and small hotels, and facilities for boating, bird-watching, diving, and sportfishing. Xcalak has a landing strip as well as ferry service to Chetumal.

Banco Chinchorro: About 18 miles offshore from Costa Maya is Chinchorro, the largest atoll in Mexico and part of the second longest barrier reef in the world, offering superb snorkeling and diving. Larger than the island of Cozumel, the atoll covers about 500 square miles, most of it taken up by a lagoon of crystal-clear water that is 3 to 25 feet deep and drops to 600 feet and more outside the atoll. Chinchorro also has three mangrove areas: Cayo Norte, Cayo Sur, and Cayo Centro, the main one for tourists and local fishermen.

On the reefs, divers and snorkelers can see a great variety of coral—elkhorn, staghorn, brain, star, and soft corals—and sponges of all sizes. Angel, parrot, damsel, and tang are some of the colorful tropical fish that inhabit the atoll, while turtles feed on seagrass beds, and barracuda, snapper, bass, and grouper visit constantly.

Chinchorro has another attraction: sunken ships. Spanish galleons, nineteenth-century merchant ships, and modern cargo boats all have foundered on the reefs. Gear for rent and boats to Chinchorro are available in Majahual and Xcalak.

Costa Maya Excursions

The following samples of shore excursions offered by Carnival Cruise Lines, MSC Cruises, and Royal Caribbean are similar to those available from other lines calling at Costa Maya. Prices vary, however. Recently, the cruise lines and Costa Maya have created many new excursions that provide the opportunity to learn more about the region's rich history, visit more of the Mayan sites that are described later in this chapter, and participate in a wider range of sports. Be sure to review the online listings of shore excursions offered by your cruise line in advance of your trip.

Hiking at Pueblo Chiclero: Three hours; US$82. After an hour's drive, you will hike to a chiclero camp where you can see the chewing gum (Chiclets) production process. En route the guide will tell you about this little-known culture and its traditions. Jungle trails require comfortable walking shoes, sun protection, and bug spray.

Beach Snorkel Adventure: Three and a half hours; US$44 to $56 per person, including transportation, equipment, and guide. A forty-five-minute ride to a site where snorkelers have easy entrance into water. Wear your swimsuit and bring a towel and sunscreen. Scuba packages are also available from some cruise ships; consult your cruise line's shore excursions.

Bike and Kayak Adventure: Two to three hours; US$48 to $59 per person. Biking south along a dirt road, you pass long stretches of beach, a mangrove lagoon, and a tiny fishing village en route to the beach. After a swim, you paddle along a nearby reef in a two-person kayak. The return to pier takes a different route. Guides outfit you with bikes at the pier.

Beach Horseback Riding: Three hours; $92. Saddle up for an adventure along the Caribbean coast and take in the natural surroundings; spend time at the beach. Minimum age: twelve years; maximum weight 250 pounds.

Dolphin Swim/Encounter: Three to four hours; $125 adult; $113 child. From a submerged platform in the water, participants interact with dolphins after an entertaining explanation by trainers of the dolphins' characteristics. Minimum age: twelve years.

Chacchoben Mayan Ruins: Four hours; US$72 to $79 per person. (See the description later in this section.) Situated in a jungle setting about an hour's drive from the port, the site covers almost ten acres, but only a small part has been excavated. Excursion requires walking and climbing over uneven surfaces. Bring sunscreen, sunglasses, hat, and insect repellent.

Beach Day: Five hours; US$55 per person. Half day $37 adult; $33 child. Spend the day at Uvero Beach and enjoy a swim in the ocean, a walk along the beach, some nonmotorized water sports, and a snooze in a hammock. There's a bar, a restaurant, freshwater showers, restrooms, and changing rooms.

Kohunlich Mayan Ruins: Seven hours; US$82 to $149 per person. (See the description later in this chapter.) The immense site, west of Chetumal, is a two-hour drive from the port. The ruins are among the most extensive in the region and encompass a broad range of architectural styles. They are known especially for the enormous masks sculpted on the temples. The excursion involves walking and climbing. Bring sunscreen, hat, sunglasses, and insect repellent.

Bacalar Highlights & Seven Color Lagoon: Five hours; $95 to $115 adult; $88 to $104 child. Visit San Felipe, the Spanish fort overlooking Bacalar and its lake, which the Mayans called the "Birthplace of the Rainbow." Enjoy a Yucatán-style lunch in a family-owned restaurant on the lakeshore.

Fishing Excursion: Five to six hours; $219. In this fisherman's paradise, try your hand at fly fishing on a personalized excursion with a professional guide to help you. There might also be bonefish, tarpon, and other fish available for catch and release.

Exploring the Interior

For cruise passengers who prefer to explore the interior, the region offers attractions as interesting and beautiful as the seashore. Cruise lines are offering a variety of basic tours that include two, three, or perhaps more of the following highlights. (The road west from Majahual meets Highway 307, the main road between Tulum and Chetumal, at the village of Limones. Directly west is the Mayan site of Chacchoben; a turn south leads to Bacalar and Chetumal, 87 miles.)

Chacchoben: In a wooded area a few miles inland from the main road is an important Mayan site that is only now being excavated for the first time. Here the jungle has won: Trees and thick vegetation cover most of the site. Nonetheless, as many as two dozen mounds and pyramids can be distinguished. Of them, nine buildings have been identified and are being studied, and two are being restored.

Three layers of building can be distinguished, indicating a continuation of a dynasty—that is, the son of the ruler built atop his father's structures, and the grandson did likewise. What makes the site particularly fascinating is its state of preservation. In studying and restoring the site, archaeologists are retaining the huge trees growing out of the ancient structures, removing vegetation only in places where they must for research or to stabilize the structures.

A short distance from Chacchoben is the Mayan village of Nohbec, on a small lagoon. Some cruise lines may offer a visit to the village for culture/adventure-type excursions. Also, the nearby hamlet of Pedro A Santos has one of several Mennonite communities in this area.

Bacalar and Bacalar Lagoon: The main Tulum–Chetumal highway south skirts the 30-mile-long Bacalar Lagoon to the resort town of Bacalar. Known as the "lagoon of seven colors" for its stunning shades of blue and turquoise, Bacalar Lagoon flows into the Rio Hondo (on the Belize border) and into Chetumal Bay via a network of shallow channels. The banks of the mile-wide lagoon are dotted with vacation villas of Chetumal's prosperous families and waterside cafes serving excellent local seafood and regional cuisine. Boating, fishing, waterskiing, kayaking, and windsurfing can be arranged at the Yacht Club (Club de Yates), a restaurant and boat dock, which is likely to be a stop on shore excursions.

Bacalar, 23 miles north of Chetumal, was the most important Mayan community in the region at the time of the Spanish conquest and put up great resistance to it. After the conquistador Gaspar Pacheco won a victory of sorts, he founded Villa de Salaminca de Bacalar in 1545. But the settlement was never a success due to the Mayas' hostility and refusal to work. Nonetheless, with access to the sea via Chetumal Bay, the Spaniards were able to develop Bacalar as a port for goods bound for Europe. Among the most important products was palo de tinte or dyewood, a source of dye prized by Europeans for royal garments.

Fort of San Felipe: The city's wealth made it a target of pirates; it was attacked so often that in 1729, the governor ordered the construction of a fort. Now restored and housing a small museum,

the fort is an excellent example of eighteenth-century military architecture. The layout is a square plaza surrounded by thick stone walls, a deep moat planted with sharp stakes instead of water for defense, and four rhomboid-shaped ramparts mounted with cannons. The compound had a food storage place, weapons room, sleeping quarters, and watchtower. Originally, the fort had a drawbridge.

Cenote Azul: Directly south of Bacalar is the Cenote Azul, one of seven cenotes in the area and said to be the deepest sinkhole in the Yucatán. Surrounded by lush vegetation, Cenote Azul is filled with cold, clear water almost 200 feet deep. Swimming and diving are allowed. At the entrance is a restaurant serving regional cuisine, and there are changing rooms. Some native wildlife—parrots, toucans, agoutis, spider monkeys—are kept in cages beside the steps leading down to the cenote.

Chetumal

A Maya center in antiquity covering the area from Bacalar to the Rio Hondo, the natural border between Mexico and Belize, *Chetumal* means "the place where the red cedar is plentiful." Despite their conquest of Mexico, the Spaniards were never able to subjugate the fiercely independent people of this region and, after several attempts, abandoned the area, leaving the Maya to their own devices.

The present town, set on the Bay of Chetumal, was founded in 1898 and is the capital of Quintana Roo. Today, as in its past, it serves as a gateway to Belize and Central America.

A typical Mexican town with a central plaza and market, Chetumal is the real Mexico and the antithesis of Cancún. Its tree-shaded streets are lined with modest, single-story buildings and homes. It has a modern airport, hotels, restaurants, car rental offices, travel agencies, and a ferry linking it to Xcalak across the bay on the Costa Maya. The town market is strictly a local one. For incurable shoppers, Chetumal is famous for its many shoe stores full of inexpensive footwear.

Surprisingly, Chetumal is a more developed and sophisticated town than you would expect in this seemingly isolated corner of Mexico. A pretty town with parks and gardens, it has a graceful parkway skirting the bay, a large botanical garden, three museums, two universities, and an interesting ethnic population of East Indians, Lebanese, Chinese, Western Europeans, and other foreigners who began arriving here in the early 1900s.

Museum of Mayan Culture: Located in the center of town next to the market, the **Museo de la Cultura** (983-832-6838) is by far the most important attraction here. This small museum is exquisitely conceived and executed, and—through the use of sophisticated multimedia—it provides an invaluable introduction to the ancient Maya and their world. The exhibits include miniature displays of important Mayan temples from Chichén Itzá to Tikal to Copan. All exhibits are labeled in Spanish and English. Hours: 9:00 A.M. to 7:00 P.M. Tuesday. Admission: adult $3; child $1.

The exhibits are divided into eight sections, each dealing with a different aspect of Mayan culture:

- *The Maya* reflects the people themselves, from their physical appearance and language to their natural environment and history.

- *Between the Mountain and the Sea* portrays the Mayas' relationship with the environment, the technology they developed, and other cultural advances. The section uses stelae, videos, interactive media, scale models, and illustrations.

- *The Place of Thrones and High Places* displays Mayan architecture and cities, models of civic and ceremonial buildings, and information on urban planning.

- *The Men of Corn* depicts the Mayan economy, daily life, and activities such as hunting, fishing, gathering, farming, and trading.

- *Cosmovision of the Mayan People* focuses on the ties between people and the spiritual world, the myth of creation, and funerary customs. A display on the ceiba tree reflects its importance as a symbol of the Mayan universe and its three interconnected planes: the underworld; the earth, home of humankind; and the heavens.

- *The Wisdom of the Ancients* showcases the Mayas' knowledge of the stars, time, and numerical and writing systems.

- *The Foreigners* shows the Mayan cultural contacts and links they forged with peoples such as the Teotihuacan and Toltec, among others.

- *The End of the World* highlights the arrival of the Spanish conquistadores and their deeds and the prophesies predicting the fall of the Mayan civilization. The courtyard of the museum is meant to be like a village house.

Chetumal's other museums are the **City Museum** and the **Museo de Constituyentes,** which features a scale model of Payo Obispo, the town's original name, as it appeared in the 1930s when the streets were lined with colorful wooden houses built in the Caribbean style.

Touring the city, you will pass the **Palacio del Gobierno,** or state administration building; the **Congreso del Estado,** or state congress hall; and a monument, *Homenaje al Mestizaje,* depicting a white man, his Indian wife, and their offspring. The statue honors the mestizo race, said to have begun at the dawn of the Spanish era with the union of a Mayan woman and Gonzalo Guerrero, a shipwrecked Spaniard who fathered the first persons of mixed Indian and Spanish blood and who took up the Mayas' cause against the conquistadores.

Chetumal Bay is a huge, shallow bay with beaches; it's surrounded by mangroves, marshes, and forest. It offers boating and swimming and a host of moderate waterfront seafood restaurants, such as Christy's in Calderitas, a popular beach 5 miles north of Chetumal. An isolated section in the northeast corner of the bay is a manatee sanctuary.

Mayan Sites in the Chetumal Region

Today, as in ancient times, Chetumal is surrounded by agricultural land and dense forest. Hidden in the jungle fastness are an estimated 800 Mayan sites, according to infrared surveys. Only about two dozen have had serious study and are being restored. Instead of clearing the land that results in the manicured look of Chichén Itzá, the encroaching jungle is being retained, giving scientists a clearer picture of the site's history and providing visitors with a remarkable view. All Mexican archaeological sites are protected areas and therefore are havens for wildlife, especially birds.

Oxtankah: (north of Chetumal on the road to Calderitas; turn left at km 11.5 and follow the signs). *Oxtankah* means "three neighborhoods" in the Mayan language, and it has also been translated as the "place of the ramon." The ramon, or breadnut tree, bears a nut gathered by the ancient Mayas and ground into flour. The site was first settled by the Maya during the Early Classic period, A.D. 200 to 600. Remnants from the period have survived at the Plaza of the Bees and Plaza of the Columns, the two areas open to visitors.

The buildings, like others in southern Quintana Roo, show the influence of the Peten (Tikal) region of Guatemala, with which the inhabitants traded. Sometime after A.D. 600, Oxtankah was abandoned, and the site was overrun by the jungle. Eight hundred or so years later, the Maya returned and used the stones from ancient structures to build a modest settlement. Some of these have survived also.

By 1531 the Spaniards had arrived and christened the settlement Villa Real de Chetumal. But the Mayas' hostility forced them to leave within two years. The Spaniards built a church, of which the archway that supported the roof over the altar and remnants of the baptistery remain. The presence of Mayan and European buildings in one locale makes Oxtankah unusual. Admission: US$2.20.

Kohunlich: (40 miles southwest of Chetumal via the Escarcega–Campeche Highway 186; exit south at km 60 to the hamlet of Francisco Villa and follow signs for last 5 miles). One of southern Quintana Roo's most important archaeological sites, Kohunlich was a ceremonial center and home of a powerful dynasty with links to cities in Campeche and Tikal in Guatemala. Despite external influence, experts say, they developed their own distinctive art and architecture. Kohunlich and its surrounding sites were probably inhabited throughout the Classic period, A.D. 250 to 900, and abandoned after 1200.

Kohunlich is named for a nearby logging camp called Cohoon Ridge—a reference to the cohune, a gigantic palm tree abundant here and growing on the ridge (*licht*). The site was discovered in 1912 by explorer Raymond Merwin and excavated in the

1960s by Victor Segovia, who found three periods of construction.

Erected on a slope, the Temple of the Masks is the most important temple on the site and gets its name from the monumental, 6-foot-high stucco masks that line the staircase and reflect the complexity of ancient Mayan society. Experts believe these outstanding works of art represent ancient rulers who portrayed themselves as the sun god, Kinich Ahau, in order to legitimize their rule. The masks are framed with anthropomorphic figures associated with the jaguar, god of the underworld. Thus the symbolism of the masks places the rulers at the center of the universe.

The ceremonial heart of the city during the Late Classic period was dominated by the Palace of the Stelae and the buildings around it, aligned east–west on the central axis and probably used for civic events and administrative functions. The Acropolis, on the northwest, is positioned so that during the spring equinox the moon shines through an opening in the building.

There are many other structures. The majestic North Palace was the residence of a great ruler, built on top of an older building. Another group known as the Complex of the 27 Stairs housed the nobility. It is accessed via stairs that lead to a courtyard with various rooms and terraces. Several tombs have been found in the area. Admission: 30 pesos.

The Explorean Kohunlich

A few miles from the antiquity site might be the biggest surprise in southern Quintana Roo. To call it a rustic jungle lodge, as do the owners, Fiesta Americana, is a little misleading. True, it's a hotel, it's in the jungle, and from a distance the thatched roofs of the cottages piercing the forest canopy appear rustic, but make no mistake, this resort is luxury in every way.

The lobby, fronted by a reflecting pool, sits under a tall palapa and opens onto a view stretching across the treetops of the surrounding jungle for as far as the eye can see. The reception area steps down to a lounge, fitted with stylish casual sofas and chairs and accessories in natural woods and textures.

To one side is the open-air dining room; to the other, a long, narrow swimming pool with lounge chairs and umbrellas perched at the jungle's edge, a health club and spa, and a small meeting room. In the garden at the foot of the pool are two small, igloo-shaped structures where a steam bath treatment is given using local herbs based on a Mayan ritual to drive away bad spirits.

Narrow paths wind down through the forest along stone walls to the cottages, each with two suites. Each suite has a large bedroom, marbled bath, and a terrace furnished like a living room with views overlooking the jungle canopy—an ideal perch for early-morning bird-watching—and a hammock, just waiting for an occupant.

The decor, uncluttered and understated throughout, uses earth-tone fabrics and local wood, stone, and marble with sophisticated renderings of Mexican motifs. There is an exquisite attention to detail—instead of a metal drain in the shower floor, tiny holes in the marble allow water to drain; instead of curtains, wooden panels with woven straw tapestries slide in place to cover the windows.

Explorean Kohunlich (5-201-8350; fax 52-5-201-8450; www.theexplorean.com.mx) has twenty-one cottages (forty-two rooms), two with Jacuzzi. Daily rates are approximately US$200 per person and include meals, tours to nearby antiquity sites, and hiking, canoeing, and other adventure excursions. Some cruise lines make the resort a stop on itineraries that include Kohunlich.

Dzibanche: (Highway 186 via the turnoff to Morocoy; Dzibanche is 2 miles beyond). Dzibanche, deep in the forest north of Kohunlich, was a powerful city that flourished from A.D. 300 to 1200 and traded with Mayan centers in Campeche and Guatemala. The site was discovered in 1927 by Thomas Gann, who named it *Dzibanche,* meaning "carved in wood," after carvings that deal with the settlement's important dates found on lintels of zapote wood in Temple VI, or the Temple of the Lintels. The Maya used timber in their art and architecture, but few wooden artifacts have survived due to the region's tropical climate.

Temple I, an Early Classic pyramid and Dzibanche's finest structure, was adorned with giant masks on each side of the staircase. The pyramid is also known as the Temple of the Owl

after a fine vessel with a sculpted lid in the shape of an owl, found in the tomb. Here, too, the tomb of an ancient ruler surrounded by offerings of jade, alabaster, obsidian, shell, and ceramic was uncovered. Elements in the design of the buildings on the north and south are said to symbolize the nine levels of the underworld, leading experts to think that they were associated with burials.

Temple II, or the Temple of the Cormorants, the oldest part of the town, has been excavated and restored. The complex owes its name to the polychrome burial vessel decorated with cormorants discovered during excavation. Gann Plaza is a courtyard surrounded by seven buildings, including Structure XII, known as the Temple of the Captives due to the carving of captive warriors on the steps.

Kinichna: (House of the Sun). About a mile north of Dzibanche is a small outlying site that appears to have been part of the ancient city. It consists of small buildings grouped around a plaza dominated by a long, symmetrical structure known as the Acropolis. Stairs lead to palaces and temples on different levels. Offerings of jade associated with a burial were found in the upper temple. The Acropolis, dating from between A.D. 200 and 600, appears to celebrate the power of Dzibanche and is built in Peten (Tikal) architectural style.

Natural Attractions

Southern Quintana Roo has large protected areas of wetlands, where bird life is abundant with more than 300 species, and jungle that is home to the endangered jaguar, howler monkey, tapir, peccary, and other animals. Farmers in villages such as **Tres Garantias,** on the edge of the forest reserve west of Chetumal, live off the land and harvest hardwoods from the forest. A few have converted portions of their land into ecotourism projects designed to protect the land and generate income. La Piramide camp, within the reserve, is an example. It offers rustic cabins with basic services and guided tours.

Cenote del Crocodilo Dorado (Sinkhole of the Golden Crocodile). Located by the Hondo River near La Union, the cenote is inhabited by a golden crocodile, according to a local legend, that occasionally makes an appearance. The area is popular for bird-watching and hiking on jungle trails. Excursions can be arranged through agencies in Chetumal.

Rio Hondo: Known to the Mayas as *Nohoch Ucum,* or great river, the jungle river is the natural border between Mexico and Belize; both countries have equal rights to it. The 63-mile-long river is entirely navigable and was used extensively for trade in ancient times. Particularly lucrative in colonial times was harvesting dyewood, from which a dye prized in Europe was extracted. Illegal logging camps that flourished along the Rio Hondo were a thorn in the side of the Spanish authorities, with pirates often becoming loggers or raiding the area for dyewood. Rio Hondo has mangrove islets, and its banks are alive with deer, tapir, agouti, and a variety of birds. Cruising the river, you will see herons, ospreys, iguanas, monkeys, and perhaps manatees.

Central America

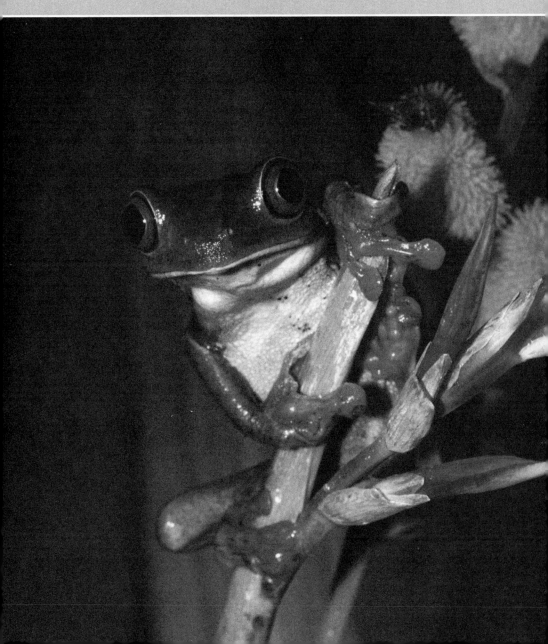

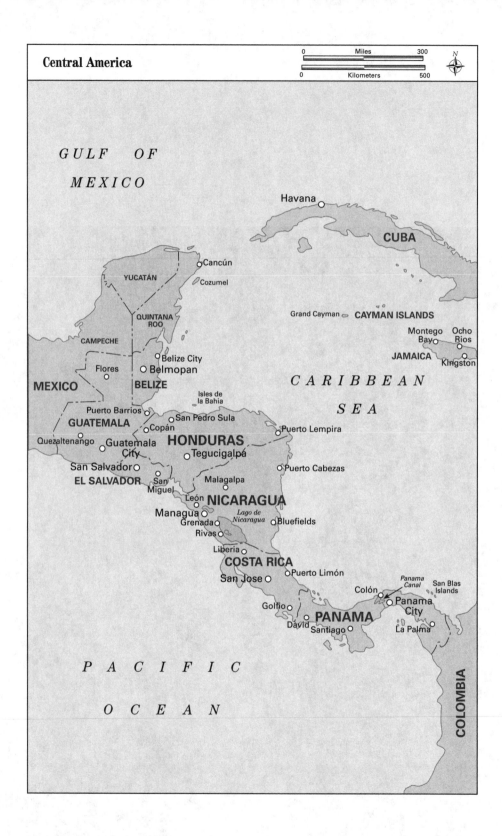

Central America

Miles 0 — 300

Kilometers 0 — 500

N

GULF   OF

MEXICO

Havana

CUBA

Cancún

Cozumel

YUCATÁN

QUINTANA ROO

Grand Cayman   CAYMAN ISLANDS

CAMPECHE

Montego Bay   Ocho Rios

Belize City

JAMAICA   Kingston

Flores   Belmopan

MEXICO   BELIZE

CARIBBEAN

Isles de la Bahia

SEA

Puerto Barrios   San Pedro Sula

Puerto Lempira

GUATEMALA   Copán

Quezaltenango   HONDURAS

Guatemala City   Tegucigalpé

San Salvador   Puerto Cabezas

EL SALVADOR   San Miguel   Malagalpa

León   NICARAGUA

Managua   *Lago de Nicaragua*   Bluefields

Grenada

Rivas

Liberia

COSTA RICA   Puerto Limón

San Jose   *Panama Canal*   San Blas Islands

Colón

PACIFIC   Golfio   PANAMA   Panama City

Dávid   Santiago   La Palma

COLOMBIA

OCEAN

Central America

The land that forms a bridge between North and South America is a complex of seven nations—Belize, Guatemala, Honduras, El Salvador, Nicaragua, Costa Rica, and Panama—dissimilar as often as they are alike. Although the landmass stretches across some 2,000 miles from Mexico to Colombia, separating the Caribbean Sea from the Pacific Ocean, the area is actually quite small: The seven countries together are not as large as Texas.

To most of us from the United States, the countries of Central America seem exotic and distant, but they are, in fact, among our closest neighbors. All except El Salvador have coastlines washed by the Caribbean Sea. Yet with the exception of Panama and the Panama Canal, the cruise world has largely ignored these countries as places to visit.

Topography, tradition, and turmoil can probably share equal blame. A look at the map reveals a spine of high mountains running almost unbroken from Mexico to Panama and reaching more than 12,500 feet at its highest peaks. From their clouded and rain-forested slopes, the terrain, carved by many rivers, drops to a skirt of lowlands bordering the Caribbean Sea. The Spaniards who arrived on these shores in Columbus's wake found a hot, humid, hostile climate. Little wonder that after they conquered the highlands, with their springlike weather, the Spaniards stayed and built their capitals there. The majority of people who came later did likewise. Hence, the Caribbean coast was never widely populated and was largely ignored, except perhaps by banana growers such as the United Fruit Company, which built some of the towns and ports of the lowlands that exist today.

As for tradition, the countries of Central America, except for Belize and to some extent Honduras, are not usually associated with the Caribbean; their history and culture have been more closely related with the Latin world than with the West Indian one. But then Cuba, the Dominican Republic, and Puerto Rico are tied to the Spanish-speaking world, yet they are the very soul of the Caribbean. And, too, Mexico had very little relationship to the Caribbean in modern times until the creation of Cancún and the development of Cozumel. Now these destinations are promoted as the "Mexican Caribbean" and have become standard ports of call on Western Caribbean itineraries.

More relevant, perhaps, was the political turmoil that dominated the headlines of the 1980s, particularly regarding El Salvador, Guatemala, and Nicaragua, and kept tourists away from much of the region. Coincidentally, the decade paralleled the burgeoning of Caribbean cruising when there was, as yet, little demand or necessity for cruise lines to break out of their traditional itineraries, which sailed east from Florida to the Bahamas and the Eastern Caribbean.

Now that has changed. As Caribbean cruising began to mature in the 1990s, and even today, as the number of ships continues to increase, cruise lines are being driven by competition to develop new itineraries. At the same time, the reservoir of repeat passengers, eager to visit new destinations, is growing steadily. No area of the Caribbean would seem better suited to satisfy these needs than Central America.

Most Central American countries are still held back from any rush of cruise ships by the lack of adequate docking facilities, a developed tourism plant, and other infrastructure requirements. However, a start was made by some small cruise lines with small ships offering adventure-type cruises, usually focusing in depth on one or two destinations. Now major cruise lines with larger ships have added some of these countries to their Western Caribbean and Panama Canal itineraries with regular weekly calls, and more can be expected to do so in the future. Currently cruise ships visit Belize, Guatemala, Honduras, Nicaragua, Costa Rica (although more frequently stopping at attractions on its Pacific coast than the Caribbean one), and Panama.

No doubt interest in the area is growing as these nations, young in tourism, develop in the twenty-first century. Meanwhile, anyone who selects a cruise that touches on the region will not be disappointed.

History buffs will find colonial cities, Indian villages, and some of the most important sites of antiquity in the Western Hemisphere; shoppers will be thrilled with the colorful markets filled with excellent and unusual crafts; and outdoor enthusiasts have many new worlds to discover, from palm-fringed coasts with porcelain beaches to mighty mountains with rain forests, volcanoes, and wildlife preserves that are the last refuge for some of the exotic animals and birds once abundant in the Western Hemisphere.

Fronting the Caribbean coast from Mexico to Honduras lies the longest barrier reef in the Western Hemisphere, second in the world only to the Great Barrier Reef of Australia. These pristine waters, particularly off the coasts of Belize and Honduras, offer outstanding snorkeling and diving and some of the best fishing in the world. Several cays, or tiny islets, are nesting places for significant numbers of birds, while mainland marshes and river deltas provide habitat for the manatee and other endangered wildlife.

Belize
www.travelbelize.org
www.belizetourism.org

Long before conservation and environmental protection became fashionable causes, this small country earmarked more than a third of its territory for preservation. Within these borders lie spectacular Mayan ruins, forests, mountains, rivers, waterfalls, and a great variety of wildlife that includes 500 species of birds, 250 types of orchids, howler monkeys, pumas, ocelots, and the 100,000-acre Cockscomb Basin Wildlife Reserve, the world's only jaguar sanctuary.

Belize also has one of the longest chains of caves in the Western Hemisphere and the world's seventh highest waterfall. Its coast faces the world's second longest barrier reef, dotted with hundreds of islets encircled by white-sand beaches and fantastically clear waters rich in coral gardens and teeming with fish.

Formerly known as British Honduras, Belize is bordered by Mexico on the north and by Guatemala on the west and south. About the size of Massachusetts, it is one of Central America's most stable countries, with an English- and Spanish-speaking multicultural population of 250,000. Belmopan, a small interior town, is the capital, but Belize City, on the coast, is the center of commerce, trans-

portation, and activity, as well as a port of call for cruise lines.

Passenger arrival has greatly improved with the US$10 million Cruise Tourism Village, opened in 2002. The main arrival hall has tour operator and other tourist services, a water taxi terminal to take visitors to outer islands for diving and snorkeling, and shops with local crafts and duty-free goods. There is a restaurant and bar, a tender terminal, and other hospitality facilities. Car rental services are also available. A list of rental agencies can be found on the Belize Web site www.travelbelize.org.

Shore Excursions

As Belize has improved its infrastructure over the past decade, local tour operators and cruise lines, working in tandem, have become more sophisticated and creative in the types and variety of excursions they offer. Those listed here are a sampling of the more adventurous excursions that are offered by Carnival Cruises and Holland America Cruises. They are typical of those available from most lines and are still difficult to do on your own. Basic offerings, such as city tours and nearby sites, are noted in the descriptions on the following pages.

Yet keep in mind that while Belize has come a long way, it is still a rough diamond. Roads are often very bumpy and the climate, hot and humid. Participants should be in good physical condition; most of these tours are not suitable for those with physical limitations. You will need insect repellent, sunscreen, hat, and bottled water; wear comfortable lightweight clothing that covers arms and legs.

Biking in Belize: Six hours; US$55. An hour's drive takes you to the rain forest, where you get a brief orientation before guides lead a four-hour bike adventure on some of Belize's best trails. You might see such indigenous wildlife as iguanas, possums, anteaters, foxes, forest rabbits, a variety of birds, and natural ponds with crocodiles.

Goff's Caye Snorkeling: Four hours; US$55. A snorkel boat leaves directly from your ship for a forty-minute ride to the remote atoll, 12 miles east of Belize. Goff's Caye, about the size of a football field, is a coral island in Belize's barrier reef. A guide takes you snorkeling around the whole island to see abundant reef life and coral formations.

Population: 294,000, comprising Creoles (African-European), Garinagus (African-Amerindian), mestizos (Spanish-Indian), Mayas, Europeans, and Americans.

Government: A democratically elected parliamentary government and a member of the British Commonwealth.

Climate: Hot and tropical year-round; the dry season, from October to May, is the most comfortable time.

Clothing: Comfortable, casual light clothing for the coastal areas; hiking clothes and shoes for jungle excursions.

Currency: Belize dollar or BZ. US$1 equals BZ$1.96. In 2006 Belize replaced the value-added tax (VAT) with a general sales tax of 10 percent on goods and services, except hotel accommodations, for which the tax remains 7 percent.

Departure Tax: US$35, and must be paid in US currency only.

Electricity: 110 volts AC.

Entry Formalities: No visa required for US or Canadian citizens, but you must have a valid US passport.

Language: English.

Time: Central Standard Time.

Telephone Area Code: 501.

Vaccination Requirement: None.

Airlines: American, Continental, Delta, TACA, USAirways. Local Airlines: Tropic Air: (800) 422-3435 (from the United States) or 226-2012; Maya Island Airway: (800) 521-1247 (from the United States) or (501) 226-2435.

Information: www.travelbelize.org; www.belizetourism.org. Belize Tourist Board, P.O. Box 325, 64 Regent Street, Belize City, Belize; 227-2420; (800) 624-0686; fax 227-2423.

Horseback Adventure and Nature Walk: Seven hours; US$90. A one-hour bus ride takes you to a ranch and lodge near Belmopan, the capital. A short river crossing on an old ferry system takes you to the beginning of your horseback ride through some of Belize's most beautiful rain forest trails, with diverse vegetation, birds and wildlife, and scenery. Lunch is served at the lodge. Minimum age twelve years; maximum weight 220 pounds. Long pants and closed-toed shoes are recommended.

Shark/Ray Alley Snorkel: Seven hours; US$79. Four miles south of Ambergris Caye, the Hol Chan Marine Reserve and shark/ray alley area are among the most popular snorkeling/dive sites along the barrier reef. For years local fishermen cleaned their catch in this area; now it is a popular site for southern stingrays and nurse sharks. A speedboat leaves directly from your ship for the one-and-a-quarter-hour ride along the mangrove channels to the reef. There you swim and snorkel from the boat among stingrays and nurse sharks in shallow 8 to 10 feet of water.

Belize City: Belize's main city is something of a hodgepodge, with elevated tin-roofed wooden buildings beside British colonial ones, such as the Court House, rebuilt in the 1920s after a fire destroyed the original, and modern ones overlaid with a West Indian atmosphere. Its Cathedral of St. John, built in 1812, is the oldest Anglican church in Central America and today houses a museum. Among the other historic sites spanning two centuries, you will see the nineteenth-century hand-cranked swing bridge over Haulover Creek, apparently named because cattle were once roped together by their horns and hauled over the river. Nowadays it is opened at 6:00 A.M. and 5:30 P.M. to let ships pass. The **Museum of Belize,** Belize City's first museum, opened in 2002. It is dedicated to the country's history and culture with exhibits pertaining to Belize's past and present. Otherwise the town is short on sightseeing attractions, but it makes a good base for reaching some of Belize's most interesting sites. City tour: Two and a half hours; US$39.

Belize Zoo (www.belizezoo.org): Topping the list of attractions is the unusual, if not funky, Belize Zoo, 30 miles west of town. Here, amid hand-printed, funny, and hokey but charming signs, you can see more than one hundred species of native

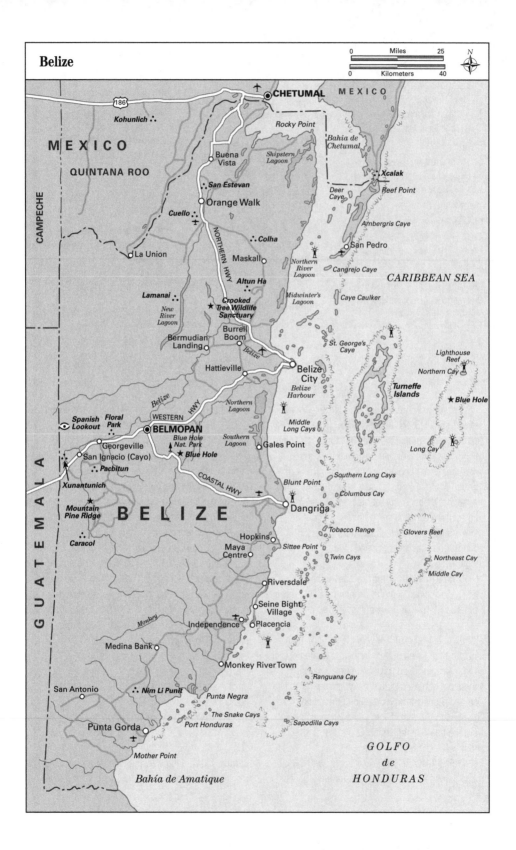

Belize

0 Miles 25
0 Kilometers 40

N

MEXICO ●**CHETUMAL**

186

Kohunlich ∴

MEXICO

QUINTANA ROO

CAMPECHE

Rocky Point

Bahía de
Chetumal

Buena
Vista

Shipstern
Lagoon

∴ San Estevan

Orange Walk

Cuello ∴

∴ Colha

La Union

Maskall

Northern
River
Lagoon

Xcalak ∴

Deer
Caye

Reef Point

Ambergris Caye

San Pedro

Cangrejo Caye

CARIBBEAN SEA

Altun Ha ∴

Lamanai ∴

New
River
Lagoon

★ Crooked
Tree Wildlife
Sanctuary

Midwinter's
Lagoon

Caye Caulker

Burrell
Boom

Bermudian
Landing

Belize

St. George's
Caye

Lighthouse
Reef

Northern Cay

Hattieville

Belize
City

Belize
Harbour

Turneffe
Islands

★ Blue Hole

NORTHERN HWY

Belize

Northern
Lagoon

Middle
Long Cays

Spanish
Lookout

Floral
Park

WESTERN HWY

●**BELMOPAN**

Blue Hole
Nat. Park

Southern
Lagoon

Gales Point

Long Cay

Georgeville

San Ignacio (Cayo)

★ Blue Hole

∴ Pacbitun

COASTAL HWY

Blunt Point

Southern Long Cays

Columbus Cay

Xunantunich

★ Mountain
Pine Ridge

B E L I Z E

Dangriga

Caracol ∴

Hopkins

Maya
Centre

Sittee Point

Tobacco Range

Twin Cays

Glovers Reef

Northeast Cay

Middle Cay

Riversdale

Seine Bight
Village

Independence

Placencia

Medina Bank

Monkey

Monkey River Town

Ranguana Cay

San Antonio

∴ Nim Li Punit

Punta Negra

The Snake Cays

Punta Gorda

Port Honduras

Sapodilla Cays

Mother Point

**GOLFO
de
HONDURAS**

Bahía de Amatique

GUATEMALA

animals, including jaguars, tapir, howler monkeys, toucans, and more. The zoo was created originally by happenstance. Sharon Madola came to Belize in 1982 to care for a group of native animals that were being used in a nature film, but the project ran out of money before it could finish. The fate of the animals was a big concern.

Since Belize did not have a zoo, Sharon asked, why not start one? And she did. Through the schools particularly, she raised interest and awareness, enabling her to get government and private help, and in a decade of hard work she turned the zoo from a noble idea into a Belize institution everyone loves. A half-day city tour and zoo visit combination is one of the shore excursions offered by cruise ships and costs about US$49 per person.

Altun Ha: About 30 miles north of Belize City are the country's most accessible Mayan ruins, where thirteen temples and residential structures have been uncovered. Here a jade head—the largest carved jade object ever found in the Mayan region—was uncovered during excavations by David Pendergast of the Royal Ontario Museum from 1964 to 1971. It represents the sun god Kinich Ahau, a national symbol of Belize that can be seen on the nation's currency. Altun Ha was a major ceremonial center in the Classic period from A.D. 250 to 900 and a trading center linking the Caribbean coast with Mayan centers in the interior. A full-day tour departs from Belize City by boat and cruises up the scenic Belize River. En route you might see troops of black howler monkeys and crocodiles basking in the sun on the riverbanks. The site has a gift shop and restrooms.

Belize City combined with Altun Ha: Four hours; US$59; **Altun Ha and Belize River:** Seven hours; US$100. The river trip is about one and a quarter hours; boats are uncovered.

Bermudian Landing Baboon Sanctuary: The 18-square-mile reserve, an hour's drive north of Belize City, was established in 1985 to protect the black howler monkey through an unusual voluntary grassroots conservation program dependent upon the cooperation of landowners and villagers in farming communities bordering the monkey's habitat on the Belize River.

The black howler monkey, known in Belize as the baboon, is an endangered species whose range is now limited to Belize, southern Mexico, and isolated areas of Guatemala. When the Bermudian Landing community learned of the need to preserve the howlers' dwindling habitat and the benefits they could derive from conservation, its members responded by signing pledges to abide by certain guidelines. These include protecting forests along riverbanks, leaving food trees when clearing land, and maintaining corridors of forest around farmed areas. In turn, the landowners have benefited by reducing erosion, preventing silting of the river, and allowing for more rapid replacement of forests. The community derives some revenue from visitors as well.

In addition to seeing the monkeys, hikers on the reserve's forest trails can see iguanas, coati, anteaters, and other exotic animals along with some of the nearly 200 bird species observed here. A visitor center and exhibit are supported by the World Wildlife Fund and the Zoological Society of Milwaukee County.

Baboon Sanctuary and Belize City: Four hours; US$65. As they are neither shy nor quiet, you are likely to see and definitely hear these primates that live in the riverine forests by the Belize River. The sanctuary visit is followed by a short tour of Belize City.

Crooked Tree Wildlife Sanctuary: A 3,000-acre preserve of lagoons and marshes 33 miles northwest of Belize City, this is a bird-watcher's mecca. There are dozens of species to be seen, but the sanctuary is best known for the thousands of jabiru storks, the largest flying bird in the hemisphere, that reside here during the dry season, from October to early May. Local tour companies can arrange a visit, but it is unlikely that your cruise ship will offer a shore excursion here, unless it is a nature or bird-watching type of cruise.

Hummingbird Highway and Mountain Pine Ridge: For hiking, the most accessible area is the 300-square-mile Mountain Pine Ridge, west of Belize City and south of Belize's capital, Belmopan, along the Hummingbird Highway, an area known for its scenic pine forests, streams, caves, and the 1,000-foot Hidden Valley Falls.

Caves Branch River: The Hummingbird Highway gives access to the Caves Branch River, which winds through the mountains into a tunnel that leads to an underground cave system through which the Caves Branch River flows. From artifacts found here, it is thought that the caves were used by ancient inhabitants for ceremonial purposes. Today visitors can enjoy an unusual "cave tubing" excursion.

The full-day excursion departs from Belize City by bus for a one-hour ride into the lush tropical countryside to where the cave excursion begins. Participants are given a flashlight to wear during their two-hour ride in an inflated inner tube, carried along by the slow-moving currents, and can view the stalactites and stalagmites that line the cave system. At the end of the journey, they are greeted with a picnic lunch. Changing facilities are available.

Cave Tubing and Rain Forest Exploration: Seven hours; US$79. Carrying your equipment and walking about forty-five minutes on a rain forest path, you reach the Sibun River site where your tubing adventure begins. Waterproof camera, sturdy closed shoes, sunscreen, hat, and change of clothes are recommended. The operation of the tour depends on weather conditions.

Other Mayan Sites: Among other important Mayan ruins in western Belize are the ceremonial center of Caracol, the most impressive Mayan site in Belize, accessible by road only in the dry season (a new, all-weather road is being developed, which is expected to make the area more accessible year-round), and Xunantunich, a major center during the Classic period, 2 miles from the Guatemala border.

Xunantunich: Seven hours; US$109. The site, two hours by bus from the port, is situated on a limestone ridge with views of the hilly Cayo district, and it's composed of six large plazas surrounded by more than twenty-five temples and palaces. Lunch in San Ignacio.

West of the town of San Ignacio, just across the Belize–Guatemala border, is Tikal, one of the largest, most important Mayan sites in Central America. People often visit it from Belize. (See the Guatemala section that follows for information.)

Tikal Expedition by Air: Nine hours; about US$499. From the airport (10 miles from the port), a fifty-minute flight to Peten in Guatemala provides great views of Belize. In Peten your bus travels along Lago Peten Itza to Tikal for a three-hour tour of the famous Mayan site. Lunch is served at the site. Wildlife, such as howler and spider monkeys, coatimundi, parrots, keel-billed toucans, and other birds, is abundant. Deep in the forest of the Orange Walk district, north of Belize City and only accessible by boat, is Lamanai, another of the major Mayan antiquity sites.

The Cays

A short distance offshore is a string of tiny islands along the 185-mile-long barrier reef, the longest in the Western Hemisphere. Development is concentrated on Ambergris Caye, 35 miles to the north of Belize City, and Caye Caulker, 14 miles south of Ambergris Caye; another dozen have one or two hotels. San Pedro, the main town on Ambergris Caye, is usually a stop for small cruise ships where passengers can enjoy fabulous white-sand beaches, excellent deep-sea fishing, and snorkeling on the shallow-water reefs of the Hol Chan Marine Preserve, a 5-mile-square area of shallow-water coral gardens at the southern tip of Ambergris. Trips to Mayan sites and jungle retreats on the mainland depart daily from San Pedro.

Other locations along the reef that are often stops for small cruise ships are the Turneffe Islands, 18 miles east of Belize City, a large atoll with abundant fish and large rays; Lighthouse Reef, about 30 miles farther east, where Half Moon Cay is a sanctuary for nesting red-footed boobies and magnificent frigate birds; and Glovers Reef, 30 miles east of the southern coastal town of Dangriga.

The coastal villages of Placencia and Punta Gorda in Belize are occasional ports of call by small ships. Some continue, although rarely, to Livingston in Guatemala, where a ship can turn into the Rio Dulce, a jungle river near the Honduras border. Small ships can sail upriver to Lake Izabel for passengers to visit the Mayan ruins of Quirigua.

Guatemala
www.visitguatemala.com

Guatemala is a land of superlatives. It has Central America's highest, most active volcano; the most prodigious Mayan ruins; the largest population; and the largest, most authentic population of indigenous people, who have clung the most tenaciously to their ancient culture and customs.

To many, Guatemala is the most beautiful and most interesting of the Central American seven. Certainly, the magnificent scenery, the Mayan antiquities, the colonial treasures, and the native Indians, with their exotic faces, dazzling dress, and colorful markets, make the country a photographer's dream.

About the size of Ohio, Guatemala offers an amazing variety of landscapes, from volcanic highlands clad with forests and dotted with lakes to lowlands covered with coffee, banana, and sugar plantations. From its lofty and rugged mountain peaks at more than 12,500 feet, the land is carved by dozens of rivers and falls west/southwest to the Pacific and east to a short coast on the Caribbean and a long border with Belize. To the west and north/northeast is a very long, irregular border with Mexico; to the south and southeast, El Salvador and Honduras.

Guatemala City, the capital, is the gateway to the country's western highlands, where the majority of the native Indians live. The town is a convenient base for touring the main attractions of the region, and its two superb museums alone would make it worth a visit.

Antigua: The former capital and oldest Spanish colonial city in Guatemala is one of the loveliest in Central America, with churches, houses, and flower-filled plazas dating from the sixteenth and seventeenth centuries. It has been declared a National Monument of the Americas.

Lake Atitlan: Northwest from Antigua, the Pan-American Highway leads to the breathtakingly beautiful landscape of a mile-high lake surrounded by towering volcanoes. Around the shores of the lake are Indian villages whose people are directly descended from the Mayan tribes—Cakchiquel, Tzutuhil, and Quiche—who peopled the region when the Spaniards arrived in 1524. A road west continues to Quezaltenango, the country's second city and another good base for exploring more remote villages and hiking.

Chichicastenango (north of Lake Atitlan; 90 miles from Guatemala City). Perhaps the most popular market town in all Central America, Chichi, as

it is known, is certainly the most photographed for the colorful Quiche Indians who inhabit the area, their crafts, and the town's colonial churches.

The Caribbean Coast

Guatemala has only a small strip of land fronting the Caribbean where the Rio Dulce empties into the sea. Livingston, an old port that can only be reached by sea, is on the north side of the river; Puerto Barrios and Santo Tomás de Castilla, the newer port and the usual dock for cruise ships, are on the south.

Puerto Barrios: This was built as a company town by the United Fruit Company when it put in the railway to ship its bananas to the coast, where they were loaded onto ships destined for the United States. Laid out in a grid, Puerto Barrios has wide streets and typical Caribbean wood frame houses, many on stilts. In the 1960s Santo Tomás de Castilla, a short distance to the southwest, was built to serve as the main port.

Livingston: Located just across the border from Belize, Livingston, with its lush tropical landscape and brightly painted wooden buildings, is a village caught in time. It has no airport and no road to the outside; the only way in is by sea. The gateway to Guatemala at the turn of the twentieth century, when it was the principal port for goods transported down the Rio Dulce, it lost its raison d'être when the railroad and Puerto Barrios were built.

For some cruise ships, it is still a port of call and starting point for the journey up the Rio Dulce to Lake Izabal. In addition to small cruise ships that sail up river, the excursion can be made by cayucos, motorized dugout canoes that take groups of tourists on river trips for about US$10 per person.

Livingston's population of 2,000 or so is made up mostly of the Black Caribs, known in Central America as Garinagus or by their language, Garifuna. They are descendants of African slaves who escaped or were shipwrecked off the coast of St. Vincent and commingled with the Carib Indians there. In the late eighteenth century, after a major revolt against the British who had colonized St. Vincent, most of the Black Caribs were shipped off to Roatan, an island off the coast of Honduras.

Population: Eight million.

Climate: Hot and humid on the coast; springlike weather in the highlands.

Clothing: Comfortable, casual, light clothing for coastal areas.

Currency: The Guatemalan quetzal (Q) is divided into 100 centavos. The quetzal fluctuates between Q7.60–8 to US$1.00.

Departure Tax: US$30.

Electricity: 110 volts AC.

Entry Formalities: Valid U.S. passport.

Language: Spanish; some English in coastal areas.

Time: Central Standard Time.

Telephone Area Code: 502.

Vaccination Requirement: None.

Information: *Guatemala Tourist Commission,* Guatemala City; (888) 464–8281. *Guatemala Consulate,* 57 Park Avenue, New York, NY 10016; (212) 686-3837.

Over time they migrated to southern Belize, Guatemala, and Nicaragua, intermarrying with shipwrecked sailors of other races and with the indigenous Mayas and developing a distinctive culture and language made up of African, Carib Indian, Mayan, and European elements. They also speak Spanish and English with a lilt similar to others in the Caribbean.

An interesting side note to history: At the time of the Columbus Quincentennial, the Caribs of Dominica, the last of the Carib tribes populating the Caribbean when Columbus arrived, established contacts with the Garinagus in Central America to try to learn more about their heritage by sharing their cultural traditions. If you compare the traditional crafts of the Caribs of Dominica and those of the Garinagus in Belize, the connection between the two peoples becomes obvious, particularly in the art of straw weaving, where the type of weaving, straw, and patterns used are so distinctive.

Rio Dulce Cruises: A boat trip up the Rio Dulce is, as one writer described it, an adventure straight out of *The African Queen.* From Livingston, the river passes through a steep-walled gorge thick with jungle greenery and streaming waterfalls and alive with egrets and other tropical birds. At the base of the gorge, the sulfurous water from a hot spring provides a delightful place for a swim.

Upon emerging from the gorge, the river widens into an area known as El Golfete, whose north side borders a 7,200-hectare nature reserve, **Biotopo Chocon-Machacas.** In addition to the beautiful river landscape, the reserve protects mangroves, tropical flora, and exotic wildlife, particularly the manatees that inhabit the waters. The reserve runs for about 7 miles along the river and has a network of boat routes around the jungle lagoons, enabling passengers to get a close-up look at the wildlife. A nature trail begins at the visitor center.

At the western end of El Golfete is a restored seventeenth-century fortress, **Castillo de San Felipe de Lara,** built at the entrance to Lake Izabal (Lago de Izabel) to keep out marauding pirates, who ruled the seas of the Caribbean at the time and preyed on local villages and the commerce traveling on the river. Apparently the fortress was only minimally effective, as pirates were able to capture and burn it in 1686. Once the pirate threat was removed from the Caribbean, the fortress was used as a prison.

Lake Izabal, a large body whose fresh waters shelter the manatee, has not been developed for tourism, but some small cruise ships sail around the lake, stopping to visit the fort and take passengers from the village of Rio Dulce (also known as El Relleno) by bus to the region's main antiquity sites.

Carretera al Atlantico, the highway from the capital to the sea, is on the south side of the lake. At the Morales–La Ruidosa junction (Carretera al Atlantico, km 245), the highway west leads to Los Amates, less than a mile from the Maya archaeological site of Quirigua, in a lovely park setting. It is famous for the huge, intricately carved stelae that

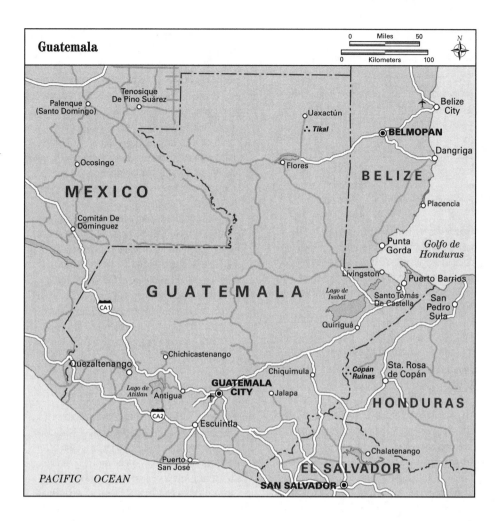

Guatemala

can be seen there. The site is open 7:00 A.M. to 5:00 P.M. daily; there is a small admission fee.

The Morales–La Ruidosa junction north crosses to the village of Rio Dulce, where a road leads to Flores, the gateway to El Peten, a vast lowland forest of which 50 square miles are a national park, with some of the most important antiquities in the Western Hemisphere.

Tikal National Park: In the dense jungle of El Peten, in the northeast region, is Tikal, the crown jewel of Guatemala's Mayan antiquities and the largest, most impressive ruins from the Classic period in the Mayan world. The vast area holds the ruins of approximately 3,000 structures. In the Great Plaza two awesome temples have been excavated, while the tops of three pyramids tower above the jungle's canopy to heights of more than 145 feet. In addition to the prodigious antiquities, the forest is alive with exotic flora and wildlife, including brightly colored parrots that squawk from the treetops and howler monkeys that swing noisily through the branches.

Flores is about a forty-five-minute drive away. Several lodges are situated near the site, enabling visitors to remain overnight. Some cruise ships offer excursions that travel by motorcoach in one direction and by plane in the other. Tikal is located near the Belize border and is often visited from there.

Honduras

www.letsgohonduras.com

Stretching east–west between Guatemala and Nicaragua, with El Salvador on the south, Honduras is the second largest of the Central American seven and boasts a long, beautiful Caribbean coastline backed by tropical-jungle-clad mountains that climb to more than 7,000 feet. Much of the coast, with its beaches, wetlands, and lagoons full of manatees, howler monkeys, and other wildlife, is protected in coastal and marine parks.

A short distance off the Caribbean coast lie Honduras's best-known attractions—the Bay Islands, idyllic hideaways surrounded by fabulous coral reefs, an extension of the barrier reef off Mexico and Belize. The country's other well-known star is the spectacular Mayan ruin site at Copán, near the Guatemalan border.

Honduras's interior comprises mostly mountains and highland valleys—80 percent of its total 59,160 square miles is made up of terrain ranging from 1,800 feet to almost 9,500 feet above sea level.

Tegucigalpa, the capital, is situated in the central highlands at 3,217 feet in a bowl-shaped valley surrounded by pine-covered mountains and enjoying a springlike climate year-round. The hilly town, with its tile-roofed, pastel houses along cobblestone streets, has retained its colonial atmosphere. The main highway of the region connects Tegucigalpa with San Pedro Sula, the country's principal commercial center, and the coast.

In 1502, on his fourth and final voyage, Christopher Columbus sailed from Jamaica to explore the Central American landmass. He came ashore near Trujillo on the north coast and named it Honduras, meaning "depths" in Spanish, for the deep waters there.

The town of Trujillo, founded in 1525 near the site of Columbus's landing, was the first capital of the Spanish colony, but soon the Spanish became more interested in the cooler highlands of the interior. Meanwhile the British grabbed the coast for its timber and the Bay Islands for their hidden bays and inlets, from which British pirates could prey on Spanish ships. It is said that by the early 1600s, Roatan had an estimated 5,000 British pirates. The notorious eighteenth-century pirate Henry Morgan, who later was rewarded by the British Crown—which named him governor of Jamaica—was among those who used the islands as a base.

To harvest the mahogany and other hardwoods from the forests, the British brought Jamaicans and other West Indians to Honduras. Today their descendants are largely people from the Caribbean coast, along with the mestizos of indigenous Indian and Spanish blood, and the Garinagus, who are a mixture of African and Carib Indians and known in the Eastern Caribbean as the Black Caribs.

In the late eighteenth century, after a revolt of the Black Caribs in St. Vincent, the British rounded up the survivors and shipped them to Roatan. From there the Garifuna, as they are sometimes called after their language, migrated to the mainland, creating fishing and farming communities along the coast from Belize to Nicaragua and developing their own religion, music, dance, and language, Garifuna, a mix of West African, Arawak, and European speech.

The Bay Islands

Islas de la Bahía, an archipelago of three main islands—Roatan, Guanaja, and Utila—and many tiny cays, is located about 30 miles off the north coast. These islands are Honduras's prime tourist attractions, offering great diving and snorkeling on their extensive coral reefs. The marine gardens are a continuation of the barrier reef that starts off the coast of Mexico and extends for 185 miles to Honduras, making it the largest reef in the Western Hemisphere and second in the world only to Australia's Great Barrier Reef.

Culturally as well as scenically, the Bay Islands are a world apart from the mainland, having been occupied by the British from the seventeenth to the nineteenth centuries. Christopher Columbus landed on Guanaja in 1502, where he found a fairly large indigenous population. In less than twenty-five years, though, the population was decimated by the Spaniards who followed him, enslaving the islanders and sending them to work on the plantations of Cuba and in the silver mines of Mexico.

Before long English, French, and Dutch pirates took over the islands, and from these convenient

Population: 6.2 million.

Government: A democratically elected government.

Climate: Hot, tropical year-round in the lowlands; perpetual spring in the highlands.

Clothing: Comfortable, casual, light clothing for the coastal areas; hiking clothes and shoes for jungle excursions.

Currency: Lempira. There are 100 centavos in a lempira. US$1=L19.

Departure Tax: US$25.

Electricity: 110 volts AC.

Entry Formalities: Valid US passport; on arrival, tourists get tourist cards valid for up to ninety days.

Languages: Spanish and English on the Caribbean coast and Bay Islands.

Time: Central Standard Time.

Telephone Area Code: 505.

Vaccination Requirement: None.

Airlines: AeroHonduras, American, Continental, Delta, Northwest, TACA, United.

Information: www.letsgo honduras.com; www.hondurastips .com; www.travel-to-honduras.com; *Honduras Tourist Board*, 2828 Coral Way, Suite 305, Miami, FL 33145; (305) 461-0600; (800) 410-9608.

---

bases they raided the Spanish galleons laden with gold and other treasures from the New World en route to Spain. Then, in 1782, after many attempts, the Spanish successfully wiped out the pirates' stronghold, and once again the islands were left uninhabited. A decade later, after the Black Carib uprising in St. Vincent, the British shipped the survivors to Roatan. Although most made their way eventually to the mainland, Roatan still has one settlement of Garinagus at Punta Gorda.

The Bay Islands, along with the large Mosquitia territory in northeastern Honduras, remained British until 1859, when Great Britain ceded the territory to Honduras. Yet only in recent times, after Honduras required that Spanish be spoken in all schools, did the islanders begin to speak Spanish. English, spoken with a typical Caribbean lilt, remains their preferred language as well as their cultural orientation.

Roatan: Situated off the coast from La Ceiba, Roatan is the largest and most developed of the Bay Islands, with a population of about 10,000. The island, 30 miles long and only 1 to 3 miles wide, is surrounded by more than 60 miles of reef, making it a mecca for divers. Carnival Corporation and the government of Honduras are building a new $50 million port on the southwest coast of Roatan in an area known as Dixon Cove. Situated on twenty acres of waterfront, Mahogany Bay, as it will be called, is expected to open in 2009. The concept is similar to Carnival's port at Grand Turk, with a state-of-the-art pier with two berths for megaships and passenger facilities. Next to the pier is a welcome center with retail shops, restaurants, and bars, along with a 60-foot lighthouse, a lagoon, and a nature trail. A transportation hub for taxis, car rentals, tour buses, and shore excursions is also planned. Mahogany is located next door to Coral Cay, a marine and nature park, and will be connected to it by a foot bridge.

The most beautiful part of the island is at West End, a small village with an idyllic, palm-shaded, white-sand beach washed by turquoise waters filled with colorful fish. Coxen Hole, the main town, is about a ten-minute drive from the airport. The island has a deluxe resort, **Anthony's Key** (800-227-3483; www.anthonyskey.com), with good dive facilities. It also has dolphins that can be seen daily in a thirty-minute show and a talk by a specialist on dolphin behavior: 10:30 A.M. and 4:30 P.M. Monday through Friday; 10:30 A.M., 1:30 and 4:30 P.M. Saturday and Sunday, US$4. Also available is a swim, for US$84 for non-hotel-guests; and a dive for $112 ($149 as a cruise ship shore excursion). Swims are scheduled at 9:00 A.M., noon, and 2:30 P.M. The dives start at 8:30 and 11:30 A.M. and 2:30 P.M., maximum eight people. Also on the premises is a well-organized, well-displayed museum exhibit on the region's history and anthropology, which is funded by the resort, and a gift shop.

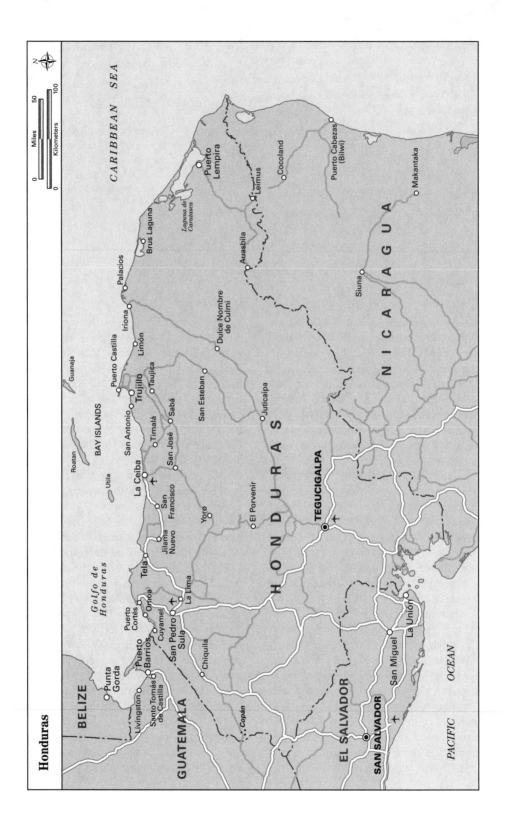

Honduras

The Tropical Treasure Bird Park, begun in 1998 by Tennessee native Lloyd Davidson, a local businessman, has a large variety of tropical birds, most brought to the park after being injured. An entrance fee (US$5 adult; $3 children) goes toward maintaining the birds.

You can easily hire a taxi at the cruise ship dock in Coxen Hole for about US$40 for a two-hour tour, or rent a bicycle in the tiny town for about $2. An information kiosk and outdoor market with local crafts are at the pier.

The most popular excursion that cruise ships offer is a day at the beach and snorkeling at Tabyana Beach or at West End. The price ranges from US$39 to $59, depending on the length of time, equipment, and food service. Some cruise ships also offer kayaking.

Guanaja: The most easterly of the three islands, Guanaja has rugged, mountainous terrain covered with forests and appears to be a mainland breakaway. Only about 11 miles long and 4 miles wide at its widest point, the island is surrounded by miles of coral reefs and a dozen or more cays. About 90 percent of the island has been declared a national forest reserve and marine park. The island caters mostly to affluent travelers.

Guanaja Town, known as the Venice of Honduras and called "Bonacca" by its inhabitants, is on a small cay just off the main island's east coast. Its wooden houses with sloping roofs are packed tight and rest on stilts. There are no roads and no cars on the cay; a labyrinth of walkways winding around the houses and narrow canals enable residents to bring their boats right up to their houses.

Utila: The smallest, least developed of the group has modest tourist facilities, appealing to budget travelers, and is, as yet, probably the cheapest place in the Caribbean to learn to dive.

Actually, all three islands are relatively inexpensive by Caribbean standards and have excellent diving facilities. The dive shops offer a range of options, from an introductory resort course to full certification. The islands are linked by daily air service from La Ceiba and San Pedro Sula to Roatan.

The North Coast

Honduras's entire north coast of 384 miles fronts the Caribbean Sea, with mountains of tropical jungle rising to more than 7,000 feet behind it. The towns of the north coast are Puerto Cortés, the main port where cruise ships usually dock; La Ceiba, the largest coastal town and jumping-off point for travel by air or boat to the Bay Islands; and Tela and Trujillo, known for their lovely, palm-fringed beaches and good fresh seafood. Rain, heaviest on the coast from September to January, can sometimes make the roads impassable.

Puerto Cortés: Located on the sea near the Guatemala border and 34 miles from San Pedro Sula, Puerto Cortés handles more than half of the country's exports. The docks are in the heart of town and are normally busy with cargo ships loading bananas, pineapples, and other produce for the two-day sail to Miami. There are some good beaches within a short drive, and the Spanish fortress at Omoa is a half-hour bus ride west from town.

Tela: In addition to its beaches, Tela has the Lancetilla Botanic Gardens and Research Center, begun in 1926 by United Fruit Company as an experimental station for tropical plants. The huge estate is a park with a visitor center and specimens of about every fruit tree and flower that grows in Central America. It's also a birder's haven: The gardens attract more than 200 species.

La Ceiba: Situated on the narrow coastal plain between the towering Cordillera Nombre de Dios mountains and the Caribbean, La Ceiba is a rich fishing and farming community surrounded by banana and pineapple plantations, mostly owned by Standard Fruit. Pico Bonito National Park, a few miles behind the town and covering about 300 square miles, is Honduras's largest national park and has magnificent forests and wildlife. On the coast 12 miles west of La Ceiba is the Cuero-Salado Nature Reserve, a large estuary formed by the Cuero and Salado Rivers that protects a multitude of animals, including manatees, howler monkeys, and many bird species.

Inland from the North Coast

San Pedro Sula: Honduras's second largest city is 34 miles south of Puerto Cortés in the Ulua River Valley, a large plain that is one of Honduras's most fertile, productive areas and the heart of banana country. Here Standard Fruit and United Fruit, which own a large part of northern Honduras, grow bananas and pineapples for export to the United States. Several of the vicinity's towns, ports, roads, and railways were built by the banana companies.

San Pedro Sula is a lively town with a population of about 325,900. It has an archaeological museum and a good central market where the National Association of Honduras Artisans has a wide selection of crafts from throughout the country.

Founded by the Spaniards in 1536, the town is today Honduras's major industrial and commercial center as well as the main center for the region's agricultural products. It is also the transportation hub for western Honduras and the gateway to Copán.

La Lima, 8 miles east of San Pedro, is a company town built by United Brands of Chiquita bananas fame, where you can visit the banana plantation and watch the packing operations. **Cusuco National Park,** 12 miles west of San Pedro, is a mountainous cloud forest with its highest peak at 7,398 feet; there is a visitor center. The 300-foot **Pulhapanzak Waterfall** and **Lago de Yojoa,** about 30 miles to the south, are popular recreation areas.

The Mayan Antiquities of Copán

Southwest of San Pedro Sula, via a 125-mile road that climbs the hills and upland valleys through coffee, tobacco, and cornfields and terraced hillsides, are the ruins of Copán, among the most magnificent antiquities in the Americas, rivaling Tikal in Guatemala for top honors as Central America's most important archaeological site. Called the Athens of the Mayan World, Copán was a flourishing city for hundreds of years and reached its peak between A.D. 465 and 800 in the Mayan Classic period, when it was the artistic and scientific center. The region was inhabited by the Maya for about 2,800 years.

The main ceremonial center covers about seventy-five acres. The principal group of ruins includes the Great Plaza, with dozens of intricately carved stelae portraying the rulers of Copán, and the Hieroglyphic Stairway, the most dramatic monument. The stairway, 30 feet wide and 60 feet high, is covered with more than 2,200 glyphs that record the history of the Copán rulers. It is the longest pre-Columbian text ever found. Indeed, the temples and monuments of Copán have more reliefs and artistic embellishment than any other in the Mayan world—one reason they are so significant. The entire site is thought to have been built over earlier temples and other buildings.

The park has three other basic areas: The Ball Court was the social center of the city, and its unique features are the markers on the side walls, resembling macaw heads. Work here dates from the thirteenth ruler, known as "18 Rabbit," A.D. 711 to 736.

The Acropolis is divided into two large courts. The west court houses the elaborate Temple 11, built during the reign of Yax-Pac and meant to be his portal to the other world; and Temple 16, set between the east and west courts, which has the unique Altar "Q" at its base. Altar Q has been "read" completely and depicts each of the sixteen members of the Copán Dynasty, seated on their own glyph. In that of Yax-Pac, dynasty founder Yax-Kuk-Mo is passing the scepter of power to Yax-Pac.

The Tunnels: Archaeological excavations in Copán have led to the digging of more than 2½ miles of tunnels under the Acropolis, which have allowed scholars to view earlier stages of Copán's urban structure, as well as finding important tombs. Two tunnels are open to the public on a limited basis; only ten persons are allowed in at one time, and they must be accompanied by a guide. Rosalila Tunnel, under Temple 16, is said to be the best-preserved stucco building in the Mayan world. A full-size replica can be seen in the Mayan sculpture museum. Los Jaguares Tunnel is more than 2,100 feet long, with Galindo's Tomb (discovered more than a century ago), among other highlights.

Las Sepulturas Archaeological Site: Located 1 mile from the main Acropolis, this small site has been important in understanding how the Mayan elite lived in Copán's heyday. No guides are on the site, but one can be hired at the visitor center. New discoveries are made continuously; these findings are housed in the Mayan sculpture museum adjacent to the visitor center and in the town museum. Entrance fees: main park, US$15, including Las Sepulturas Archaeological Site; Museum of Mayan Sculpture, US$7; Museum of Archaeology (in town) US$3; Rosalila and Los Jaguares Tunnels, US$15. Normally cruise ship shore excursions include the cost of the park and museum entrance fees.

Casa K'inich: An interactive museum for children is located in the town of Copan Ruinas's main square. Here children learn about the Mayan culture by trying on ball game equipment and watching a game reenactment, practicing Maya math and writing, and counting in Ch'orti', a Mayan language. Casa K'inich—"house of sun"—is open Tuesday through Saturday from 8:00 A.M. to noon and 1:00 to 5:00 P.M.; Sunday 8:00 A.M. to noon only. Entrance is free, contact 651-4105.

The pretty little town of **Copan Ruinas** is less than a mile from the ancient ruins. Its cobblestoned streets are lined with typical whitewashed adobe houses with red-tiled roofs; a colonial church anchors the plaza. Copán is a three-hour drive from San Pedro Sula and four hours from Puerto Cortés; there are hotels within walking distance of the Mayan site.

The Mosquito Coast

Located in the northeastern part of the country, La Mosquitia, or the Mosquito Coast, is one of Central America's largest wilderness areas, rich in wildlife. This swampy, heavily forested region is sparsely inhabited by the Miskito and Sumo Indians. Travel is mostly by boat, as there is only one road. Adventure and nature tours reach their destinations in the region by bush plane, four-wheel-drive vehicle, cayuco (dugout canoe) and mule pack, or on foot.

The **Rio Platano Reserve,** established by Honduras with the United Nations in 1980, is often described as the most beautiful nature reserve in Honduras. It protects a pristine river system that flows through a tropical rain forest and has abundant wildlife. Travel is by boat on the river, with camping in the forest. Air service to Palacios, a lilliputian hamlet and the most accessible locale to visit the reserve, operates from La Ceiba. There is also air service to Puerto Lempira, a small village and the largest coastal settlement in the Mosquito region, near the Nicaraguan border.

Nicaragua
www.intur.gob.ni

Although it has been more than a decade since a democratically elected government was voted into power and peace fell over the land, neither US tourists nor cruise lines seem ready, as yet, to embrace Nicaragua as a major travel destination. When they do, they will find a beautiful country of tall mountains with pine-forested slopes, volcanoes, and lakes (including the largest lake in Central America), rain forests, lowlands drained by twenty-three rivers often traversing thick tropical jungles, and long shorelines on both its Caribbean and Pacific coasts. They will also see some of the Western Hemisphere's most historic towns, such as Granada and León, with lovely Spanish colonial architecture, and enjoy music, folklore, festivals, and markets brimming with handicrafts.

The largest country in Central America, with 57,143 square miles, Nicaragua is sandwiched between the Caribbean Sea on the east and the Pacific Ocean on the west. It is separated from Honduras, its neighbor on the north, by the 411-mile Rio Coco, Nicaragua's longest river; on the south, much of its border with Costa Rica is formed by the 120-mile Rio San Juan. Geographically, Nicaragua has three distinct regions: (1) the north-central mountains that fall east to the Caribbean in (2) a vast area of rivers and lowlands known as the Caribbean or Mosquito Coast, and (3) the Pacific lowland, which has the majority of the towns—including Managua, the capital—and people. The Pacific region also has about forty volcanoes, some reaching upward of 6,000 feet. The Momotombo volcano, on the southern shore of Lake Managua and clearly visible from the capital, is the national emblem. Just outside Managua is the **Masaya National Park,** with the Masaya volcano. It is one of the few summits of an active volcano that can

Population: 5.2 million.

Government: A democratically elected government.

Climate: Hot and humid on the coasts; springlike in the highlands.

Currency: Cordoba, divided into 100 centavos. US$1 = 18.5 cordobas.

Departure Tax: US$32.

Electricity: 110 volts AC.

Entry Formalities: A US passport valid at least six months after entry date and a tourist card, issued for US$5 on arrival.

Languages: Spanish; English on the Caribbean coast and Corn Islands.

Time: Central Standard Time.

Telephone Area Code: 505.

Information: *Nicaraguan Institute of Tourism,* 011-505-222-3333; 011-505-254-5191; fax 011-505-222-6610; *Consulate of Nicaragua,* 1627 New Hampshire Avenue, NW, Washington, DC 20009; (202) 939-6570; fax (202) 939-6542; www.intur.gob.ni.

---

be reached by car. A road leads directly to the lip of the cone, where you can look down into the smoking crater. The town of Masaya, 15 miles from Managua, is well known for its artisans, whose wares are on display in the town's colorful market.

The rich volcanic soil has made the Pacific corridor Nicaragua's most productive farming region. The region also has many lakes, including 5,067-square-mile Lake Nicaragua, Central America's largest and the tenth largest freshwater lake in the world. Granada, 28 miles from the capital at the foot of the Mombacho volcano on the northwestern shore of Lake Nicaragua, is Nicaragua's oldest city, founded by Hernandez de Córdoba in 1524. It is known for its Spanish colonial architecture and its conservative ways and rivals León, long a liberal stronghold and almost as old.

León Viejo, or Old León, at the foot of Momotombo, was also established by Hernandez de Córdoba in 1524, but it was destroyed by an earthquake in 1610 and covered with layers of ash from subsequent eruptions of the volcano. The present city of León is 19 miles away; it served as Nicaragua's capital until 1857, when the capital was moved to Managua. Among León's many attractions, the massive Metropolitan Cathedral, begun in 1746 and completed a century later, is the largest in Central America and is famous for its huge paintings of the Stations of the Cross, considered masterpieces of Spanish colonial art.

Tourism has grown with peace and already ranks second as a source of national revenue.

Hotel and resort development is moving along on the Pacific coast; the Caribbean shores, however, remain undeveloped and almost inaccessible, except at Puerto Cabezas in the north and Bluefields in the south.

Nicaragua is recapturing some of its past appeal to visitors through travel programs focusing on nature and light adventure. These might include visits to ranches and coffee plantations or a cruise on the Rio San Juan through the Indio Maiz National Reserve. The trip follows the course of the river from Lake Nicaragua to the Caribbean Sea along Nicaragua's border with Costa Rica. Once a major highway of commerce, the waterway was viewed by many as a more viable route than through Panama for building a channel to connect the Caribbean with the Pacific when various plans were being studied for the Panama Canal.

Now, for the first time, a few cruise ships are calling at **San Juan del Sur,** a small village on the Pacific coast that provides access to some of Nicaragua's main attractions. Given the town's limited facilities, you are probably better off taking one of your ship's shore excursions. They are likely to be similar to those that Holland America Cruises offers. One combines a visit to the heart of the coffee country with an equestrian show, $99 per person; another is a half-day trip to Granada, $49 adult, $29 child; yet another is a half-day shopping tour to Masaya for its crafts market and shops, where handicrafts and leather goods are inexpensive, $39 adult, $24 child; and still another is a full-

Nicaragua

day tour combining Granada, Masaya market, and Masaya Volcano National Park, with lunch at a local restaurant: eight hours; $99 adult; $55 child.

The Mosquito Coast

Hot, humid, and sparsely populated, the Caribbean or Mosquito Coast covers about half of Nicaragua and, with an average width of 60 miles, forms the widest skirt of lowlands in Central America. Much of it is covered with tropical rain forests that in some places are impenetrable jungle. The 325 miles of Caribbean shores are broken up by many river deltas and large lagoons created by the coursing of twenty-three rivers from the central mountains to the Caribbean Sea.

Nicaragua's Caribbean ports can be reached from Managua by air, but a preferred tourist route is via the town of El Rama and downriver by boat to Bluefields, a colorful old port on the Caribbean. The Mosquito region was never colonized by Spain, and indeed, tribal leaders asked for—and got—protection from the British against the Spaniards. Britain relinquished the territory to an independent Nicaragua in 1860, but English is still spoken on the coast and nearby islands, and, like so many pockets along the Central American coast with their mixed populations, there's a West Indian flavor here, too.

About 40 miles or so offshore from Bluefields are the tiny, idyllic **Corn Islands** (Islas del Maíz)—Grande and Pequeña—currently the only Nicaraguan Caribbean destinations visited by cruise ships. The larger of the Corn Islands is only 4 miles square; the smaller is about 1 mile square. Both are fringed by sandy beaches, crystal-clear waters, and coral reefs and are ideal for swimming, fishing, snorkeling, and diving, including exploring the wreck of a Spanish galleon a short distance offshore. The islanders are English-speaking Creoles and Garinagus.

Costa Rica
www.visitcostarica.com

Costa Rica is often called the Switzerland of Central America. A mountainous land with a long democratic tradition, no army, and one of the highest literacy rates in the Western Hemisphere, the country has managed miraculously, in recent years, to stay out of trouble.

A small, friendly country about the size of West Virginia, Costa Rica is bordered on the north by Nicaragua and on the south by Panama—countries plagued by political turmoil and armed conflicts throughout the 1980s. Yet peaceful Costa Rica succeeded in staying out of the conflicts that were tearing apart its neighbors while remaining their friend and, at the same time, maintaining a good relationship with the United States and often serving as mediator for all.

Most visitors come to Costa Rica to see its natural wonders, and cruise passengers are no exception. Costa Rica has become the very definition of ecotourism through its pioneering environmental efforts. Approximately 20 percent of the nation's land is under protection in more than thirty national parks, forestry reserves, wildlife refuges, and biological and private reserves (compared with 3 percent in the United States).

The designated areas protect a diverse landscape ranging from volcanic peaks and rain and cloud forests on mountain slopes, to dry and swamp forests in the lowlands, to dense mangrove and coral reefs along the coasts. The country has twelve distinct ecological systems containing 8,000 species of plants, including 1,200 varieties of orchids; 750 species of birds—more than in all of North America—and 10 percent of the world's butterflies. In the national park system, which is made up of forty-five areas, at least one example of each ecosystem is represented.

Three chains of volcanic mountains form the Central Highlands, where the capital of Costa Rica, **San José,** with its year-round springlike weather, is located at an altitude of 3,805 feet. Depending on their ship's itinerary, cruise passengers often spend either the first or last night of their cruise in San José; visit the nineteenth-century National Cathedral and the wonderful National Museum, with a wealth of pre-Columbian artifacts; and shop at the Central Market.

Sarchi, a short trip from the capital, is a handicraft center known for its workshops that create the traditional, brightly painted oxcarts and interpret the colorful art onto many practical souvenirs. Shops sell other hardwood products as well as hammocks, straw, and leather.

San José is the gateway to many of the country's parks, with drive-to volcanoes, rain-forested mountains, and a lush countryside fresh with rushing rivers and rich with fertile valleys.

Poas Volcano National Park, an easy one-and-a-half-hour drive north of San José (22 miles north of Alajuela), is one of the most accessible and hence most popular parks. It provides the rare opportunity to drive almost to the crater rim of an active volcano at 8,000 feet, to peer down into it (when clouds don't obscure the view), and to hike in the surrounding forest. The crater is almost a mile across and 1,000 feet deep. There are small eruptions from time to time, but normally not enough to close the park (as in 1989, when eruption sent volcanic ash almost a mile into the air). A trail through a dwarf cloud forest heavy with mosses, lichens, and bromeliads and abundant with hummingbirds and other species leads to an extinct crater with a pretty lake.

Farther to the northwest, **Arenal National Park** protects the majestic Arenal volcano, the largest and most active in Central America. From its perfect cone, the 5,389-foot-high volcano puts on a spectacular display, sending smoke, ash, and exploding rocks into the air and lava tumbling down the slopes. At night, when the streams of orange-red lava glow, the sight is awesome. East of San José, **Irazu Volcano National Park** has Costa Rica's highest volcano, at 11,325 feet altitude.

Population: 4.13 million.

Government: A democratically elected government.

Climate: Springlike climate in San José and the highlands; hot and tropical year-round on the coast; the dry season from October to May is the most comfortable period.

Clothing: Comfortable, casual, light clothing for the coastal areas; hiking clothes and shoes for jungle excursions.

Currency: Colón. US$1 = about 518 colónes.

Departure Tax: US$26.

Electricity: 110 volts AC.

Entry Formalities: No visa required for US or Canadian citizens, but you must have a valid US passport.

Languages: Spanish and English.

Time: Central Standard Time.

Telephone Area Code: 506.

Vaccination Requirement: None.

Airlines: LACSA, Aero Costa Rica, American, Continental, Delta, Northwest, Spirit, United, USAirways.

Information:
www.visitcostarica.com; *Costa Rica Tourist Bureau,* P.O. Box 777-1000, San Jose, Costa Rica. The Tourist Board has a toll-free line to its San José offices, where English-speaking operators answer questions: (800) 343-6332.

The Caribbean Coast

Like so much of Central America, Costa Rica's Caribbean coast is sparsely settled and is the least accessible, less developed area of the country. Puerto Limón, the eastern gateway, almost at the center of the country's Caribbean coast, is a three-hour bus ride from San José. A hot, humid port city of about 60,000 people, Puerto Limón owes its creation in 1880 to the railway and banana industry, both of which have seen better days. In 1871 the government, eager to get the country's principal crop, coffee, more expeditiously to foreign markets, contracted Minor Keith, an American engineer, to build a railway from San José to the coast. The track took some twenty years to lay and cost thousands of lives because of malaria and yellow fever. It also changed Costa Rica forever by introducing Jamaicans into the population and bananas into the economy.

At first Keith brought workers from China and Italy, but in time he found that Jamaicans were better able to withstand the weather and disease. To help defray some of the cost of building the railway, he planted bananas alongside the track, and in Limón, he built a pier and collected a share of the fee for its usage.

The banana business was so successful that by 1884, Keith was able to help Costa Rica pay its national debt and in exchange received a ninety-nine-year lease on the railway and thousands of acres of land along its route, where, of course, he planted more bananas. Five years later Keith and a rival company joined hands to form the United Fruit Company. It extended its base of operation from Guatemala to Panama and to a great extent controlled the power and politics of Central America's "banana republics" for almost a century.

After the railway had been completed, most of the Jamaicans stayed to work the banana plantations and railroad. Today the descendants of these English-speaking Jamaicans make up the majority of the population, which has largely retained a Jamaican or West Indian culture. However, that they kept their separate identity is not surprising considering the fact that the rest of Costa Rica did not accept them. Not until 1952 were they allowed Costa Rican citizenship. Even half a century later, there is little evidence of assimilation.

A cruise ship terminal at Puerto Limón, where two large cruise ships can dock at one time, has greatly improved the arrival experience for cruise passengers. Immediately outside the exit gate is a thriving market crammed full of inexpensive Costa Rican goods and crafts. For example, a beautifully carved, wooden salad bowl that could cost US$200 in New York can be had for $20. A kilo (2.2 pounds) of fine Costa Rican coffee is US$2.

Tortuguero National Park

North of Puerto Limón is a huge area of jungle-thick forests, swamps, and marshland crisscrossed

Costa Rica

by rivers and canals, a large part of which is protected by the Tortuguero National Park and, to the north, the Barra del Colorado National Refuge. Both are rich with birds and other wildlife.

Tortuguero takes its name from the large numbers of turtles that nest here from August to November. The national park, created in 1975 after a two-decade effort by conservationists, protects the nesting sites of four species—hawksbill, green, leatherback, and loggerhead turtles—on the beaches in the 50-mile stretch between the Matina River, which empties at Moin, and the Colorado River near the Nicaragua border.

The protected areas also include the low-lying hills, swamps, and forests that are home to monkeys, jaguars, raccoons, tapirs, and hundreds of species of birds. In addition, inland waterways support a wide variety of fish and other wildlife, including storks, herons, crocodiles, otters, manatees, and the gar, an unusual prehistoric fish said to be little changed for ninety million years.

Boat trips start at Moin, about 2 miles from Puerto Limón, and make their way through the swamps and marshes via a network of jungle-bordered canals, with signs like a highway, used by the people of the region as transportation. The area offers good sportfishing, while divers head to the reefs south of Limón.

Cahuita National Park

Cahuita, a small village about 25 miles southeast of Limón, is expanding as a tourist destination, attracting visitors for its laid-back lifestyle and the pretty beaches and reefs protected by the Cahuita National Park. Here the Caribbean Sea rolls in sometimes with force and breaks against the reefs. Behind the palm-edged beaches is a coastal rain forest full of birds and other wildlife.

Shore Excursions

With the growth of cruise traffic into Puerto Limón has come an increase in the number and diversity of excursions that cruise ships offer. The following samples are available from Princess Cruises and Holland America Cruises and are typical of those offered by other lines.

Tortuguero Canals: Four and a half hours; US$64. An hour's bus ride from the pier takes you to the Matina Embarcadero, where you are treated to a buffet of tropical fruits, soft drinks, and beers along with native music, before boarding a small boat to cruise through the jungle river system of natural and human-made canals used as waterways for transportation and exploration. The canals, paralleling Costa Rica's Caribbean coast, are surrounded by rain forest rich in flora and fauna, where you might see birds, monkeys, crocodiles, sloths, and toucans.

Rio Reventazon White Water Rafting: Eight hours; US$99. The Reventazon River has some of Costa Rica's best 10 miles of Class II and III rapids. You travel southeast from Limón through fertile valleys and mountains with endless stretches of banana plantations. The river run starts near an abandoned railroad town in an area called Florida and passes through the beautiful valley where you might see toucans, herons, kingfishers, tanagers, and iguanas. En route, you'll stop for a buffet lunch prepared by the guides. *Participants must be able to swim.*

Costa Flores: Five hours; US$64. Located on the border of the Braulio Carrillo National Park, Costa Flores is a 300-acre farm with more than 600 varieties of tropical flowers. Created in 1988, Costa Flores is said to be the largest tropical flower farm in the world. A mile-long, tree-shaded road leads to serene gardens with ponds, fountains, small waterfalls, and thousands of flowers that attract a large variety of birds.

Cahuita & Puerto Vargas National Park: Five hours; US$79. Puerto Vargas Reserve forms part of Cahuita National Park and has a variety of wildlife, such as the howler monkey and raccoon. Among the bird species in the swamp forest are the green ibis, green and rufous kingfishers, yellow-crowned night heron, and northern boat-billed heron; there are also four species of frogs. The Cahuita area is one of the most scenic regions of Costa Rica's Caribbean.

Rain Forest Aerial Tram: Eight hours; US$129. The Aerial Tram, a two-hour drive from Puerto Limón, is a decade-old ecotourism and research facility. The tram takes visitors on a one-and-a-quarter-hour ride through the rain forest canopy, with extraordinary biological diversity of great beauty. The tram, located on a 1,000-acre private nature reserve adjacent to the northern border of the Braulio Carrillo National Park, has one of the richest canopy communities in the world.

Rain Forest Canopy Adventure: Four hours; US$99. Ten platforms up to 197 feet high and 1,700 feet across give visitors an eye-level look at rain forest trees and spectacular views of the countryside. Cables are progressively more challenging, and guests have the option of experiencing only the first two platforms.

Sloth Sanctuary and Canoe Adventure: Five and a half hours; US$89. Seventy minutes of canoeing on the Estrella River. Expect to see rain forest denizens including monkeys, otters, caiman, butterflies, and amphibians. Guests will be introduced to sloths close-up at the Avioaros Center Sloth Sanctuary, followed by a guided walk through a humid tropical lowland forest.

The Pacific Coast

On Panama Canal cruises, Puerto Caldera, a modern container port about 6 miles from Puntarenas, the traditional port, is frequently used by cruise ships for passengers beginning or ending their cruise in San José, where they arrive or fly back to the United States. Depending on your ship's itinerary, you are likely to visit some of the national parks of the Pacific coast, some of which are remote from the capital and more readily accessible by ship.

Manuel Antonio National Park, near the Pacific coastal town of Quepos, is the smallest of the country's parks and one of the most popular. It protects beaches, rocky headlands, and a tropical forest that hosts a great variety of wildlife, including ocelots, three-toed sloths, squirrels, and howler and white-face monkeys—all often seen during hikes on the park's maintained trails. The park is three and a half hours by bus trip from San José.

Santa Rosa National Park, the first park to be established, covers 260 acres in the Pacific northwest and is the nesting ground for three turtle species: huge leatherbacks, the olive ridley, and the Pacific green. The park protects ten different habitats ranging from beaches and mangroves to dry forests and wooded savannas. The wildlife includes monkeys, anteaters, coatimundi, peccaries, and deer. **Palo Verde National Park,** a huge swampy refuge for migratory waterfowl, is also in the northwest.

Corcovado National Park, in the south on the Osa Peninsula near the Panama border, is remote from the capital. A popular stop for cruise ships, Corcovado's tropical rain forest and diverse habitat counts more than 500 species of trees, 285 species of birds, and 139 species of animals. Cruise ships often visit the **Marenco Biological Reserve,** which cannot be reached by road. There they hike a trail to the Rio Claro for swimming in freshwater pools and along beaches shaded by almond trees. This region is one of the last refuges for the rare scarlet macaw, often spotted in the trees by hikers.

Panama

The San Blas Islands

Of all the exotic destinations cruise ships visit in the Western Caribbean, none is more unusual than the San Blas Islands, an archipelago of low-lying islands off the northeast Caribbean coast of Panama. Upon approach, their thatched-roof dwellings shaded by crowds of palm trees look more like the islands of the South Seas than the Caribbean.

These islands are the home of the Kuna Indians, the only tribe of island dwellers in the Caribbean who have both survived and been able to maintain their ancient folkways more or less intact despite 500 years of contact with Europeans and other foreign cultures.

The San Blas Islands comprise about 400 islets plus a strip of land on the Panamanian coast, over which the Kuna claim sovereignty and maintain self-rule. There are forty-eight Kuna villages, with a total population of about 40,000, represented in a tribal council. The people move between the islands in dugout canoes, little changed from those of their ancestors. Their main crop is coconut, which they use as currency. Despite their isolation on these islands, they are unusually worldly and have accepted certain innovations, such as communications and education, while retaining their traditional way of life.

Normally, your first glimpse of the Kuna will be from your cruise ship, where as many as ten boats, full of Kuna women, will be doing a brisk business selling their colorful, unique molas, for which they are famous. Do not think these are the last of their stock. When you go ashore to visit a Kuna village, you will see the molas displayed on clotheslines strung the entire length of the village. Some are squares that can be made into pillow covers or framed; others appear on shirts and dresses. All are remarkably inexpensive, ranging from US$10 to $40 depending on the intricacy of the design. There is no need to try bargaining; these women may not be able to speak your language, but they understand money.

Molas represent a Kuna woman's wealth, like a dowry. They are elaborate reverse appliqué in bold, bright colors, incorporating stylized flowers, animals, birds, and supernatural motifs, and are made originally for the front and back panels of the blouse that the petite Kuna women wear. Occasionally you will see a mola that incorporates current events, such as the US landing of troops in Panama, which crept into designs in 1990. To a newcomer molas may all seem alike, but upon

Population: 3.2 million.

Government: Democratically elected government.

Climate: Hot, tropical year-round.

Clothing: Comfortable, casual, light clothes.

Currency: Balboa, on par with US$1.

Departure Tax: US$20.

Electricity: 110 volts AC.

Entry Formalities: No visa required for US or Canadian citizens, but you must have a valid US passport. Tourist card, $5.

Languages: Spanish and English.

Telephone Area Code: 507.

Time: Central Standard Time.

Airlines: American Airlines, Avianca, Continental, Copa, Delta, Taca, Mexicana.

Information: www.pancanal.com; www.visitpanama.com; www.ipat.gob.pa

Instituto Panameño de Turismo, Apartado 4421, Panama City 5, Republic de Panama; (800) 231-0568; 226-7000; fax 011-507-226-5043.

closer examination the fineness of the stitches and sophistication of the motifs are the telling signs of a master craftswoman.

Kuna women also wear beaded bracelets drawn tightly on their arms and legs, gold nose rings, and layers of gold around their necks. They are a colorful bunch, irresistible to photographers. Most are happy for you to take their picture, often posing with a bright green parakeet, monkey, or iguana, but you must pay them 25 cents per click minimum.

The villagers are friendly, although rather stone-faced unless you take the time to admire someone's beautiful child—a gesture that usually draws a broad smile from the young mother. Their straight hair is jet black, and their facial features are similar to those of other Indian tribes of South America's Caribbean coast, whose common ancestors were the Arawaks, once populating all the islands of the Caribbean.

More and more, the San Blas Islands are being included on transcanal itineraries, particularly the westbound ones sailing from the Caribbean to the Panama Canal.

The Panama Canal

Building the Panama Canal

History is replete with great endeavors, but few were as bold, difficult, dangerous, and controver-

sial—yet successful and beneficial—as the Panama Canal. An engineering triumph by any measure, the Big Ditch, as it is often called, is a 50-mile-long channel traversing Panama at the narrowest point between the Atlantic and Pacific Oceans. A vital link in international trade for nearly a century, it has had a profound effect on world economic and commercial development. Annually, as many as 20,000 ships pass through it, carrying more than 200 million tons of cargo bound for destinations in the four corners of the world.

From the time the Spanish explorer Vasco Nuñez de Balboa crossed from the Atlantic to glimpse the Pacific in 1513, the dream of a waterway through the Isthmus of Panama was born. Under Charles I of Spain, the first survey for a proposed canal was made in 1534. The California gold rush of 1849, when the lack of a safe way across the country by land hampered those in the eastern United States from participating in the bonanza, helped the search for a shortcut across Panama find new motivation. With the permission of Colombia, which controlled the isthmus area, a group of New York businessmen financed the building of a railroad, completed in 1855. It provided travel from the eastern United States to Panama by sea, crossing the Isthmus of Panama by rail, and sailing up the Pacific coast to California.

Yet the idea of a waterway persisted. In 1876 Colombia gave a French financial syndicate,

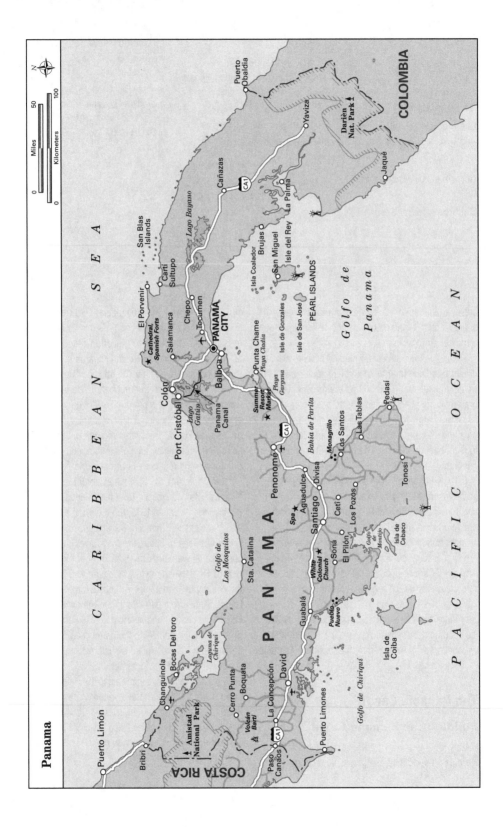

Panama

headed by Lt. Lucien Napoleon Bonaparte Wyse, a French army officer, permission to construct a canal. The syndicate engaged Ferdinand de Lesseps, who had built the Suez Canal, for the project. De Lesseps, with little evidence to support it, said that a canal at sea level was feasible.

Despite tremendous support, enthusiasm, and feverish activity, the project was doomed from the start. For reasons of geography and topography, engineers say, digging a canal at sea level would not have worked regardless how much money, labor, and machinery de Lesseps had used. And if technical miscalculations had not been enough to defeat the French, tropical diseases were. Approximately 20,000 men died from yellow fever, malaria, and other illnesses in the two decades the French toiled. To these trials were added mismanagement and financial chicanery by no less than de Lesseps's son Charles and Gustave Eiffel, builder of the Paris tower. After $300 million in payout, the syndicate went bankrupt in 1889.

Meanwhile Theodore Roosevelt, a visionary who personified the American spirit of the times, wanted the United States to build a canal, which he saw as strategic for an expanding America and the link between the eastern United States and its new Pacific possessions—Hawaii and the Philippines, gained from the Spanish-American War in 1898.

After engineers studied sites in Nicaragua and Panama and a long, public debate was held, Congress approved Panama in 1902. But the battle was not over. Colombia said no and demanded more money for granting permission to the United States. The Panamanians, wanting the canal and eager for independence from Colombia, had their own ideas. With French aid and US encouragement, they revolted; US troops prevented Colombia from moving forces to stop them.

In 1903 the United States and Panama signed a treaty allowing America to build the canal. The following year, the United States bought the rights, property, and equipment of the French Canal Company for $40 million. Ironically, the equipment had deteriorated so much by then that most of it was worthless.

Faced with the difficulties of removing the rock necessary to create a sea-level canal, US engi-

neers, headed by Col. George W. Goethals, an Army Corps of Engineers career officer, concluded that a lock system would be less costly and provide better control. But the first order of business was to improve health conditions and particularly to control the mosquitoes that carried yellow fever and malaria. The job was given to Col. William C. Gorgas, who set about draining swamps and installing sewer systems. By 1906 yellow fever had been brought under control and malaria reduced dramatically.

Building the canal entailed three major projects on a grand scale: cutting a channel through the Continental Divide; digging an earthen dam—the largest ever built up to that time—across the Chagres River to create Gatun Lake, which became the largest artificial lake of its time; and designing and building three sets of enormous parallel locks and gates.

Cutting the 9-mile channel through Panama's mountain spine at the Culebra Cut—later named Gaillard Cut for Col. David DuBose Gaillard, the engineer in charge—was the most difficult part and took ten years. Enormous amounts of rock and shale were removed and hauled by rail to the Pacific to fill in marshes and build a causeway. Like the French, the US team was plagued by rock and mudslides caused by the area's heavy rains.

The canal opened to traffic on August 15, 1914, six months ahead of schedule and at a cost of $387 million—$23 million below estimates. In the years since then, the United States has invested more than $3 billion in the canal, 70 percent of which was recovered, but basically the original structure is intact. Even though ships have gotten larger, the canal can still handle 90 percent of the world's oceangoing liners. By the time the canal had marked its seventy-fifth anniversary in 1989, more than five billion tons of goods and 700,000 ships had transited it. Currently more than 922,000 vessels have used the waterway since its opening.

In his *The Path Between the Seas,* the leading book on the history and construction of the Panama Canal, author David McCullough says that of its many achievements, perhaps the most remarkable is that "so vast and costly an undertaking . . . [was] done without graft, kickbacks, payroll padding [or] any of the hundred and one forms of corruption endemic to such works. . . . nor has there been even a hint of scandal . . . [or] charge of corruption in all the years that it has been in operation."

The canal's value is impossible to calculate. Just one example provides a dramatic illustration: From San Francisco, the voyage around South America is 13,000 miles and takes three weeks; to reach one side of the continent from the other via the canal, it's 4,600 miles and can be made in a week.

For Panama, it has meant jobs—more than 9,000 employees—and income from tolls and other revenue of about $921 million a year.

A New Day

At the stroke of midnight on December 31, 1999, while the world ushered in the new millennium, Panama celebrated its own once-in-a-lifetime event: the transfer of the Panama Canal, along with about $4 billion worth of property, from the United States to Panama. It included 569 square miles of real estate, transforming the barracks, hospitals, schools, airstrips, churches, houses, offices, and manicured lawns into private housing, hotels and other tourist facilities, a university, sports centers, and industrial parks.

Long before the big day, Panamanians had already laid plans and committed resources—an estimated $1 billion from Panamanian and foreign investors—to develop the Canal Zone for tourism, primarily in two directions: Colón 2000, an umbrella project to develop the city of Colón at the western mouth of the canal into a major Caribbean deepwater port for cruise tourism and trade and as a convention center with the makeover of the city's historical waterfront; and a similar, smaller development at the Pacific entry point. In between Panamanians are creating a tourism infrastructure with an eye to ecotourism particularly, with preservation of the Panama Canal watershed a top priority.

Panama claims to be giving more than lip service to ecotourism and expects the Panama Canal region to play a major role. Almost one-third of Panama is under protection through its national park system, which shelters more than 10,000 species of plants, including 1,200 orchid species,

and 940 types of birds. Because the canal is surrounded by pristine rain forest, alive with wildlife, such projects as the **Gamboa Rainforest Resort at the Panama Canal** (877-800-1690; 314-9000; www.gamboaresort.com) seem to be ideal.

Located about midway across the Isthmus of Panama, about 25 miles from the Atlantic and Pacific Oceans, the resort sits at the fork of the Chagres River and Gatun Lake, in Soberania National Park, which is part of the watershed. In addition to its facilities—145 deluxe rooms, three restaurants, a pool, a spa, a marina, and meeting facilities—the resort has an education and research program, partly in cooperation with the Smithsonian Tropical Research Institute, which has trained the resort's guides. It has hiking trails; an observation deck over the canopy allows birdwatching, fishing, and other nature-oriented activities. River excursions and visits to nearby Indian villages are offered.

Among Panama's other ambitious projects, the $60 million restoration of the Panama Railroad has enabled passengers to travel by rail from ocean to ocean. The eighty-two-acre site of the former School of the Americas, 5 miles from the Canal Free Zone, has been transformed into the **Meliá Panamá Canal** (470-1100; www.solmelia.com), managed by the Spanish hotel chain Sol Meliá. The 285-room hotel has a large pool, three restaurants, and a marina.

To expand the benefits of the cruise traffic, Panamanian authorities have encouraged cruise lines to design new itineraries that begin and end in Panama as well as having some ships turn around in the Gatun Lake at midpoint. The effort has paid off: Now many cruise ships have added Panama and the Canal Zone as shore excursion destinations in their own right.

Recently a $5.25 billion expansion project was approved that will build a new lane of traffic along the Panama Canal. A third set of locks will accommodate supertankers and larger cargo ships carrying 12,000 containers each—as opposed to the 5,000 containers carried by Panamax ships, the largest that can currently run the canal—doubling capacity and allowing more traffic and longer, wider ships, including the mega-cruise-ships that are too large to transit the present canal.

On Friday, July 13, 2007, the first bid to widen the canal was issued to a Panamanian company, Constructora Urbana SA (CUSA). This firm's $41 million bid calls for digging 4.1 miles of new channel to accommodate larger ships, moving an estimated 46 million cubic feet of sediment and earth on the Pacific side of the canal. Work is to begin in 2008 and end in 2010. The project, controversial for its environmental impact, calls for the work to be completed in 2014, with the new locks open for transit in 2015. Some 14,000 ships use the canal annually.

Shore Excursions

Samples of the excursions available to cruise passengers in the canal area follow. Your ship is also likely to have the more traditional city tours of Colón at the canal's eastern end and Panama City on the west.

Rainforest Aerial Tram: Four and a half hours; US$99 adult; $79 child. The Gamboa Rainforest Resort at the Panama Canal is located on the Chagres River amid the 55,000-acre Soberania National Park. Here in this spectacular setting, the Aerial Tram enables you to see the forest canopy and get a bird's-eye view of the countryside. The tram rises from the forest floor and understory into the sunlit canopy to an observation tower. The Serpentarium, a butterfly house, botanical and orchid gardens, a reptile exhibit, and a model Emberá Indian village are also on the tour. (Were you to visit on your own, the resort charges US$43 for the aerial tram tour. The cruise ship excursion includes transportation and perhaps another stop.)

An Ecological Adventure on Gatun Lake: Five and a half hours; US$49 adult; $39 child. At Gamboa Pier you board a 25-foot boat and travel to cargo ships waiting to cross the canal to Cerro Balboa on Gatun Lake, where the ecological tour begins. Your guide explains the flora and fauna here and its surprising importance to the canal operation. The visit continues to Monkey Island, where it's common to see monkeys and hopefully other wildlife. The last stop is the Miraflores Locks to watch the operation of the Panama Canal and see a model of the canal with a narrated video on its building and operation. Here, too, is the visitor center, with excellent exhibits.

Discover the Emberá Indian Culture: Five and a half hours; US$99 adult; $73 child. Panama's rich and diverse indigenous population accounts for about 8 percent of the total populace and comprises seven tribes. Although threatened by environmental degradation of their lands and incursions by outsiders, these tribal people have managed to preserve much of their culture. Upstream along the Chagres River, you will come into contact with the Emberá Indians.

Also called Choco Indians, the Emberá live in houses built on stilts with cone-shaped roofs made of palm leaves. They sit on the floor, sleep on straw mats, and use a stepladder to climb up to their houses. Both men and women create crafts: basket weaving and ceramics for the women; woodcraft—cooking utensils, walking sticks, ritual sculptures, and altars—for the men. Perhaps their best skill is making piraguas or dugout canoes from cedar or yellow pine.

El Valle Ecological Paradise: Eight hours; US$69 adult; $54 child. The one-and-a-half-hour drive from Panama City to El Valle on the Pan-American Highway crosses the Bridge of the Americas and passes through beautiful, lush countryside. El Valle, at the edge of an extinct volcano, is famous for its ecological environment resplendent with flora and fauna; the town is a popular weekend escape for Panamanians. Visits are made to El Chorro Waterfall and Nispero Zoo.

Portobelo: The Pirate's Trail: Four and a half hours; US$43 adult; $31 child. Portobelo, one of the most important Spanish settlements in the New World, is an hour's scenic ride east from Colón on a road bordering the Caribbean coast much of the way. An excellent harbor (visited by Christopher Columbus), Portobelo was connected by a stone highway to Panama City—both transshipment ports for riches destined for Spain—and the end of two trails that crossed the jungles of the isthmus. When enough treasure had been accumulated here, caravans of sailing ships began their voyage back to Spain, trying to avoid pirates lying in wait.

Sir Francis Drake died of fever before he could capture the port and was buried in the bay, but other English buccaneers sacked it several times, including Sir Henry Morgan in 1688. In those days Portobelo was said to be the most heavily fortified

Spanish coastal control point in the Americas. After viewing the early Spanish fortifications and customs house, you visit the Church of the Black Christ and hear its legend.

Atlantic to Pacific Railway Journey: Four and a half hours; US$149 adult; $119 child. The dome railway car, a refurbished 1938 Vintage Deluxe Observation Car, has full-length observation windows and booth-style seating. There are no preassigned seats, and capacity is limited. The air-conditioned car has restrooms and a bar. It shares an outside observation area with an executive train car.

Transiting the Panama Canal

More than two dozen cruise ships offer transcanal cruises regularly in the winter season, and another three dozen offer them seasonally in spring and fall, when they make their way between the Caribbean and Alaska; or the West Coast and the East Coast; or en route to and from South America in winter and Europe for the summer.

The Isthmus of Panama lies northeast–southwest across mountainous, tropical jungle terrain. Because of the lay of the land, ships sail mostly on a north–south course, rather than east–west as might be assumed.

Ships approaching from the Caribbean enter the waterway at Port Cristobál in Limón Bay; Colón, Panama's second largest town, is to the east. Port Cristobál is also the northern terminus of the railroad that runs alongside the canal. There may be as many as fifty ships waiting to transit, but cruise ships are given priority over cargo vessels. Normally, cruise ships complete the crossing in about eight hours, but it can take longer, depending on the number and speed of the ships ahead. Pilots from the Panama Canal Commission board all ships to guide them through the canal. The commission also provides every cruise ship with a commentator who gives a running account over the ship's public address system of the vessel's passage through the canal and of the history and operation of the canal.

From Port Cristobál, your ship follows a 6½-mile course at sea level along a 500-foot-wide channel south to the Gatun Locks, the first of three locks, where the vessel is lifted 85 feet in three stages to the level of Gatun Lake. As your ship inches forward on its own steam into the first and lowest of the three chambers, a towline is tossed to a Panamanian seaman, who connects it to a messenger line from an electric fifty-five-ton towing locomotive known as a mule, which runs on rails at the top of the lock on each side, pulling the ship into place in the chamber. Each mule can pull 70,000 pounds; the number attached to a ship is determined by the ship's size.

Above the first chamber is the control tower where the operator controls the flow of water through huge 18-foot culverts, or tunnels, located in the center and side walls of the locks. When the pilot gives the signal, the mules begin to roll forward to position your ship into the first chamber; slowly the great doors at the stern close.

With your ship inside the huge chamber, the tower operator opens the valves, and water spills out through the culverts at the rate of three million gallons a minute. It is like being on the bottom of a gigantic swimming pool, watching your ship rise as water fills the enclosure. No pumps are used to fill or empty the chambers; the system works by gravity, with water flowing from one level to another through the large culverts to smaller culverts that open to the floor of the chambers.

The huge chambers—1,000 feet long by 110 feet wide—have concrete walls from 8 to 50 feet thick and floors from 13 to 20 feet deep. Each set of locks has parallel chambers of the same size to allow passage in both directions at the same time. Each lock holds 65.8 million gallons of water; every time a ship makes a complete transit, 52 million gallons of water flow into the sea. The colossal steel doors or gates—still the originals—at the end of each chamber are 65 feet wide and 7 feet thick, and vary from 47 to 82 feet in height; the largest weighs more than 700 tons. Yet they can be opened and closed with only a forty-horsepower motor.

When the water in the first chamber reaches the level of the water in the next lock, the gates between the two open, the mules pull your ship forward, and the doors behind your ship close. Again, water fills the chamber, and your ship rises to the water level of the third and final stage. When that step is completed, your ship sails onto Gatun Lake.

Covering an area of 163.38 square miles, Gatun Lake was created by carving out an enormous earthen dam across the Chagres Valley at the north end of the canal. The Chagres River flows into Gatun and Madden Lakes on the north side of the Continental Divide and, together with Miraflores Lake on the south side, supplies the water to operate the locks. The lakes' water levels are controlled by dams, ensuring a constant supply.

Your ship sails under its own power for 24 miles across Gatun Lake to the Gaillard Cut through a pretty landscape of forested hills and islets (the tops of submerged hills), where you can observe some of the region's wildlife. The most frequent visitors around your ship are brown pelicans; the treetops are often heavy with vultures; and high in the sky, magnificent frigate birds glide overhead. If you are good at spotting birds, off in the forest you might see toucans and macaws, and as the ship moves closer to the Pacific, you might begin to see boobies.

You will also be able to watch ships transiting the canal from the other direction; most will be cargo vessels, but occasionally a small private yacht or another cruise ship will pass, too. Expect a shower or two; depending on the time of year, the air can be balmy and pleasant or steamy. This is, after all, the middle of the jungle, even if it appears mechanized and manicured.

Some cruise ships on one-week Caribbean cruises go only as far as Gatun Lake, where they turn around and depart through the Gatun Locks back to the Atlantic side.

At about the midpoint of the canal, your ship leaves Gatun Lake and sails into the Gaillard Cut. This V-shaped channel, cut from granite and volcanic rock, is the narrowest stretch of the canal and was the most difficult to build. More than 230 million cubic yards of earth and rock were excavated from the 9-mile stretch to make it navigable. Originally the channel was 300 feet wide; later it was widened to 500 feet, and there is discussion about widening it further. It has a depth of 42 feet. While the sides have been stabilized, they are monitored constantly, and dredging never stops. About halfway along the cut on the west side, a bronze plaque honors the builders of the canal and the workers who died.

The cut ends at the entrance to the first of two sets of locks: Pedro Miguel Locks, with only one step of 31 feet, followed by the Miraflores Lake and the Miraflores Locks, which drop 54 feet in two steps. Here the process is reversed. Your ship will enter a chamber full of water, and as the water is drained out, your ship is lowered to the next level, and finally to the level of the Pacific. At the exit of the final lock is the Port of Balboa and, off in the distance to the south, Panama City. Directly in front is the lofty Bridge of the Americas, the bridge connecting the two sides of the waterway and part of the Interamerican Highway between North and South America.

Trivia buffs may like to know that for years the largest cruise ship to pass through the canal was Cunard's *QE2*, which is 963 feet long with a beam of 105—just 5 feet short of the locks' 110-foot width. However, most of the new large ships built to the specifications that allow them to transit the canal, referred to as Panamax ships, are a fraction longer and/or wider than the *QE2*. For example, NCL's *Norwegian Star* is 971 feet in length and has a 105.6-foot beam. The amount these large ships pay has increased as well, normally up to $300,000 or more, but the least is still the 36 cents paid by Richard Halliburton to swim the canal in 1928.

Canal Operation

The Panama Canal operation is a model of efficiency. The canal operates 24 hours a day and 365 days a year, with as many as forty ships passing through daily. For most ships, the average Canal Waters Time—the total time spent at the Panama Canal, including waiting time and in-transit time—is just under 24 hours. A reservation system is available to provide a guaranteed priority transit upon request.

The canal's ability to work at peak efficiency is attributed to its skilled technicians and year-round maintenance, which accounts for about one-quarter of its annual operating budget, or about $100 million.

Miraflores Visitors Center

Located on the east side of the Miraflores Locks, the center enables visitors to watch vessels transiting the canal from a very short distance and learn about the canal's operation and watershed, the history of its construction, and its vital role in world trade. The center has a fully equipped theater, three observation terraces, snack bars, a panoramic-view restaurant, a gift shop, and four exhibition halls. The exhibitions include historic pieces, interactive modules, video presentations, models of the canal, and objects used in its operations.

The History Hall provides background, explains the technical innovations that were integral to the canal's construction, and honors the hundreds of men and women who made it possible.

The Hall of Water emphasizes the importance of water; the protection of the Canal Watershed, environment, and biodiversity; and the Canal Authority's commitment to managing this resource and the surrounding region.

The Canal in Action is an amusing depiction of the canal operation and enables viewers to be inside a navigation simulator and one of the lock culverts and to view a virtual ocean-to-ocean transit. It also features the canal's ongoing improvements, modernization, and maintenance projects.

The Canal in the World focuses on the importance of the canal to world trade, the trade routes it serves, its users, the types of vessels that transit, and the commodities they carry. It also gives an overview of studies conducted to guarantee the canal's future competitiveness and benefits to Panama.

Center admission for nonresidents: $8 adult; $5 ages five to seventeen; under five free. Hours: 9:00 A.M. to 5:00 P.M. daily; restaurant noon to 11 P.M. Information: 276-8325; fax 276-8469; cvm@pancanal.com; www.pancanal.com.

Chart of Cruise Ships Sailing the Caribbean

Every effort has been made to ensure the accuracy of the information regarding the ships' ports of call and prices, but keep in mind that cruise lines often change itineraries for a variety of reasons. Before you make plans, you should obtain the most current information from your cruise line, its Web site, or your travel agent.

Prices are for "cruise only" unless indicated otherwise and are based on per-person, double-occupancy rates, ranging from the least expensive cabin in low season to the best cabin in high season. Prices include port charges unless noted otherwise, and they are full-rate brochure prices. However, almost all cruise brochures now include early-bird saving prices, which are often discounted 50 percent and more. Holiday, special, or positioning cruises are not included.

Cruise Line/Ships	Ports of Call	Price Range	Duration/Season
American Canadian Caribbean Line			
Grande Mariner	Bahamas/Turks & Caicos from Providenciales to Nassau via Mayaguana Island, Long Island, Acklins Island, Exuma Cays, Staniel Cay, Norman's Cay.	$2,970–$3,795	11 days/winter
	Caribbean from St. Thomas to St. John, Tortola, Salt Island. Or St. Maarten to Antigua via Marigot, Saba. St. Kitts, Nevis.		
	Bahamas round trip from Nassau to Spanish Wells, Eleuthera, Harbour Island, Governor's Harbour, Exuma Cays, Staniel Cay, Warderick Wells Cay.		
Carnival Cruise Lines			
Carnival Conquest	Western Caribbean round trip from Galveston to Montego Bay, Grand Cayman, Cozumel.	$1,669–$2,619	7 days/year-round
Carnival Destiny	Southern Caribbean round trip from San Juan to St. Thomas, Dominica, Barbados, St. Kitts, La Romana (overnight).	$1,669–$2,619	7 days/to April
	Round trip from San Juan to St. Kitts, Antigua, St. Lucia, Barbados, Dominica, St. Thomas.		From March 2, 2008

Cruise Line/Ships	Ports of Call	Price Range	Duration/Season
Carnival Cruise Lines *(continued)*			
Carnival Dream (debuts 2009)	tba		
Carnival Freedom	Alternating Eastern/Western Caribbean round trip from Miami to San Juan, St. Thomas, St. Maarten; or Cozumel, Grand Cayman, Ocho Rios, 3 days at sea; or Half Moon Cay, St. Thomas, San Juan, Grand Turk.	$1,419–$2,869	7 nights/to April 2008
	Western Caribbean round trip from Fort Lauderdale to Key West, Grand Cayman, Ocho Rios. Alternating Western/ Eastern Caribbean round trip from Fort Lauderdale; or to Costa Maya, Limón, Colón or San Juan, St. Thomas, Antigua, Tortola, Nassau.		6 days/November 2008– April 2009; or 8 days
Carnival Glory	Port Canaveral to Nassau, St. Thomas/St. John, St. Maarten; or Cozumel, Belize City, Costa Maya, Nassau.	$1,669–$2,619	7 days/year-round
Carnival Legend	Western Caribbean round trip from Tampa to Grand Cayman, Cozumel, Belize; Costa Maya with 2 days at sea.	$1,669–$2,619	7 days/year-round
Carnival Liberty	Alternating Western/Eastern Caribbean round trip from Fort Lauderdale to Costa Maya, Puerto Limón, Colón, or San Juan, St. Thomas/ St. John, Antigua, Tortola/Virgin Gorda, Nassau; or Freeport, Grand Cayman, and Cozumel; or Freeport, Key West or Nassau, Grand Cayman and Costa Maya or Ocho Rios.	$1,419–$2,869	6, 8 days/winter to May 2008
	Eastern Caribbean round trip from Miami to Half Moon Cay, St. Thomas, San Juan, Grand Turk.		7 days/May–October
	Alternating Eastern/Western Caribbean round trip from Miami to San Juan, St. Thomas, St. Maarten; or Cozumel, Grand Cayman, Ocho Rios.		7 days/June 2008– May 2009
Carnival Miracle	Alternating Southern/Western Caribbean round trip from Fort Lauderdale to St. Maarten, St. Lucia, St. Kitts or Colón, Limón, Belize.	$1,819–$2,869	8 days/to Feb 2009
	Eastern Caribbean round trip from New York to San Juan, St. Thomas, Tortola with 4 days at sea.		8 days/June, August– October 2008
Carnival Splendor (debuts 2008)	Eastern Caribbean from Fort Lauderdale to San Juan, St. Thomas, Casa de Campo/ La Romana.	$1,819–$2,819	7-day/November 22, 2008–February 2009
Carnival Triumph	Alternating Eastern/Western Caribbean round trip from Miami to Half Moon Cay, St. Thomas, San Juan, Nassau or Grand Turk; or Cozumel, Grand Cayman, Ocho Rios.	$1,669–$2,619	7 days/to April 2008
Carnival Valor	Alternating Eastern/Western Caribbean round trip from Miami to Nassau, St. Thomas, St. Maarten; or Grand Cayman, Belize City, Roatan, Costa Maya.	$1,669–$2,619	7 days/year-round

Cruise Line/Ships	Ports of Call	Price Range	Duration/Season
Carnival Cruise Lines *(continued)*			
Carnival Victory	Alternating Eastern and Western Caribbean round trip from Miami to San Juan, St. Maarten and St. Thomas, or Costa Maya, Grand Cayman, Ocho Rios.	$1,669–$2,619	7 days/winter
	Bahamas round trip from Charleston to Nassau and Freeport or round-trip from Norfolk.		5 days/May, June, October
	Southern Caribbean from San Juan to La Romana/Casa de Campo, St. Kitts, Barbados, Dominica, St. Thomas.		7-day year-round from November 2, 2008
Celebration (leaves Carnival fleet April 2008)	Jacksonville (FL) to Freeport, Nassau (4 days); or Key West, Nassau (5 days).	$849–$1,749	4, 5 days/year-round
Carnival Ecstasy	Galveston (TX) to Cozumel (4 days); or Cozumel, Calica/Playa del Carmen (5 days).	$849–$1,549	4, 5 days/year-round
Carnival Fantasy	Western Caribbean round trip from New Orleans, 4 days, alternate Thursdays to Cozumel; 5 days, alternate Mondays and Saturdays to Costa Maya and Cozumel.	$849–$1,549	4, 5 days/year-round
Fascination	Miami to Nassau (3 days); or to Key West, Calica/Playa del Carmen or Cozumel (4 days).	$699–$1,279	3, 4 days/year-round
Holiday	Western Caribbean round trip from Mobile alternate Thursdays to Cozumel (4 days); or alternate Mondays to Cozumel, Calica/Playa del Carmen or alternate Saturdays to Cozumel, Costa Maya (5 days).	$849–$1,749	4, 5 days/year-round
Carnival Imagination	Miami to Key West, Calica/Playa del Carmen (4 days); or Grand Cayman and Ocho Rios (5 days).	$849–$1,549	4, 5 days/year-round
Carnival Inspiration	Tampa to Cozumel (4 days); or to Grand Cayman, Cozumel or Calica (5 days).	$849–$1,549	4, 5 days/year-round
Carnival Sensation	Bahamas round trip from Port Canaveral, Thursdays to Nassau (3 days); Sundays to Freeport and Nassau (4 days).	$699–$1,279	3, 4 days/year-round
Celebrity Cruises			
Azamara Quest	Eastern Caribbean round trip from Miami to Virgin Gorda, Dominica, St. Vincent, Tobago, St. Barts, St. John, USVI, Ponce, Samaná, Dominican Republic; Grand Turk, Turks and Caicos. Or Mayaguez and Ponce, Puerto Rico; St. John, Antigua, Dominica, Guadeloupe, St. Barts, Samaná, Grand Turk.	$2,129–$6,049	14 days/winter
Celebrity Century	Western Caribbean round trip from Miami to Key West, Cozumel or Cozumel, Grand Cayman; or Grand Cayman; Key West.	$389–$2,849	4, 5 days/winter
	Bahamas round trip from Miami to Nassau.		2 days/January 2008

Cruise Line/Ships	Ports of Call	Price Range	Duration/Season
Celebrity Cruises	*(continued)*		
Celebrity Constellation	Eastern/Western Caribbean round trip from Fort Lauderdale to St. Thomas; St. Kitts; Barbados; St. Lucia; St. Maarten; or Grand Cayman, Aruba; Cristobál/Panama; Cartagena, Cozumel.	$1,149–$5,149	10, 11 days/winter
Celebrity Galaxy	Southern Caribbean round trip from San Juan, to Tortola, St. Maarten, St. Lucia, Barbados, Margarita Island, Curaçao, Aruba (10 days) or Dominica, St. Kitts instead of St. Maarten (11 days); or Aruba, Curacao, Grenada, Barbados, Dominica, St. Kitts, Tortola.	$769–$3,199	10, 11 days/winter
Celebrity Infinity	Between Fort Lauderdale and San Francisco via Montego Bay, Cartagena, Panama Canal, Puntarenas, Costa Rica; Huatulco, Mexico; Acapulco, Cabo San Lucas.	$1,549–$4,299	15 days/spring/fall
Celebrity Millennium	Eastern Caribbean round trip from Fort Lauderdale to San Juan, St. Thomas, Casa de Campo, Dominican Republic; Labadee, Haiti.	$699–$3,949	7 days/winter
Celebrity Summit	Southern Caribbean round trip from San Juan to St. Maarten, Dominica, Grenada, Bonaire, Aruba.	$669–$3,299	7 days/winter
Costa Cruises			
Costa Fortuna	Alternating Western/Eastern Caribbean round trip from Fort Lauderdale to Cozumel, Grand Cayman, Ocho Rios (or Montego Bay), Grand Turk. Or to San Juan, St. Maarten, Tortola, Nassau or San Juan, St. Thomas, Catalina Island/La Romana, Nassau.	$999–$2,799	7 days/winter
Costa Mediterranea	Alternating Eastern/Western Caribbean round trip from Fort Lauderdale to San Juan, St. Thomas, La Romana, Grand Turk, or Key West, Grand Cayman, Roatan, Cozumel.	$1,049–$2,999	7 days/winter
Crystal Cruises			
Crystal Serenity	Caribbean/Panama Canal from Miami to Costa Rica via Grand Turk, Tortola, St. Barts, Aruba, Panama Canal; reverse. Or round trip from Miami to Tortola, St. Maarten, St. Barts, Antigua, St. Lucia, Barbados, Curaçao, Aruba.	$7,090–$51,915	11, 14 days/December
Crystal Symphony	Caribbean/Panama Canal from Miami to Costa Rica via St. Thomas, St. Maarten, Antigua, Aruba, Panama Canal; reverse.	$5,195–$28,585	11, 13, 16 days/ December–January
	From Miami to Los Angeles via Cozumel, Panama Canal, Acapulco, Cabo San Lucas; or from Los Angeles to Miami via Cabo San Lucas, Costa Rica, Panama Canal, Aruba, St. Kitts, San Juan.		

Cruise Line/Ships	Ports of Call	Price Range	Duration/Season
Cunard			
QM2	Panama & Caribbean round trip from New York to Limón, Cristobál, Curaçao, Bonaire, St. Lucia, St. Thomas.	$1,289–$30,119	4 days/February–March
	Caribbean between New York and Fort Lauderdale via St. Kitts, Grenada, Bonaire. Or round trip from Fort Lauderdale to Curaçao, Grenada, Barbados, St. Lucia, St. Kitts, St. Thomas. Or to Panama, Bonaire, Grenada, Barbados, St. Lucia, Dominica, St. Kitts, Tortola.		8, 10, 14 nights/ November–December 2008–2009
Disney Cruise Line			
Disney Magic	Alternating Eastern/Western Caribbean round trip from Port Canaveral to St. Thomas, Castaway Cay or Key West, Grand Cayman, Cozumel, Castaway Cay.	$849–$6,199	7 days/year-round
	Bahamas round trip from Port Canaveral to Nassau with 2 days at Castaway Cay.		5 days/September
	Round trip from Port Canaveral to Costa Maya with 2 days at Castaway Cay.		7 days/September– December
Disney Wonder	Port Canaveral to Nassau, Castaway Cay (3 days) plus a day at sea (4 days).	$429–$3,999	3, 4 days/year-round
	Cruise can be combined with Disney World packages for a 7-night vacation.		
Holland America Line			
Eurodam	Eastern/Southern Caribbean round trip from Fort Lauderdale to Nassau, Half Moon Cay; or Grand Turk, Tortola; or Puerto Rico, St. Thomas, Half Moon Cay; or Half Moon Cay, Aruba, Curacao.	$499–$4,799	3, 7 days, winter
Maasdam	Eastern/Southern Caribbean round trip from Fort Lauderdale to St. Maarten, St. Lucia, Barbados, Martinique, Tortola or Half Moon Cay, St. Thomas, Dominica, Curacao, Aruba.	$1,789–$14,764	10, 15 days/winter & fall
	Or Fort Lauderdale to San Diego via Half Moon Cay, Cartagena, Panama Canal, Golfo Dulce, Puntarenas, Puerto Chiapas, Santa Cruz Huatulco, Acapulco, Cabo San Lucas. Reverse via Cabo San Lucas, Mazatlan, Puerto Vallarta, Puerto Quetzal, San Juan del Sur, Panama Canal, Cartagena, Nassau.		
Noordam	New York to Grand Turk, Tortola, St. Maarten, St. Thomas, San Juan.	$999–$5,999	10, 11 days/winter & fall through March 2008

Cruise Line/Ships	Ports of Call	Price Range	Duration/Season
Holland America Line *(continued)*			
Prinsendam	Caribbean/Amazon round trip from Fort Lauderdale to Grand Turk, Aruba, Bonaire, Grenada, Devil's Island, Amazon River, Santarem, Boca de Valeria, Manaus, Parintins, Alter do Chao, Barbados, Dominica, St. Thomas, Half Moon Cay.	$4,199–$31,999	26 days/November
Statendam	Southern Caribbean round trip from Fort Lauderdale to Half Moon Cay, St. Thomas, St. John's. St. Lucia, Barbados, Trinidad, El Guamache, Curacao, Aruba, Grand Turk. Or round trip from Tampa to Key West, Belize City, Santo Tomas de Castilla, Costa Maya.	$1,879–$11,199	14 days/December
Veendam	Caribbean round trip from Tampa to Half Moon Cay, St. Thomas, Dominica, Barbados, Grenada, El Guamache, Bonaire, Aruba. Or to Costa Maya, Montego Bay, Grand Cayman.	$649–$31,396	14, 7 days/winter & fall
	From Tampa to San Diego, or Vancouver via Grand Cayman, Cartagena, Panama Canal, Golfo Dulce, San Juan del Sur, Puerto Chiapas, Santa Cruz Huatulco, Acapulco, Cabo San Lucas.		15–19 days/April
	Panama/Amazon/Caribbean from Vancouver or San Diego to Tampa via Victoria, San Diego, Cabo San Lucas, Acapulco, Santa Cruz Huatulco, Puerto Chiapas, Puerto Caldera, Panama Canal, Aruba, Grenada, Santarem, Boca de Valeria, Amazon River, Barbados, Grand Turk, Half Moon Cay.		32, 36 days/ September–October
Volendam	Caribbean/Panama round trip from Fort Lauderdale to Half Moon Cay, Aruba, Curaçao, Panama Canal, Limón Bay, Manzanillo Bay, Puerto Limón; or reverse.	$1,199–$13,349	10 days/winter to April 2008
Westerdam	Eastern Caribbean round trip from Fort Lauderdale to Grand Turk, San Juan, St. Thomas, Half Moon Cay.	$499–$4,959	7 days/winter & fall
	Or alternating Eastern/Western Caribbean round trip from Fort Lauderdale to Half Moon Cay, Grand Turk, Grand Cayman, Costa Maya or Grand Turk, St. Maarten, Tortola, Half Moon Cay.		
	Eastern Caribbean from Fort Lauderdale to Nassau and Half Moon Cay.		3 days/April & October
Zuiderdam	Eastern Caribbean round trip from Fort Lauderdale to Grand Turk, Tortola, Half Moon Cay, or San Juan, St. Thomas, Half Moon Cay.	$649–$4,959	7 days/winter & fall
	Caribbean/Panama round trip from Fort Lauderdale to Half Moon Cay, Aruba, Curaçao, Panama Canal, Limón Bay, Manzanillo Bay, Puerto Limón; or reverse.		From November 2008

Cruise Line/Ships	Ports of Call	Price Range	Duration/Season
MSC Cruises			
MSC Lirica	Fort Lauderdale to San Juan, St. Maarten, St. Lucia, Antigua, Tortola, and Cayo Levantado (Dominican Republic); or to Cozumel, Puerto Limón, Cristobál, Cartagena, Cayo Levantado.	$699–$3,500	10 days/winter
MSC Orchestra	Alternating Eastern and Western Caribbean round trip from Fort Lauderdale. Itineraries tba.	From $499	7 days/winter 2009
Norwegian Cruise Line			
Norwegian Dawn	Eastern Caribbean round trip from Miami to Samaná (Dominica Republic), Tortola, St. Thomas, Great Stirrup Cay.	$449–$2,099	7 days/winter
Norwegian Gem	Southern Caribbean round trip from New York via St. Thomas, Antigua, Barbados, St. Maarten and Tortola; 11 nights add Grenada and Dominica, instead of St. Maarten.	$1,099–$2,999	10, 11 days/ January–February
	Bahamas round trip from New York via Grand Bahama, Nassau, Great Stirrup Cay, Port Canaveral.		7 days/February–April and December; January-April 2009
Norwegian Jade	Miami to the Bahamas via Grand Bahama Island.	t.b.a.	December
Norwegian Jewel	Alternating Southern Caribbean round trip from Miami to Samaná, Tortola, Antigua, Barbados and St. Lucia.	$299–$3,999	9 days/winter
	Western Caribbean round trip from Miami to Cozumel and Grand Cayman.		5 days/winter 9 and 5 day itineraries can be combined into 14 day cruise
Norwegian Majesty	Charleston (SC) to Grand Cayman, Cozumel, and Key West.	$429–$2,849	7 days/winter
Norwegian Pearl	Alternating Southern/Western Caribbean round trip from Miami via Samaná, Tortola, Antigua, Barbados, and St. Lucia. Or 5 nights, via Cozumel and Grand Cayman.	$329–$2,779	9, 5, 14 days/winter
	Or 9-day and 5-day can be combined into 14-night round trip from Miami.		
Norwegian Spirit	Western Caribbean round trip from New Orleans to Roatan (January to March sailings) or, to Costa Maya (November to December sailings), Santo Tomás de Castilla (Guatemala), Belize, Cozumel.	$499–$4,399	7 days/winter
Norwegian Sun	Western Caribbean round trip from Miami to Roatan, Belize City, Cozumel, Great Stirrup Cay.	$399–$1,899	7 days/winter

Cruise Line/Ships	Ports of Call	Price Range	Duration/Season
Oceania Cruises			
Regatta	Eastern Caribbean round trip from Miami to Virgin Gorda, St. Barts, Dominica, St. Lucia, Antigua, Tortola, Samaná, Grand Turk and reverse.	$2,998–$16,598	10–12 days/winter
	Or Western Caribbean/Panama from Miami to Los Angeles via Playa del Carmen, Cozumel, San Andres, Panama Canal, Puntarenas, Puerto Quetzal, Acapulco, Cabo San Lucas.		
	Or Western Caribbean/Central America round trip from Miami to Playa del Carmen, Cozumel, Belize, Santo Tomas, Roatan, Puerto Limón, Colón, Cartagena, Grand Cayman.		16, 14 days/winter
Princess Cruises			
Caribbean Princess	Fort Lauderdale to St. Thomas, St. Maarten, Princess Cays.	$799–$4,349	7 days/winter
	Eastern Caribbean round trip from New York to Grand Turk, San Juan, St. Thomas, Bermuda (West End) and reverse.		
	Bermuda/Eastern Caribbean between New York and San Juan to St. Kitts, Antigua, St. Thomas.		May–August
	Southern Caribbean between Barbados, St. Lucia, Antigua, Tortola and St. Thomas; or Aruba, Bonaire, Grenada, Dominica and St Thomas.		7 days/October November 2008– May 2009
Coral Princess	Panama Canal round trip from Fort Lauderdale to Aruba, Cartagena, Panama Canal to Gatun Lake, Cristobál, Costa Rica, Ocho Rios or Montego Bay.	$1,199–$3,624	10 days/winter
	Eastern Caribbean round-trip from Fort Lauderdale to Princess Cays, St. Maarten, St. Thomas, Grand Turk.	$599–$4,349	7 days, October 2008– May 2009
Crown Princess	Southern Caribbean round trip from San Juan to Barbados, St. Lucia, Antigua, Tortola, St. Thomas. Or to St. Kitts, Grenada, Bonaire, Aruba; or San Juan, Tortola, St. Thomas, Antigua, St. Lucia, Barbados.	$599–$3,249	7 days/summer
Emerald Princess	Alternating Southern/Eastern Caribbean round trip from Fort Lauderdale to Aruba, Bonaire, Grenada, Dominica, St. Thomas, Princess Cays.	$899–$4,149	10 days/winter
	Or round trip from Fort Lauderdale to Princess Cays, St. Thomas, St. Kitts, Barbados, St. Lucia, Antigua, or reverse.		
	Or, Princess Cays, St. Thomas, Dominica, Grenada, Bonaire, and Aruba; or Antigua, St. Lucia, Barbados, St. Kitts, St. Thomas, and Princess Cays.		October 2008– May 2009

Cruise Line/Ships	Ports of Call	Price Range	Duration/Season
Princess Cruises	*(continued)*		
Grand Princess	Western Caribbean round trip from Fort Lauderdale to Ocho Rios, Grand Cayman, Cozumel, and Princess Cays.	$599–$4,349	7 days/winter
	Aruba, Curaçao, Trinidad, Barbados, St. Vincent, St. Kitts, St. Thomas, La Romana, and Grand Turk.		14 days, December 2008–April 2009
Island Princess	Panama Canal between Los Angeles and Fort Lauderdale via Huatulco, Puerto Quetzal, Puerto Corinto, Costa Rica, Panama Canal, Cartagena, Aruba, Ocho Rios. Or Fort Lauderdale and Acapulco to Ocho Rios, Panama Canal, Fuerte Amador, Costa Rica, San Juan del Sur, Puerto Quetzal, Huatulco; reverse adds Puerto Corinto, Cartagena, Aruba.	$1,199–$4,824	15 days/winter
	Panama Canal between Acapulco and San Juan to Huatulco, Puerto Quetzal, Puerto Corinto, Costa Rica, Panama Canal, Cartagena, Aruba; reverse adds Curaçao, San Juan del Sur.		10–11 days/winter
Royal Princess	Caribbean/Amazon River between Fort Lauderdale and Manaus to St. Barts, St. Lucia, Tobago, Devil's Island, Amazon River ports of Santarem, Boca da Valeria, Parintins, and Manaus; and reverse.	$2,049–$6,449	14 days/winter
Ruby Princess	Western Caribbean round-trip from Fort Lauderdale to Ocho Rios, Grand Cayman, Cozumel, Princess Cays.	$599–$4,349	7 days, November 2008–May 2009
Sea Princess	Alternating Eastern Caribbean round trip from Barbados to St. Lucia, Antigua, St. Maarten, St. Thomas, Grand Turk, Montego Bay, Grand Cayman, Aruba, Bonaire, Caracas, Grenada.	$1,399–$4,999	14 days/winter
	Or from Montego Bay to Curaçao, Bonaire, Isla Margarita, Trinidad, Barbados, Antigua, St. Maarten, St. Thomas, Grand Turk.		
	Transatlantic between Montego Bay or Barbados and Southampton via Grand Cayman, Bonaire, Caracas, Grenada, Barbados, St. Vincent, St. Lucia, St. Maarten, St. Thomas, Antigua, Azores.		7–14 days/April
	Or from Barbados to Dominica, Antigua, St. Maarten, Tortola, Samana, Montego Bay, Curaçao, Bonaire, Isla Margarita, Grenada, Trinidad, or, St. Lucia, Antigua, St. Kitts, Tortola, Samana, Montego Bay, Grand Cayman, Aruba, Bonaire, Caracas (La Guaira), and Grenada.		14 days, October 2008–April 2009

Cruise Line/Ships	Ports of Call	Price Range	Duration/Season

Regent Seven Seas Cruises

Port and handling charges are additional. Cruise-only fares include gratuities, wine with lunch and dinner, soft drinks and juice throughout the cruise, in-cabin bar setup.

Cruise Line/Ships	Ports of Call	Price Range	Duration/Season
Seven Seas Mariner	Caribbean round trip from Fort Lauderdale.	$5,795–$27,295 + port charges	7–12 days/May
Seven Seas Navigator	Caribbean/Mexico round trip from Fort Lauderdale on varying itineraries.	$4,995–$28,295 + port charge	7–14 days/winter
Seven Seas Voyager	Caribbean round trip from Fort Lauderdale to Aruba, Curaçao, St. Kitts, and St. Lucia.	$4,995–$23,295 + port charges	7–11 days/ December 2008–January 2009

Royal Caribbean Cruise Line

Cruise Line/Ships	Ports of Call	Price Range	Duration/Season
Adventure of the Seas	San Juan to Aruba, Curaçao, St. Maarten, and St. Thomas. April–October alternate to St. Maarten, Antigua, St. Lucia, Barbados.	$599–$3,699	7 days/year-round
Brilliance of the Seas	Western Caribbean round trip from Miami to Curacáo, Aruba, Ocho Rios, Labadee.		
	Southern Caribbean/Panama Canal round trip from Miami to Aruba, Panama Canal, Cristobál, Puerto Limón, Grand Cayman (10 nights); or Labadee, Aruba, Curaçao, Panama Canal, Cristobál, Puerto Limón (11 nights); or add Grand Cayman.	$1,099–$3,299	10, 11 days/winter
Empress of the Seas (leaves fleet after March 7 sailing)	San Juan to St. Maarten, St. Barts, St. Kitts, Antigua. St. Lucia, Barbados, Isla Margarita, Curaçao, Aruba (11 nights); to St. Maarten, St. Lucia, Barbados, Isla Margarita, Curacáo, Aruba (9 nights); or St. Thomas, St. Maarten (3 nights); or St. Kitts, St. Maarten (3 nights).	$368–$1,799	3, 11 days/winter to March 2008
Enchantment of the Seas	Western Caribbean round trip from Fort Lauderdale alternating Thursdays to Key West, Cozumel; Mondays to Belize City, Cozumel, Key West; Saturdays to Grand Cayman, Costa Maya. Or Thursdays to Coco Cay, Key West.	$249–$1,309	4–5 days/year-round
	To Grand Cayman, Costa Maya, Cozumel, Coco Cay.		7 days/April
Explorer of the Seas	Southern Caribbean round trip from Cape Liberty to St. Maarten, Antigua, Dominica, Barbados, St. Kitts, St. Thomas, San Juan.	$799–$2,799	7 days/winter
	Bermuda round trip from Cape Liberty to Kings Wharf, Bermuda.		
	Or Eastern Caribbean to Labadee, Casa De Campo, St. Thomas; San Juan.		
	Or Bermuda/Caribbean round trip from Cape Liberty to Kings Wharf, St. Maarten; St. Thomas; San Juan.		9 days

Cruise Line/Ships	Ports of Call	Price Range	Duration/Season
Royal Caribbean Cruise Line *(continued)*			
Freedom of the Seas	Western/Eastern Caribbean round trip from Miami to Labadee, Ocho Rios, Grand Cayman, Cozumel. Or to San Juan, St. Thomas, St. Maarten.	$699–$3,599	7 days/year-round
Grandeur of the Seas	Western Caribbean round trip from Tampa to Grand Cayman, Progresso, Belize, Cozumel.	$599–$2,049	7 days/winter
	Bermuda, Caribbean, and Canada/New England from Norfolk, Virginia and Baltimore, MD.		5, 7, 9 days/summer
Independence of the Seas	Eastern/Western Caribbean round trip from Fort Lauderdale to San Juan, St. Thomas, St. Maarten, Labadee, or Belize, Costa Maya, Cozumel.	$549–$2,299	Winter 2008–2009
Jewel of the Seas	Eastern/Western Caribbean from Fort Lauderdale to San Juan, St. Maarten, St. Thomas, Tortola, Nassau or Key West, Cozumel, Playa del Carmen, Belize.	$549–$2,299	8, 6, days/winter
Legend of the Seas	Southern Caribbean round trip from Santo Domingo to St. Kitts, Guadeloupe, Martinique, Barbados, St. Lucia. Or St. Maarten, Dominica, Grenada, Margarita Island, Aruba.	$649–$5,299	7 days/winter
Liberty of the Seas	Western/Eastern Caribbean round trip from Miami to Labadee, Montego Bay, Grand Cayman, Cozumel. Or to San Juan, St. Maarten, Labadee.	$649–$3,699	7 days/winter
Majesty of the Seas	Miami to Nassau, Coco Cay (3 days) plus Key West (4 days).	Starting at $279	3, 4 days/year-round
Mariner of the Seas	Eastern/Western Caribbean round trip from Port Canaveral to Coco Cay, St. Thomas, St. Maarten; or to Labadee, Ocho Rios, Grand Cayman, Cozumel.	$599–$2,249	7 days/year-round
Navigator of the Seas	Western Caribbean round trip from Fort Lauderdale to Cozumel, Belize, Key West; or to Cozumel, Key West; or to Cozumel, Belize; or to Ocho Rios, Grand Cayman, or Cozumel.	$349–$2,059	6, 5, 4 days/year-round
Radiance of the Seas	Eastern Caribbean/Western Caribbean round trip from Fort Lauderdale to San Juan, St. Thomas, Antigua, St. Maarten, Nassau; or Key West, Cozumel, Grand Cayman, Montego Bay.	$509–$1,349	8 days/winter
Serenade of the Seas	Eastern/Southern Caribbean round trip from San Juan to St. Thomas, St. Maarten, Antigua, St. Lucia, Barbados.	$549–$2,599	7 days/winter
Sovereign of the Seas	Port Canaveral to Nassau, Coco Cay (3 days) plus a day at sea (4 days).	Starting at $279	3, 4 days/year-round
Voyager of the Seas	Western Caribbean round trip from Galveston to Montego Bay, Grand Cayman, Cozumel; or to Cozumel, Roatan, Costa Maya, Progreso.	$699–$2,849	7 days/winter

Seabourn Cruise Line

Cruise-only fares include gratuities, wine and spirits, and a complimentary shore experience when itineraries allow.

Seabourn Legend	Panama, Belize & Costa Rica, from Fort Lauderdale to Puerto Caldera, Belize, Roatan, Costa Rica, Panama Canal transit, Puerto Quepos, San Juan del Sur.	$8,325–$61,031	14–28 days/winter
	Panama Canal & Caribbean, from Fort Lauderdale to St. Thomas via Panama Canal, Puerto Moin, Roatan, Belize, San Juan, St. John, Guadeloupe, Antigua, St. Martin, Virgin Gorda.		7–25 day/winter

SeaDream Yacht Club

SeaDream I	Eastern Caribbean round trip from San Juan to Culebrita, Esperanza, St. John, St. Martin, St. Barts, Virgin Gorda, Jost Van Dyke.	$4,900–$14,750	7 days/winter
	Round trip from St. Thomas to San Juan via St. John, St. Barts, Guadeloupe, Nevis, Jost Van Dyke.		
SeaDream II	Southern/Eastern Caribbean round trip from Barbados to St. Thomas, San Juan, Antigua or from St. Thomas to San Juan; San Juan to St. Thomas; St. Thomas to Barbados; Barbados to Antigua.	$3,900–$29,500	4–14 days/winter

Silversea Cruises

Cruise-only fares include all gratuities and beverages aboard ship, including select wines, champagnes, and spirits.

Silver Wind	Barbados to San Juan round trip; or reverse on varying itineraries.	$3,895–$14,695 + port charges	7–8 days/March

Star Clippers

Royal Clipper	Barbados to St. Lucia, Iles des Saintes, Antigua, St. Kitts, Dominica, Martinique; or Grenadines, Grenada, Tobago Cays, St. Vincent, St. Lucia, Martinique.	$1,745–$4,865 + port charges	7 days/winter

Windstar Cruises

Wind Spirit	St. Thomas to St. Martin, St. Barts, Tortola, Jost Van Dyke, and overnight on board in St. John and Virgin Gorda.	$1,849–$3,449	7 days/winter
Wind Surf	Caribbean round trip from Barbados to either Tobago, Bequia, Dominica, St. Lucia, Mayreau, Grenada, Tobago; or Nevis, St. Martin, St. Barts, Isles des Saintes, St. Lucia.	$1,749–$3,649	7 days/winter

French West Indies, xxi
Frost, Robert, 88

G

Garinagus (indigenous people), 6, 199–200,
    202, 203
Garland, Colin, 126
George Town. *See also* Grand Cayman, 139, 140
Goethals, George W., 217
golf, 8
    Bahamas, 64, 69–70
    Cancún, 160, 174
    Cozumel, 168
    Grand Cayman, 142, 143–44, 150
    Jamaica, 116, 119
    Key West, 95
    Montego Bay, 111
    Nassau, 49
    Ocho Rios, 129
    Playa del Carmen, 160, 171, 176
Goombay (festival), 66–67
Gorgas, William C., 217
Grand Bahama Island. *See also* Bahamas, 46,
    67–72
    boat trips, 71
    dining, 71–72
    driving around, 72
    shopping, 68–69
    sightseeing, 70–71
    sports, 69–70
Grand Cayman, 139–52
    dining, 148–49
    driving tour, 143–47
    nightlife, 152
    port profile, 139–41
    shopping, 147–48
    shore excursions, 141–42
    sightseeing, 142–43
    sports, 149–52
Greater Antilles, 5
Grenada, xxi, 5, 8
Grenadines, xxi, 5
Griffin, Merv, 44, 46
Groves, Wallace, 46, 67
Guadeloupe, xxi, 5, 8
Guatemala, 5, 8, 198–201
    Caribbean coast, 199–201
    fast facts, 200

map of, 201
ports of call, xxi

H

Haiti, 5, 6
    ports of call, xxi
Hartford, Huntington, 44, 59
Hemingway, Ernest, 74, 75
    in Key West, 79, 80, 88–89, 90–91, 92, 97
Holland America Line, 28–29, 194
    chart of ships, 227–28
Honduras, 5, 8, 202–7
    Bay Islands, 202–3, 205
    Copán, 206–7
    fast facts, 203
    map of, 204
    Mosquito Coast, 207
    north coast and inland, 205–6
    ports of call, xxi
honeymoons, 12
horseback riding
    Bahamas, 64, 70
    Belize, 195
    Cancún, 160
    Costa Maya, 185
    Cozumel, 159, 168
    Grand Cayman, 150
    Jamaica, 119–20
    Montego Bay, 111
    Ocho Rios, 129

I

Inagua Island. *See also* Bahamas, 76
internet access
    Grand Cayman, 140
    onboard, 19
Isla Mujeres. *See also* Cancún, 160, 175–76

J

Jamaica, 5, 8, 99–133
    costs, 103, 105
    cuisine and dining, 107–8, 118
    drugs in, 105
    fast facts, 104
    festivals, 109
    geography and culture, 101
    at a glance, 101
    history of, 101–3

Truman, Harry S., 80, 87
tubing
  Belize, 198
  Jamaica, 122
Tulum, 157, 169, 178–79
Turks, 5

U

underwater trips
  Bahamas, 49, 65, 71
  Cozumel, 159
  Grand Cayman, 142, 152
  Jamaica, 120
US Virgin Islands. *See* Virgin Islands
Uxmal, 157, 182

V

Virgin Islands, 5, 8
  ports of call, xxi

W

wardrobe, onboard, 17
water parks. *See* beaches
waterskiing, 65
water sports. *See* beaches; specific sports
weddings, onboard, 12

Western Caribbean. *See* Caribbean; specific
    locations
wildlife sanctuaries
  Belize, 194, 197
  Costa Rica, 213
Williams, Tennessee, 79, 80, 89, 93–94
Windstar Cruises, 37, 234
windsurfing
  Bahamas, 65
  Cayman Islands, 152
  Cozumel, 169
  Jamaica, 120
  Ocho Rios, 129
Windwards, 5

X

Xcaret. *See also* Playa del Carmen, 159, 176–77

Y

Yucatán Peninsula. *See also* Mexican Caribbean, 5

Z

zoos
  Belize, 195, 197
  Nassau, 57

About the Author

Kay Showker is a veteran writer, photographer, and lecturer on travel. Her assignments have taken her to more than a hundred countries—in the Caribbean and around the world. She is the author of *The 100 Best Resorts of the Caribbean* (Globe Pequot Press, 2007); *Caribbean Ports of Call: Eastern and Southern Regions* (Globe Pequot Press, 2008); *Caribbean Ports of Call: Northern and Northeastern Regions* (Globe Pequot Press, 2000); *The Outdoor Traveler's Guide to the Caribbean* (Stewart, Tabori & Chang, updated 1992), which was named first runner-up as Travel Guidebook of the Year in 1990; and two Fodor guides—*Egypt* and *Jordan and the Holy Land.* Her book *The Unofficial Guide to Cruises* (Macmillan Travel, 2008) was named Best Travel Guide Book of the Year by Lowell Thomas Awards of the Society of American Travel Writers in 1995 when it was first published.

Ms. Showker has written for *National Geographic Traveler, Travel + Leisure, Caribbean Travel and Life,* and many other magazines and newspapers across the country. She has appeared as a travel expert on network and cable television and on America Online. She served as senior editor of *Travel Weekly,* the industry's major trade publication, with which she was associated for eleven years.

A native of Kingsport, Tennessee, Ms. Showker received a master's degree in international affairs from the School of Advanced International Studies at Johns Hopkins University and a BA from Mary Washington University. She was the first recipient of the Caribbean Tourism Association Award for excellence in journalism, and in 2003 her book *Caribbean Ports of Call: Western Region,* sixth edition, was named Best Guide Book of the Year by the Caribbean Tourism Organization. She was named Travel Writer of the Year by the Bahamas Hotel Association in 1990, and she received the 1989 Marcia Vickery Wallace Memorial Award for Travel Journalism given by the Jamaica Tourist Board in conjunction with the Caribbean Tourism Organization. In 1996 she became the first travel journalist to receive the Sucrier d'Oro award from the Martinique government for "her outstanding coverage of the Caribbean scene."